# Crusade

*Also by the same author*

Double Dealer
Twins
War on the Mind
The Nazi's Wife

# CRUSADE

## Peter Watson

HUTCHINSON
London Melbourne Auckland Johannesburg

For my mother

This edition first published by Hutchinson, an imprint of Century Hutchinson Ltd, Brookmount House, 62–65 Chandos Place, London WC2N 4NW

Century Hutchinson Australia Pty Ltd, PO Box 496, 16–22 Church Street, Hawthorn, Victoria 3122, Australia

Century Hutchinson New Zealand Limited, PO Box 40–086, Glenfield, Auckland 10, New Zealand

Century Hutchinson South Africa (Pty) Ltd, PO Box 337, Berglvei, 2012 South Africa

British Library Cataloguing in Publication Data

Watson, Peter, *1943–*
    Crusade.
    I. Title
    823'.914[F]        PR6073.A87/

    ISBN 0–09–168480–3

Phototypeset by Input Typesetting Ltd, London SW19 8DR
Printed and bound in Great Britain by
Mackays of Chatham Ltd

# Prologue

Benedetto stared at his cup. What was happening to it? He had taken coffee in Enzo's bar every Sunday morning for – oh, eight years at least. He waited there after early mass for his son who sang in the cathedral choir. Then, when the boy arrived, he would have another before going home for breakfast. There was no hurry – Pasqualina, his wife, liked them both out of the house so that, on this one day of the week, she could have a lie-in. The coffee at Enzo's was always excellent, the best in Foligno. But today . . . it had tasted fine when Benedetto had taken his first sip. But now, as he looked down at his cup, he noticed what looked like a number of rings on the surface of the thick liquid. As if it was being shaken from below. Odd. He couldn't feel anything.

At that moment – 8.19, according to the newspapers next day – he did. The black and white marble tiles beneath his feet suddenly began to vibrate, as if there were someone below, trying to drill his way out of hell. Cups and ashtrays were rattling – then suddenly an entire shelf of glasses fell to the floor.

Benedetto never heard the crash, for the sound was obliterated from across the square as, not fifty yards away, a huge piece of gold and blue masonry slammed on to the piazza stones, destroying the newspaper kiosk and sending showers of fist-sized rocks everywhere, like exploding shrapnel. Dimly, Benedetto recognized those gold and blue colours: at the top of the cathedral, on its main wall, there was a famous mosaic, showing Christ and the pope who had donated it. But that was hardly his main thought now as, along with Enzo and one or two other early-morning coffee drinkers, he cowered at the back of the bar. None of them had been in an earthquake before but they were Italian, so knew what was happening.

The shaking and the terrible sound of falling masonry went on for several minutes. Before long the front wall of the bar fell outwards – though mercifully the roof didn't cave in – enabling Benedetto and Enzo to see the appalling damage being done to their town. The arch linking the cathedral to the Palazzo Trinci had completely gone. The north wall of the cathedral, normally a beautiful mixture of pink and white stone put together over eight hundred years, was no more. The main rose window had gone, too – that appeared to have fallen inwards, into the cathedral, taking the roof with it.

Now, as Benedetto watched, two of the huge columns on the Palazzo Trinci, red as the blood oranges of Italy, fell outwards into the piazza. The sound was worse than thunder, the clouds of red dust making the square like a Second World War battlefield. Still the ground boiled. Sounds of buildings cracking, then smashing on to the pavements of the town could be heard from all around. Finally, to Benedetto and Enzo's helpless horror, the cupola of the cathedral, a dome as smooth as a skull and the dominant shape on the town's skyline, caved in. First the south side settled, giving the dome a drunken appearance: then it gave way entirely and disappeared inside what was left of the cathedral. The crash boomed across the town like the pain of an anguished giant.

At last the shaking stopped and the earth settled back to where it had always been, more or less. Benedetto, Enzo and the others waited for a few minutes. So far they had survived: they had no wish to abandon their haven until they were certain the worst was over.

It seemed to be. Wiping the dust from his face with a handkerchief, Benedetto stepped forward into the rubble. It was, incongruously, a wonderful day, the sun streaming down as if all were well with the world. He picked his way across the piazza, past the remains of the kiosk, its green wood smashed into a thousand pieces; past the battered hulks of cars; past what he recognized with a groan was the mangled accordion which used to belong to Aldo, the cripple who played in the piazza all day long. His body must be here somewhere, under the stone.

He aimed for the north door of the cathedral. Of Romanesque origin and flanked by two red stone lions, it was not only the most beautiful feature of the building, but also the strongest. It was still standing, and the wall around it – some of it, anyway – was intact: he could get inside the building from there. By now a fresh crop of sounds was coming from the town, the sounds of suffering – groans from the injured, shrieks from the survivors as they discovered loved ones who had been killed. But Benedetto pressed on.

The centre of the church was the most inaccessible. This was where the north wall and the rose window had fallen, and then the cupola had crashed down on top of that. The pink bricks, stone runnels and twisted lead from the dome were in some cases piled nine or ten feet high. Benedetto picked his way around all this. He noticed things he recognized – a stone statue of Saint Barnabus, its head broken off, that used to stand in the north transept. Then he saw the remains of the baldacchino, a copy of the one in St Peter's in Rome and designed by the great Bernini. That meant he was getting close.

6

The baldacchino was a kind of canopy, made of bronze, which stood over the high altar and behind which was the organ and the choir. Only now did Benedetto begin pulling away what stones he could. He was wearing his best suit, or what had been his best suit until minutes before. But he paid no heed. He moved two or three stones, then stopped to listen. There was still no shortage of screams from elsewhere in the town, but where he stood the silence was ominous.

He moved more stones and stopped to listen again. He repeated the process desperately. He discovered his first body after five minutes of searching. It was the Gasparris' boy, no more than fifteen and still dressed in the lace-edged surplice of the cathedral choir: the boys always stayed behind to gossip after their singing had ended. He laid the boy's body gently by the edge of the rubble and went back to his digging. The cathedral was by no means the only building destroyed that day in Foligno, but it was the biggest and, at that hour, was the only structure with any number of people in it. So Benedetto was already being joined by others scrabbling in the remains.

Twice more he encountered bodies before he found what, or rather who, he was looking for. One was the nineteen-year-old corpse of Frederico Sangrilli, son of Vito, the baker. The other was too badly mangled to identify. Benedetto shuddered but laid the three bodies side by side where the rescue teams, or relatives, when they finally caught up with him, could not fail to spot them. Then he went back again to where the choir stalls should have been.

He came to a piece of fresco first, and recalled that the ceiling of the cathedral in the apse above the altar was decorated in blues, pinks and whites, scenes from the life of St Feliciano, to whom the church was dedicated. The piece Benedetto found showed a winged angel, brandishing a sword with a twisted blade. The colours were spattered with blood and, as he shifted the angel, a bolt went through him: the crumpled body of his own son was revealed beneath. Lorenzo was covered in pale dust but underneath that his head was black and sticky with blood, his legs twisted in awkward and unnatural ways. His eyes were open. As Benedetto scraped the piece of ceiling still further out of the way one of Lorenzo's arms slipped down and, for a cruel moment, the movement made Benedetto think his boy was still alive. He bent down and shook him.

'Lorenzo! Lorenzo!'

Nothing. The life had been crushed out of his son just as it had been crushed out of all the other eighteen boys in the choir.

Benedetto kissed his son, touched the sticky patch at the side of his head and felt the jagged cracks in the boy's skull. Now the tears started to run. As he pulled at the rubble it seemed as if he would never free the dusty, ungainly body of his dead child. His eyes filled, the tears ran down his cheeks and fell, warm as life, into the dust on his hands as they scratched at the stones. At last the boy's feet, clad incongruously in running shoes beneath his cassock, were uncovered. At seventeen Lorenzo was as tall as his father but had yet to fill out. Still, it took Benedetto a while to sort out his balance. Oblivious to the others who were searching in the debris, he lifted the boy across his shoulder: there was no sign of any rescue team. Slowly, carefully, Benedetto picked his way back across the stones. Shattered wood from the choir stalls mingled with sharp and jagged splinters of stained glass. Once-ornate brass work, twisted hideously, poked up from beneath curved terracotta roof tiles. Flowers – fresh that day – lay scattered over what had once been a marble sarcophagus. Reaching the edge of the rubble, he rested, leaning Lorenzo's body against the still-standing door arch. He wiped his eyes with his sleeve – dust was caked to his moist cheeks.

More and more people were coming into the grand piazza now as the town picked itself up and word spread that the cathedral area had been worst hit. Benedetto was watched in silence as others realized he had already found what they most dreaded: a relative dead in the ruins. He mustn't wait, he told himself. He had to get home. He was just lifting the boy's body again when he heard the scream. He knew what he would see even as he lifted his gaze: Pasqualina. She was standing outside Enzo's bar, where the front had fallen in minutes before. She had searched for them first in the bar. She had pulled about her the blue coat Benedetto had given her at Easter. Unbuttoned, it flopped open as she raised her arms in anguish. Lorenzo was – had been – their youngest child, her favourite, her only son. For what seemed like an eternity her screams filled the square.

Hours later, long after Benedetto and Pasqualina had taken their grief into the privacy of their own home, the mayor of Foligno, Sandro Sirianni, stood with his old friend, Father Umberto Narnucci, on the town football field. It was situated about half a kilometre outside the walls of the old town, on the road to Terni and Rome. Like many towns in Italy, Foligno was ruled by the communists. But Italian communism is like no other, and Father Narnucci was Sirianni's oldest sparring partner, a good friend since schooldays and still a drinking companion and fellow director of the football team. The mayor had been relieved to learn that Narnucci, who had been scheduled to say the later masses at the cathedral that day, was visiting nearby Assisi at the time of the earthquake, staying with friends at the monastery. Sirianni's own son who, against his father's wishes, had once been a chorister in the cathedral, was now, fortunately, miles away at university in Milan.

It had been a grim day. Both men were exhausted. So far, and it was now six o'clock in the evening, the number of dead was put at 900; 1,500 were seriously injured, roughly 2,000 were homeless – and there were close to 350 people unaccounted for.

Narnucci had spent the day comforting the bereaved, overseeing the emergency funeral arrangements, finding accommodation for the homeless. Sirianni had, if anything, worked even harder: fixing water supplies that had been broken, finding beds, organizing makeshift electricity links to the much-damaged hospitals, tracking down the owners of shops which sold camping equipment and requisitioning tents. He had had some help from the army locally but there was still no sign of the government rescue teams. The same old story; both men were in despair.

This was the second time that Sirianni had been out to the football field. The first was to greet Carlo Volpe, the Italian president who had helicoptered in from Rome as soon as news of the earthquake had reached him. He had been to see the damage for himself and had promised aid. This second time was to see off the Pope who was also paying a visit by helicopter. The Holy Father had cancelled all his engagements that day to make his own tour of the town. The new pontiff – he had been in office barely three months – had arrived two hours earlier, inspected the damage, especially the cathedral, comforted the injured in hospital and said mass at a school which had miraculously survived more or less intact and which would now be home for many Folignese for some time.

As Sirianni and Narnucci waited together the Pope was talking with the local archbishop before boarding his helicopter for the flight back to Rome. It had been a shock at first when, after a long, thirteen-day conclave, the Sacred College of Cardinals had elected an American as pope and in Italy it had not been a popular choice. His age hadn't helped, either – fifty-nine was young for a Pope, and promised a long era with a foreigner in charge. But Pope Thomas – he had kept his own name as pontiff, only the third holy father in history to do so – spoke fluent Italian, had a weakness for ice cream and, he confessed to an interviewer, old Bugattis. He was rapidly winning the Italian people round.

There were three helicopters on the field, their drooping blades beginning to rotate. After the attempt to assassinate John-Paul II, the Italian airforce at first kept the Pope's helicopter under close surveillance by radar, with a squadron in readiness should any attempt be made to intercept the aircraft. More recently a second, 'shadow' helicopter had been introduced as simpler, cheaper and more effective. The third helicopter contained the press. Wherever he went nowadays the American Pope was news. The bright arc lights and pushy cameramen of the TV networks were as much a part of the papal entourage as cherubs in a Renaissance painting.

As His Holiness and the archbishop finished their talk this entourage moved towards Sirianni and Narnucci. Pope Thomas was a tall man anyway but his pure white cassock, bespattered with mud, made him seem all the taller. As he drew near, with that distinctive limp, Narnucci dropped to one knee and kissed the Pontiff's hand. Across the field the helicopter blades swirled faster, drumming their own wind. It swept through the entourage, and one cameraman, moving backwards and momentarily off-balance, stepped on a young girl of eight or nine who was waiting with a few other children to be blessed by the Pope. She gave a cry of pain and pushed at the man's leg. The moment soon passed and the young girl was not really hurt anyway, but for Sirianni that minor accident caused something inside him to ignite. He was wound up anyway, and aching from the day's exertions. The camera-man's behaviour was too much – and it was typical. He had turned to apologize to the young girl, but briefly – more important work was at hand.

The Pope was now in front of Sirianni. Thomas, of course, had been alerted by his staff to the fact that the mayor was a communist, so he was under no illusions that the man before him would kneel and kiss his ring. Instead, he held out his hand for Sirianni to shake. The nearest cameraman was no more than ten feet away.

'You look tired, Signor Sirianni. We shall get out of your way. We've held you up long enough. There is still much for you to do.'

The Holy Father's arm was still extended. Sirianni had not yet grasped it. Thomas tensed, sensing trouble. The camera was trained on them.

'You have our support,' the Pope went on, careful not to use the word 'blessing'. 'Our thoughts will go with you.' He didn't say 'prayers'. 'We shall give you what help we can. Priests, nurses, drivers. I shall see to it myself.'

Sirianni still said nothing. The Pope looked quickly at Narnucci, then back to the mayor again. Sensing unease in the Pope, the nearest cameraman intuitively moved closer. Narnucci was staring at his old friend.

'Come,' said Thomas, taking a step forward to grasp Sirianni's arm. 'We have to work togeth – '

That was as far as he got. In an explosive gesture that would be flashed around the television sets of the world in the next few hours. Sirianni shook off the Pope's proffered arm and screamed at him:

'Work! Shaking hands isn't work! Blessing people, doling out comfort isn't work!' He glared at the cameramen. 'Being on television isn't work!'

Narnucci tried to calm him but the mayor shook off the priest as well. He turned back to the Pope whose face had paled. 'Hundreds of us have died here today. Thousands. Those of us who are wretched enough to have survived are homeless, bereaved, our bones and our hearts broken. You promise us priests and prayer – ' He spat into the ground. 'The President came earlier and left us with promises too. But then he, like you are about to do, went back to his cosy apartment in Rome.'

10

The mayor screamed louder. 'Where can *we* go?' There were tears in his eyes as Sirianni pointed at his watch. 'Six o'clock! Six o'clock! Nearly ten hours since the shock and still no rescue teams. Not a single blanket, carton of food, not even a tent that we haven't had to organize for ourselves.'

The Pope stood very still as Sirianni railed and the cameras recorded every detail. 'Keep your priests, your prayers and your promises. We need money. *Money!* Lire, dollars, pounds, francs, gold – we don't care. Just don't send us blessings and promises and prayers that make *you* feel good but leave us as wretched and as helpless as we already are.'

Breathless, and still weeping, Sirianni stood glaring at the Pope, who towered above him, still silent. Then Sirianni's face collapsed into sadness, the hatred of the Catholic Church drained from him by the emotions of the day. The breeze from the helicopter blades riffled through his hair as, still sobbing, he turned round and trudged off across the field, back to his ravaged town. Pope Thomas, and the cameras, watched him go.

# PART ONE

# 1

David Colwyn sipped his whisky and water and looked down at the Lombardy plain 25,000 feet below him. The landscape was hazy; motor-ways and rivers unravelled like different coloured ribbons. At this height, the crowded countryside of Italy looked clean and calm. But David was anything but calm. As chief executive, and chief auctioneer, of one of the world's oldest salerooms, he travelled a lot. The Carlisle in New York, the Mandarin in Hong Kong, the Beau Rivage in Geneva – these hotels were almost as much home to him as his house in London. Normally, however, he knew his travel plans weeks in advance. The big sales – of Old Masters, impressionist pictures, furni-ture or jewellery – had their own rhythms which he followed eagerly, year in, year out. But not this trip. This flight to Rome was very last-minute.

He had planned a fairly uneventful Monday. Morning in the office would be spent going through the preparations for the forthcoming sale of MacIver House, yet another of the British stately homes that was in financial straits and the contents of which were being put on the market. Lunch at Wiltons in Jermyn Street was with the fine arts' correspondent of the *New York Times*, who was passing through London. There was nothing much in the afternoon, if you could call a visit to the dentist nothing much, and in the evening he had an excur-sion to Covent Garden as a guest of Sir Roland Lavery, director of London's Tate Gallery. He had suspected that Lavery would use the occasion to tell him more about the gallery's thinking on the new paintings it would be looking to acquire in the coming months. But all that went by the board when his telephone had rung at seven-thirty that morning.

He had just returned to the house, after his swim, and snatched at the receiver, half angry that anyone should call so early but expectant too because, presumably, it was urgent. Maybe it was from somebody who worked in the firm's offices halfway round the world. No. A man's voice, which sounded so close it could have come from the next room, said: 'Excuse me. Is that Mr Colwyn, of Hamilton's?'

'Yes – who is that?'

'Just a moment, please. I have Monsignor Hale for you.'

Monsignor Hale. David placed his swimming things on a chair and turned to lean against the edge of his desk. A troop of horseguards clattered by outside, early morning exercise for men and beasts. Why would Hale be calling at this ungodly hour? David had met the apostolic delegate in London only once, at a reception to mark some exhibition. But he knew that Jasper Hale was a much-liked figure in the capital – urbane, witty, a connoisseur of wine, a linguist of prodigious achievement.

The line clicked as the delegate took the receiver at his end. 'Don't be too angry with me for calling you this early, Mr Colwyn. His Holiness says it's urgent.'

'His Holiness?' David frowned into the receiver. He wondered if Hale knew he was a Catholic.

'I'd hoped you would be impressed,' chuckled Hale. 'I was, I can tell you, when he telephoned me himself from Rome not half an hour ago. Of course,' he sniffed, as if it explained everything, 'they are one hour ahead over there.'

David smiled but said nothing. The Monsignor would get to the point soon.

'I'm sure you've heard the saying that "the Lord moves in mysterious ways", Mr Colwyn. In my job I'm used to it, but not everyone is. I've got a mystery for you.'

He paused. David suspected Hale was trying to gauge his reaction to what he had said so far. So he obliged: 'Good. I'm a sucker for mysteries.'

'Thank you for making it easy for me, Mr Colwyn. Very civilized. Well, here's the story. The Holy Father wants you to go to see him. Today, I mean. The mystery is, he won't say why in advance. It's all top-secret. He came through me and not the Archbishop at Westminster since they are an even bigger bunch of gossips than we are here. But His Holiness wouldn't tell me anything at all about the reason why he wants to see you. He just said: "Make Colwyn come. It's urgent." '

Thoughts crowded into David's brain. This was weird, surely, this type of request? Or did it happen all the time, only most people never knew? He could change his plans – no problem there, it was a humdrum day. But did the invitation involve business, or something else?

'Am . . . am I being invited personally, Monsignor, or professionally?'

'I wish I knew, Mr Colwyn, I wish I knew. All I do know is that I must telephone one of the Holy Father's secretaries once you have made up your mind. If you agree to go my car will pick you up wherever you want in time for the Alitalia flight at two this afternoon. You have an appointment with His Holiness at six-thirty tonight. A room will be reserved for you at the Hassler – I hope that's convenient. You will be free to return to London tomorrow.'

David had not got to the top of his profession without possessing a full set of instincts and these now told him to say yes at once. After all, it is not every day a Pope asks to meet you, especially a brand new one. Nonetheless, he hesitated.

'Monsignor – I take it you know that I am a Catholic?'

'Yes, Mr Colwyn.'

'And do you know also that I am separated from my wife – who is not – a Catholic, I mean?' Sarah and he had been apart for more than a year now. She had left him, more or less overnight, for a junior minister in the Government. Ned, their son, lived with her and that had been the worst blow. After months of depression David was only now beginning to come round.

'Yes. I'm sorry.'

'I didn't mean that. There may be a divorce at some point. I can't say. But I wouldn't want to embarrass His Holiness.'

'You sound like a conscientious Catholic, Mr Colwyn, but remember, Pope Thomas is an American. Not as hard-headed or as hard-hearted as their President, Mr Roskill, but a realist all the same. The Church will change under this Holy Father, have no doubt. On birth control, on divorce, maybe even on priests being allowed to marry – though I am against that myself. Rome has been backward for too long. That is why he was elected, after all. If that is your only worry, you need have no fear. You will find Thomas Murray an intelligent and likeable man. Above all, a doer.'

Above David's house the early morning transatlantic jets growled into Heathrow, unseen because of the low cloud. It would be nice to feel the sun of Rome.

'Very well then,' said David. 'There's nothing I can't get out of today. I shall look forward to meeting His Holiness.'

'Thank you,' breathed the delegate, obviously relieved. 'One other thing. You will have a confidential secretary, I expect. She will no doubt have to know where you are going, in case of emergencies. But the Holy Father would be grateful if no one else were to be told. I hope that's acceptable.'

'Yes, I suppose so. My secretary is called Sally Middleton, in case it should matter.'

'Good. I shall call Rome right away. My car will pick you up at your office – when? Twelve-thirty? You will of course be met at Rome airport.'

'I should have thought that, if secrecy matters, the sight of *your* car picking *me* up would be riskier than me taking a common or garden taxi. You can reimburse me later.' David raised the tone of his voice to make it obvious that the last quip was a joke.

'I think you are right Mr Colwyn and, if you don't mind, that's what we will do. Now, I must wish you a pleasant flight . . . and I hope the mystery has a happy ending.'

In fact, the mystery had only deepened during the day. By the time David arrived at Heathrow he had read the papers and listened to the radio news in the taxi. Everywhere the lead item was the earthquake at Foligno the previous day, where the dead were now estimated at nearly 1,200. But also prominently displayed on the front pages was the extraordinary attack made on the Pope by the communist mayor of the stricken town. Everyone was outraged that Pope Thomas had been abused so badly after he had specifically cancelled his appointments that day to fly to Foligno and share in the grief of the victims. Only the communist papers in Italy had supported Sirianni. In some of the more popular papers, David noted, the attack on the Pope even outweighed the earthquake itself. Newspaper values, he told himself. There had been earthquakes before but attacks on the Holy Father were much rarer. He would have thought the Pope would have been far too busy to see him, today of all days.

The Alitalia flight touched down on schedule. As soon as he came out of the green channel he saw a driver holding a card with his name, and he was shown straight into a small, black, very discreet Mercedes. David was an authority on Roman painting, the fifteenth, sixteenth and seventeenth centuries especially. He therefore knew the churches, palazzos and libraries of the city very well. That included St Peter's, the Vatican museums and the Secret Archive, but he had never been inside the city-state proper, where the Pope and the top curia lived, and he was intrigued to see what it was like.

At the Porta Sant'Anna, the business entrance of the Vatican, on the Via di Porta Angelica, they were stopped by a Swiss guard, dressed in a navy beret, a blue blouse, blue knickerbockers, long blue woollen socks, and white gloves. He didn't hold them up for long: he recognized the driver and David was expected.

What then happened was mystifying. As they drove inside the gate the driver pointed out the Vatican Bank – the Institute for Religious Works – on the left, and the papal apartments behind that. But David wasn't taken there, the obvious destination, he thought, for a papal audience. Instead, they drove straight through an arch ahead of them, into a courtyard with what he recognized as the Borgia apartments on the left and the Secret Archive on the right; then on through another arch which, this time, led inside a building. They turned left, up a cobbled ramp, which was in a kind of tunnel and were in no time out into a courtyard surrounded by high walls. The driver had to stop for another guard, this time dressed like an ordinary policeman. As he slowed to be recognized, he waved casually at the building on the left and murmured: 'Capella Sistina' – the Sistine Chapel.

David craned his head up. *'Grazie,'* he said. He had not realized the chapel was so tall.

Past the guard they went through another arch and David could see the apse of St Peter's and the Vatican gardens ahead of him. But the car turned sharp right, through yet another arch and raced along a dead straight road for about a quarter of a mile. A huge, straight building was to the right – David calculated it must be part of the Vatican museums. To the left were the gardens – covered walkways, box hedges, conifers, Japanese maples, a waterfall. The car came to a halt at the end of the straight road, where there was a right-angled bend. Another large building faced them and, set in the corner between these two facades, was a small grey-green door. The driver got out and led the way to it. The door was opened immediately by a security guard, who showed David into a small room. It was someone's working office rather than a waiting room proper, but he was not there long. A small nun, in a grey habit, soon came in and said, in English: 'Mr Colwyn? Follow me please.' She set off at a brisk pace up a flight of wide stone steps. At the top they turned back on themselves and went up another flight. At the top this time there was a large hall and yet more security guards. The nun showed David into what he at first thought was a long corridor, since the view stretched for some hundred and fifty yards. 'You may wait here, Mr Colwyn. The Holy Father will not keep you long.' The guards remained but she was gone.

David could see that it was by no means a simple corridor where he was being left. To his amazement, he had been shown into the Vatican picture gallery.

He stared ahead of him. The gallery consisted of a number of rooms in a straight line, with the doorways between rooms all in line as well, so he could see from one end to another. It felt like a hospital with pictures. He had been here before, of course, but not for some time. He looked back. The security guards were talking among themselves; there seemed no sign of the Pope. Glancing at his watch, he noticed that it was in any case not quite six-thirty. Pope Thomas was a busy man: presumably he would be a few minutes late at least. David strolled into the gallery. Why *had* the Holy Father decided to meet him here? The apostolic delegate had said more than he meant when he called the whole business a mystery.

The first rooms contained the early paintings, primitive, icon-like pictures with thick gold backgrounds, mostly fourteenth century, from Siena, Florence, Rimini. David knew collectors who would kill for paintings of this type but they were not to his taste. Further down came a room he liked better, containing pictures by Pinturicchio and Perugino. David loved Pinturicchio's exuberance, his cheerful greens and reds. There was always something going on in his pictures.

Suddenly, before he could go any further, David heard a commotion.

He looked back. Coming towards him from the large hall where the security guards had been waiting, limped the Pope, glowing in his white cassock. A number of other figures spilled around His Holiness. David walked towards the group, not sure what greeting to use. Should he kneel? Or just shake hands? The Holy Father's limp seemed pronounced today. But David had only ever seen it before on television so perhaps the cameras softened and blunted it in some way. David had forgotten, if he had ever known, why the Pope limped. In the event His Holiness put him at his ease by calling out, when he was a few paces away, 'Thank you for coming so promptly, Mr Colwyn. I know how busy you must be. I am in your debt. But we shan't be wasting your time, I hope.' And he held out his hand in such a way that he clearly expected it to be shaken, not kissed.

'Monsignor Hale was very persuasive, your Holiness.'

The Pope smiled. He was slightly taller than David expected and the predominant impression he gave on first meeting was of a man who, apart from his leg, was remarkably fit. His hair, though flecked with white, was shiny and bushy; his eyes – greenish unless the light was playing tricks – were never still; and his mouth was wide, the lips full but not sensual so that the impression was of an open – but controlled – face. As they shook hands – a firm, not overlong handshake – David was faintly surprised to register that the Pope smelled very fresh, as though he had just taken a shower and doused himself in cologne.

His Holiness was turning now, introducing the other people he had with him. First, out of politeness rather than precedence, came a face David did recognize, Elizabeth Lisle, the Vatican press secretary. After his election, controversial enough in itself, Thomas Murray had immediately followed up with this equally controversial appointment. Elizabeth Lisle was also American but that wasn't what made her controversial so much as the fact that she was a woman. In fact, appointing a woman as press secretary was not quite the revolutionary move some of Thomas's enemies made it seem. The Pontifical Commission on Social Communication – Vatican-speak for press office – had long been staffed at lower levels by women, very often American women. The Pope had merely noticed that, in giving the top job to a female and drawing her into his confidence, he was able to bring the other sex centre stage in the Vatican without any fundamental change of policy. He was thus able to send signals to the outside world, that things were changing in Rome, without any interior wrangling. It was a simple, bold, astute move that marked Thomas as an instinctive politician. On reflection, many of his early critics had conceded as much.

David shook hands with the woman now. She was dressed in a dark, two-piece suit, over a white silk shirt. The most striking thing about her, he thought, was her neck, long like a swan's. 'Welcome to the

Vatican, Mr Colwyn. I am responsible for the arrangements. If you have any criticisms, shoot at me.'

David smiled back and shook his head. 'No problems so far. The Hassler has always been my favourite hotel here.'

His attention turned to the figure on her left, a severe-looking man in glasses, whom he also recognized. Cardinal Ottavio Massoni was the second most powerful man in the Vatican, Thomas's Secretary of State. An Italian and a conservative, he had been Thomas's main rival for Pope. The two men were as different as Peter and Paul. It had been a surprise when Thomas offered the job to Massoni but not as big a one as when the Italian had accepted. Still, the arrangement seemed to be working well so far, though it was early days. Massoni, now in his late sixties, had a rather cadaverous skull, and was famed for his taciturn manner. To the wags in the Secretariat of State he was known as 'P.A.' which stood for 'Pronto – Arrivederci', the only two words which, it was alleged, he ever said on the telephone. So it was no surprise to David when the Cardinal merely took a pace forward, shook hands, said 'Buona sera', and stepped back again.

A second cardinal presented himself. This was Luciano Zingale, introduced to David as President of the Patrimony of the Holy See. Bald and fat, he looked more like a boxer than a religious man, his appearance not helped by the rimless glasses he wore. But he was civil enough and bowed as he shook David's hand.

Of the three other men in the party one was Father Patrick O'Rourke, the Pope's principal private secretary. The second was Dottore Mauro Tecce, general secretary of the Pontifical Monuments, Museums and Galleries, and the third was actually someone David knew, Dottore Giulio Venturini, curator of the picture gallery where they all now stood. David had seen him often at exhibitions and even one or two sales. He had read his books. They had sat next to each other in the Vatican's Secret Archive. Venturini gave him a small smile but it was scarcely warm – more wary. What *was* going on?

He was about to find out. 'This way, Mr Colwyn,' said the Pope, and moved further into the gallery. The rest of the party followed. Thomas walked past a number of Tuscan statues of the thirteenth and fourteenth centuries, back past the Pinturicchios and the Perugino and into a large hall at the end. Lit from above, partly by natural light – what was left of it – this room had a 'blue-green' feel to it: the marble of the floor contained much green, while the tapestries around the walls were the pale, watery blue that old thread assumes with great age.

On the far wall, which Pope Thomas now made for, there were three large paintings. In the middle one Jesus seemed to float in the air, above some two dozen individuals all lost in wonder, pointing, staring, gasping. The right-hand painting showed, in its top half, the Virgin being crowned and, below, grouped around an empty tomb, the twelve apostles looking up. But the Pope stood before the painting on the left.

Thomas turned and signalled for the security guards, who had followed the papal entourage, to leave. When they had gone he said: 'Mr Colwyn, our discussions this evening are confidential. I take it I may have that assurance?'

David nodded.

'Good. To be frank, I hope that we shall be able to do some business but in case we cannot this meeting never took place. Yes?'

'I understand,' said David, thinking he would burst if the man in white didn't get to the point soon.

Pope Thomas looked at the pictures in front of them. 'I understand that as well as being chief executive of Hamilton's you are also an authority on Roman painting. You will therefore probably be more familiar with these three works than I am.' The Pontiff looked hard at David, assessing, challenging, waiting.

David had made his name in the art world by being a scholar-detective as well as an auctioneer. His discoveries, his 'coups', had won him international recognition. The first had been made early on in his career when he had discovered a set of documents belonging to an old Roman family which had set him on the trail of a missing sculpture by Gianlorenzo Bernini, the great Baroque master. He had tracked that down to a family in Germany who hadn't a clue what treasure they housed in their conservatory. The second had earned him promotion over the heads of at least two older colleagues. This was his discovery of a small 'Madonna' in a private collection in Sweden. It had been miscatalogued, but David was able to show it was a Raphael that had once belonged to the Hapsburg Emperor, Rudolph II of Prague, and then to Queen Christina of Sweden, whose troops had looted the Prague pictures in the Thirty Years War. The delighted Swede had sold the picture, through Hamilton's, of course, when it had fetched over ten million pounds. So yes, he reflected, he did know the pictures in this room quite well. He gazed at the painting above the Pope. It showed a Madonna and Child in its top half, the Virgin seated in a large golden halo surrounded by clouds in the shape of cherubs. In the bottom half several saints craned their necks upwards. The picture was full of rich reds, gold, smoky blues, deep lush greens.

The Holy Father still looked at David, still waiting. For a moment, David was mystified by the silence. He looked again at the picture in the middle of the wall. This was Raphael's great 'Transfiguration'. On the far side was the equally arresting 'Coronation of the Virgin'. Then it came to him. Rehearsing the titles of the pictures did it, helped him make the link the Pope was waiting for. How could he have been so slow! The picture above them was Raphael's 'Madonna of Foligno'.

21

'I want to sell this picture, Mr Colwyn, and give the proceeds to the victims of Foligno.'

'What!' David half-shouted. The Pope put his hand on David's arm as if to steady him. David looked at Elizabeth Lisle: her expression was concerned but she was smiling faintly. He looked at Massoni: that famous cold stare. At Venturini: a sad, almost hunted look.

'I'm sure you've seen the newspapers today, or the television, or listened to the radio. You will know that I was shouted at – screamed at – by the mayor of Foligno, a man who happens to be a communist. I should be thankful, perhaps, that so much of the press appears to be on my side. But it's a poor leader who starts believing the publicity about himself, especially when he's only been in the job for a few months. Like me you may have noticed that, in some cases, the news of Signor Sirianni's outburst outweighed even the news of the disaster itself. A sad reflection on our times.'

The Pope shifted his stance and rubbed his thigh. David remembered now that he had been shot at and injured as a young man while on church business in Kampuchea which had left him with a weak left leg. 'You're in shock and my leg's playing up, Mr Colwyn. Let's sit down.' He pointed to some wooden Roman-style chairs on the far side of the gallery, beneath the tapestries. They crossed, and sat down side by side. The rest of the party hovered about them.

'Tecce! Am I allowed to smoke in here?'

'Of course, Holiness.'

The Pope reached into his cassock and took out a packet of cigarettes. He offered one to David, who shook his head.

Thomas flicked the lighter and breathed blue smoke into the gallery. 'You know, being a smoker these days is lonelier than being Pope. I don't know anyone except me who has this dreadful habit.' He smiled. 'Are you on the trail of any other missing paintings just now?'

David shook his head. 'No, I've become seduced by one of the oldest mysteries in the art world. I spend all my spare time investigating that.'

'Oh yes, tell me.' Thomas was being polite, letting David get used to the outrageous idea he had just put forward.

'It concerns Leonardo da Vinci. You may or may not know, Sir, but the National Gallery in London and the Louvre in Paris each has a picture by him called the 'Virgin of the Rocks'. They are nearly identical. The puzzle is: one of them is real, but the other is not, and no one knows which is which. Leonardo left so much unfinished work it is inconceivable he produced two highly finished paintings of the same subject. He got bored so easily: he would never have finished two. The problem is the documentation which exists suggests that the London picture is genuine, but the Paris picture, in terms of style, is the earlier.'

'And what have you discovered so far?'

'Well, there's a missing year in Leonardo's life – 1482. I have found

22

some documents, in the Vatican here, relating to that year. They may throw light on the great man's activities.'

'I was going to be a scholar once. Archaeology. But I was led astray – and ended up here.' The Pope smiled again and drew on his cigarette. He let a short silence hang between them. Then he said: 'The point is, Mr Colwyn, the Foligno mayor was right. He wasn't speaking as a communist, but as a man, a tired and frustrated man who had seen his town destroyed. And he was right to say that the Church – like the Government – doesn't do enough for the victims in a tragedy such as this one. Remember the Naples earthquake in 1981?' The Pope punched a fist into his hand. 'A disgrace. It took hours – days – for any relief supplies to arrive. Even when they did the Mafia stole half the blankets, much of the food – whole lorries disappeared.' He fingered the pectoral cross on his chest. 'Think back to the Ethiopian famine of 1984. What did governments or the churches do then? Not very much, I can tell you – I've looked it up. It was left to the people. Remember that mammoth concert – Live Aid? That was followed by Fashion Aid, Sports Aid, all manner of events which, *in toto*, raised millions of dollars.'

Thomas changed tack. 'I am told by my Secretary of State here, who is an experienced man, that it would be wrong for a Pope to be seen to be influenced by a communist mayor. That it makes me seem weak and it admits the Church has done less than it can – or should – do.' He drew again on his cigarette. 'I think the Church *has* been wrong, Mr Colwyn. That we *could* have done more. And I don't see it as being weak to be influenced by someone who is correct in what he says, whatever his politics. I prefer to see it as an example of the Church's humility. If a Pope can't be humble, who can?

'This is why I want to sell the picture. The world at large thinks that we have enormous riches. In a sense, we do. But that doesn't mean we have a lot of ready cash to give away. We have investments which generate income, but we have commitments, too – schools, hospitals, missionaries, the churches themselves. As a going concern – as a management consultant might put it! – the Holy See loses a little money each year. If it were not for bequests and the St Peter's Pence collection every year we should be even deeper in the red. As it is, those things help us to break even, more or less. By selling this picture I can kill several birds with one stone. I can convince the world that, whatever theoretical riches we have, they are not in liquid cash. At the same time this is a perfect occasion to show the world that the Catholic Church is humble, but caring.'

David suddenly noticed what he should have noticed before. There was no one from the financial side of the Vatican in the Pope's entourage.

The other man was speaking again. 'The match between the disaster and the Raphael is perfect. The painting was commissioned as an

23

offering of thanks to the Virgin by someone who believed she had saved his home from a bolt of lightning. For many years it hung in the church of Santa Anna in Foligno. It was brought here after Napoleon looted it, but a copy hung in the cathedral which was destroyed yesterday. You know Raphael better than I do – that's why we chose you – but for my part I am sure even he would have approved what I have in mind. Now, how much do you think it will fetch?'

David's brain, normally nimble, was numb. It was as if there was a black hole at its centre. Was the Pope being entirely serious? Would he be allowed to be? Sell a Vatican Raphael! It was impossible, disgraceful. It was also sensational, fantastic, spectacular. David tried to shake those last words out of his head, but couldn't. He was a businessman, after all, not just a Catholic; but he understood why Venturini looked so miserable.

The Pope's green eyes were on him again. Elizabeth Lisle was staring too, and the others. David took a deep breath.

'I am sure you have done your homework, your Holiness. So you know that prices have been rising steeply. Lord Clark's Turner was sold in 1984 for over seven million pounds, and that the Northampton Mantegna fetched eight point one million pounds in 1985. The Swedish Raphael I discovered fetched ten million pounds. In 1987 there was a jump, when Van Gogh's "Sunflowers" fetched nearly twenty-five million. Since then we've had the De Schael Van Eyck and the Orresman Duccio.'

The more David thought about it, the more fantastic this conversation was. The Pope *couldn't* sell a Raphael. Could he? The outcry would be enormous. But he pressed on. 'A Raphael of any kind has to be worth those prices at least. Only this isn't just any Raphael. It is one of the Vatican's three great Raphaels. It is not just a picture, it's part of the Church's history, has hung in the Vatican itself for more than a hundred years. Napoleon looted it, it was returned. It is now being sold by a Pope for a most unusual reason. Quite frankly, sir, there are no precedents for this kind of thing. It could fetch forty million pounds, even more perhaps.' David smiled. 'Even the thought of it brings me out in a sweat.' Before anyone else could say anything, he spoke again. 'Your Holiness, it would be a tremendous honour for Hamilton's to sell this picture on your behalf, if that is what you have in mind. But . . . but is it right? There will be a massive outcry, surely. Selling off the Vatican's heritage, and Italy's. Can you do it – legally as well as morally, I mean?'

Massoni, Zingale and the others moved closer now. Clearly this was their view, that the Pope had no right to follow the plan he proposed. David began to realize that he had found himself slap in the middle of the first split between the Pope and his Secretary of State.

Pope Thomas put his hand on David's arm once more, this time as if to offer moral support.

'It *will* be controversial, Mr Colwyn, that I grant you. But there is no doubt in my mind that it is right. The Church has been losing members, no secret about that. Worse, perhaps, it has been losing *authority*. We have to try to put both things right. Here is a clear-cut opportunity.'

'And legally?'

Pope Thomas flushed slightly at this challenge but all he said, very gently, was: 'Legally, I can do as I wish, Mr Colwyn. There are no muddy waters there. There are traditions and customs, yes. But as Pope I am, in temporal matters, an absolute monarch. In the Vatican City State, what I say *is* the law.' He went on more loudly, 'But that's not the real point. What matters is what's right. We have to act – and be seen to act. And we have to act promptly. We have to give the people of Foligno hope.'

Another thought occurred to David. 'I may not be right about the exact figures, your Holiness, but one thing I do know is that it will take weeks – months, even – to mount the sale. It will be ages before the money comes through. By then it will be too late for the people of Foligno.'

The Pontiff's eyes twinkled. 'I am ahead of you there, Mr Colwyn. The Vatican could borrow the money against the sale of the picture, if it came to that. But I have a better idea. I'm told that auction houses operate as bankers themselves these days, in order to secure business. That's what I want you to do now. You say the picture is worth – let's talk in dollars: say sixty million. I want you to advance me a third of that – twenty million dollars, much less than you think the picture will safely achieve – as a condition of getting our business.'

In theory, and until that day, David had always been in favour of the new Pope. He also believed the Church needed to change, to modernize itself. It was ironical, he reflected, that he had been drawn so precipitously into that very modernizing process he had thought he approved of. But the Pope's banking ideas were a little *too* modern for his taste.

He was aware of the others waiting for him to say something. But what?

His brain was at last beginning to boil with ideas. There would be an almighty rumpus when this news got out, no doubt about that. Whatever the Pope might say, however he might dress it up, many Catholics would be outraged. For a start, the Italians would be livid. All European countries, Britain, France, Spain, Greece, Italy most of all, had strong legislation, and strong pressure groups, to guard their artistic heritage from being exported. That the Pope was prepared to sell off a Raphael would appal every one of them. So far as Hamilton's was concerned, such a commission would bring enormous publicity. It

25

would be the biggest sale ever – certainly since Napoleon's adventures. It would firmly establish Hamilton's as the premier auction house across the world. That, too, would be put beyond doubt. Yet what if the publicity backfired? What if the Pope's plan met with such resistance that, once announced, the picture had to be withdrawn? What if the sense of outrage was so strong and so widespread that demonstrations took place outside the Hamilton galleries? These days it could happen. Yet for all his doubts, David's instincts still told him to say yes. It was a bold idea, imaginative and good in the best sense, and it deserved to succeed. What's more, if it worked as well as it might, and millions of pounds reached the earthquake victims, it would do Hamilton's no harm to be associated with it.

'How long have I got? When do you want your answer?'

'Now, of course. I must give the victims hope. To do that I have to make an announcement very quickly. If not tomorrow then the day after. I've given you first refusal, Mr Colwyn, because you know Rome, are a scholar and not just a businessman – and yes, because you are a Catholic, though an unhappy one, I am told. But if you can't handle the business, I need to move on quickly. I'm sure someone from the other London salerooms can be here by tomorrow night.' The Pope's green eyes burned into David. 'Well, what do you say?' Thomas smiled. 'Is it white smoke or black smoke?'

David got up and walked back over to the 'Madonna'. It certainly was beautiful. So serene, balanced, crisp. Twenty million dollars. He could raise the money, no doubts there. Hamilton's overdraft facility with its bankers – a pompous set of peacocks, in David's view – would amply contain even this development. Strictly speaking he was supposed to consult the board for any expenditure over five million pounds, but he also had emergency powers and this was certainly that. He turned to face the rest.

'The answer is yes, your Holiness. It will be a great honour to help. I'm sure I can get your money here to Rome by the close of business on the day after tomorrow, at the latest.'

'Splendid! I was told I could count on you.'

David looked at Massoni. He appeared to have grown more cadaverous than ever, his lips drawn tightly into a straight narrow line. He would not meet anyone's eye. Yes, thought David, another round in the old battle inside the Church – liberals v. the conservatives – it starts here, tonight.

His Holiness was speaking to Elizabeth Lisle and O'Rourke, his secretary. 'I want to make an announcement tomorrow, in time for the evening news on television and for Wednesday morning's papers. Make sure everyone in the press has a photograph of the painting. In a few days this is going to be the most famous picture in the world.' He turned to Venturini. 'Giulio, I want the "Madonna" taken down right away and packed up. We don't want tourists interfering with it.' He came over to David, shepherding Elizabeth Lisle with him. 'I can't tell you how grateful I am, Mr Colwyn. You are a brave man and I hope your bravery is rewarded. I am sure there are many details to sort out. Unfortunately, I have another engagement now but I suggest Elizabeth and you go through the problems that are likely to arise. You can trust her, Mr Colwyn. I do.'

O'Rourke was trying to snatch the Holy Father away. He was already late. But before Thomas went, limping off back down the smaller galleries, he insisted, like any businessman, on shaking hands on the deal.

David sat back, drank his wine, and looked around the restaurant. On the wall opposite, rows of deep red jugs caught the light. Above them, a line of portraits – eighteenth-century engravings of much earlier originals, he judged – stared back at him. Beyond, the restaurant stretched on and on, the noise and the smells forming a rich, thick, comforting cloak.

They had a table in Manetti's on the Via Piedmontese, just off the Borghese Gardens. It had been Elizabeth Lisle's idea. To begin with she had suggested that they meet next day in her office in the Vatican. But David had wanted to get back, to alert Hamilton's board before the Holy Father made his announcement, so he had pressed for a meeting tonight.

She had allowed him time for a quick shower at the Hassler, then had picked him up and brought him on here. 'Nowhere too touristy tonight,' she had said. 'We can't have you being recognized. And nowhere Vaticany either. *I* don't want to be spotted. Manetti's is somewhere we can talk.'

There had been an embarrassing mix-up over the seating. The head waiter, misreading the situation, had shown them to a banquette, where they could sit side by side. They insisted on sitting at an ordinary table, face to face, where they could talk. The wine waiter had misread the situation, too, giving David the Merlot to taste. Elizabeth had put the man firmly in his place.

But at last they were settled. David drank more wine and closed his eyes in pleasure. 'Who – or what – is Manetti?'

'An enemy of Savonarola's. The restaurant is based on the idea that the proper use of burning is cooking. It's a rather bloodthirsty Italian joke. But there's no need to make conversation, Mr Colwyn. We have enough to talk about, don't you think?'

David nodded. 'I'll say.' He defused her tartness with a grin. 'But *I* talk – and think – better on a full stomach and all I've had today is an Alitalia whisky and soda. Let's order first and get it out of the way. Then we can concentrate.'

The waiter took their order and disappeared. The events of the day, and the wine, were overtaking David. Despite the fact that this was a business dinner, a feeling of well-being arose in him that he found incongruous but impossible to control.

Elizabeth Lisle began to speak again.

'The "Madonna" has already been taken down, Mr Colwyn. It will travel to London first thing tomorrow morning, in the diplomatic bag. Just to be on the safe side. For a few days it will be kept in the residence of the apostolic delegate. New photographs can be taken there for your catalogue and for publicity. Presumably you have to arrange insurance. Once you have done that, and once the money has been received – the twenty million dollars, I mean – we shall hand the painting over to you. His Holiness would obviously like to know as soon as possible when you have some idea when the sale might be.'

The first course – rigatoni – arrived and David waited for it to be served before answering. 'Let's see. We are now in the second week of April. We shouldn't hurry things too much. There will be a lot of press attention following the announcement tomorrow, but after that we want to let the drama build. If Venturini has any unpublished research about the picture, we could release that at a later date. We – Hamilton's, that is – might invite the mayor of Foligno to London to be present at the sale. At our expense, of course. The timing of that announcement would help keep the publicity alive, too – add to the sense of theatre. We could make a feature out of the security arrangements: they will obviously have to be rather special. Nearer the time we can organize a series of special receptions for particular notables to view the picture. There's a lot we can do to keep the picture in the public eye – once I set my mind to it.'

Elizabeth Lisle smiled, fingering the gold cross held on a simple chain around her neck. 'Good, I like all those ideas. I suppose you had better let us have a report on your security arrangements before we let the "Madonna" leave the delegate's residence.'

'Before the end of the week.'

'Will it be a special sale – an auction all to itself?'

'I don't know yet. I'll ask my colleagues about that. Our big Old Master sale of the season, when everyone who can afford a picture like this is in London, is on 11th July this year. The "Madonna" could be the last lot in that sale – but I honestly don't know. An evening sale of just one picture – black tie, champagne, TV cameras etc. – may be the best way for us to help you. But we shouldn't rush that decision. Also, I'd like to gauge the public's reaction, once the news gets out. If there's a lot of protest then a quick sale is probably called for, so that protesters have less time to organize themselves. If not, if Pope Thomas convinces others that what he is doing is the right thing, we can afford to wait, to create a sense of anticipation.'

The waiter removed their plates.

'This is an unusual sale, remember. Unique. At the moment we have no way of knowing who, besides the obvious galleries, will be interested in it. It could be that big businesses run or owned by Catholics might want to own a picture that was once in the Vatican. Even among the galleries, I can never be sure from one month to the next who is going to have the funds. Apart from the European and American museums, the Japanese are showing more and more interest. And now the Australians are following in their footsteps. Then again it might be that devout Catholics in a rich parish – New York or Chicago, say – might club together to buy it for their cathedral, especially in view of the Holy Father's motive for selling. Who knows? The possibilities are not endless but, with the right kind of presentation, the right kind of research, we may persuade a lot more people that they could own this painting.'

David had Elizabeth Lisle's full attention. When she concentrated she had the habit of gripping the tip of her tongue between her teeth. The action flexed the muscles in her neck.

David was enjoying himself now. One of the most creative auctioneers in the business, he was only just warming to the situation. He had only really started thinking about it in the shower at the Hassler, but he already knew that there were some wonderful possibilities, the chance to break new ground. And it would put Hamilton's far ahead of its rivals . . . He smiled at Elizabeth Lisle, a smile that said he was on her side in wanting to make a success of the sale, and a smile of confidence which showed her that he knew what he was talking about, he was a professional. From the warm smile which she returned to him, he knew he had convinced her.

The main course arrived, and he refilled their glasses. Elizabeth Lisle had chosen a Tuscan dish, *arrosto misto*, mixed roasts of chicken, rabbit, pigeon. They ate in silence for a moment, then she said: 'Mr Colwyn, we shall be working together a great deal in the next few weeks. I think we should get the terms of your commission out of the way tonight, don't you?'

This was the critical part of the evening, he knew. He suspected she was going to try to beat him down – with charm. He said, as levelly as possible, 'Ten per cent is the normal arrangement.'

'But this is an unusual sale, Mr Colwyn, you said so yourself. The very fact that it is a Vatican picture means that most of your publicity is done for you. Say the picture does fetch sixty million dollars. The auction will last – what, two minutes? At most . . . don't you think that six million dollars is a little excessive for two minutes' work?'

'Miss Lisle,' he said, wondering if she had French blood, 'you know perfectly well that we do a lot more for our ten per cent than two minutes' work. The organization, arranging the money, helping to research the picture, checking its condition. I'm already here, working, and the sale is ages away. As for the publicity you talk about . . . this sale could backfire, so it's a risk from our point of view. And there's always uncertainty over price. It might only fetch twenty or thirty million dollars. There are those receptions I was talking about, the photography. We shall send people around the world, talking the picture up. You came to us, don't forget, and ten per cent is our rate.'

'What about the reason for the sale? The earthquake victims. Don't they mean anything to you? If you were to reduce your commission to – say – five per cent that could be *your* contribution to the victims.'

'No. Our contribution is organizing the sale so that we get you the best price for the painting. Our contribution is advancing you twenty million dollars for maybe three months and not charging you interest – which, after all, would be about five hundred thousand dollars at current rates.' He bit into his *ossubucco*. 'But I won't go on arguing with you over money, Miss Lisle. I will reduce our commission this time to eight per cent but no further. If that's not good enough, you'll have to find someone else to sell the "Madonna".'

'Done,' she said quickly. 'I can see that's as far as I am going to get. Thank you for coming down a bit, anyway. His Holiness will be pleased when I tell him. It means more for those poor people of Foligno. Now let's drink to a successful sale.'

# 2

The outrage created by the Vatican's announcement that it intended to
sell the 'Madonna of Foligno' was quite as shrill as David had predicted
and he wondered whether, in involving Hamilton's, he had made the
right decision. Europe's – and particularly Italy's – anti-Americanism
surfaced: a spokesman for the Italian government condemned the
proposal, claiming that, whatever the strict legal position of the Vatican
as a sovereign state in its own right, the Pope did not have the moral
authority to sell off treasures that had been on the Italian mainland for
so long. He ended, bitingly, 'An Italian Pope would not have done
this.'

This was almost certainly true. But the government spokesman had
missed the real point of Thomas's plan, which was to take the Church
into new waters. Change was coming to Rome.

The conclave which had elected Thomas had been the longest and
most bitterly contested in nearly two centuries. Although the previous
Pope, Pius XIII, as unlucky and as unpopular as his number implied,
had reigned for only three years, for many people those years had
been a disaster. Introspective and deeply conservative, Pius had much
resented the liberal turn which the Church had taken under *his* predecessor, a man who had instinctively understood the role of the media
in the modern world and who, by making the Church seem more
relevant, had in fact made the Papacy more popular and effective. But
Pius chose to see only showmanship where others saw substance, moral
decline where others saw liberalization, self-indulgence where others
saw happiness. As a result, on assuming office, Pius had sought to
undo much of the work of the previous years. A series of papal encycli-
cals castigated the modern world and, albeit in beautiful Latin, reiterated and upheld traditional practices. Chaos ensued. Priests found
themselves having to teach almost the opposite of what they had taught
before. As an inevitable result, numbers attending mass declined
sharply. Collections slumped. The press became hostile. Men left the
priesthood in droves. Pius didn't seem to care. 'Better one Holy soul

than a thousand Hollywood ones,' he liked to say in his tortured English.

To make matters politically even worse, before dying Pius fell ill and lapsed into a coma for three months. During that time the Church had no real leadership and ambitious cardinals began manoeuvring for position, an unedifying sight that did not go unnoticed in the world at large. When Pius finally did die there were three broad camps which converged on Rome for the conclave. The liberal faction was mainly made up of cardinals from the Anglo-Saxon countries, the more conservative group was from the Latin and Mediterranean areas, while the Third World cardinals were in general uncommitted.

The liberal candidate in the early conclave was Cardinal Hans Wendt, archbishop of Berlin, a man who had made his reputation by being rigidly anti-communist in political matters but was very flexible on social issues. It was an attractive mix for many people. His conservative opponent was Massoni, then Prefect of the Congregation for the Doctrine of the Faith, the old Holy Office which had once been responsible for the Inquisition. As such, Massoni was felt to be one of Pius's preferred successors, a fact which probably lost him as much support as it earned him.

In the early ballots both men attracted a similar number of votes and after two days it was clear that the conclave was deadlocked in a way unknown in recent times, though perhaps not uncommon in earlier centuries.

Normally, in such a case, the search for a compromise candidate, though never easy, would not take more than a day or two. On this occasion, however, the compromise choices all ended up with more opponents than supporters and a week passed with no agreement. As the deliberations went on and every day black smoke poured from the chimney on the roof of the Sistine Chapel, indicating that agreement had not been reached, world interest grew in the Catholic Church's evident crisis. Then, after a further forty-eight hours of deadlock, it was rumoured outside the Sistine Chapel that a group of Third World cardinals, frustrated by the Europeans' obduracy, had sought to find a compromise candidate of their own. At first they had put forward the cardinal from Chad but he had not accepted the nomination. Their second choice was the archbishop from Buenos Aires. But it then became clear that, since the new military government of that country was so dictatorial, an Argentinian Pope would be considered too controversial for the church at such a dangerous time. It would look as though the Church condoned dictatorships. That was when eyes had first turned to North America.

Attention almost immediately focused on two people: the archbishop of Montreal, and Thomas, who was then working in Rome as Prefect for the Congregation of Bishops. Many of the European cardinals, from long experience, took the view that if they were so divided among themselves, they should elect an elderly Pope, one who could not be expected to reign for too long. And then, by the time of his death, a natural successor might be apparent. At seventy-four, the cardinal from Montreal was this school's obvious choice.

The Third World cardinals took a different view. They argued, strongly, that the Church had just come through several short papacies, and the resulting upheavals had been disastrous for the Church, had made it confused and rudderless. *Their* dioceses needed the stability of a long papacy. At fifty-nine, Thomas might be young to be Pope, but as Prefect of the Congregation of Bishops, his responsibilities included the Pontifical Commission for Latin America and a similar commission for the pastoral care of migrants and itinerant people, and many of the black and yellow bishops already knew and liked him.

There were other reasons why they supported him. As a young man, after studying in Rome, Thomas had been sent on a special mission by the then-Pope to Thailand. From there he had secretly entered Kampuchea where he had been shot at by guerillas, and wounded in the leg. His account of life under the Khmer Rouge had been a best-seller and turned into a film, and his royalties had been used to help the refugees of the Khmer atrocities. In later years, too, he had spent time in South America, Argentina especially, where his talent for secret missions had again paid off. He had helped to trace several people who had been 'disappeared' by the military authorities. Three of these had already been executed but the publicity associated with his discoveries had eventually brought about the release of the others. To the third-world cardinals, no less than to Jasper Hale, Thomas Murray was a *doer*. Furthermore, he had been a cardinal now for five years and so was widely known throughout the Church.

Thomas's election was anything but straightforward, however, even with the third-world faction behind him. Though all agreed in principle that, sooner or later, an American as Pope had to come, neither Wendt's liberals nor Massoni's conservatives were happy with the idea. The deadlock had been eased but not entirely removed. After twelve days Thomas was still short of the necessary majority – two thirds of the votes plus one. Then two things happened.

First, the cardinal from Brussels, Jaime Salvin, died. He was seventy-one but even so, his death made the lack of agreement in the conclave begin to look frankly irresponsible. Second, the cardinal from Toulouse, a supporter of Massoni, was found with a radio transmitter concealed about him. He had been using it to communicate with a French TV station which had thus been able to broadcast unsuitably accurate accounts of the divisions within the conclave. This so disturbed his fellow cardinals that Thomas quickly obtained the extra votes he needed, and after thirteen days white smoke above the Sistine Chapel roof finally showed a by now rather disenchanted world that it at last had a new Pope.

A Holy Father from North America was a novelty, of course, and Thomas had added to that novelty by retaining his name on assuming office – only the third Pope to do so and the first since Renaissance times. In this, and in many other ways, he was obliged to move swiftly. Unlike any of his predecessors, he was faced with the fact that the whole world knew of the divisions within the Church, knew what unholy bargaining had gone on in the conclave. His authority was thus fundamentally undermined and, from the word go, Thomas had to fight to rebuild it.

Thomas was a liberal by temperament, and of the other candidates, Massoni was the most different, the most unlike in his attitudes, beliefs, in his whole approach to Vatican affairs. That was why Thomas had offered him the job of Secretary of State. He was sending a signal to the rest of the Church, and to the world, that he would remove the divisions they had been gloating over. It wasn't quite a joint leadership he was offering Massoni. Nonetheless, by the time of the Foligno earthquake, although few really understood his intentions yet, the papacy was changing. The Raphael sale was the first, bold move in Thomas's crusade for change.

It was not only the Italian government which objected when the news about the Raphael sale was divulged. Demonstrators outside the Vatican museums and the American embassy in Rome carried placards saying: 'Take your Pope home!' Customs officers at Rome's Leonardo da Vinci airport said they would examine all London-bound baggage for the picture and refuse to load it. When they learned that the painting had already left, they mounted a go-slow. Car stickers were printed by the million in Italy which showed the Raphael above the words: 'The Missing Madonna – have you seen her?' Overnight, the 'Madonna of Foligno' became the most controversial painting on earth.

In London, David was invited on to the BBC late-night current affairs show to defend Hamilton's involvement. A group of art historians – Italian, British and American – had written to *The Times*, condemning the sale as outrageous and arguing that it was illegal. Italian students in London had protested outside Hamilton's St James's offices. David was faced on the programme by Sir Anthony Hardy, a retired director of the National Gallery, and Monsignor David Mulreahy, assistant to the archbishop of Westminster. Hardy spoke first, repeating the arguments of the letter in *The Times*, which he had co-authored, saying that the Vatican was the natural home for religious art of the quality of Raphael and that under the terms of the Lateran treaty, which the Holy See had concluded with Mussolini in 1929, the Pope was not allowed to sell off the Vatican's art anyhow. He also threw in a criticism of

Hamilton's saying they were 'aiding and abetting the crime of the decade'.

The presenter of the programme then turned to Mulreahy, as a noted canon lawyer, for clarification of the law on the sale of the painting. Mulreahy was a smooth Irishman. David knew of him as a Northern Ireland priest, a frequent thorn in the side of whatever British government was in power. He had not realized Mulreahy was a canon lawyer as well and was apprehensive of what he might have to say. Hamilton's legal advisors had done their homework, but there were always grey areas.

'Sir Anthony is quite wrong, I'm afraid,' purred Mulreahy, and David relaxed. 'The law is perfectly clear. His Holiness is an absolute monarch in temporal matters. His word is absolute from the moment he is elected Pope, provided it is by a proper conclave, until the moment his successor is elected, also by a proper conclave. There are all sorts of conventions and traditions in Vatican life – but that's all they are. For example, it has been the convention for recent Popes to donate to charity only the gifts they have received themselves, or gifts presented to their immediate predecessor. Anything else is deemed to be part of the patrimony of the Holy See. But, I repeat, this is only a convention and a Pope may change it at any time if he wants to. And especially if he sees there is a pressing need, as I believe there is now. As to the Lateran Treaty, I have actually read it, which Sir Anthony may not have.' David could see that Mulreahy was enjoying himself. He wondered if there was some personal animosity between the two men. 'It consists of twenty-nine clauses, of which only clause eighteen relates to the treasures of the Vatican. It is three lines long, and although hardly a complicated legal document it is in fact a touch vague in the original Italian. It says that His Holiness must keep the *tesori* of the Vatican open at all times, for the public, students and scholars. Now *tesori* has two meanings: treasures and treasuries. If the Pope wanted to, therefore, he could choose to understand the treaty as reading that his obligation is to keep open the treasuries, the treasure *houses* of the Vatican, the museums and galleries! The Lateran treaty does not necessarily apply to any one single work of art.'

David was delighted now that Mulreahy had gone before him. He had entirely redressed the balance after Hardy's attack.

The presenter turned back to Sir Anthony for his reply.

'I think Father Mulreahy is quibbling. Maybe the Pope is not acting illegally, strictly speaking, but he is certainly doing something he ought not to. And, in my view, he wouldn't be able to if he wasn't abetted by auction houses like Hamilton's. They seem to think that the most important thing about a painting is its price. They are profiting by other people's misfortune.'

Swiftly and smoothly the presenter turned to David. 'Mr Colwyn, what do you say to that? Accessary to a crime, profiting by others' misfortune: heavy charges, eh?'

'And entirely mistaken,' said David quickly, trying to get into his voice all the enthusiasm he felt about the sale. 'I think we've just heard from Father Mulreahy here that there's no question of the sale of this painting being a crime. I never for a moment imagined that there was. As to Sir Anthony's argument that a great painting should not be bargained for I think that's a wholly misplaced view, too. Many of the paintings in the National Gallery, of which he was the distinguished director for several years, were themselves bargained for in just this way – as, for example, when large numbers of works of art came on to the market after the French Revolution and the Napoleonic wars. This painting, too, was looted by Napoleon's troops, so it is not all that dissimilar.'

'Forget the law, then,' said the presenter. 'What about the charge that the Pope has no *moral* authority to sell the painting?'

'Who is to decide?' said David. 'If a Pope doesn't have moral authority, who does? But even if he were not Pope, think about the reason why the sale is taking place: 1,200 dead, thousands homeless. What better moral authority can there be than Christ's own words, that we should help the poor?'

Again the presenter slid in. 'And what about the charge that Hamilton's are profiting from other people's misfortunes, that the most important thing for you is the price of a picture?'

'Those arguments are naive and not a little snobbish,' said David. 'It's like saying that doctors profit from misfortune, or nurses, or the police. Our organization will be helping to make a huge amount of money available to the disaster victims: that has to be a good thing.'

'But the prices are obscene.' It was Hardy again.

'Are they?' said David, taking a slip of paper out of his wallet. 'I did a bit of research before coming to the studio. Back in 1909 Holbein's "Duchess of Milan", now in the National Gallery, changed hands for £72,000: that would be over six million pounds today. The Leonardo cartoon, not even a proper painting, cost £800,000 in 1962, close to twelve million pounds now. That's in the National Gallery too. I could go on: Velasquez's "Juan de Pareja" was sold for £2,320,000 in 1970, nearer nineteen million pounds today.' These details had everybody's attention, so David swept on. 'Sir Anthony says we in the auction houses are only interested in prices. Not true – but we don't try to pretend that art is *only* about aesthetic appearance. That's the most important thing, yes, but not the only one. That's why I think he and a number of other academic art historians are naive and snobbish. Should artists work for nothing? Of course not. And unless you want art kept only in museums, which is clearly nonsense, there are going to be private collectors. Why then shouldn't museums and collectors buy and sell their collections, like anything else? That's all the art market is. Yet Sir Anthony Hardy, and his colleagues, when they write art history, write only about the *appearance* of pictures. Why ignore the fact that money changes hands, and why ignore the fact that art works are more expensive at some points in history than at others? When the Duke of Orléans wanted to raise money during the French Revolution to finance his political ambitions and settle his gambling debts, he sold the family's collection of paintings, the best in all France, perhaps in the whole world. Who was the first man to whom it was offered? James Christie, the very same who founded the distinguished house that still exists today. Who brought some of our greatest pictures, like the Altieri Claudes, all the way from Italy in the face of the entire French navy patrolling the Mediterranean and the Bay of Biscay? Not art historians but art dealers.'

'When the Orléans collection finally arrived in England who was it who arranged an exhibition unlike any that had been seen by the British public before, which changed our tastes for ever and was so popular it ran for six months? Michael Bryan, a dealer.'

David's mouth was dry by now, but while he had the floor he pressed on. 'As to the claim that the Vatican is the spiritual home of the picture I would like to point out that the "Madonna" has not been hanging in St Peter's or any other church. The picture is in a museum and, after the sale, will most likely go to another museum. So just as many people will be able to see it as in the past. It's not being destroyed – it's simply being sold.' He could see the studio manager waving at the presenter to wind up the show so he finished quickly. 'We have advanced His Holiness a substantial sum against the sale of the Raphael, so that he can offer aid to the earthquake victims promptly – in fact, even as this programme is taking place. That could not have been done before modern banking techniques and modern auction house practices. It could not have been done by anyone else in the art world. That *has* to be a good thing.'

The presenter was trying to slide in again but David had one more sentence. 'And, in view of the reason for the sale, we have agreed to reduce the commission we are charging.'

David sat back and reached for the glass of water on the desk in front of him. As the presenter began to wind up the programme, Hardy, a television professional, had the last word. Loudly, he shouted across the studio: 'Conscience money, Colwyn. Blood money.'

David slept badly that night, afraid that Hardy's final comment might have ruined the impression he had been trying to make.

When he got to Hamilton's office in St James's Square next morning, however, all of his colleagues had seen the show, and they thought he had had by far the best of the argument. The Earl of Afton, chairman

of Hamilton's and a descendant of the original Hamilton family, foun-
ders of the auction house in the eighteenth century, was very encouraging. 'Always thought that Hardy fellow was unstable,' he confided
in David. 'Now I know he's not only unstable, but nasty, too. Blood
money indeed.' He sniffed.

Afton had appointed David three years before, after his discovery of
the Raphael 'Madonna' in Sweden. Since then David had always found
the old man very supportive. When David had told him, two days
before, about the deal with the Pope, he had slapped his thigh and
chuckled. 'Bet you're nervous, eh? Don't be. Of course there'll be a
fuss, but always keep at the back of your mind poor old Stanley. If this
thing comes off we'll really have given him something to cry about.'

Stanley Rice was the millionaire owner of Steele's, Hamilton's main
rivals, and a man who, notoriously, always looked miserable. Together
Afton and David had pushed the Vatican sale through the emergency
board meeting that had to be called to ratify the decision to advance
twenty million dollars to the Pope. David had his rivals on the board,
an American called Sam Averne especially. But Afton had despatched
him. Indeed, David thought that Afton was enjoying all the 'fuss'
more than he was himself. And the Earl would be seventy-eight next
birthday.

Not that opposition to the sale was quite as great as David had feared.
Staff at the small office Hamilton's maintained in Rome reported after
a couple of days that, in fact, the Italian press was curiously split on
the issue and far less hostile than the Italian government. After all, the
press, although much criticized by people it attacked, was actually more
in touch with public opinion than anyone else, and its editors clearly
realized that, away from Rome and the rarified world of art historians,
the Pope's decision to sell the painting was very popular. A snap
opinion poll in the Milan-based *Corriere della Sera*, for instance, showed
that fifty-nine per cent of people approved of the sale of the painting,
only twenty-three per cent were against, and eighteen per cent didn't
know.

Another reason why press criticism was blunted was provided by
Elizabeth Lisle. In a very astute move, before making the announcement, she had obtained a reaction from Sirianni, the mayor of Foligno.
Not unnaturally he was absolutely delighted, effusive in his praise
of Pope Thomas, and he immediately withdrew the much-publicized
remarks he had shouted at the Holy Father. Thus anyone who attacked
Thomas's plan was by implication forced into taking a position against
the earthquake victims. Moreover, since Sirianni was a communist, the
communist papers in Italy, which might have been expected to be
virulently anti-Vatican, were in fact very welcoming of the Pope's
initiative. Opposition leaders in Italy sided with His Holiness also,
making the telling point that the government itself had done so little

to help the Foligno victims – the old story – that they were ill-equipped to speak about 'moral authority' in anything.

Around the rest of the world, it seemed to David, following the press cuttings closely, that once people got over the shock of a Pope actually having the courage to sell the painting, most of them approved. Indeed, press criticism soon gave way to speculation about who the most likely buyers were, and what the 'Madonna' was worth. When asked, the directors of the National Gallery in London, the Louvre in Paris, the Metropolitan Museum in New York, the Getty in Malibu and the Alte Pinakothek in Munich all said they would love the picture for their collections. But not one of them would discuss the price. They weren't about to talk the picture up.

By the weekend, it seemed to David that the Pope had won the argument, as he had predicted he would that evening in the Vatican picture gallery. The final accolade came on the following Tuesday when the American President, James Roskill, himself a Catholic, was asked by a reporter at his weekly news briefing to comment on the new American Pope's ambitious plan.

'As you know,' said the President, 'the United States has promised half a million dollars aid for the Foligno victims and as yet we are one of only a very few foreign governments – Great Britain and West Germany are the others – who have done so. I therefore welcome this initiative by Pope Thomas. It seems to me he's bringing American-style imagination, as well as true compassion, to his sacred duties. As an American, and as a Catholic, I applaud what he is trying to do. And I am sure that, were he alive today, Raphael of Urbino, itself not so very far from Foligno, would also approve the Pope's actions.'

In Italy, although grumbles continued spasmodically and art historians in general remained unconvinced, elsewhere everyone quickly got used to the idea. Nevertheless, because of all the publicity, it did not prove at all difficult for David to keep the 'Madonna' newsworthy.

To begin with, Venturini, the Vatican curator, was mortified by the thought of selling the Raphael; but, now put his back into ensuring that everything went off as well as possible – and he soon came up with a spectacular discovery in the Vatican's Secret Archives. He found a document, dated Christmas 1519, in which the then Pope, Leone X, Giovanni de' Medici, had written to Raphael offering to make him a cardinal. This was a story that had often been rumoured but invariably discounted by the historians. But here was the document, confounding even the best authorities. Its importance lay in the way it established the enormously high status of artists at the beginning of the sixteenth century: they were no longer just craftsmen but on a par with cardinals and, by implication, Popes. There was no reply from Raphael in the archive – at that point he didn't have long to live anyway – but it didn't

39

matter. Venturini's discovery made the front pages of the newspapers and even began to soften up the Pope's critics among professional art historians. This new research would not have taken place, and produced results, but for His Holiness's initiative.

As Elizabeth Lisle had promised, the picture was transferred to Hamilton's care after insurance had been arranged. David used the transfer as an opportunity for a photo-call: he guessed rightly that most picture editors would not be able to pass up the chance of being in the company of such a great painting, and the turnout by the press and networks was magnificent. Also, since he had decided the picture would not go on public display just yet, the sale being some way off, for a select few, distinguished collectors, government ministers in the relevant departments, art historians, other prominent personalities, the word was put round that a private viewing could be arranged. He was taken to task about this, however, when Elizabeth Lisle came to London after a month or so to check that everything was going smoothly. It was his chance to repay her hospitality, so he picked her up at Westminster Cathedral, where she was attending mass, and took her on to dinner at Wiltons in Jermyn Street.

In the car on the way to the restaurant David noticed her fiddling with her watch and holding it to her ear. 'What's wrong? Not working?'

'Listen.' She held up her wrist. Faintly, he could make make out a voice, speaking in Italian.

'A speaking watch?'

'Sort of. It's a watch and a radio. I have it tuned to the Vatican station so I can keep up when I'm away.'

He must have looked perplexed for she added, with a smile, 'Don't mind me. I'm gadget crazy. You'd be amazed at the junk I collect.'

After they were seated at the restaurant, Elizabeth Lisle chose the whiting, waited till it was on the table, then challenged him. 'I hear that if someone is fancy enough he can get to see the "Madonna". But you have to be on a list of – what's it called? – the "Great and the Good".' Her brown eyes were fixed on him. Again, he noticed her grip her tongue between her teeth. 'Is that the right image we want to give? Thomas asked me to ask you.'

'I'm absolutely certain it is,' David replied without hesitation. 'I'm trying to make the picture "fashionable". And to do that I need to make it exclusive. I have to limit its accessibility – just as the South Africans limit the accessibility of diamonds or gold. We'll put it on general show later, but the present arrangements are part of my overall plan. For instance,' he went on, 'I don't just let people see the picture. It's made perfectly clear to them that, in return for the privilege, they are expected to make a donation to the Foligno appeal. Now, some of the people we've invited have been leaving cheques for quite impressive amounts. We've had three for a thousand pounds already. That way the Foligno fund benefits and for the people we are talking about, the viewing becomes not entirely self-indulgent: they can go off and tell their friends that they are not only privileged to have seen the picture, but they are holy too.'

She swallowed some fish and smiled wryly. 'Ingenious – but a shade cynical, uh?'

'Not really,' David countered. 'Don't get me wrong – I like the people I'm talking about. They may have their foibles, but then so do we all. And to be a businessman, an art dealer, and entrepreneur, you have to know how people are, what makes them get up in the morning. Now,' he went on in a less serious tone, 'tell me your news.'

Elizabeth Lisle put down her fork. 'Well, first off I'm instructed to tell you that the Holy Father is delighted with the way things are going. He was most impressed when the twenty million turned up on time. We had the hospitals fixed in two days. Within four days everyone had electricity and enough food. The water took a bit longer but even that was operational within a week. The prefabricated houses arrived by the Monday eight days after the quake and the school was able to begin classes after two weeks. We've put in extra teachers, extra nurses, extra plumbers and electricians. We've given a thousand dollars each to roughly two thousand families. Demolition experts have been hired to clear the rubble. They started at the end of last week. Fresh building starts the week after next but we're obviously hampered by not knowing exactly how much we can spend until the painting has actually been sold. What about that? Are you tagging it on to your ordinary Old Master sale, or is it going to be a one-off?'

'Oh, it has to be a special event, don't you think?' said David. 'Everything points to that. The opposition is actually *less* fierce than I expected and in fact I think people are already looking forward to the sale. We'll make it as much of an occasion as we can and sell the Raphael the evening *before* our regular Old Master auction – black tie, by invitation only, preceded by a champagne reception at which Monsignor Hale and the Earl of Afton will receive the guests. We'll hold the sale at 7.30, in time for the evening television news and the following morning's papers. We're compiling a special catalogue. Most of the people attending the sale with a view to bidding will already know the painting very well but there's still scope for making the catalogue something of a memento. Photographs and a condition report on the "Madonna" have already gone out to dealers, galleries, collectors – anyone we think is likely to be a contender at the auction. I've also got one or two other things up my sleeve.'

Elizabeth Lisle finished her whiting and sat back in her chair, relaxed and smiling. 'You're making me a great success in my job, you know. Up to now things haven't been easy. Can you imagine what it's like in the Vatican being a woman, the only woman in charge of anything? I

41

tell you, at the start I was about as popular as termites in timber. But things are going well now: the Holy Father's getting a great reception in the press, I'm in his good books – and I guess we owe a lot of this to you.' She paused. 'You were brilliant on television, I hear.'

'Only lucky,' said David, grinning. 'Mulreahy handed it to me on a plate.'

She eyed him thoughtfully. 'I have to admit I was suspicious of you and the whole plan to begin with. I was suspicious of all art dealer types and auctioneers – too many phonies, too many fat men with striped shirts and chequered pasts. But you sure showed me I was wrong, David Colwyn. And coming from a Mississippi girl that's quite an admission.'

David inclined his head in a mock bow. 'I'm pleased you're pleased,' he said, and meant it.

Mississippi – he should have realized Elizabeth Lisle was a southerner from the husky eddies in her voice. Here was an opportunity at last to take the conversation away from business. 'Tell me about the American South,' he said. 'I'm ashamed to say I've never been there.'

So she told him about her childhood. Her family were French originally, and had lived in Louisiana since before it was an American state. They owned a substantial stretch of the Mississippi river frontage. She told him about the family business, 'Lisle Liquors', bourbon especially. She had always wanted to write, so after school and a time in Switzerland, she had gone to Columbia School of Journalism in New York.

'I started on a couple of small papers in the mid-west, then joined the *Boston Times*, covering local politics at first, then the Third World.'

'And how did you come to leave?'

'I'd always been used to travel. Well, movement anyway. At home we were surrounded by rivers and swamps. Louisiana is one swamp after another. Pa had a plane, one that landed on water. He used to take us children all over the state, skimming the dogwood trees, scooping down on the creeks and bayous, scaring the alligators. You haven't lived till you've landed on water. But as soon as I was old enough I wanted to go beyond the swamps, they were so goddam flat! Later, after I'd been in journalism a few years, I got frustrated, being so close to power but never actually having any. It happens to lots of journalists but usually later in their careers.'

'And why Rome?'

'Well, Louisiana was French of course, before it was American. But that also means it's very Catholic. Near where we lived was the oldest church in the state – so Pa flew us there every Sunday. It was exciting, flying to church – we always wanted to go. What with the church, and the flying, and swamps being so darned flat, I was always hankering after abroad. To a girl abroad seemed more mountainous, more *interesting* somehow. Then I met Thomas when I was working in Boston. I wrote a piece about him which he saw and liked. I guess it impressed him. Anyway, he told me to look him up if ever I was in Rome – he'd just been made a cardinal at that time. So I did exactly that: bought a plane ticket, called him up out of the blue. We had lunch. Anyone could see the Vatican press office needed beefing up. At that stage they had no one covering the Third World's press, so I suggested myself. With his South American background Thomas was enthusiastic and, although it took a month or two, he finally got me the perfect job. Living in the old world, dealing with the Third World, in a field I knew, but with some real power at last. And I was only thirty. I had two and a half wonderful years – then he went and got himself elected Pope. The rest, as they say, is history.'

'And you're enjoying life?'

'What do you think? Apart from everything else, I meet people like you.' She reached for her wine glass. 'And that's *your* cue to do the talking for a while. It's thirsty work, all this remembering.'

'What would you like to know?'

'Why go into art? Why not politics, the law, the church?'

'Can anyone properly answer such questions? I think one reason must be that, in the arts more than anything else, it's clear that the people who came before us were just as skilled, just as wise, as we are now. Michelangelo's sculpture has never been equalled, let alone surpassed. Neither have Shakespeare's plays or Beethoven's music. Goya's insights were as profound as Freud's. Turner knew how beauty hides just as much as it reveals. There's been change in art but the very idea of direction or progress, in painting say, is ludicrous. I find that comforting. Another reason could be that I like the way art seeks to find beauty in what *is*, rather than what might be. Politicians and lawyers, like Americans these days, are so used to putting things right, they think they can do anything. They'rd so pleased with themselves.'

'You don't like Americans?'

'I like their enthusiasm; it's their overconfidence I'm not so sure about.'

She let that pass. 'But you're a scholar *and* an auctioneer. Why both? Why not one or the other?'

'Scholarship is wonderfully satisfying. It's all about solving mysteries. At the moment, for instance, I'm trying to discover which of two paintings allegedly by Leonardo is genuine and which is the copy. There ought to be a clean answer, if only I could find the right documents. Auctions, on the other hand, are about people and therefore untidy. There are no clean answers in the art market: what is true one minute is not true the next. And the uncertainties are as gripping as the straight-forward, clean answers of scholarship. Some people find only the one or the other attractive. I like them both. So far, I've been lucky – I can have them both. It may not last.'

'You sound as if you're as much married to your job as I am to mine.'

'Never been properly married?'

She shook her head.

He hesitated. 'I was. Still am, in fact, but it's over. And a real mess. I'm a Catholic, but my wife is not. So she can get divorced and remarry, of course, but I can't. Not if I take my religion seriously. Which leaves me beached, stranded. I try not to think about it.'

Elizabeth Lisle looked at him. Her brown eyes caught the light. 'I shouldn't really tell you this. But the Holy Father has plans for the Church which will revolutionize Catholic marriages – and Catholic divorces. Your situation may not be so bleak as you think. You may not be beached at all. But – ' she bent down and picked up her napkin from the floor where it had fallen ' – it all depends on how this sale of the "Madonna" goes. It's the Holy Father's first attempt to do some-thing new, to shake up the old traditions. If it succeeds, Mr Colwyn, you may have done yourself a favour in more ways than one. But it *must* succeed.'

The date of the sale approached. David had told Elizabeth Lisle over dinner at Wiltons that he had 'one or two things up his sleeve.' The first of these related to the catalogue. Instead of showing the 'Madonna' on its cover, as would have been expected, Hamilton's had commissioned Fulvio Cippolini, a leading Italian photographer, to take pictures of Foligno in the aftermath of its agony. The cover of the catalogue showed the ruins of the cathedral and inside there was a selection of Cippolini's views, including one of the tattered copy of the Vatican Raphael that had hung in the cathedral transept. The tactic succeeded gloriously: Cippolini's pictures were works of art in them-selves, and David made a much-publicized round-the-world flight, taking with him copies of the catalogue for all those gallery directors and collectors who might be interested in the 'Madonna'.

David's second revolutionary notion was to charge the public for admission to view the picture before the sale. The charge was to be flexible, whatever people could afford, and would then be passed on to the Foligno fund. Some board members said this ran the risk of being misunderstood, that people might think Hamilton's themselves were profiting from the charge. They also claimed it would keep away large numbers and in that case would create the impression that there was less interest in the picture than there actually was. That could affect the sale.

David argued vigorously. He believed that the Pope had judged the public's enthusiasm accurately and that charging would actually *increase* the attendance, since the object of going would no longer be simply 'arty' but also charitable.

David's proposal, passed by the board only narrowly, with the

Averne faction against him as always, was triumphantly vindicated. People came in droves to see the painting. The queues at Hamilton's stretched all the way down to Pall Mall, around the corner and, ironically enough, past the main door of Steele's. Meanwhile the rescue work and reconstruction was still continuing at Foligno, so the two stories fed on one another, making each more newsworthy.

Even so the sale might have passed off very differently had not Nature suddenly intervened, and in such a horrifyingly dramatic way.

The *Waitara Chief* was a 29,000 ton refrigerator vessel out of Christchurch, New Zealand. At 4.03 on the morning of 5th July, laden with a cargo of frozen lamb and bound for Manzanillo in Mexico, she was steaming due east at fifteen knots about fifty miles west of Nuku Hiva in the Marquesas Isles in the south-east corner of the Pacific. Not many people at that moment could have pointed to the Marquesas Isles on the map, but before the day was out countless millions would know exactly where latitude 9° south, longitude 140° west was.

First officer Ross Napier was on the *Waitara Chief's* bridge. At that hour only he and four others were needed to man her: she was hardly the last word in ships but she was modern enough. The rest of the crew was below decks sleeping. Nuku Hiva, the main island of the Marquesas, was too far away to be visible even in full sunshine, let alone then, in the faint grey wash of dawn. But Motu Iti, a smaller island but much closer, might just be seen, depending on the visibility. Napier brought his binoculars up to his eyes to check, and in so doing missed the enormous eruption of water that suddenly rose from nowhere out to his right. He felt it soon enough, though. The ship heaved and he turned rapidly as a huge wall of grey-green water approached, towering over him. It must have been twenty metres high. He stared, horrified. 'Oh my god!' he gasped. Almost immediately another mass of water appeared to the left and the ship was thrown violently back on itself. Napier's first thought was that the ship had run into a family of huge whales – but the sonar should have picked that up. He turned to the screen. It had gone hyperactive now, but it wasn't the kind of pattern you got with whales. What in heaven's name was happening?

Then the whole ocean boiled.

In no time, a matter of seconds, the night's calm sea was transformed: huge mountains of water were punched up into the air as if by some hidden fist. The ship rolled steeply, first this way, then that. Vainly the helmsman spun the wheel. Napier grabbed for the intercom, stabbed a button. The captain needed no rousing. Everyone on the ship was awake; no one could sleep in this turmoil.

'You'd better come and see for yourself, Tom. The sea's gone mad.'

The captain was never to make it. By now, among the enormous cliffs of water, stinking, sulphurous gases were escaping into the morning air, with a dreadful, high-pitched hiss, and bringing with them stones, rocks, gigantic boulders that were hurled into the air by some huge hidden force deep down below the surface. Napier noticed, the way one does in a crisis, something irrelevant: Motu Iti *was*, after all, visible to port. He grabbed the phone again and jabbed another button.

'Mitchell! Mitchell – are you there?'

The radio officer came on the line. 'Sir. What in god's – '

'Send out a Mayday! D'you hear? We'll never make it.'

At that moment a boulder half as big as a bus landed on the bridge, crushing it. Both Napier and the helmsman died instantly. Mitchell, in his radio shack, still lived, but by the time he had sent off the Mayday call it was too late. As Captain Thomas Boswell climbed hand-over-hand up the last few stairs to the main deck, the *Waitara* suddenly rolled and pitched back, the sea beneath her bow swelling up with all the force of the devil himself. Boswell lost his grip and fell. The ship checked with a deadening jolt and a loud cracking scream as her back was broken. A black gash appeared across her decks forward of the bridge and with one final, terrible, screech, the stern section separated. No one had any time to take to the boats. Those crew members who managed to get on deck jumped for it. They were the first to perish. As they hit the water their screams of agony were added to the uproar around them. For, in addition to everything else that morning, the sea about the *Waitara Chief* was boiling hot. The seamen were scalded to death before they could drown.

Moments later the ship herself disappeared as the full force of the erupting underwater volcano was felt. An area of sea hundreds of yards across rose into the air as if a new country was being born below it. Immense boulders were thrown into the air, and hissing, steaming lava, only to fall back, leaving just the escaping gases and a gathering tidal wave as evidence of the cataclysm.

The *Waitara's* Mayday call was picked up in Pitcairn Island but it was academic. It took the tidal wave caused by the eruption barely twenty minutes to reach Nuku Hiva so it was shortly after 4.30 that a wall of water about sixty feet high swept across the island. Nothing below the one hundred feet line was left intact and whole villages and towns, including Hakamui on Ua Pu, were obliterated. But, with the mountains there reaching 11,000 feet and more, the radio masts and telephone aerials were left intact so that the world knew about the Marquesas Isles disaster in a matter of minutes. Survivors would later describe in vivid terms the moment they first spotted the monster wave, miles out to sea, like a huge silver band upon the horizon. The silver band had got larger. Then a terrible hissing had been heard as the wave rushed everything before it. Already there had been widespread panic. Now the water slammed into areas that were still largely asleep so that hundreds – the death toll was put at six hundred next day – were drowned almost instantly.

The retreat of a tidal wave does almost as much damage as its advance. Whole families were sucked back into the sea and never seen again. But the eeriest event of that black day was the fate of Ross Napier. Pulled from the battered bridge of the *Waitara Chief* as she went down, Napier's body must have been borne high on the crest of the tidal wave, for it was eventually flung to rest on a hillside on Nuku Hiva, fifty miles away. His dead hand still gripped the intercom phone.


'He wants to do *what?*'

David listened incredulously as Elizabeth Lisle on the other end of the line in her office in Vatican City, gave him the news again. He pushed his hand through his hair. 'I don't believe it. I mean I *do* believe it – what I mean is, if I can just pick myself up off the ground, this boss of yours is brilliant. It's a fantastic idea.'

Elizabeth began speaking again and now David took notes. It was late, after six. Sally Middleton, his secretary, had gone home, and he had poured himself a small whisky in the office. He sipped it now as Elizabeth Lisle continued to talk. More notes. Then, he said: 'Ten probably, eight certainly, five I can do right away, as before. And we'll need photographs. How will you get it to us – the same way as last time?'

He jotted down the details. 'Right,' he said, 'It's a marvellous idea, stunning. But there's a lot of work to do. I must get started right away. I'll talk to you again very soon.'

He hung up, then immediately made an internal call. 'Jack? You're still there, good. Can you come down here, straight away please. I've got some news that will curl your hair.'

Jack Pringle arrived. A tall, handsome, balding Canadian, Pringle was Hamilton's press and publicity officer. 'Here,' said David, holding out a glass. 'You're going to need this.'

He waved Pringle to a seat. 'I'm not trying to tell you how to do your job, Jack, but, to save time, I'm going to dictate a press release to you. We haven't much leeway. With the "Madonna" sale only a week off we've got to contact all the news boys right away.'

'Nothing wrong, is there?' said Pringle anxiously.

'On the contrary.' David grinned. 'Sharpen your ballpoint and pin back your ears.' He picked up a large yellow legal notepad on which he had been scribbling while he waited for the other man. 'This isn't very polished, Jack, but I'll leave that to you. It gets across the essentials. Are you ready?'

Pringle nodded.

'Right. Copy begins: Following the disaster in the Marquesas Isles, when a massive tidal wave killed six hundred inhabitants and rendered

47

thousands homeless, His Holiness Pope Thomas has decided to offer another painting from the Vatican collection for sale – '

Pringle whistled.

'Save it,' said David. 'Hear the rest first . . . another painting from the Vatican collection for sale to aid the victims. As with Raphael's "Madonna of Foligno", which is being sold to help in the aftermath of the Foligno earthquake, this second painting too will be sold by auction at Hamilton's in London on July 10th, at 7.30 in the evening. This further painting is to be Paul Gauguin's "Nativity", painted in 1898 and only recently acquired by the Vatican. Art lovers will need no reminding that Gauguin, himself a poor man, died at Atuona in the Marquesas Isles in 1903. His Holiness feels therefore that, as with the Foligno earthquake, this perfect match between the work of art in the Vatican's possession and the particular disaster, provides an opportunity for the Catholic Church to help, and to give a lead across the world in trying to alleviate acute hardship wherever it occurs. In the few days remaining before the sale, Hamilton's will place the Gauguin on show alongside the Raphael, at its St James's Square galleries. The voluntary admission charge will continue but from the moment the Gauguin goes on display the amount of money received will be divided among the two charitable appeal funds.

'Note to editors – and don't forget this, Jack,' David added. 'Most of them will know about Raphael but less about Gauguin, so a brief art lesson seems in order: "Gauguin's paintings, especially those produced in the South Seas, are very rare outside France. Britain and America, for example, have hardly a single example of this period of his work between them. In London the National Gallery is known to be particularly keen to acquire one, so too the Tate. Bidding is, therefore, expected to be extremely keen".'

David sat back and refilled his glass. 'What do you think?'

'How much does the Pope hope for this time?' Pringle believed in getting straight down to basics.

'The figure I suggested he might expect was twenty million dollars. Fifteen certainly. I've agreed to advance them ten.'

Pringle sucked the end of his pen. 'It's great business – and wonderful theatre. I love every minute of it. But if this sale catches on, sir, if we make a lot of money for the Vatican and if selling your art for a good cause becomes the smart thing to do, where will it end? I have a feeling these are deep waters, Mr Colwyn, very deep waters.'

# 3

David looked down from the rostrum at the faces in front of him. Sir Roland Lavery was there, in the first row where he couldn't be missed. Sir Alaistair Brown, his opposite number at the National Gallery and normally an ally, sat three rows back, his mane of silver hair framing his ruddy face and black velvet bow tie. The Americans, for some reason, all liked to sit at the back: Smallbone from the Getty, Holmes from Houston, Jakobson from the Metropolitan, Villiers from Boston, McGinty from Chicago. Von Hohenburg had a whole team over from Berlin with him: he sat in the auction hall now at the end of his row where David could see him easily. The French, the Italians, the Australians, the Japanese were all here. There was even a Russian from the Hermitage, an almost unprecedented visit and one which underlined, if it needed underlining, the sensational impact of the Vatican sale.

For David, for Elizabeth Lisle and for the entire Hamilton staff the past few days had been unbelievably hectic. The announcement of the Gauguin sale had left people stunned. An Italian government spokesman again attacked the Pope's policy of selling off treasures, but in the face of the scale of the damage in the Marquesas Isles, his were graceless words. Most people applauded the Pope's compassion, his imagination and, above all, his will to act. Newspapers the world over despatched reporters to the scenes of devastation and their reports, first of the damage, then of the Vatican aid arriving, provided the sale with the best kind of publicity. When the Gauguin went on show at the Hamilton gallery, the lines swelled further. Many people, interviewed in the queues, told reporters that they were coming for the second time.

David's ambition to make the sale the event of the season succeeded magnificently. He was aware of the bitter irony that helping the poor required so much glitter but, as he wrote in a specially commissioned article for the *New York Times* which appeared on the morning of the sale, he honestly could see no better way. Of those invited to the sale, almost no one refused and extra public rooms had to be prepared, linked to the main hall by closed circuit television.

The arrival of the communist mayor of Foligno, Sandro Sirianni, on the day before the sale was heavily covered in the British press, and his introduction in the catalogue, praising the Pope for what he was doing, was reprinted in abridged form in the London *Times* on the same day as David's New York piece.

Elizabeth Lisle had arrived at the saleroom early, but David had seen very little of her by the time he mounted the rostrum to begin the sale. They exchanged a word during the reception, when they had wished each other luck, but no more.

Jasper Hale, the apostolic delegate, had also arrived early, ready to receive the guests with Afton. 'So, Mr Colwyn,' he murmured as they stood together at the top of the great staircase at Hamilton's, 'it looks like the mystery will have a happy ending after all.'

David smiled. The old fox had the memory of an elephant. He held up crossed fingers. They had then bowed and smiled and shaken many hands as the room filled up.

Amid such glitter, the communist mayor of Foligno might have been expected to look out of place. Except of course that, as an *Italian* communist, Sirianni arrived in black tie, his grey hair immaculately groomed – and with a gift for David and for Hamilton's.

He was introduced by the Italian ambassador, who acted as interpreter. 'Foligno is not a rich town, Mr Colwyn,' he said. 'But we are proud and not ungrateful.' What he then held out moved David very much. It was a mounted fragment of the marvellous mosaic, the vivid gold and blue picture of Christ being worshipped by the earlier Pope that had once adorned the main facade of Foligno Cathedral, which had crashed to the ground near Enzo's bar on that fateful Sunday. It was very beautiful and very appropriate.

'As you can see, Mr Colwyn, it has been framed by local carpenters in Foligno, men who survived the earthquake and have been helped by the Pope's funds. It is a – well, a kind of memorial to this whole episode. I hope you will accept it, with our thanks.'

Elizabeth Lisle was standing beside the Italian ambassador and Sirianni and David could see that she was as touched as he was.

'I am honoured, Signor Sirianni. And I am delighted to accept it on behalf of Hamilton's. We shall display it prominently, I assure you.'

By then it was a quarter past seven and David hastily excused himself and disappeared up to his office on the fourth floor. He needed to comb his hair, straighten his tie and to collect his own copy of the sale catalogue. For an ordinary sale, with many paintings to be auctioned, it would have been marked in his own private code, with reserves, bids, details of those lots which, although spread throughout the catalogue, actually belonged to the same buyer – all the details that went into a successful sale but which also made being an auctioneer a rather more difficult job than it might appear to an outsider.

For this sale, however, preparation of that kind was not necessary. To begin with, of course, there were just the two lots, the Gauguin, which was to be sold first, and the 'Madonna'. But this sale was also exceptional in that Hamilton's had received *no* telephone bids whatsoever. Quite simply, everyone had been determined to come themselves, wanting to be present at what was so obviously an historic occasion. He knew, because the publicity department had made a count for a diary item in that morning's newspapers, that twenty-three directors of national galleries around the world were here, all forty-seven of the top Old Master dealers and all sixty-six of the top modern French dealers except Louis von Lutitz who, he knew, was ill in hospital in Paris. And even he had sent a deputy. David also knew that there were, perhaps, no more than twenty or thirty private collectors in the entire world who could afford the prices likely to be seen tonight, and ninety per cent of them were taking their seats in the main hall at that very moment.

During the reception Jasper Hale had been in his element. He knew everyone and, David could see, he obviously adored Elizabeth Lisle, introducing her flamboyantly to every guest. Though there was a serious side to the evening, the reception had very soon taken on the flavour of a party. Photographers from the press, who David had also insisted wear black tie so as not to spoil the mood, moved among the guests, their lights flashing like fireworks.

In his office, as he scooped up the catalogue and one or two other items he would need on the rostrum, David realized that, despite his nearly twenty years in the business, and despite the fact that everything had gone so well so far, he was horribly nervous. At the end of the day the paintings had to sell. If, for some unanticipated, dreadful reason the pictures failed to reach the millions he had advanced to the Pope, it would be the biggest embarrassment, and the most expensive disaster the art world had ever known. He, David Colwyn, would certainly be out of a job – but worse, the Holy Father's ambitions for his Church would be severely crippled.

Firmly dismissing such thoughts, he went down to the main hall. He had timed his entry well. It was a matter of pride at Hamilton's that auctions started punctually. On this occasion, however, David judged that a three or four minute delay would underline the sale's importance and add to the drama. The main saleroom was packed, men and women representing millions of pounds in nearly every seat. As David appeared, nodding to acquaintances, giving last-minute instructions to his staff and mounting in a leisurely way the steps to the rostrum, the buzz in the room died away. He spread his papers on the desk before him, took his gavel from his pocket and settled into his chair. He looked down to check that all the Hamilton staff dotted about the room were in place. They were there to spot any bids he missed.

The huge saleroom suddenly brightened as the television lights were turned on. Well, thought David, this is it. The greatest sale of my career, of anybody's career. The greatest auction ever. It was time to begin.

'Ladies and gentlemen, welcome to Hamilton's. Before we begin the main business of the evening I have two announcements.' He looked down and to his left. A blue-coated porter placed the Foligno gift, the blue and gold mosaic, on the display easel. David beamed. 'This, I hasten to say, is not for sale. For those of you who don't recognize it, this is an exquisite fragment of a work of art from Foligno Cathedral. As you can see it has been framed by carpenters in the town, men aided by Pope Thomas's efforts. Earlier this evening it was presented to Hamilton's as a thank-you gift by Signor Sirianni here' – and David indicated with a nod of the head where the mayor was sitting. 'Since one of you here tonight is actually going to buy the "Madonna" I think you deserve his thanks far more than we.'

A burst of chatter broke out and a ripple of applause. David indicated to the porter to take away the mosaic. Then he spoke again, to quieten the hubbub. 'My second announcement . . .' – he allowed the murmurs to die away completely – 'My second announcement is equally pleasant.' He held aloft a slip of paper, obviously a cheque. 'As you know, in connection with tonight's sale, and as a way of raising more money to help the disaster victims, Hamilton's took the unusual step of requesting payment at public viewings of the Raphael "Madonna" and then, after the Marquesas Isles disaster, the Gauguin. I am happy, therefore, to present this cheque now to Monsignor Jasper Hale, the apostolic delegate in London.'

Hale got to his feet, the cameras trained on him and David.

'The amount, incidentally,' said David, pausing with a fine sense of the dramatic, 'the amount from the voluntary admission charges, together with the sale of the special catalogue, comes to £613,176.'

This time the applause was heavier. David leaned down and handed the cheque to an astounded Hale who took it, kissed it, and pushed his way between the packed rows of chairs to shake Sirianni's hand enthusiastically. David had deliberately not told the delegate about the cheque: he had wanted to catch him off-balance. Some television networks were carrying the auction live and this was too good an opportunity to miss. Now, while the chatter about the cheque continued, David nodded to the senior porter to put up the Gauguin. Immediately the noise died away to stillness: faces and cameras turned to the easel.

'And now, without further delay, the main business of the evening. The first lot in the sale tonight is Paul Gauguin's "Nativity", painted in the South Seas in 1898. This painting is being sold on the authority of His Holiness Pope Thomas, the proceeds to benefit the survivors of the Marquesas Isles tidal wave disaster. I shall start the bidding at five million pounds – any more? Five million? . . . five million pounds . . . Any more . . . ?' This was the moment David always hated. Quite often, between the opening statement by the auctioneer and the first bid from the floor there was a ghostly silence, a dead time when it seemed as if nothing further would happen. David looked around the room: all faces were on him now but no one moved. No one spoke. Then a man removed his glasses, waved them briefly. It was a dealer from New York.

'Five million. Five million is bid,' said David. The sale was on and he breathed again.

As often happens, once the ice was broken, an avalanche started. Dozens of people – Americans, Europeans, and the Australians particularly – were raising their hands, or nodding their heads, or waving their catalogues in David's direction. The bidding rose to ten, twelve, fifteen million pounds. Eighteen million. Then it slowed as people reached their limits and dropped out of the bidding. David breathed more easily as the bidding crested eighteen million. In common, seemingly, with most of the trade, he had set the picture's value at between eighteen and nineteen million, and had told Elizabeth Lisle as much over the phone. He would have felt he had let the Pope down if the Gauguin had not made eighteen million pounds.

But it had and now, as the figure approached nineteen million, only three bidders appeared to be left: the National Gallery of Tokyo, the Houston gallery and a dealer who, David thought, was bidding for either the National Gallery in London, or the Tate. At twenty Houston dropped out. The bidders were more reflective now, taking as much as thirty seconds to make up their minds on each offer. The three Japanese from Tokyo even had mini-conferences among themselves.

At twenty-one million, just when both sides seemed to be exhausted, a new bidder entered: the New York Metropolitan Museum. David admired the skill and experience of Norman Jakobson who had sat there patiently, letting the others wear each other out, then entering at just the right psychological moment. At twenty-two million Tokyo dropped out. Most surprising the Met, having come in at twenty-one million pounds, dropped out immediately after. An interesting tactic, thought David. Jakobson had done nothing to drive the price up, was willing to pay slightly over the odds for the picture, but no more than that. Very professional.

And so David found himself saying: 'twenty-three million . . . twenty-three million pounds . . . any more? . . . any more? . . . twenty-three million pounds . . . fair warning . . . twenty-three million pounds . . .' His gaze searched the room. ' . . . Any more? . . . twenty-three million . . . twenty-three million . . . Any more? . . . twenty-three million . . . all done at twenty-three million pounds . . .' He banged his gavel. As another wave of excited chatter began to break, he looked at the winning dealer, ready to call out his name. But this man, an old acquaintance of Hamilton's, looked across to where Sir Alaistair Brown, director of the National Gallery of London was smiling happily. Sir Alaistair nodded to David, meaning his identity could now be revealed. Delighted, David banged his gavel again and said in a loud clear voice, 'The National Gallery, London.' You old rogue, he thought. Hiding behind a dealer was not exactly a new ploy but it had paid off gloriously this time. The Gauguin was a great catch for the National.

David had expected to move straight on to the Raphael but the hubbub was such that a short break was obviously needed. He realized that no one wanted to rush the occasion and that for some of the people in the hall, the two sales were related. The National Gallery was presumably cleaned out and wouldn't be bidding any more tonight, whereas other galleries, having failed to spend money so far, might go higher to get the 'Madonna'.

So, for a minute or two, David sat sipping water from the carafe on his desk and patiently surveying the room. Then, after what he judged a suitable interval, he said loudly to the head porter, 'Put up the Raphael.'

The 'Madonna' was lifted onto the easel. Whereas the Gauguin had seemed to David somewhat unassuming in the vast dimensions of the auction room, the Raphael was more obviously imposing, its reds and blues losing none of their vividness in the bright television lights. The room was reverently hushed now, totally silent, as if these art lovers realized they were seeing a picture the quality of which would never be repeated at auction. David hardly had to raise his voice to make himself heard. 'Raphael's "Madonna of Foligno", painted between 1511 and 1512 for Sigismondi dei Conti, originally at the church of Aracoeli in Rome, and then later at Sant' Anna in Foligno. It was looted by Napoleon's troops in 1797 and transferred onto the canvas in Paris. Since it was returned to Italy this picture has been in the Vatican and is now sold on the authority of His Holiness Pope Thomas, the proceeds to benefit the victims of the earthquake which struck Foligno earlier this year.'

David picked up his gavel, double-checked again that all his aides were in place, and began. 'This time, ladies and gentlemen, I shall start the bidding at ten million pounds . . . ten million . . . ten million pounds . . . ?'

Again the dead seconds. No one in the room moved.

The five hands went up together and the next three minutes were the most exhilarating in David's life. He had never known so many bidders. There was activity in all parts of the room and his assistants were calling out bids he didn't even see. It seemed at times that *everyone* wanted to bid, perhaps just to say they had taken part in this historic auction. Quickly the bidding climbed to twenty-eight million pounds.

By then the competition was down to six: Berlin, Sydney, the Getty, Tokyo, the Louvre, and the Metropolitan in New York. David held his breath as thirty million pounds approached. When he had first discussed numbers with the Holy Father he had known the picture would break all records – but now, as the magic figure of thirty million approached, he still couldn't quite believe it.

But the figure was reached. And still the drama wasn't over. At thirty million pounds Tokyo and Sydney dropped out but – sensation – the Hermitage came in!

Where Ivan Shirikin had got the money from David didn't know but there he was, lifting his catalogue in an unmistakeable bid. At thirty-two million pounds Berlin and the Louvre gave up but Shirikin's presence only seemed a challenge to the Americans. Thirty-five million was reached. Then the Russian, as suddenly as he had entered, dropped out. That left just the Getty and the Met.

Or did it? Sitting slightly apart from the other Americans was a small, spare man, who now raised a well-manicured, rather bony finger. David recognized him as Douglas Fillimore, director of the Frick Collection in New York, a wholly private collection which many people in the know regarded as the greatest *collection* in the world, certainly in America. Founded by Henry Clay Frick, the coke and steel millionaire, the Frick made very few acquisitions but, when it did, they were always the very best. Fillimore's intervention was a masterstroke, and brilliantly-timed psychologically. By coming in now he had signalled to the other two, the Getty and the Met, that he would fight to the end. The Frick had the funds and did not have other acquisitions to make as they did. The price was already in the stratosphere. Quickly, Jakobson, for the Met, and Smallbone for the Getty, realized that a prolonged battle would be ruinous for all concerned. The Met dropped out first, at thirty-six million, with the Getty following one bid later.

David surveyed the room. However clear the situation was, he had to go through the motions. 'Thirty-seven million pounds . . . any more? . . . any more? . . . fair warning at thirty-seven million pounds . . . any more? . . . any more at thirty-seven million pounds? . . . fair warning . . . thirty-seven million . . . thirty-seven million pounds . . .' As the gavel smacked down thunderous applause broke out and not a little cheering. David's words, 'The Frick Collection' were utterly overwhelmed by the noise of shouting and stamping of feet. Fillimore was being surrounded by reporters and television crews.

David did some quick sums. Thirty-seven plus twenty made sixty million pounds. Eight per cent of that was four point eight million pounds. It had taken rather more work than the two minutes Elizabeth Lisle had once accused him of, but, with its ten per cent buyer's commission on top of that, Hamilton's was ten point eight million pounds better off now, while the Pope's relief fund had benefitted by more than fifty-five million. That felt good. He descended from the rostrum into the mass of people. No one wanted to go home it seemed, the occasion was too special. Sirianni shook his hand. So did Hale. The Earl of Afton gave him the thumbs up from across the room. Jack Pringle, the press officer, raised his arms and clasped his hands together above his head like a victorious boxer. David noticed Elizabeth Lisle beckoning to him, and he fought his way through the crush towards her. As he approached he saw that she was on the phone. She smiled. Her deep voice carried above the general clamour.

'It's the Holy Father,' she said. 'He wants a word.'

David took the instrument from her.

'Mr Colwyn, I've just been watching you on television. You were magnificent! Congratulations and thank you. You've managed everything perfectly. If I can ever repay the favour, don't hesitate to ask.'

'Thank you, your Holiness. I'm simply relieved it's all gone so well, believe me.'

'I *do* believe you, Mr Colwyn. I know what it's like, being exposed the way you were tonight. Well, a marvellous night for us all, the disaster victims especially. I shall sleep very well, ready for a busy day tomorrow – I'm going to Foligno again, as it happens. Goodnight. And God bless you.'

The line went dead. David turned as Monsignor Hale, flanked by Sirianni and Elizabeth Lisle, came up. 'Colwyn, I'm taking the Italian contingent to dinner. Care to join us?'

'I'd love to,' said David. 'Unfortunately, there are things I have to do here. Also, I've got to be up early tomorrow.'

Hale held out his hand. 'Then I'll say goodnight. What you have accomplished here this evening is truly God's work. You have all our thanks.'

David shook hands and watched them leave the great hall. Then he went to check on the security of the pictures. It would take the money men at least thirty-six hours to clear the cheques, and in the meantime Hamilton's would keep the Gauguin and the Raphael in its vaults. He felt rather flat, now that the excitement was all over. One of the attractions of auctioneering he hadn't mentioned to Elizabeth Lisle was its theatrical atmosphere on great occasions. This evening had been like a first night. He was keyed up and would have loved to go on with Hale and the others. But work had to come first.

His house in Pelham Crescent, when he eventually arrived home after doing all the chores that follow a major sale, was dark and empty. The morning mail always arrived after he'd left for the office, so it was there stacked neatly on the hall table, put there to greet him by his ever-tidy daily woman whom he rarely saw, Mrs Mackeson. One of the letters, however, turned out to be a pretty poor greeting. It was from his wife's lawyer, and it made a miserable ending to a day that had been the peak of his career as an auctioneer. Sarah had decided to get remarried and so wanted an immediate divorce.

David had to be up early next day for the usual reason: he had a plane to catch. As an expert on Roman art, with an expertise that had profited Hamilton's handsomely, he had, as part of his contract, negotiated a certain number of days a year when he could pursue his scholarly interests. Today and tomorrow were just such a time. The Renaissance Society was meeting in Milan and David was due to give a paper. He would describe his preliminary findings arising from his discovery of new documents in the Vatican archive which concerned Leonardo's early works.

As he was driven to the airport he flipped through the morning papers. The *Daily Mail* had a short piece about the Vatican auction on page one, headlined 'THE MULTI-MILLION DOLLAR MADONNA!' while the *Daily Telegraph* had as its second lead, 'POPE'S PICTURE PULLS IN THE PENNIES'. But it was the letter from Sarah's lawyer which still kept nagging at him. He sighed. Why was it that bad news was always so much more compelling than good? David had met Sarah when he was twenty-five and had just joined Hamilton's. She was working as a librarian in the House of Commons. He'd had girlfriends in his last years at school, and affairs at Harvard. But Sarah was something else. She'd had poor health as a child but by then she was a forceful young lady and very passionate. They'd married within months, and had been crazily happy, even happier when their son, Ned, arrived. For years they had a marvellous life. The auction business was expanding, David was travelling more and more, Ned was a source of constant amazement and pleasure. Life changed enough each year to keep them fresh. Ironically, looking back, David thought it was the Bernini discovery which had started the rot. It wasn't only the publicity his discovery had attracted, or the boost it gave to his reputation in the trade. It was the change it had wrought in his appetite for success. With hindsight he now realized that one discovery took some living up to: he had to make another, if possible even more exciting. He'd spent all his free time on the trail of the Swedish Raphael.

Unfortunately, all this had coincided with Ned going away to school. That meant Sarah had less to do. David was in favour of her going back to work: he liked a wife with her own career. The question whether that was what Sarah wanted didn't cross his mind. A librarian's skills don't become obsolete quite as quickly as some other professions. There were no jobs at the House of Commons but because of her experience in Parliament, she was lucky and got something in the library at the Foreign Office. It was a time when a trade mission was being planned to the Far East. It mainly involved questions of commerce but even so the FO had to be involved. That was how she had met Michael Greener, Member of Parliament for a London constituency, Minister for Overseas Trade and a coming man in the Conservative Party.

It had all been very civilized. She had told David about the affair one night about thirty minutes before Greener was to arrive at Pelham Crescent. David supposed that Greener had been really quite brave. He had come to support Sarah in what was bound to be a difficult scene. He was *with* her, which was more than David had been in the preceding months. Everything had gone off as calmly as these things can be expected to – but maybe that had been the problem. At no time during the break-up had there been any *show* of emotion. As a result his grief had found no outlet but had festered. Now, twenty months later, he supposed he was beginning to come round. All the same, reminders like yesterday's letter still had the power to set him back.

Yet neither Sarah nor Greener was being unreasonable. Greener had now been promised a seat in the cabinet but first the Prime Minister wanted him to put his private life in order. Was he going to marry Sarah Colwyn or not? To be a cabinet minister one needed a regular private life. One could lose the party votes otherwise.

The letter was considerate in its tone. But David was still upset. He wondered how Ned was. So thoughtful had Sarah been that she had initially told David about Greener only a week after Ned had gone back to school. In this way they had both had almost a term to adjust to the new situation, to get their feelings under control before facing their son. Greener had kept tactfully in the background and things had begun to settle down. Ned spent his holidays with his mother, of course, but David could see him when he wanted. They remained close.

David gazed out at the dirty sky above the M4. Even the clouds looked soaked in diesel.

Ned was a delight and a puzzle. Half the time he seemed much older than thirteen, his actual age. His jokes, his thoughtfulness, his *understanding*, made his company second to none. Then, unpredictably, he would retreat into himself, regress into solitary, childish games. He was like a lighthouse whose beam only came round when you were least expecting it.

David would give Sarah the divorce, of course. But it only emphasized what he had told Elizabeth Lisle: he felt hopelessly beached. What was that Elizabeth had said about his situation? That the Pope would be making changes, but it all depended on the Raphael sale? Well, that had gone off splendidly enough so maybe something would happen to ease his situation. He felt he had earned it now.

If anything could lift David's spirits it was the company of fellow scholars or a few days spent under the warm skies and dusty colours of Italy. The Renaissance Society meeting in Milan, therefore, was perfect. His paper, too, was a success. The Secret Archives of the Vatican are notoriously badly organized; no one knows exactly what is contained in them, nor, since there is so much, can anyone be sure exactly what is where. It had been a hunch of David's to search in them for documents relating to Leonardo da Vinci. A lot was known about him, of course, except for that missing year: 1482.

David's paper to the conference was entitled, dryly, 'Leonardo's missing year: some documentary discoveries.' His talk was to the point. All he had done, he said, was look at certain papers that *might* throw light on the problem. First, he had drawn up a list of events in Italy around 1482 which could, by some stretch of the imagination, be said to be relevant. These events included the contract for some frescoes in the Sistine Chapel (1481/82), the death of the painter, Luca Della Robbia (1482), the death of Pope Sixtus IV, Francesco della Rovere, the death of the Duke of Urbino (1482) and the accession to power as Duke of Mantua of Francesco Gonzaga (1484). These last three, David reminded the meeting, were all well-known patrons of the arts. He had, he said, visited libraries in Florence and Mantua and Naples to check out some of the events, but it had been in the Vatican that he had first come across something of significance. This was in a long note to Pope Sixtus IV from the papal nuncio at the court in Urbino, notifying His Holiness of the death of Frederigo da Montefeltro, Duke of Urbino. The letter included a brief list of the people who had been in Urbino for Montefeltro's funeral, and mentioned one 'Leonardo the engineer', who had been trying to interest the Duke of Urbino, before his death, in a new kind of bridge.

That was all he had found so far, David admitted. Yet it was known that, a year later, Leonardo da Vinci had tried to interest the Duke of Milan in some designs for military fortifications, when he had again described himself as an engineer. It wasn't much, concluded David, but it was a start. His discoveries clearly showed that in 1482 Leonardo spent some time in Urbino, and he was continuing to plough through the reports of the papal nuncio at Urbino, to see if Leonardo was mentioned again.

The paper attracted considerable scholarly attention. It was hardly front-page news, but in its way it was important and the others at the conference appreciated it. David was approached and congratulated by academics from as far away as Moscow and Montreal.

On his last night in Milan, David had dinner at Casa Fontana with Edward Townshend, from the Fogg Library at Harvard, Jean-Claude Sapper of the Louvre, and Ivan Shirikin of the Hermitage in Leningrad. It was a truly international gathering and, over three bottles of Trebbiano, the wine the house recommended, the conversation ranged from Veronese to vodka, Boston to Bramante and Pope Thomas to Trotsky.

On the flight back to London David reflected that it had almost taken his mind off his divorce.

Almost, but not quite.

Roberto Vizzini was a handsome man and, for a Sicilian, exceptionally tall. Wherever he was he stood out, not a bad attribute for a priest. He certainly stood out now, among all these school children. He looked down on them seated in rows in St Agatha's school hall in front of him. This was work he enjoyed, giving prizes to the successful pupils, telling a few simple jokes, then sitting with the headmaster as focus for the school photograph.

He enjoyed other kinds of work also. And in consequence there were some people in Sicily who called Father Vizzini a saint. It was not often a priest went 'under cover' and acted like a policeman or an investigative journalist. But Vizzini had done just that. First, in the remote Burgio area of Sicily, high in the mountains, by making use of information obtained possibly through the confessional, he had succeeded, about a year before, in exposing a heroin processing plant run by the Mafia.

Then three months later, he had exposed a Mafia racket at Punta Raisi, Palermo airport. One evening, after dark, a spiked chain had been drawn across the main runway, ripping open the tyres of a small plane that was landing. Unbalanced by the blown-out tyres, the plane had crashed and burst into flames, killing the two aircrew and three occupants. This 'accident' had been caused because the airport authorities had refused to pay protection money. After it the local underworld had got what they wanted – until Vizzini, again using the confessional, was able to give the police some names.

More recently he had had a third spectacular success. In a disconcerting move the Mafia in Palermo had, about three months before, stolen all the blood in the city's blood bank. It was an easy theft since blood was hardly something the hospital authorities had imagined anyone would want to steal. And in any case the stocks could be replenished by new donors . . . Except that the Mafia then let it be known that anyone offering to give blood would be 'dealt with' – maimed or murdered. The number of donors dwindled and, after two people had their feet shattered with bullets, dried up completely. Within a matter of days the hospital was in crisis. Blood could only be obtained from the Mafia, inevitably at astronomical prices. The state hospital system refused to pay and so only rich patients in private hospitals could afford transfusions. After several people in the state hospitals in Palermo and Messina had died because there was no blood for them, Vizzini had set to work. Again his methods were probably doubtful. Almost certainly he got a lead in the confessional from the wife of one of the black market dealers. In any case, something put him on to the

Mafia link man and a raid by Sicilian police on a warehouse in Trapani uncovered the blood bank.

The island was jubilant and, when it was revealed that Vizzini had once again been instrumental in outwitting the Mafia, he was feted as no other priest in Sicily. The archbishop of Palermo invited him to preach in his cathedral there and thousands pleaded for a visit from this unconventional man of God.

St Agatha's School was one of many which had begged him to honour them at their prize-giving. He had accepted for two reasons. St Agatha's was in a pitifully poor region, Mussomeli, and one of the policemen wounded in the raid on the warehouse in Trapani had originally come from here.

When the prize-giving itself was at an end the school trooped outside for the photograph. A number of chairs had been arranged in a curving line in the broad sunshine: this was where the staff would sit with the headmaster and Fr Vizzini in the centre. The younger pupils would be cross-legged on the ground in front of the staff, others would stand behind the chairs, and still others would stand on benches behind them to make up four rows. The school's headgirl, who looked as though she might one day be as tall as Vizzini, showed the priest to his seat. She, he remembered, had won the prize for art and had been given a book on Caravaggio. He noticed that she was still holding it.

Vizzini sat down. As the other children milled around, getting into place, several of the prizewinners came up to him, shyly, and asked him to sign their books. As he scribbled his name and a short inscription, wishing them luck and God's protection, he noticed a number of proud mothers standing against the wall of the school, watching the show. 'Why don't you get the mothers in the shot?' he said to the headmaster, who had just taken his seat.

The headmaster laughed. 'Don't make my job harder than it is already, Father, please. It's bad enough trying to control children, as you can see, without trying to control their parents as well. And don't forget this is a poor area: many mothers work in the fields with the fathers. We could never get everybody in one place at one time and to include only some would annoy those who have to be left out.' He turned and looked at the lines. 'I think we are ready – yes?' he said to the headgirl, standing just behind him.

'Yes sir,' she replied. 'Everybody is here.'

'All right everybody,' shouted the headmaster. 'Now keep very still. This won't take long.' He motioned to the photographer, standing by a tripod about ten yards away. The man bent to his work.

Just then a motorbicycle, a small scooter, could be heard approaching beyond the school wall. It came in at the school gate and across the yard towards the photographer. It was ridden by a swarthy young man in sunglasses who had something – perhaps a guitar – slung across his back. It was only when the scooter skidded to a halt just to one side of the photographer and slightly in front of him that those watching realized the object was a gun.

Calmly, unhurriedly, the rider unslung his machine gun and fired at Vizzini. Children and teachers ran screaming in all directions. Mothers, near the wall, stumbled towards their children. The photographer picked up his tripod and made to hit the rider with it. The gunman simply fired a short burst into the photographer's face. Then he turned back and fired a final round into Vizzini now writhing on the ground. The priest jerked, and lay still.

Just as unhurriedly as he had arrived, the gunman swung his gun back over his shoulder, put the scooter into gear, and rode off. Behind him he left Vizzini already dead, the headmaster shot through the heart, two other teachers killed, as well as the photographer, and eleven children, including the headgirl. In her hand she still held her prize, the book on Caravaggio.

'David Colwyn. I am expected.'

The guard, dressed in yellow, blue and red pantaloons, consulted a list in his glass booth. He came out again. 'Yes. Do you know how to get to the Commission on Social Communication?'

David shook his head; he didn't know this part of the Vatican at all.

'Very well. You go straight ahead to begin with, keeping the Holy Office here on your left, and the audience hall. Then, to your right you will see two arches; go through both of them. Ahead of you then will be the Vatican gardens and, on your left, a large building with two petrol pumps in front of it. That is where Signorina Lisle's office is.'

'Thank you,' said David as his taxi eased forward.

David had not counted on seeing Elizabeth Lisle again so soon. This trip had not been arranged in quite such a hurry as the last, but once again he was here at the invitation of the Vatican and once again he had no advance knowledge of what to expect. Except that he had been summoned only days after news had broken of the appalling Mafia killings in Sicily.

The 'Mussomeli massacre', as it had come to be called, had shocked all Italy, all the western world. For a priest and children to be mowed down in cold blood confirmed how utterly ruthless, how savage the Mafia was prepared to be in defence of its interests. The mobsters had shown that not even children were safe when they allied themselves with the likes of Vizzini. At the priest's funeral, to which the Pope had sent a representative, the archbishop of Palermo had hit out at the Italian government for its lack of action. He hinted openly at what many people suspected: that several government members were on the take from the mob and so were unwilling to do anything. But the final brutality was perpetrated during the night after the priest's funeral. In the morning it was found that the flowers had been removed from Vizzini's grave and replaced with poppies, the source of heroin. The Mafia were reminding people why Vizzini had died so that no one would feel like following in his footsteps.

Later that day Elizabeth Lisle had called David.

The taxi turned in through the second arch. To his right David could see the enormous apse of St Peter's. An entrance, looking for all the world like an opera house stage door, was open to reveal a long sloping floor up into the hidden recesses of the building. Ahead he could see the gardens, steep terracing and lush trees. The taxi pulled over to the left and stopped, as the Swiss guard had said, near to some petrol pumps. Elizabeth Lisle's office was on the third floor and from it could be seen both St Peter's and, over the wall, the outside world. Appropriate, David thought, for a press office.

Elizabeth poured coffee, black as boots. She had in her office what looked to David like a Victorian relic of some sort but was in fact the latest in stylish Italian coffee makers. He put it down to her obsession with gadgets. Today she had her hair pinned up. It made her neck seem longer still. He noticed that she had pierced ears. She said, 'He wants to do it again, Mr Colwyn. The Holy Father would like to sell another picture.'

'But there's been no disaster – has there?' David tried to think. 'There was that building which collapsed in France, but there weren't many killed . . . seventeen wasn't it? And there was that fire at the football stadium in – '

'No, it's different this time. It's not a natural disaster His Holiness is concerned with; it's a man-made one.' When David showed no sign of understanding, she went on: 'The Mussomeli massacre.'

David whistled. 'Thomas is willing to tangle with the Mafia?'

'Someone has to. If not the Church then who shall it be?' She sighed. 'Thomas believes, like countless Popes before him, that the Sicilian Mafia proves that the devil is alive and living among us. He has had it in his mind to take some action ever since he was elected but this incident has spurred him to start now. It was, after all, a priest who was the main target of the attack, a priest who had shown exceptional courage and imagination in trying to battle the Mafia. Thomas feels he cannot let Vizzini down.'

'What's he going to do?'

'He has several plans but for the moment, I'm afraid, they're secret.'

'And what do you want from me?'

'We have chosen the picture and we would like you to sell it again. Like before.'

'Which picture?'

' "The Deposition", by Caravaggio.'

63

David shook his head slowly. He held his cup out. 'I think I had better have some more coffee.'

She lifted the jug and poured. She looked anxious. 'You approve?'

'In a purely commercial sense, yes. I know the picture and it's fantastic, brilliant. Probably my favourite in the whole Vatican. And I think I'm right in saying that there *are* only sixty-odd pictures by Caravaggio, so he is *very* rare. His pictures simply never come on to the market. But . . . but . . . well, how is he appropriate?'

'I'm not an art historian, Mr Colwyn, you know that. But what I'm told is that Caravaggio himself worked in Sicily in the years before his death and one of his late pictures, a Nativity, was actually stolen from a church in Palermo by the Mafia. In a sense, therefore, I guess Caravaggio was a victim of the mob, like Vizzini and those children. It's also the case, as you may have read, that one of the girls killed was carrying a book about Caravaggio. She had won it as a prize only minutes before the gunman arrived. So the picture is doubly appropriate.' The coffee was finished. Elizabeth Lisle got to her feet. 'Why don't we go over and look at the picture? I'll show you the Vatican gardens and we can talk as we go.'

They went down the stairs and out into the sunshine. A light breeze swished up the hill the Vatican was built on, easing the oppressive heat. She pointed to their left. 'The helipad is up there, beyond the railway station and the HQ of Vatican radio.'

They walked halfway up the hill and then turned to their right. A huge grotto-like fountain appeared on their left, its noise soothing yet pervasive. David now recognized the Vatican art gallery ahead of him but some way off. In between were a number of delightful shaded walkways with palm trees, aralia, acanthus and a lot of plants he couldn't put a name to.

Elizabeth Lisle stopped and breathed in the sweet-smelling air. 'I come here every day. This has to be one of the most beautiful, and peaceful, spots on earth. Hardly the best environment to talk money, Mr Colwyn, but I am afraid we must. How much do you think the Caravaggio is worth?'

They moved on again. David frowned thoughtfully. 'Probably not as much as the Raphael – but it's difficult to know. Caravaggio has become very popular in the last ten to fifteen years. His realism suits the modern taste. He's rare, as I said, and again, like the "Madonna" it's a Vatican picture.' They were coming to the end of the shaded path. The picture gallery towered over them, with its statues of Raphael, Titian and Giotto. 'You would certainly get twenty million – and it could go to thirty. But closer than that I can't say.' He wondered if he would ever get used to dealing in these sorts of figures.

Elizabeth Lisle led the way into the art gallery. They ascended the stairs and turned into the exhibition halls themselves. The 'Deposition' was in the opposite row of galleries to where David had first waited for the Pope, in an octagonal room which overlooked the gardens. Light streamed in through the window as they stood in front of Caravaggio's masterpiece. Other paintings might look dull in sunlight but not this one. The pale body of Christ was held by two very real, rather ugly and obviously poor people. The expressions were modern, not idealized as in a Raphael, and at the bottom of the picture a large slab of stone seemed to jut out at the viewer, hard and rough and real enough to touch. It was magnificent, thought David. Yes, Caravaggio *was* his favourite.

There were at least half a dozen museum directors around the world who would kill for this picture and David suddenly sensed that the auction for this painting might be an even bigger tussle than for the Raphael. He turned to Elizabeth Lisle. 'We can't sell this before September. The art world goes on holiday from now until then. October would be better still. Does it matter?'

'Well, we would like *some* money now, as before. Say ten million. And the rest the sooner the better. But obviously we want another successful sale and that's up to you.'

David nodded. 'I think ten million is fine. Let's go back to your office and I'll make a couple of calls to London.'

They walked back. She took him the long way round, via the English garden, the Fontana delle Cascatelle and the church of Santo Stefano degli Abissini. During their walk she offered to take him to L'Eau Vive for lunch. He had heard of the restaurant but had never been to it. It was French, in the Via Montesome near the Pantheon, a place where many senior cardinals liked to eat and which was sometimes referred to as the Vatican canteen. It was owned by a Catholic mission and all the waitresses, who belonged to the mission, sang a hymn during coffee.

'I shall look forward to it,' he said.

'But first the Holy Father would like a quick word with you.' She looked at her watch. 'He's celebrating a special mass in one of the chapels in St Peter's in about fifteen minutes. There is a party of poor orphans from Canada here in Rome, who wanted to see him. He can never resist. I don't know whether you know this, but he's an orphan himself. So come, make your phone calls.'

The first was to Lord Afton, the second to Hamilton's bankers. Both were as supportive as David knew they would be but it was prudent of him to bring them both in at an early stage this time. Today he didn't *need* to act alone and Sam Averne, his opponent on the board, could make less trouble if David could point out that he had sought advice from the chairman and the bank in advance. He didn't want to be accused of high-handedness.

'The money should be with you the day after tomorrow,' he told Elizabeth Lisle as they walked across to the basilica.

'Good. The Holy Father will be delighted. We can tell him now. This way.' She led him into the 'stage door' he had noticed earlier, on his arrival. They took a passage curving upwards first to the left, then round to the right in a wide circle. 'We are inside the wall of the apse, just here,' Elizabeth Lisle said. 'It was originally designed as an emergency exit, in case the seventeenth-century popes should ever face invading forces like back in 1527.'

'I hope Thomas never needs it.'

She smiled back at him and pushed at a door.

David found himself deep inside the magnificent church. White baroque tomb sculptures, like the shapes in an underwater grotto, were all around. To the right, Bernini's baldacchino, or canopy, rose majestically above the high altar, its twisted bronze pillars shining, deep as damson.

'Thomas will be down here.' Elizabeth Lisle led the way into the north transept. A small throng of tourists indicated where Thomas was, but they were kept back from entering the chapel where the mass was taking place. The attendant recognized Elizabeth Lisle, however, and she and David were admitted immediately.

The service had already started. David sat and watched as, in batches of five or six, the children went forward and knelt in front of Thomas to receive communion. Standing before them, the Holy Father looked even taller than David remembered. One by one the children returned to their seats. The nun in charge tried to make them keep quiet, but they were too excited by what had just happened to them. Older people might be awed, but they were thrilled.

Thomas, smiling and understanding the girls' reactions instinctively, brought the service to an end, but then came forward and sat down among them. They crowded round as he asked their names and their ages. They answered tentatively at first, but with increasing confidence. One of the girls was accused by some others of exaggerating her age, to appear older than she was. 'So she can wear make up,' said one.

The girl in question looked crestfallen but Thomas laughed. 'That reminds me of a story,' he said. 'About when I was an orphan.' The girls crowded in.

'I was looked after by someone just like Sister Mary here. Only we had a priest, Father Flab we called him, since he was so fat.' The girls laughed. 'In the town where I grew up, in a very out-of-the-way place in America, we had just one movie house. There was very little television in those days – none at all in orphanages – so we loved to go to the movies. But the best movies of all, or we thought so anyway, were the horror movies which we weren't allowed to see because we were too young. Because we couldn't see them, we thought they had to be the best. In those days you had to be fifteen to see a horror movie. Well, as you can see, I am very tall and I was very big as a boy. Even though I was thirteen and a half, I *looked* fifteen. So, one day, when I had saved up my allowance, I decided to brave my way into the movie house. There was quite a line outside and I was very nervous as I got to the ticket office. What if the girl guessed I was only thirteen and turned me away? I would have been mortified with embarrassment. It was my turn to pay. I put the money in front of the girl.' The children around Thomas were silent, gripped by his story. He opened his eyes wide. 'The ticket girl didn't even look at me. She took the money and pushed a blue ticket at me. *I was in!*' David heard the children gasp. They knew what an achievement that was to a thirteen-year-old.

'I couldn't afford popcorn so I went straight to my seat. The lights were still on but I didn't look round, just in case any teachers were there. Boy, was I thankful when the lights went down. Anyway, eventually the horror movie started. I don't remember what it was about now, but I do remember that, after about twenty minutes, it got very scary. In fact, it got so scary *that I started to cry!* I was really frightened, scared out of my skin, so much so that I had to leave. The ticket girl was amazed to see this boy stumble out of the theatre, his eyes as red as radishes. I've never been to see a horror movie since.'

The children were smiling. It was a lovely story they could repeat to all their friends. The Pope had been just like them when he was small. Thomas held out his hand to the girl who had 'exaggerated' her age. 'Come, let's all go for a walk around the church. I'll show you some things.'

The girl hung on as Thomas walked out towards the main part of St Peter's. To David, his limp didn't seem so pronounced today.

When he saw Elizabeth Lisle and David, Thomas stopped. 'I'm sorry. How stupid of me. I'd forgotten you'd be waiting. Well? What do you think, Mr Colwyn? Will it work again?'

'I think so, sir. Caravaggio has never been more popular.'

'You've disucssed the financial side?'

'Yes, and I've spoken to London. No problems.'

'Good, good. Thank you for coming to Rome, Mr Colwyn. We thought that, because of the Mafia link, you might not wish to be involved this time. That's why Elizabeth had instructions not to speak about this on the telephone. Now you have agreed, I can make the announcement.' Thomas looked down at the girl who was still clutching his hand. 'But first I have to show this young lady a few things here in St Peter's. She "improves" her age just as I did when I was a boy. Who knows? By the time she's as old as I am now, she could be Pope. Or perhaps not.' He winked and led the straggle of girls off into the nave.

*

'Does he mean it? About a woman being Pope, I mean.'

They were in L'Eau Vive, about to tackle two large mounds of salad. Around them were off-duty cardinals, as Elizabeth Lisle put it, men in black suits, inconspicuous but for the small white collars at their throats, grey-haired men who clearly relished their food and savoured the wine in front of them. David took comfort in that. You can never trust a man who doesn't enjoy his food.

'He was exaggerating a bit, like he did about his age at the movies. But, sure, Thomas would like to see the Church change. He's lived a large part of his life in the Third World so he knows that it's necessary – and he's American, never forget that. Americans like change.'

'If you change too fast, people get hurt. You provoke a backlash.'

'Whatever pace you change at, it'll be too fast for somebody. You're looking at it from the wrong side, Mr Colwyn. You can't *impose* changes that people don't want. You have to feel your way, test out what can and cannot be done. You have to start with the things you *can* do, so people see that change actually does happen. Then they get used to the idea that such things are possible. Look at my own appointment. The old school hated it at first; now they are beginning to get used to it. More important, the outside world is getting used to the idea of a woman with some authority in the Vatican. This is why the picture sales are so important, why you are so crucial to us. They attract attention to the Vatican, to the Holy Father's policies. And they make a difference. I've already hinted to you that changes are in the offing concerning birth control, divorce, re-marriage. But Thomas is feeling his way. There has to be change, but change that people want, that they feel is fair, just, and necessary. Then it will happen *and stick*. If all that works, then the pace will increase and yes, maybe we shall see a Holy Mother one day.' She paused. 'Leadership consists of knowing what pace of change will keep the imagination of your supporters without provoking your enemies.'

David gathered a forkful of lettuce. 'Does Thomas act all by himself? That must be dangerous.'

'He does and he doesn't. Technically he is an absolute monarch, so he could function like a medieval king if he wanted to. But he has the curia, his Secretary of State – and a kitchen cabinet.'

'Which consists of whom?'

'You're looking at one of them. On certain evenings, when the Holy Father keeps his diary free of any official functions, I dine with him and his two private secretaries, O'Rourke and a man you haven't met. We throw around ideas. I chip in and say what I think a woman's reaction would be to this or that. O'Rourke is tuned into the Vatican and the curia; he gives their reaction. The other man isn't a cleric, he's a businessman from a well-known Mexican family. Thomas met him on his travels. His role is to give the non-western view of things.'

'Is that enough?'

'Enough people? Perhaps not. But a leader needs around him individuals he can trust – speak of the devil,' she said suddenly, changing her tone. She fingered the cross on her necklace and looked down.

David turned to see Ottavio Massoni leaving the restaurant. He had been lunching further inside where they had been unable to see him. It struck David that Massoni's bone-tight skin looked as though it had been vacuum wrapped over his hairless skull. He was followed by a man David knew all too well, Diego Giunta, a prickly Spanish prelate who ran the Secret Archive in the Vatican. The two men didn't see them and were soon gone. He turned back to face Elizabeth Lisle. 'What is it? You've gone rigid as a rifle.'

'I know. I can't help it.' She lowered her voice. 'I shouldn't say this, but I don't trust that man. I sometimes think he's the only enemy Thomas has. Every time Thomas has a success the scowl on Massoni's face seems to get wider, blacker. I think he wants the Church to be feared, not liked.'

'Maybe he would say "respected".'

'Maybe he would. I know better. After all, it was Massoni's people who gave me such a hard time when I started. They still do, some of them. It's extraordinary: they venerate the Virgin Mother yet they don't appear to like women.' She started on her salad. 'Not this woman anyway.' Her brown eyes gleamed.

'Is he close to Giunta?'

'He's an old friend from the Gregorian University. Besides running the archive, Giunta is writing the official biography of the last Pope, Pius XIII. I'll bet they're up to no good, plotting away. You know, I sometimes wish I had a training in eavesdropping. There are so many people I'd like to bug.'

'You're amazing. No, paranoid. If they're old friends why can't they just be enjoying their lunch, like us? What do you mean, plotting? Plotting what?'

'Yes, I *am* paranoid where Massoni is concerned. I think Thomas is starting to feel that way, too. It all went so well to begin with. The Holy Father and the Secretary of State are so different and yet they really did seem to unite the Church. But the sale of the pictures caused a rift. Massoni was against the sale – you must have picked that up the first time you came here. Having lost that first battle he was rather hoping, I think, that the auction would fail. When it didn't, that made him even more bitter.' She lowered her voice again. 'He doesn't even know about this new scheme – the Caravaggio, I mean. If it works – ' she managed a smile '– and I'm sure it will, it will make Thomas even more popular. Massoni will be livid.'

David let it rest. He changed the subject. He told Elizabeth Lisle about Caravaggio, the fact that though he was a great painter he had once killed a man during a fight in Rome and had spent a lot of his life on the run. She talked a little more about the Mississippi. She explained her fascination with gadgets.

'Pa was an inventor. Not professionally. But being a liquor distiller he was always trying to produce a better still. He had a collection of old ones – and other inventions. There's a place in Louisiana, very famous, called Fort Humbug. Back in the Civil War the locals were afraid of being attacked by some general or other so they hollowed out some tree trunks and painted them black to make it seem as though they had more cannon than they really did. Pa had one of those as well.'

She finished her salad and wiped her plate with some bread, a very European gesture, David thought. 'Pa was always making toys for my brother and me. There was supposed to be a sacred lake near us – sacred to the Indians, that is. Except it was just their way of keeping everybody else away so they could keep all the good fish to themselves. Pa invented a special fishing rod so we could take fish well back from the bank and not be seen.' She smiled wryly. 'That was wrong of us, I suppose, but Pa knew that doing anything secretly only adds to the fun.' She sighed. 'And it *was* fun.'

After lunch, they walked together in the hot sun towards the Corso Vittorio Emanuele, where David could catch a taxi to the airport. A small Fiat was the first available cab that came his way. David was always amazed at how small Italian taxis could be. He shook hands with Elizabeth Lisle and repeated his promise to have the money in Rome by the next day. She refused a lift, saying she wanted to walk back to her office. He watched her from a distance as she strode along the Corso, towards the river and the Via della Conciliazione. Her bearing was upright but not entirely self-assured. Only when he was in the taxi, folded up and speeding along the autostrade towards Fiumicino Airport, did he reflect that she may have refused him because, for once, she had revealed some of her feelings to him. For the first time it occurred to David that, although Elizabeth Lisle was in a position of power and although she regularly dined with the Holy Father, deep inside herself, she was possibly very lonely.

The announcement about the Caravaggio sale came from the Vatican later in the week – which turned out to be just as well from David's point of view.

When he got back to London, he found there was serious opposition this time from his fellow board-members. A minority, but a sizeable one, led by Averne, took the view that the sale was potentially very risky, that the Mafia should not be tampered with. They argued that the mob had a long memory, was vindictive and that Hamilton's was an easy target, with offices in New York where the Mafia was very

70

strong. The divisions in the board room were quite bitter. However, the Earl of Afton produced a telling argument in support of David, saying that it would look very bad if it got out that Hamilton's had backed down because it was scared of the Mafia. David won the final vote: 11 to 5.

The Vatican announcement, however, went well. The day before the sale was announced, Elizabeth Lisle, working closely with Sirianni, the mayor of Foligno, presented to the press the architectural plans for the new cathedral to be built in the town. As a gesture it was a perfect symbol of what the Holy Father stood for: rapid, imaginative action. Furthermore, on the same day and entirely coincidentally, the news-papers carried stories of the completion of the 500th house built in the Marquesas Isles since the tidal wave and funded by the Gauguin money. They weren't large stories but coming on top of everything else it showed that the Pope's plans really did work. The Catholic Church was making things happen.

But the main reason the announcement was such a success when it came was the revelation of the Pope's plans for spending the money raised. David now knew that the shape of those plans had been worked out with Elizabeth Lisle and the Holy Father's secretaries at their private dinners in the papal apartments. Three uses were planned for the cash. In the first place compensation was to be paid to the families who had suffered at the hands of the gunman. Second, a number of social projects were announced, not just for the Mussomeli region but all over Sicily. Clinics were to be built, training schemes set up, grants made to help small businesses. There would be no large capital expenditure but what was done would help to create the new jobs which Mussomeli, and Sicily, so desperately needed. And in each case the project would be named after one of the murdered children.

But the most combative use of the money, the use which caught the world's attention and signalled the fact that Thomas brought to the problems of Sicily the same inspiration he had brought to the problems of Foligno and the Marquesas Isles, was the Vizzini Fund. Since Fr Vizzini had died fighting the Mafia, Thomas decided that his memorial would continue the same work. Two hundred million lire – or some $100,000 – was promised to anyone who offered information leading to the conviction of any Mafia figure of a serious crime: extortion, major theft, assault, murder, violence of any kind.

There were those, of course, who said it wouldn't work, that the Mafia would soon enough appropriate the fund money for its own ends. But Thomas had set up the fund with care. The sums offered were large enough to be truly tempting and the money was to be paid out in secret wherever the informant wished. Since the Vatican was a state in its own right, there were no exchange control problems. The archbishop of Palermo, Cardinal Ligorio, added his own touch. He said that if people were frightened to go to the police with information, they could use the confessional. That had been how Vizzini got his information: the technique had an honourable precedent. Information flooded in.

'Now, look at the edge of this picture, look at the grain of the panel it's painted on.'

'So?'

'So, that's a very important grain to recognize, Ned. It's mahogany and mahogany panels were not used as panels for paintings until the mid-eighteenth century. Now look at what's written on the frame.'

'Pierre Mignard (1612–95).'

'Can't be,' said David with a smile. 'The picture is at least forty years later. Put it in the book.'

Ned kept an account of the fakes they found on their jaunts around antique shops and this was the second they had found today. He was pleased: he was due to give a lecture on fakes at school.

It was Ned's last weekend out from Hamble before the summer holidays and it was marked with a large 'N', for Ned, in David's diary. David and Ned were on what they called their Number Two tour of London's art and antique shops. Number One was the West End, Number Three the Portobello Road, Number Four Camden Passage. Number Two was Kensington and Chelsea. This meant they could lunch at Il Quirinale, an Italian restaurant just off the Fulham Road, which reminded David of Rome. By rights, he should have been there now, working in the Vatican's Secret Archives. But his son came first.

They made for the restaurant where David had reserved a table. David naturally hoped Ned would get the same pleasure from the arts as he did. But it was early days yet. The only aspect of the art world that seemed to interest the boy was the 'underside' – fakes and forgeries. Still, that was something. It involved being able to distinguish the good stuff from the bad. Their fake-spotting tours had become great days out, enjoyed enormously by both of them. David looked at Ned across the lunch table at Il Quirinale. The boy was thirteen, exactly the age of Thomas when he had tackled that horror movie. How times changed. David couldn't imagine a film that would send Ned out of the cinema, in tears. 'Are you shaving yet, Ned?'

'No, Dad. I don't go to nightclubs or take drugs either. Do you mind? I'll have a glass of wine if you want me to be more grown-up.'

'Good god, no,' said David smiling. 'And you'll have a coca cola, like you always do.'

He gazed at Ned as the boy studied the menu. By no stretch of the imagination could he be called classically good-looking but he had a charm, a sense of humour that was rare in adults, let alone thirteen year olds. 'What will you have?'

'If you're paying, Dad, I'll have a main course to start with, followed by two puds. Say veal chop followed by trifle followed by zabaglione.'

'You're sure that's enough?'

'You're nervous, Dad. That means, sooner or later, you're going to get heavy. If *you're* going to get heavy, *I* need some weight, too.'

'What do you mean: nervous? How do you know?'

'You keep nibbling the inside of your cheek. It makes you look like a cross between our cook at school and a camel. I know the signs.'

David paused. It could be avoided no longer. 'Well, it's true. I *am* nervous. Your mother has mentioned the divorce? And that she wants to remarry? We have to talk about it, Ned. I want to know what you think.'

'Try longer sentences, Dad. Maybe it'll relax you.'

'Ned! Don't be flippant! This is serious.'

No sooner had he said the words than David wished he could have taken them back. The boy was crying. Too late, he realized that in this conversation his son was ahead of him.

'Ned, I'm sorry,' he whispered. 'I didn't mean to shout. I don't want you to be upset by all this – but . . . but I don't know what else I can do.' He passed Ned his handkerchief. Boys never had such things.

A waiter appeared, tactfully ignoring Ned. David ordered, pretending the trifle was for him, the zabaglione for his son.

Ned wiped his eyes and blew his nose. He handed back the handkerchief.

'I'm sorry, Ned. For the divorce, I mean. It hurts, but . . .' He couldn't think how to finish the sentence.

'Lots of people at school have divorced parents.'

'Ned! Forget other people! Divorce is different for everybody. It's not just a final break, though that's bad enough, I know. But now your mother wants to get remarried . . . that means more changes.'

Ned was crying again but David had to finish. 'While people are separated, all sorts of things go on below the surface, but people rarely talk. Your mother and I never did, and perhaps that was a mistake. I hoped – maybe you hoped – that Sarah and I would get back together again. But that's not going to happen – '

That was as far as he got. Ned, still crying, slipped out of his seat and bolted for the door, almost crashing into a waiter as he went. David left money on the table and followed. Outside, the sunshine was painfully bright and cheerful. Ned was walking slowly away from the restaurant, close in against the shops that lined the pavement. His body shivered with sobs.

David caught up and put his arm around him. After a moment, he said: 'Look on the good side. You'll get three sets of birthday presents and three sets of Christmas presents.'

'Oh Dad, that's like having shirts with three arms, or playing football with three goals.'

David would have laughed, except that he was nearly in tears himself. They reached the Fulham Road. 'Do you want to go on with our tour?'

Ned shook his head.

'Rather be back at school, by yourself?'

'Do you mind, Dad? Just this once?'

'Like me to drive you?'

'I'd prefer the train.'

David hailed a taxi and accompanied his son to Waterloo Station. They had to wait twenty minutes before the next train to Hamble. It was a silent, painful vigil. When the train left, David watched it go but Ned never looked back.

At Pelham Crescent, David sat in his study as the day began to sink across the gardens. He didn't cry, he just stared at the reddenning sun. He had never felt so wasted, so blank, so *lonely*. He wanted to telephone someone, but no one in particular. There was no one in the firm he was close to; it was easier to do his job if he kept his distance from colleagues. Most of his friends were friends of Sarah's, too, and he couldn't face their inevitable questions or their concern. The two close friends he had kept up with since university were both away on holiday, he knew that. Then he found himself thinking of Elizabeth Lisle. Could he call her? He had mentioned his marriage to her once before, so she would understand his mood. She had been a little forthcoming about herself too, the last time they had met, when he had listened to her problems. He had sensed that she was a solitary person, also. And she didn't know Sarah so there wouldn't be any of the questions he dreaded from their London friends.

He glanced at his watch. In Rome it was nearly five o'clock – she'd still be at her office. But why should he call her up, out of the blue? he asked himself. She would think it very odd. Even as he thought this, however, he was looking up her number in his book. He dialled, but it was the Vatican switchboard operator who answered. Signorina Lisle was not in her office, she said. She was ill and was at home. Nothing serious, said the operator, but the signorina was having a couple of days off to recover. She gave David the home number and he didn't hesitate to call. Maybe she needed cheering up as much as he did. The call went through and, a thousand miles away, he heard the phone ring once, twice, three times. When it was answered he had been prepared for Elizabeth Lisle's illness to have made her sound different. What he hadn't expected was that the voice which answered would be a man's.

# 4

David lay on the beach and gazed out to sea. The sand was burnished like barley and clean, the sea was as blue as a kingfisher and clean, the air was clean. He tried to imagine what the horizon would look like when a sixty foot wave was approaching.

He was in the South Pacific, the Marquesas Isles. He was licking his wounds. After his disastrous lunch with Ned, and the abortive phone call to Rome, he had decided to bring his holiday forward by a few days. He'd had enough of London, of Europe, for the time being. Ned was spending the first part of his holiday with Sarah and Michael Greener; David would see him later. So there had been nothing to keep him in London. The major sales of the season were over and there was nothing he couldn't put off or that Sally Middleton couldn't cope with. He had chosen the Marquesas Isles partly to get away completely, but also to look at the rescue work being done in the wake of the tidal wave. He had brought his camera and had taken a few rolls of film from which something would be selected for Hamilton's annual report.

It was amazing how quickly things got back to normal. Atuona, where he now was, had been the most sheltered when the wave had swamped the islands. It was on the island furthest from the sea-bed volcano and faced south-east, away from the direction of the wave. It wasn't exactly the most popular spot for a holiday just then, but that suited David. The weather was fantastic, the rum had the right kind of kick and he had a biography of Paul Gauguin to keep him company. Atuona was where the great painter had died and it interested David to see the place. Gauguin had given up being a stockbroker to become a painter and the South Seas had always attracted him. At the moment David felt the same way.

Even on holiday, however, David couldn't resist the English-language newspapers when he saw them: he scanned them eagerly for any news of the actions of the Holy Father. The best news came from Sicily where, as a result of money promised by the Vizzini Fund, the police had found the quality of their information about the Mafia dramatically improved. No trials had taken place yet – it was too soon – but a number of arrests had been made and these rather pointedly coincided with a drop in crimes of violence and extortion on the island. It was also rumoured that several Mafia gangsters who had not yet been informed against had nonetheless taken the precaution of leaving Sicily. The Pope's imaginative foray against the mob was hailed as a success, and the Caravaggio had not even been sold yet.

The Holy Father's prestige was enhanced by two other developments. Fillimore, at the Frick Collection in New York, had taken a leaf out of Hamilton's book, and when the Raphael was put on show at the gallery it was as a special exhibit with its own entrance fee – this fee being sent to the Foligno disaster fund. It was a perfect piece of marketing psychology and lines even longer than in St James's Square snaked along 70th Street and round the corner into Fifth Avenue. Pope Thomas's popularity also increased when a survey by IIRS, the Italian Institute for Statistical Research, revealed that attendances at mass were up, not just in Italy but worldwide, as were the revenues from St Peter's Pence. The interest in the Catholic Church generated by the sale of Vatican Old Masters and the compassion epitomized by Thomas's initiatives, were drawing people back to worship, especially young people so that Thomas was now seen not only as a good businessmen but also as a charismatic leader. Even the US President was moved to remark, speaking from his summer retreat at Anchor Bay, Lake St Clair, near Detroit, that Pope Thomas's crusade was 'as inspiring, as effective and as American as the Declaration of Independence – or the FBI.'

David wondered if even Massoni had been won round by now. Or was he still 'plotting' as Elizabeth Lisle had put it that day at L'Eau Vive? He found himself thinking quite a bit about Elizabeth Lisle. It was strange. Their meetings together had always been very professional, impersonal, efficient, almost formal. He had never thought about her at all, except as the Pope's press secretary, until that afternoon in the taxi, on his way to Rome airport. He hadn't thought about her again until the day he put Ned on the train for Hamble and had been feeling so low. Why then had he been so surprised, and let down, when a man had answered the phone at her apartment? Instinctively, David had hung up without speaking.

David knew himself. She wouldn't have drifted into his mind, he wouldn't be having this conversation with himself, if something wasn't going on beneath the surface of his consciousness. He tried to think what Elizabeth Lisle looked like (and why did he still refer to her by her full name?). She was tall, with long brown hair and, as he recalled, apart from her neck her best feature was her mouth, wide and attractively sensuous. More Renoir than Rubens, he told himself. But why was he thinking like this? Her job put her off limits, she had never shown any personal interest in him, she almost certainly had a man and he, David, was a beached Catholic, married but not married, soon to be divorced but not divorced. Not an attractive proposition for anybody. Forget it, he told himself.

He stuck out his holiday. Two weeks on the beach by himself. He finished the Gauguin biography and turned to a mass of material he had brought with him on Leonardo's life. There was little in it of use to him except a short item referring to some unusual pigments which the master used. Back in London he patched things up with Ned. They had both recovered their equilibrium. Ned had been on a barge with his mother and Michael Greener, exploring the *Canal du Midi* in France, between the Atlantic and the Mediterranean. He was therefore happy to spend the rest of the school holidays in Britain with his father, making a slow, gentle tour of West Country antique shops, spotting fakes.

Occasionally Ned would relapse into private, puzzling silences but David learned to ride them out. At the end of their ten days, when he put the boy into the taxi taking him back to his mother, before the new term at Hamble, they shook hands gravely. David was half-amused, half-disturbed by this. He assumed Ned had seen men in France greet each other in that way, but between the two of them it seemed sadly distancing.

When he returned to the office he was soon swept up in the flow of things. The Caravaggio sale was now less than two months away. Also, it looked as if two large country houses were coming on to the market and, with luck and some skill on David's part, Hamilton's would be selling the contents. This meant a trip to Derbyshire and to Scotland. To Argyll.

From David's point of view, his Argyll trip was by far the more interesting. The house belonged to the descendants of one of the great Glaswegian shipping barons, a man enlightened enough to have collected Italian art on a massive scale. No one else in the family had taken much interest in the family heirlooms with the result that, now they had to sell, no one had much idea what was there. David was able to assure them that there was some very saleable art indeed, including some wonderful drawings, which he would have to research, and a painting in the style of Salvator Rosa. There were also a number of diaries and papers in different hands. These he took back to London, where he asked the manuscripts department to look at them. But first he negotiated with the trustees of the estate in Argyll to guarantee them a minimum sum from the sale. This had now become standard procedure – the Pope had been right. David didn't like it but he had no choice; if he didn't do it his rivals would. He was able to say that the painting would fetch £100,000, the drawings much the same and the rest of the contents – furniture, papers, porcelain, tapestries – perhaps £800,000. The trustees were delighted and the contract was signed.

He returned to London. One of the calls received while he had been in Scotland was from Elizabeth Lisle. She was the first person he called back.

'*There* you are,' she said when she heard his voice. 'Mr Elusive.'

It was a warmer greeting than he had been expecting. He had forgotten how deep her voice was. He told her about his summer, the Marquesas Isles trip, his photographs of the relief work. She sounded eager to see them. She had taken time off while the Holy Father had gone to his summer retreat at Castel Gandolfo and had visited her parents in Louisiana. But she really wanted to talk about business.

'How's the Caravaggio sale coming along?'

'Fine – and I've had an idea.'

'Oh yes?'

'Yes. Everything is shaping up nicely. There's plenty of publicity but – quite frankly – if I know anything about newspapers we're not going to get the same build-up as we did with the Raphael and the Gauguin sale. Newspaper readers get jaded very easily. It would be nice if we could pull something new out of the bag.'

'And your idea is . . . ?'

'I think we should hold the sale *in* the Vatican.'

There was a long silence.

'Are you alive? What do you think?'

'Not for the first time, Mr Colwyn, you have completely astonished me. I don't know *what* I think. It's either a brilliant idea or it's an idiotic one. I'm not sure there aren't rules against carrying on a business venture inside the City State. There'd be opposition from certain people in the curia. And it *seems* safer to have the auction in the saleroom, as in a normal – '

'But this – '

'But this isn't a normal sale, I know. And it's not a normal business venture either, I know that, too.' She paused, thinking. David could hear her drumming her fingers. 'Anyway – I haven't the foggiest idea what the Holy Father will think. There's no point in me trying to second-guess him.'

'But we need to know fairly quickly – '

She cut him off again. 'I'm seeing him tonight. It's one of our dinners in his private apartments. I'll talk to him then. If I know him, he'll have an instinctive reaction. I'll probably be able to call you tomorrow with his reply.'

'That's good. Tell His Holiness that I'm sure the art world will leap at the chance to attend the sale. It'll be historic. The press coverage will be enormous and obviously that will translate into a higher price for the painting. So do what you can. I'm right in this case, believe me. I understand if you have reservations, but I *am* right.'

'Yeees – I'm beginning to see the possibilities myself. I'll call you tomorrow. Now, will you send those South Sea photographs, please? I know the Holy Father would love to see them. There might be an official use I can put them to.'

Now it was David's turn to hesitate. He improvised. 'I *can* post them, certainly. But . . . but I'm coming to Rome myself next week, to spend a couple of days in the Vatican archive. I'm trying to sort out this Leonardo mystery, as I think I told you. Perhaps I could deliver them personally – and show them to you over dinner.'

He shouldn't have asked. It was out of place. Not forward exactly, or familiar. More . . . well, he assumed, too much. All this he thought as he waited for her reply. The line seemed dead. He was about to speak again when she said, 'I'm not sure what my schedule is next week. But call me when you have arrived in Rome and we'll see.'

The Holy Father approved David's idea. He agreed that it would make the occasion special, would attract the right kind of publicity and was sufficiently different from the 'Madonna' sale to attract attention right up until the day of the auction itself. There was nothing in canon law, he said, which forbade this kind of transaction. After all, the Vatican museums and galleries sold catalogues and postcards, they charged for entry, the Vatican bookshop charged for the books it sold, there was a money changer in the museums and a supermarket in the Vatican itself. But the masterstroke, in David's eyes, was the Pope's suggestion that the sale actually be held in the Vatican picture gallery in the very room where the Caravaggio hung.

After some thought David decided to make less of the catalogue this time around. He remembered how a minority of the board had been against the sale because of its Mafia implications, and he thought it wise not to stress this aspect. He didn't want to frighten anyone away from the sale. What Hamilton's would produce therefore was more a brochure than a catalogue, containing an article about the history of the painting and a short account of the work under way in Sicily, paid for by the funds that had been advanced. And they would include photographs David had taken himself in the Marquesas Isles – to show what the previous sale of Vatican pictures had achieved.

With the Caravaggio sale under control, the Argyll sale signed up and one of his colleagues busy with the house in Derbyshire, David felt able to take his two days in Rome as planned. Though the Hassler was his favourite hotel, he stayed this time at the Giulio Cesare, a much more modest establishment on the other bank of the Tiber but from where he could walk to the Vatican archive each morning keeping only to tree-lined boulevards. Almost the first person he saw at the archive was Diego Giunta, hunched over a pile of papers. David assumed Giunta was working on his biography of Pius XIII, more a scholar these days than an archivist.

The beauty, and the problem, of working in the Vatican archive was its filing system. Some documents were filed according to modern systems but many weren't. David got nowhere following up the other reports from the papal nuncio at Urbino. There was not a single mention of Leonardo. Where to turn next? Leonardo had been described by the nuncio not as an artist but as an engineer. David therefore turned to the chaotic files which referred to civil engineering feats of the time – not court or religious projects, since they were all known, but buildings like hospitals, which were not always linked to the Church, irrigation techniques, and designs for new medical instruments. On his second day he was lucky. He came across a mention of a hospital ordered to be built by the Duke of Urbino. The date was January 1482 and the document included a reference to a design for a medical magnifying glass, offered by one 'Leond°', newly arrived from Rimini.'

So the great man had been at Rimini at the end of 1481! This was new information, but not yet what David was looking for. The family who had governed Rimini at the time were the Malatesta, fairly despotic, if memory served him. The papacy had eventually overrun Rimini, just as it had incorporated Urbino. So some of the Malatesta papers would be here in Rome, but others might be in Rimini itself. David had run out of time, however. He had to get back to London. Rimini would have to wait.

He thought a small celebration would be in order, however, especially as Elizabeth Lisle had consented to have dinner with him on his last night in Rome. She had been her usual self when he had called the day before. 'It'll have to be late, supper rather than dinner, but, yes, I am free. I shall look forward to it.' She was a tantalizing mixture of the reserved and the cordial.

She had suggested they meet at Gina's, her local trattoria, near where she lived on the Via dei Banchi Vecchi. The cafe turned out to be half bar, half restaurant, half inside, half outside, half a television-watching place for the neighbourhood and half a telephone answering service. Gina herself was there, small, fat, round and made up as red as a mullet. She fussed over Elizabeth Lisle as if she had been her own daughter.

There was no menu, simply a prolonged conversation between the two women. David was content with that. 'We're having *porcini*,' said Elizabeth Lisle. 'The most delicately flavoured mushroom in the world. With tagliatelle.'

'Perfect. I'm glad you ordered – but don't forget I'm paying. I want to celebrate.'

'Oh?'

He told her about his day in the archives.

'That's marvellous.' She looked at him slyly. 'But does it really matter if you prove which Leonardo is real and which is fake? If even the experts find it difficult to tell them apart then surely the one is as good as the other?'

'No,' said David firmly. This was an old, familiar argument. 'Scholarship is important for its own sake. The more we can know about an artist, the better we can appreciate him – or her. If I identify the real Leonardo, it has to make a difference. Knowing the true from the false always does. In life and in art. We must believe that.'

'I don't follow.' She had her hair down tonight. Because the sun had bleached it David counted at least three browns – whisky, walnut, wheat.

'Look at it this way. People have a lazy attitude to painting. They expect to like a picture straight away. If they don't, they assume they never will. These days people don't seem interested in trying to understand what a painter was after, what he was trying to do. I blame the impressionists. They produced pretty pictures which have an immediate appeal and that's all that people want these days. Yet that's not how it is with the other arts. Think of music or opera. Few people like opera to start with. Only with increasing association, increasing knowledge, do they find their appetite being whetted. Then their passions grow. It's the same with pictures.' He leaned across the table towards her. 'If I do identify the real Leonardo, it will change the way we look at it, and at the other painting. The different features in the two works will take on a different significance. They will inevitably refine our understanding of both works and the man who made them.'

'Hmm. I hadn't thought of it like that. You make scholarship sound exciting. I like that.'

'You wouldn't have enjoyed being in the archive yesterday. I sat next to Giunta. Do you still think he and Massoni are "plotting" against Thomas?'

Her face clouded. Instinctively, she fingered the cross at her neck. 'Massoni! Bah! Do you know what he did, after the announcement of the Caravaggio sale? He'd been invited to address the American clergy here in Rome who have a dining club at the Villa Stritch, where most of them live. He attacked what he called "American values" – putting a monetary figure on everything. And he said it was a mistake to tangle with the Mafia.'

'What happened?'

'Well, I think it backfired with a lot of the Americans, of course, but his speech was leaked to the Rome papers, and they were much more sympathetic. It means the split between him and Thomas is out in the open now. It hasn't blown up yet, but it might at any moment.'

'But isn't the Vizzini Fund proving very effective?'

'Yes, but it's beginning to look like a mistake for Thomas to have appointed Massoni as his Secretary of State. You can't have a powerful organization if it's split at the top.'

They sat for a while, letting the noises of the restaurant swirl around them. There was brass band music on the television, bored complaints from children who were still up well past their respectable Anglo-Saxon bed-time. Gina brought the *porcini* and a bottle of Rubesco. Elizabeth Lisle tasted it and nodded approvingly. She turned back to David. 'The food's so good here, and so cheap, I hardly ever eat at home.'

'Do you live alone?'

'Oh yes, just down the street here. Fourth floor. You have to walk up.'

David smiled. 'No wonder you look so slim.'

She shook her head. 'I eat like a lion. It must be my genes which stop me spreading.'

'What other genes do you have? Are you extrovert? Introvert? Optimistic? Depressive? Forgetful? Credit card crazy? I can't tell from here.'

She was smiling. 'Not the last one, certainly. And not depressive or forgetful, either. Optimistic? – yes, but with Massoni around, less and less so.'

'Lonely?'

Now she wasn't smiling. Her face was serious but gentle. 'Mr Colwyn, only a man who was lonely himself would ask a question like that.'

For a moment he was silenced. Then, recovering, he said, 'That's not an answer.'

She tossed back her hair in a gesture he hadn't seen before. It made her look years younger and he felt as if, with that simple twist of her neck, he had been admitted to her inner self. 'Lonely? Or do you mean solitary? I can never be sure which I am. Maybe I'm both.'

But she gave no more, and before he could press her further she changed the subject. 'Do you like fairs?'

'Fairs?' He was flummoxed.

'Carousels . . . dodgem cars . . . there's one on here in Rome this week, over by the Janiculum. I love fairs but it's difficult for a woman to go by herself. Life in Louisiana was full of fairs and festivals. Everybody's heard of Mardi Gras – Fat Tuesday – in New Orleans. But we also had the rice festival, the sugar cane festival, a frog festival, would you believe? My favourite was Contraband Day, rowing and boating races commemorating the famous pirates and smugglers of the seventeenth century. Their descendants are, of course, a bit snooty now.' She smiled. 'I was a bit of a tomboy as a girl – I loved all that stuff. If you'd take me to the fair, it would be a kindness.'

'It'll have to be tonight. I'm flying home tomorrow.'

She nodded.

David savoured the last of his *porcini*. 'On one condition. I can't go to a fair with someone who refers to me by my last name. If we go, and I'd like to, I'm David. And you . . . ? Whatever you are, but not Miss Lisle.'

She considered this. 'Yes. OK. But I'm not Elizabeth. That's what my grandmother's called, and my mother is Liz. In the family I'm Bess.'

He loved it. A simple name, brave and unassuming. A tomboyish name. At a stroke it put her into context.

She watched him react. 'Boney, bossy and boyish, my Pa used to say.'

'That must have been some time ago.'

She was getting to her feet so David couldn't be certain whether she blushed. But either way he was sure some barrier between them had been crossed. He paid the bill and they walked towards the Lungotevere where they took a taxi.

The rest of the evening was a great success. In the first place it was obvious that Elizabeth Lisle – Bess – really did adore fairs. For once the restraints of her Vatican life were forgotten. She had to try her hand at everything. She gave David a trouncing in the dodgems, frightened him into silence on the big dipper and laughed helplessly at him in the hall of mirrors. He retrieved some dignity by acquitting himself well on the shooting range, so much so that he wasn't allowed a second go. That impressed her. But the evening's success went deeper than that. The mass of people, the crush, the bright lights under the dark sky, the tacky food and the fizzy drinks they had at midnight, it all created a sense of intimacy between them, privacy even, that could have occurred almost nowhere else. They found they could be at ease with eath other.

David could also tell, from the earnest enthusiasm with which Bess embraced the fair, that his instincts had been sound: she *was* lonely. Solitary was her word for it, a kinder word perhaps but in this case it amounted to the same thing. Maybe the man who had answered the phone was no longer in her life. But he couldn't ask about that tonight.

They stayed late. It was gone two when they collapsed into a taxi and Bess fell asleep on the short ride back to the Via dei Banchi Vecchi. Her hair fell across David's shoulder. It smelled of lavender. Her flat was in an old building, set back beyond a courtyard. As the taxi drew to a halt, she jerked awake.

'Sorry.'

'Don't be. It's late.'

They got out and he paid.

'Aren't you going to keep the cab?'

'No, it's not far to the hotel. Just across the river. I'd like to walk.'

Now came the awkwardness. *He'd* asked her out, *he'd* agreed to accompany her to the fair. It was her place to round off the evening.

She held out her hand. 'Thank you, David,' she said softly. 'You were kind to take me. It finishes tomorrow. I would have missed it, but for you.'

'I enjoyed it, too,' said David. 'Thank you for thinking of it.' He felt as awkward as he sounded. Suddenly he wanted her to say something, to move their relationship forward. He was amazed at how much he wanted that. But she turned without speaking again and disappeared across the courtyard.

Back in London, the auction season was getting under way. With competition between the salerooms now so fierce, senior executives in each firm spent a lot of time thinking up new schemes to make their house attractive to potential sellers of art. A favourite ploy was to guarantee sellers a certain amount of money from a sale, come what may. Exactly as had happened over the Argyll Estate and with the Vatican pictures. But it was risky and each case had to be treated on its merits. At Hamilton's next board meeting, the week after David got back from Rome, the issue cropped up again. This time it was raised by Peter McBride, the director in charge of French painting.

'The situation is this,' he told the board. 'George Kinney has decided to sell his collection of Watteaus and Bouchers. For those of you who don't know him, Kinney owns large forests in North Carolina, Canada and Alaska; he supplies hundreds of newspapers in North America with newsprint and he, his father and his grandfather before him have been collecting French painting for over eighty years.'

'So why is he selling?' someone asked.

'He won't say but the best guess is that he's strapped for cash and wants to buy more forests which have just come on the market in Canada. Anyway, what we're talking about is seven Watteaus, five Bouchers, five Fragonards and twenty-three other paintings by smaller names – Greuze, Vigée-Lebrun, Vien. There's been a lot of toing and froing, but the nitty-gritty is that Steele's have guaranteed Kinney fifteen million pounds. That's way over my budget without board approval, hence this item on today's agenda.'

'And what are these pictures worth?' It was Afton speaking.

'We've done a careful estimate and our view is that the top price would be thirteen point five million pounds.'

'How come Steele's say it's worth more?' Averne sat directly across from McBride.

'We think they're taking a chance. They want the business.'

'How good is our judgement?' It was Averne again.

McBride said: 'I did the calculation myself.'

'But you've been wrong before. Didn't that David go for nearly twice the figure you put on it?'

'It's tricky trying to put a figure on a painting weeks before it comes up for auction, and there were special circumstances in that case – '

'But you were nearly 100 per cent out – yes or no?'

'Yes'

Afton spoke. 'Sam, by the tone of your voice you think we should guarantee Kinney more than Steele's have?'

'Sure I do,' said Averne. 'These are great names, Watteau, Boucher, Fragonard. If we offer, say, sixteen million pounds and they fetch nineteen, or twenty, it's good business.'

'And if they don't?'

'So we own some French Old Masters for a while. So what? The market will catch up sooner or later.'

Afton turned to his left. 'David?'

'I'm against it. We are auctioneers, not bankers. Our whole business depends on the close link between value and quality. Let that go and the whole art world falls to pieces. Also, if we follow Sam's reasoning we could end up owning more paintings than we sell. And third, if it gets out that the big auction houses act like bankers just to get business, then sellers will be playing one house off against the others in no time and we'll all be the losers. If we *have* to offer money up front, then that money should always be tied to what we think the art is worth. Of course we make mistakes but in-house surveys show that on average our estimates are within fifteen per cent of the actual prices fetched. If I know Peter McBride, he's done his homework and that figure of his – thirteen point five million pounds – includes that margin for error.'

McBride nodded.

Afton looked across to Averne. 'Want to come back, Sam?'

'Just this. We won't always have these Vatican sales to rely on. We've got to be aggressive, go out and get the business. Steele's see that; I'm not sure we do. The Kinney sale is worth a punt.'

Afton put it to a vote. Averne lost, but it was close: 9 to 7. As David went back to his office after the meeting, he reflected that, as ever in a large company, there were jealousies to contend with. Averne needed watching.

Ned needed watching too, if for very different reasons. David hadn't heard from him since term started – he hadn't even sent back his latest chess move (they played by post during every term). David didn't want to appear a fussing parent and Ned was probably in touch with his mother anyway. So he would leave it another week or so before calling the housemaster. But no longer.

As the Caravaggio sale drew near David had one or two conversations on the phone with Bess, but they were strictly professional. After the way she had just turned away at the end of their evening together, he could not bring himself to be at all familiar – not when there were a thousand miles separating them. Once he was back in Rome, though, things might be different. He'd make them different.

Before that, however, David made headlines again. Working in the National Fine Art Library in the Victoria & Albert Museum, and consulting some documents relating to seventeenth-century Rome, he came across a commission to Salvator Rosa that exactly fitted the Argyll painting. Excited, he sent a photograph of the painting, and a photocopy of the library document, to Sir Charles Senior, Director of the Fitzwilliam Museum in Cambridge and an authority on Rosa. Senior confirmed by return that the Argyll painting was a Rosa and almost certainly the one referred to in the documents. Delighted, David checked back through the records in the basement of Hamilton's. He worked late for two nights comparing the prices of similar pictures in the past. At the end of that time, he felt justified in changing the estimate on the Rosa – to £750,000. Next day, Pringle had no problem interesting the press in an object that had been lying forgotten in a Scottish manse for many years, and which was now found to be worth three quarters of a million pounds. David left for Rome feeling better than he had for weeks.

The Vatican technicians had done a superb job with the lights. The Caravaggio looked sensational, its reds and browns as deep and dark as the night outside the open window. The octagonal gallery was much cosier than any normal auction house, an impressive backdrop of Domenichino, Guido Reni, and Guercino. The visitors' black ties and dark silk evening dresses made a perfect contrast, with the colour of the evening provided by a handful of cardinals in vivid, official scarlet, there because, as one of them put it, they 'wanted to see the action.'

The temporary rostrum for the sale was to one side, rather than directly ahead of the bidders, who faced the painting. This was David's idea; he felt it suggested that the priorities of the evening were not entirely commercial.

He had been in Rome two days, checking that his staff had done their jobs. One or two last-minute hitches had been ironed out – for example, he had to smooth out the ruffled feathers of two museum directors who had inadvertently not been invited to the previous evening's reception given by His Holiness. Thomas was out of Rome for the sale tonight, but the reception had gone very well, with the Holy Father deep in interested conversation with several museum directors, Smallbone from the Getty especially. David had tried to catch Bess's eye but, to his disappointment, had failed. It didn't seem as though she was avoiding him, though. She was truly busy and had agreed to a quick supper right after the auction. At Gina's again. He was therefore in a fairly relaxed mood – which was just as well, given the job he had to do.

David tapped the microphone to check that it was working. 'Ladies and gentlemen,' he said quickly in English. 'Welcome to Hamilton's new auction rooms.' Everyone, including the cardinals, laughed. 'We have only one painting in the auction tonight, "The Deposition", by Michelangelo Merisi da Caravaggio. Before we come to the sale itself, however, His Holiness has asked me to screen a short film – just a few minutes – which will show you how the money advanced on the picture to be sold tonight is already being used.'

Almost immediately the lights of the gallery dimmed and, to the left of the Caravaggio where there was a screen, the film started to roll. It was neatly done. A few minutes only, as David had said, juxtaposing newsreel film of the Mussomeli massacre with more recent footage of the projects in Sicily and even one or two grimmer shots of Mafia suspects being rounded up. Finally, a shot of the Oratory of San Lorenzo in Palermo from where, in 1969, Caravaggio's 'Nativity' had been stolen by the Mafia and never returned, showing that Caravaggio too, like Fr Vizzini, like the children near the priest that day, had been a victim of the mob.

The film faded and the lights of the TV crews went on again. David waited until everyone had settled down. 'Ladies and gentlemen, "The Deposition". Painted for the Chiesa Nuova here in Rome, this picture was taken to Paris in 1797 for the Musée Napoleon, but returned and installed in the Vatican around 1815. The painting is dated 1602/3.' He paused, looked around the room, then carried on. 'I have two bids in the book and so shall start tonight at twenty billion lire. Approximately ten million dollars. Twenty billion lire . . . any more?'

Later, in his report of the sale, David would tell his board there must have been twenty people in the room that night who wanted to buy the picture. After an initial, inevitable hesitation, the bids crowded in. At fifty billion there were still six hands urgently raised. At sixty-six only two remained – the Met and Sydney. At sixty-eight Sydney dropped out but then, having sat immobile until now, Sol Smallbone from the Getty flicked his catalogue. So that left the Met v. the Getty, a classic fight.

The bidding was soon at seventy-two billion, but at seventy-three Jakobson of the Met was obviously worried. He wanted the picture, he seemed determined to have it, but he was clearly near, if not already over, his limit. Though the next bid should have gone to seventy-four, he called out 'Seventy-three and a half!'

David accepted the bid and looked at Smallbone. With a wonderful sense of theatre, the Getty man removed his glasses, took a handkerchief from his pocket, polished his glasses, put them back on, looked long at the Caravaggio. Then he said calmly but loudly, 'Seventy-five.'

A gasp came from several places in the room. To jump a bid, especially at this level, was unheard of. Smallbone was signalling to Jakobson and anyone else with a fancy for 'The Deposition' that he was going to get it, even if it took all of his $110 million budget for that year.

Jakobson, looking as though his world was about to end, shook his head. The sound of David's gavel falling was drowned by the cheers and applause. Seventy-five billion lire was over thirty-seven million dollars. Over twenty-four million pounds. Recovering his composure, Jakobson went over to congratulate Smallbone. The pair were photographed shaking hands and then Smallbone was ushered forward to stand in front of the painting as it was taken down. David's men took no more than ten minutes to unscrew the frame and lift the picture off the wall. The gesture was genuinely moving. As the picture went, accompanied by Smallbone, a pale and dirty patch was left on the now very empty gallery wall.

The newspaper reporters and television crews were milling around, soliciting comments. It was some time before David could get away to meet Bess – he had to arrange delivery of 'The Deposition' and make sure the Getty's cheque went through smoothly. He caught up with Smallbone in the Vatican gallery's framing room, where the carpenters worked. A packing case had already been half-constructed for the Caravaggio and the Getty man was examining it.

'Well done, Sol,' said David, holding out his hand.

Smallbone smiled and grasped his hand firmly. 'What a painting! These people are as alive tonight as the day Caravaggio had them pose for him. I could go on looking at it for ever.'

Together they stood in silence for a moment, gazing at the creams and reds, the rich skin tones of the faces, the mysterious burnt browns in the shadows.

'Are you dashing back to Malibu, Sol?'

'As a matter of fact, no. Funny thing . . . at the reception yesterday the Holy Father asked me to stay on for a couple of days. At Vatican expense, too. Said he wanted to pick my brains.' Smallbone laughed and tapped his temple. 'He's welcome to what's left. Can't imagine what he has in mind. Still, I shall be around, yes. Why?'

David glanced up at the clock. 'I thought we could tie up all the details tomorrow rather than now. I'm sure you'll be wanting your dinner. And you have some celebrating to do.'

Smallbone grinned. 'You bet. Sure, David. If you can wait, so can I. The difficult bit is over. If you're happy to wait twenty-four hours before receiving the cheque, that's fine by me. A day's interest on thirty-seven and a half million dollars is close to nine thousand five hundred bucks. I know these things. Come to the hotel at noon tomorrow. I'm at the Eden – couldn't get into the Hassler. We'll settle everything and then have lunch. OK?'

David waved goodbye. 'OK, see you tomorrow. Don't celebrate too hard.'

He made straight for Gina's. Bess was already there, a campari soda in front of her. She looked up and smiled as he arrived and held out her hand. David shook it, though the gesture implied a formality he hoped he'd got beyond. He sat down. She was wearing a red silk dress. He scanned her face. Had she made up specially for him? He couldn't be sure, but she was wearing earrings and he liked that. They were something extra.

'I've just been looking at the picture, close up, with Smallbone. It's fantastic.'

'And so different from the Raphael – yet just as spiritual.'

'Yes, it's a pity the pictures couldn't have been sold together – it would have brought out one of the ideas Thomas is trying to get across: that spirituality means different things to different people.'

She looked at him levelly. 'If they *had* been sold together, would it have made any difference to the prices paid?'

'I doubt it. Each of the three paintings His Holiness has sold are first-rate and very rare. There's always money around for the best. Why do you ask?'

She shook her head. 'It doesn't matter. Nothing.'

Gina appeared, half-hidden behind a mound of macaroni, with a tomato sauce red as her make-up.

'I ordered for you,' said Bess. 'I'm starving.'

She served the pasta and they began to eat.

'I have a question for you,' said David. 'Smallbone said the Holy Father asked him to stay on in Rome. You don't know what that's about, do you?'

Bess threw back her head, twisting her neck as he had seen her do on the previous occasion. Again her hair was swept back so that it no longer framed her face, making her look younger. The red in her dress brought out the gold in her hair as if she had sunshine inside her. 'As a matter of fact I do. But I can't tell you. What I can say is that the Holy Father would like you to stay on in Rome also – '

'What! Why?'

'I can't say, David. Please. Only for forty-eight hours, then all will be explained. It's very important, I promise.'

'I'd planned to go back tomorrow.'

'Put it off, please.'

'And you really can't say?'

'No. I hate being so secretive but, when you understand, you'll see why.'

'And Smallbone is involved?'

'I can't say any more. Please say you'll stay. It's important to Thomas.'

If it was important to Thomas, David reflected, it was important to Bess. But he was being difficult – why? Was it because, when she had agreed to have dinner with him, he had hoped they might take up from last time? . . . but now he found that she had another reason to see him, to give him news of this damn meeting.

'Why is it all so last-minute, so rushed?'

'I can't explain that either. But Thomas will, the day after tomorrow.'

89

David would have to stay, of course. It would be insulting not to, after the money the Vatican sales had brought into Hamilton's.

'If I *do* stay, Bess, don't you think you ought to make it up to me? Don't you think I ought to get something in return?' He smiled to show he was half-joking. But he was half-serious, too.

Her hair had fallen forward and yet again she tossed it back with a twist that was already becoming familiar. 'There *is* something, but I don't think it's what you have in mind.'

'You owe me, Bess.'

'All right, then. If you insist. I've bought some things, art things – '

' – And you want me to advise you.'

'No, not quite. I've already bought them – it's too late for that. They've even been delivered. That's my point. I need a man to carry them up four flights of stairs.'

# 5

Two exciting, momentous days followed. First came the world's reaction to the sale of the Caravaggio: His Holiness now had thirty-seven million dollars, less three million commission, to fight the Mafia with. This time James Roskill, the American President, was not the only political figure to praise Pope Thomas. The Prime Ministers of Great Britain, Australia and Sweden did too, as well as the West German Chancellor, the Israeli President and the Brazilian President.

And there was David's visit to Bess's apartment building, helping her haul and hoist and heft her 'art things' up 107 steps. The job took hours and his lunch beforehand with Smallbone hadn't improved matters. The Getty man had already seen the Holy Father – he still wouldn't say what about – but he insisted on celebrating his acquisition of the Caravaggio all over again. So when David arrived at Bess's flat in the Via dei Banchi Vecchi that afternoon he could have been in better shape.

The exercise soon straightened him out. From their size – they were solidly packaged – Bess's 'art things' appeared to be two very large paintings and a particularly heavy piece of sculpture. Bess herself was dressed, for the first time since had known her, in trousers and a very practical pair of espadrilles. She would supervise the operation. 'There's freshly squeezed lemon juice in the flat – when you get there,' she had said with a grin.

David took off his blazer and started lifting. What had happened to the man who had answered the phone? he wondered. Was he out of the picture now? He didn't dare ask.

Though heavy, the sculpture was in fact the easiest thing to move. The pictures, although lighter, were so large they were very difficult to negotiate up the twists and turns of the staircase. Still, when Bess's flat was reached the climb proved worth it. She had one large room, a sort of studio, off which the bedroom, kitchen and bathroom all led. The main room was dramatic enough but the view was even more so. The window looked across miles of roof tops, punctuated here and there by the majestic rising shapes of baroque church steeples and spires, the whole vista dominated by the magnificent cupola of St Peter's.

'How did you find this place?' said David, drinking his juice.

'Believe it or not, it comes with the job. But as you can see, the steps are a problem.'

David put his glass down and started undoing the packages. He noticed photographs on the walls. Bess and her family, American landscapes, a fine portrait of Thomas. Bess in a balloon, in a sea plane, on a bicycle against a backdrop that looked like the Italian lakes. Active pictures all of them – the tomboy, David observed, had not quite disappeared. There was none of an eligible man. When he had unwrapped the pictures, he placed them against the wall. One showed a mythological scene, with nude figures, some dressed in helmets, and with many animals. The second was a drawing with fantastic writhing figures in weird perspective. The sculpture was of a single nude male figure, much calmer, classically proportioned with strong abdominal muscles and a straight, aquiline nose.

'What do you think?' said Bess.

David didn't reply straight away. Then, 'What do *you* think? Why did you buy these?'

'Well, to tell the truth, you're a bit responsible. These sales of Thomas's have obviously concentrated my mind on art. And you made the scholarly side to it sound so interesting that I decided to start collecting for myself. And, you know, I reckon I may already have made a discovery.' She went over and stood by the drawing. It was almost as tall as she was. 'The guy I bought this from said it was by Domenico Tiepolo, the "wrong Tiepolo", as he called him. So it didn't cost that much. But before I bought it I looked at a few books on the Tiepolos – there were two of them, as you must know. Giambattista is the famous one, Domenico was his son and not as good. And you know, David, I found a drawing in one of these books which looks just like this. It could really be by Giambattista Tiepolo and if it is, it's worth a whole lot more than I paid for it.' She looked at him hopefully.

David helped himself to more juice. 'And the other picture?'

'Well, it was sold to me as an Antonio Carracci. I gather there were at least five Carraccis and that Antonio ranked about fourth out of the five. But I'm rather hoping it might be the same as the Tiepolo. I've looked at a few books and it *seems* in the style of Annibale – he was number one, as I don't need to tell you. That would be really exciting if it turned out to be an Annibale.'

'And the sculpture?'

'The dealer threw that in for very little. He was a picture dealer, he said. He didn't know much about sculpture. He said he thought it was probably a Roman copy of a Greek original. Even if it is, it's worth more than I paid for it. If I can identify it in any of the books, I mean.'

She sat on the sofa and poured herself some juice. 'Well, have I the makings of a connoisseur or not?'

'You've been had.'

'What!'

'By one of the oldest tricks in the book.'

'No! You're not serious. Good grief. Tell me you're joking, David. The man was so nice.'

'I've never been more serious.'

'But I don't understand! What's wrong with these things? What do you mean: the oldest trick in the book?'

'For a start, the "drawing", as you call it, is not by *Domenico* Tiepolo, it's by his father Giambattista, the famous one.'

'So.'

'But it's not a drawing. It's an old engraving – it can be hard sometimes to tell the difference. An engraver called Pietro Monaco copied quite a lot of old man Tiepolo's drawings. He did them to show what he could do. There are a lot of them around and I'm afraid they aren't worth very much – and never will be.'

Bess went over to the 'drawing' to examine it.

'You fell for an old line, I'm afraid. Dealers get a copy of a picture by a well-known artist. It's thrown in with a pile of other things. Many famous artists had families whose other members were also painters – the Carracci, the Tiepolo, the Bassano, the Veronese, the Le Nain brothers, the Breughels, the Van der Veldes. There are more than you'd think. To the dealers a copy is worth next to nothing, since the painter is so well known. So they keep it in a back room – is that where your man had this one?'

Bess nodded.

'– and when someone comes in who seems keen but naive, they pass it off as an original but by the junior member of the family. Willem van de Velde, not Adriaen, Carlo Veronese, not Paolo. Newcomers in the art world always buy carefully, or they think they do. They carry out rudimentary research in easily available books – and find what you found, that the picture is not by the junior man at all, but the famous one. People are so keen to make a coup that they never stop to ask themselves why the dealer hasn't looked in the same books.'

'So this other painting . . . ?'

'I can't be sure, but I know this much. In the eighteenth century there was a Venetian connoisseur called Filippo Farsetti. He had a wonderful collection of copies. He employed a painter, Luigi Pozzi, and a sculptor, Ventura Furlani, to do nothing else but copy great works in Rome and elsewhere.

'Pozzi copied mainly works by Raphael and the Carracci and Furlani spent all his time carving copies of classical statues. I'm afraid you haven't got a sixteenth-century painting, or a piece of classical sculpture, but late eighteenth-century copies'.

Bess was blushing, embarrassed at being taken in so easily. Anger was beginning to stir. 'What can I do?'

'How did you pay?'

'By cheque. But it cleared before they would let me take the things away. They delivered the day it cleared.'

'Who are "they"?'

'A dealer called Ludovisi in the Via del Babuino.'

David thought fast. 'May I use your phone?'

'Of course.'

He dialled. 'May I speak to Massimo Vittrice, please.' There was a pause, during which time David told her he was calling Hamilton's offices in Rome. 'Massimo? David Colwyn here. Fine, thank you – and you? Good. Listen, Massimo, I need some help. Do you know a dealer here in Rome called Ludovisi? Yes, that's right, on the Via del Babuino. Do they buy from us? A lot – good. Look, I know this is short notice but do you think you could meet me there in, say, half an hour? Thanks – I'll explain everything then. See you in thirty minutes.'

They finished their juice. David washed quickly and put his blazer back on. Then he and Bess took a taxi to the Via del Babuino. He wouldn't tell her what he planned in case it didn't come off. They waited outside Ludovisi's until Massimo appeared, then he led the way inside. The dealer's face lit up when he saw Massimo, but fell immediately he noticed Bess behind him with David. Massimo introduced David to Ludovisi and then David explained, courteously, with many expressions of Italianate regret, that unless Ludovisi returned all monies to Miss Elizabeth Lisle, press secretary to the Holy Father, and took back the works he had recently sold her, no doubt as the result of a cataloguing error, he would never again be able to enter Hamilton's auction house.

Ludovisi was a practical man, who recognized superior force when he saw it. The 'error' was admitted, apologies were made and the cheque was written out there and then. David told him he could collect the artworks in two days – when the cheque had cleared.

Later that evening, as David walked Bess home after a celebratory supper at Gina's with Massimo, she had said, 'Why didn't you let me pay for dinner tonight? After what happened today I feel as though I still owe you something.'

They had reached her courtyard. 'You do,' said David. 'You do owe me. But I'll settle for much less than dinner. I'll settle for this.' And before she could respond he leaned forward and, very lightly, kissed her cheek.

David recalled the faint, lavender smell of Bess's make-up next morning

94

as he stepped out of the lift and into the third floor of the papal apartments. Patrick O'Rourke, the Holy Father's principal private secretary, held out his hand. 'Welcome to the apostolic palace, Mr Colwyn. This way, please.'

David shook the offered hand and followed O'Rourke down a wide corridor, uncarpeted. The floor was of red and grey marble, the walls painted a surprisingly sallow, institutional yellow. Like most Catholics, David had always wanted to see inside the papal apartments at the Vatican and now, at long last, here he was. The Pope's special meeting, which David had been asked to stay on in Rome for, was about to begin.

O'Rourke turned off the corridor into a large study-cum-conference room. The windows, David could see, gave on to St Peter's Square.

He was amazed at the size of the meeting: there must have been a dozen men in the room, many of whom he didn't know. Bess wasn't among them but scarcely had David been shown to his seat at the long rectangular table than a large double door at the far end of the room opened and His Holiness appeared with Bess and his other private secretary behind. The Pope, who was limping quite badly, was carrying a bundle of papers and took his seat at the head of the table. Bess sat opposite David and smiled, rather nervously he thought. She had her hair up.

The Pope came straight to the point. 'Good morning everyone – especially to Mr David Colwyn here, chief executive of Hamilton's who has so successfully masterminded the sale of our paintings.' All eyes turned to David. His Holiness spoke again. 'Mr Colwyn, of course you know Elizabeth Lisle here, and His Eminence Cardinal Massoni, the Secretary of State.' Massoni, unsmiling, inclined his head. The Pope continued: 'You have also met Cardinal Zingale, I recall, President of the Patrimony of the Holy See, Dottore Tecce and Dottore Venturini. Next to you is Cardinal John Rich, Archbishop of New York, on his left is Archbishop Albino Sabino, president of the Institute for Religious Works, the Vatican Bank, and on *his* left Cardinal Ettore Loredan, president of the Pontifical Commission for Latin America. Opposite you, next to Miss Lisle, is Archbishop Andrzej Rozmberk, President of the Pontifical Commission Cor Unum which, as you may know, looks after development issues in the Third World. Next to me here is Cardinal Romeo Savelli, president of the Prefecture of the Economic Affairs of the Holy See; and finally, on Miss Lisle's other side, you see Cardinal Eusebio del Santander, head of the Permanent Commission for the protection of Historical and Artistic Monuments of the Holy See.'

Thomas paused to examine the papers in front of him. It struck David that His Holiness looked slightly nervous. There was not a sound anywhere in the room.

95

The Pope looked up. 'Gentlemen – and Elizabeth,' he said. 'I'm sorry for the rather cloak and dagger way some of you have been brought here, but I assure you that what we are to discuss this morning is important enough to warrant it.' He pushed his chair back. 'Let me recap a little before I come to the main purpose of the meeting. Earlier this year, as a result of the unfortunate tragedy at Foligno, and following an angry outburst by Sr Sirianni, the mayor of that town, I had an idea. As a result of Mr Colwyn's – "adaptation" of my idea, the Church has been set on a new direction, one that appears to have much to commend it: we provide funds for the poor, we offer them hope, we improve the standing of the Church in the eyes of many and we draw them back to the faith. Most important, I believe the Holy Spirit is speaking to us and this approach is the work of God. What we have been doing is *right*.

'The monies raised by the sale of the Raphael, the Gauguin and the Caravaggio have been put to good use. Foligno will be almost restored by the end of the year. The new cathedral will take two years more to complete but already the people can see it going up. Part of the relief money is being used to help build a Fiat factory, which will provide jobs and perhaps prosperity for the area. In the Marquesas Isles in the South Pacific we have built a hospital, a school, five hundred and sixty-five prefabricated houses, and a small dock. We have provided deposits for the purchase of eight fishing vessels. In Sicily most of you will be familiar with our successes against the Mafia there – the first real relief from violence the island has ever known.

'But these specifics are not really the main point. The main point is that our approach, selling off some tiny part of the Vatican treasures to help the needy, has caught the imagination of the world. The latest figures I have support this: the numbers of those receiving mass, world-wide, are up by nine per cent; entries to the priesthood are up by seven per cent; the enrolments in Catholic schools, worldwide, are up by all of fifteen per cent; the number of conversions are up and the latest figure on tourists to the Vatican shows a rise over last year of eight per cent.

'But this is not all. In many *non*-Catholic areas too, there are moves to follow our lead. In Israel, for instance, the Socialist party has called on the government to sell off some of the Dead Sea Scrolls to benefit poor people on the West Bank. In Egypt there are plans for a sale of Abydos antiquities to help the drought-stricken areas of the Upper Nile. Once more, therefore, after a long period of retrenchment, the Roman Church has become the conscience of the world. But, having created a momentum, we need to keep it up.'

Thomas paused and looked around the table. 'It is now time that we gave a fresh lead. We have, I believe, created a climate of opinion in which we can go forward at a faster, even more impressive pace. We need to show just what *can* be done, so that all those who have been moved by our successes so far will want to follow. So that is why I believe the time is right to move our plans up a gear.'

Thomas stood up. 'Now to details.' He reached forward and picked up a pile of papers from the table in front of him. He tapped them into line like a pack of cards. 'Despite our successes over the past months, two things have worried me. One is the undeniable fact that we cannot go on selling off treasures forever – eventually there will be nothing left to sell. The other is that, until now, we have been very fortunate in that the art possessed by the Vatican has included examples in some way apposite to the causes we were trying to help. We cannot expect such good fortune to continue. It is time, therefore, to consider a different approach – which is why we are all here today.'

Thomas now began to move around the table distributing sheets of paper. 'I have given the matter a lot of thought and, indeed, consulted with some of you around this table today. I have been particularly impressed by the Getty Museum's situation. The Getty, as some of you will know, have an endowment fund which provides a yearly income somewhere in the region of $110 million for spending on art.

'Yesterday, I met for an hour with Mr Sol Smallbone, director of the Getty Museum which, as you know, bought the Caravaggio. He briefed me on how the Getty endowment fund works.'

Thomas stopped at the far end of the table. 'I propose to set up a scheme which is, in a way, a Getty Fund in reverse. My plan is to sell a large number of Vatican treasures all at once – a one-off sale which will produce a capital sum of such proportions that, properly invested, it will provide the Church with an annual income sufficient to fund whatever charity work we think is appropriate.' He held up a copy of the two photostatted sheets which everyone present now had before them. 'This is the list of works I am proposing to sell. But first some explanation is necessary as to how the choice has been made.

'Clearly, there are many art works we cannot sell. We cannot sell the walls or the ceiling of the Sistine Chapel with Michelangelo's frescoes on them; we cannot sell Raphael's frescoes in the Stanza della Segnatura. Equally clearly it would be wrong to sell things that are intimately related to the Church's history and authority – documents about the Council of Trent, for instance, or the Borgia family. We would not sell rare or early copies of the Bible or relics such as the bones of St Peter.' He raised his voice. 'But that still leaves a great deal that we *can* sell. The list I have put before you today for discussion contains what, after consultation, I propose *can* be sold. It is, of course, totally confidential at the moment.'

Thomas sat down. There was utter silence in the room. David cast his eyes down the two photostats. If the Pope really did intend to sell these works, and David had no doubt now that Thomas always said what he meant, then he was doing rather more than move up a gear. It was like switching from the horse and cart to Concorde. The list was so magnificent it was frightening.

What David read was:

Vatican Works of Art
Intended for Sale by Auction
(Provisional list)

| Paintings | Estimated value (In US $) |
|---|---|
| Leonardo da Vinci (1452–1519) | 75,000,000 |
| St Jerome (1481); oil on wood panel; 103 x 75 cm | |
| Raphael (Raffaello Sanzio, 1483–1520) | 60,000,000 |
| Coronation of the Virgin (1502–03); transferred on to canvas, tempera (?); 272 x 165 cm | |
| Raphael (Raffaello Sanzio, 1483–1520) | 60,000,000 |
| Transfiguration (1518–20); oil on wood panel; 410 x 279 cm | |
| Giovanni Bellini (c. 1430–1516) | 50,000,000 |
| The Burial of Christ; oil on wood panel; 107 x 84 cm | |
| Giotto di Bondone (c. 1267–1337) | 50,000,000 |
| Stefaneschi Triptych (c. 1320); centre panel, 178 x 89 cm; left panel, 168.2 x 82.3; right panel, 168 x 82.6 | |
| Simone Martini (c. 1284–1344) | 50,000,000 |
| Christ Giving His Blessing (c. 1315–20); tempera on wood panel; 39 x 29 cm | |
| Titian (Tiziano Vecellio, c. 1490–1576) | 50,000,000 |
| Madonna di San Niccolo dei Frari (1523); oil, transferred on to canvas; 388 x 270 cm | |
| Perugino (Pietro Vannucci, c. 1446–1523) | 40,000,000 |
| The Resurrection (1502); oil on wood panel; 233 x 156 cm | |
| Lucas Cranach the Elder (1472–1553) | 40,000,000 |
| The Pietà; tempera on wood panel; 54 x 74 cm | |
| Fra Angelico (Giovanni da Fiesole, 1387–1455) | 30,000,000 |
| Scenes from the Life of St Nicholas of Bari (1437); tempera on wood panel; 63 x 33 cm each | |

| | |
|---|---:|
| Paolo Veronese (1528–88) | 30,000,000 |
| *St Helen*; oil on canvas; 166 x 134 cm | |
| Gian Lorenzo Bernini (1598–1680) | 30,000,000 |
| *Head of a Youth* (c. 1635); oil on canvas; 67.6 x 50.1 cm | |
| Nicholas Poussin (1594–1665) | 30,000,000 |
| *Gideon Vanquishes the Midianites*; oil on canvas; 98 x 137 cm | |
| Guido Reni (1575–1642) | 20,000,000 |
| *The Crucifixion of St Peter*; oil on wood panel; 305 x 175 cm | |
| Anton Van Dyck (1599–1641) | 20,000,000 |
| *St Francis Xavier*; oil on canvas; 346 x 214 cm | |
| Giulio Romano (Giulio Pippi, c. 1492–1546) | 15,000,000 |
| *The Stoning of St Stephen* (1523); charcoal on paper; 419 x 285 cm | |

*Sculpture*

| | |
|---|---:|
| Michelangelo Buonarroti (1475–1564) | 100,000,000 |
| *Pietà* (c. 1500); white marble | |
| Anonymous Roman; c. 1st century AD | 15,000,000 |
| *Belvedere Apollo*; white marble | |
| Anonymous Greek; c. 1st century BC | 15,000,000 |
| *Laocoön*; white stone | |

*Manuscripts*

| | |
|---|---:|
| Martin Luther (1483–1546) | 10,000,000 |
| *Papal Bull excommunicating same* (1520) | |
| Galileo Galilei (1564–1642) | 10,000,000 |
| *Signed confession at his Trial* | |

| | |
|---:|---:|
| Total | 780,000,000 |

The silence in the room lengthened. With nearly eight hundred million dollars in the balance, no one wanted to be the first to speak. What His Holiness proposed was so outrageous, so magnificent, so historic and yet so risky; everyone wanted time to think.

Thomas looked across to David. 'I'd like your reactions in a moment, Mr Colwyn, but first let me add this. It cannot have escaped your notice that the biggest bidders at the two sales we have already had were both Americans. So, although I still want Hamilton's to handle the sale, I'd like the auction to take place in America, in New York in fact. I've also been doing some historical research, and I've been studying Queen Christina's collection. As you may know, when the Swedish queen died in Rome towards the end of the seventeenth century her fabulous collection was sold off. Eventually, it found its way to England. When it was sold there the sellers mounted an exhibition of her paintings for some months before the auction. That's what I intend to do. That is why Cardinal Rich is here from New York. All these works to be sold will go on show at St Patrick's Cathedral on Fifth Avenue. We shall charge for admission – thus raising extra money, generating publicity, and gaining time in which copies can be made, copies which we shall keep here in the Vatican. Now tell us, Mr Colwyn, is the plan feasible? Will it work?'

David fingered the paper in front of him. He was conscious of the traffic and the bright sunshine outside in St Peter's Square. He was also aware that a critical point had been reached in the history of the Church and he had been asked to play a part in it. Yet he was unprepared. Or was he? He had no shortgage of experience, and he couldn't honestly say that this idea of Thomas's was any different in *quality* from the original decision to sell the 'Madonna of Foligno'. It was greater in scale, certainly, and would leave the Vatican museums greatly denuded. But then the rewards were incomparably more significant.

In personal terms the plan, of course, would mean great business for Hamilton's, with the bonus that he would continue to work for months with Bess. But it was perhaps the chance to affect things on a world scale that attracted him the most. Normally, no auctioneer could expect to play a role anywhere near as significant. It was an offer that wouldn't come again.

So he said: 'I quarrel with some of your figures, your Holiness. For instance, the Giulio Romano is undervalued for today's taste, and the Bernini is overvalued. But I don't quarrel with the idea. By my count you are selling twenty-one works, which aren't enough to flood the market and spoil the prices. All the museums and galleries in the world will be eager to own these works. And personally I believe the idea of putting art to work, so to speak, is a magnificent one. As for the exhibition at St Patrick's, that's an excellent suggestion – and, if I may say so, the Cathedral might make an ideal venue for the sale itself. Anyway, wherever it takes place, I can tell you that Hamilton's will be delighted to handle the sale for you.'

'Thank you, Mr Colwyn, thank you.' The Pope beamed around the room. 'Now, are there any other points? Now is the time to voice your doubts. If you can think of any problems let's hear them before it's too late to do anything about them.'

No one spoke. Then Cardinal Massoni cleared his throat. David had forgotten how weak the Secretary of State's voice was but, given what he went on to say, its softness made his case quite moving.

'Holiness, I am bitterly opposed to this plan, and you are well aware of my views. Nevertheless, for the record and in one last effort to dissuade you from what I believe is a disastrous course, I will repeat them here. Your successes so far, with sales which I freely admit I was also against, offer no guarantee that the plan you have now conceived will likewise succeed. It is too cavalier. It shows a disregard for Catholic heritage which, I believe, borders on the foolhardy. It is wrong to sell off these works because, in the first place, you have no right. Whatever you may say about papal authority, you must know in your heart that one man should not disperse what generations have collected and put in trust for those who come after him. Although Michaelangelo or Raphael or Giotto were paid by the Church of their day for what they did, the inspiration they embodied was not something a financial figure can be put on. The true home for these works is therefore in the Church here in Rome, at the heart of God's earthly Kingdom. To have it sold off, when it might end up anywhere, is a disgrace.

'What you are doing, Holiness, is wrong also because this art, and the hard work, faith and sense of beauty which it represents, is in a way part of the Church's justification. Take away those things – hard work, faith and a sense of beauty – and you take away part of the Vatican's reason for being. I believe furthermore that the scale of the charity work you intend to undertake with this fund is dangerous. Dangerous in its nature, dangerous in its extent, dangerous in the psychological impulses it plays with. The world is increasingly a small place. You cannot tamper with the world on this scale, Holiness, without producing a multitude of side effects which you can neither predict nor control. No Pope should set off on a journey when he knows so little of the destination.

'And finally I object to the style of this sale – attaching financial values to works of human genius. In this the Vatican isn't leading, Holiness, it is merely following the secular trend of our age.' Massoni's voice had gathered strength, but now it weakened again. 'In my view, Holiness, this plan, this whole expedient of selling off our wonderful Catholic treasures, is demeaning to the Church, demeaning to the tradition of St Peter, and demeaning to the office of the Supreme Pontiff.'

Massoni's figure slumped a little as he finished speaking but his eyes sparked as ferociously as ever. Silence again filled the room.

Thomas rose and limped to a window. He lit a cigarette and looked out. After a while he turned back to the room. 'Eminence, your arguments sadden me. Not only are they the arguments of privileged men throughout the ages, that any change must be bad, but they also suggest that what I am doing has no sense of history. That I am somehow out of step with my predecessors. But am I really?'

He moved again, this time to the foot of the table, as far away from Massoni as possible, David noted. 'Every expert – inside and outside the Vatican – agrees that more people left the Church under Paul VI's pontificate than at any other time. And how was Paul known? As the Hamlet Pope, the man who was so cautious he could *never* make up his mind. Paul's failure to speak out against the outrages perpetrated by the governments of Eastern Europe weakened his position fatally. His successor, Jean-Paul I, wanted change, especially in the Vatican's relationship with the Third World. He appointed a black cardinal, Bernardin Gantin, to head Cor Unum. Sadly, as we all know, Jean-Paul I died after only thirty-three days in office. But look at the achievements wrought by his successor, Jean-Paul II: look at the support he offered to the Polish solidarity workers; don't forget he wrote to the Russian President of his day, Leonard Brezhnev, threatening to resign as Pope and fight on the barricades if Russia invaded his home country. Remember the lecture he gave to the synod of bishops on the financial plight of the Church – the first time any Pope had "gone public" on the matter.'

Thomas stretched out his hands towards Massoni. 'Can you really say that what I plan is any more dangerous or controversial than that? Am I any more concerned with money for its own sake than Jean-Paul II? Or Paul VI, who embroiled the Vatican with two financial swindlers, Michele Sindona and Roberto Calvi? And as long ago as the early 1970s didn't Cardinal Heenan, of Great Britain, suggest that the Vatican might sell off some of its art to help the poor? Before that in the seventeenth century, Innocent XI sold all his earthly possessions when he was elected Pope – and he was a wealthy man – and gave the proceeds to the poor.' His Holiness returned to his seat and sat down again. 'No, Eminence, our plans aren't *that* outrageous. Merely an extension of what has gone before, and applied to what even you must concede is an ever-changing world.'

Massoni didn't reply. He shrugged, as if dismissing Thomas's arguments as worthless.

Cardinal Rich now spoke. 'Holiness, Cardinal Massoni has served the Church well, as has the caution he epitomizes. But I for one see a new response among the people I serve. Catholics are proud to be Catholics. For the first time in years the Church is talked about by everyone, not just the faithful. These sales have the attention of the world. We mustn't let that go. I am sure a sale in St Patrick's would be a wonderful success.'

Thomas inclined his head. He stubbed out his cigarette in the ashtray in front of him.

'Savelli?'

The president of the Prefecture of the Economic Affairs of the Holy See looked uneasy. 'I am divided, Holiness. I'm unhappy that we should be selling these treasures, yet I cannot overlook the fact that it

102

would ease our burdens greatly to have the income from these funds. Perhaps on balance the sale is a good thing.'

'Santander?'

Cardinal Santander shook his head mutely. He was responsible for the monuments and museums in the Vatican and he was having some of his jewels taken away from him. He wasn't happy and Thomas knew it. But the Cardinal had no arguments that Massoni had not already put, so he wisely kept quiet.

'Sabino?'

'No problems from a banking point of view, Holiness. You can expect an income in excess of seventy-five million dollars each year. That's enough to fund several capital projects – hospitals, dams, farms, factories – every year. Enough for the Church to have a real impact in poor countries.

'Zingale? Loredan? Tecce? Venturini?' No one else had anything to contribute.

'Very well,' said Thomas, summing up. 'Mr Colwyn will coordinate the necessary details with Cardinal Rich. You can keep me informed through Elizabeth Lisle, Mr Colwyn. Perhaps a sale next Spring would be suitable.'

David nodded.

'One final thing. Now that our discussions are completed, I ask – as any Pope, any leader, would – that those of you who perhaps do not agree with me nevertheless try sincerely to put our differences behind you and now work wholeheartedly for the success of the project. We cannot succeed if the Vatican is perceived as divided on this matter.'

Thomas looked around the table at the doubters. At Tecce, Venturini, Santander, Savelli. One by one they nodded. Finally, Thomas turned to Massoni, who still sat as still as death.

'Eminence?'

The Secretary of State did not reply straight away. When he did so it was in a voice scarcely above a whisper. 'No, Holiness, I want no part of this. If you insist on going ahead, then you must do so without me. I resign.'

# PART TWO

# 6

Bess's announcement, that twenty-one Vatican treasures were to be auctioned off at one sale in New York, so that the Pope could continue the sort of work he had started in Foligno, the Marquesas Isles and in Sicily, was nothing less than a sensation. No one asked to comment on the news, no editor, no television producer, no art historian, could recall such a dramatic, dazzling or *daring* idea being conceived before. Newspapers across the world covered their front pages with colour reproductions of the treasures. Special television programmes were put together which examined the works of art and the men who had made them. For weeks Michelangelo, Bellini, Giotto and Simone Martini were as much talked about as any film celebrities. 'Quickie' books appeared on the Vatican's art works and the Popes who had commissioned them. Later, more learned articles were published, assessing which museums around the world lacked which pictures, with estimates of the money likely to be involved. The enormous sums quoted kept the story on the front pages and for a few days Thomas became known in the headlines as 'Pope Midas'.

The number of people visiting the Vatican picture gallery more than doubled and the lines stretched all the way down the Viale Vaticano, round the corner and into the Piazza del Risorgimento.

Massoni's resignation had added spice to the story. The fact that the Holy Father's decision to sell the treasures had caused a top-level rift in Rome was irresistible to the pundits and separated them, Catholic or not, into the radicals who sided with the Pope, and the conservatives, who preferred things the way they were.

In general the people for the Pope far outnumbered those against him. The sheer firepower of his imagination and the glamour of the paintings themselves, carried the majority with him. Indeed, it was a measure of the esteem in which the Holy Father was now held, world-wide, that so few voices were raised against him. Admittedly the Italian government, through its spokesman, made angry noises about the loss of such treasures to Italy and managed to scrape through a vote of censure against the Pope in parliament; and many Romans viewed the departure of '*Il reaturo*' – the twenty-one – with grave misgivings. But the communist mayor, Sirianni, rapidly becoming a national figure, argued on Italian television that if the government really wanted to keep the works of art in Rome they should attend the auction in New York and buy them back. That, however, was not what the government had had in mind.

David received a formal vote of congratulations from the board of Hamilton's. Averne had stayed away. Even with a reduced commission of eight per cent, and assuming the sale realized "only" seven hundred million dollars, with the buyer's commission the auction house was guaranteed a minimum income during the next year of one hundred and twenty-six million dollars. There was even talk of floating the company on the Stock Exchange but the Earl of Afton squashed that, tartly pointing out that they must not bee seen to be profiteering from their association with the Vatican.

Massoni moved out of the official apartments which he had occupied as Secretary of State but was allowed to stay on in the Vatican, where he now spent a lot of time in the Secret Archives. Only Bess, apparently, was bothered by this.

Over a late supper at Gina's one night, she voiced her concern to David. 'He's not the type to just fade away. Have you noticed his hands? Long, sinewy fingers – good for hanging on to things. What I wouldn't give to bug Massoni's mind. You'd think the CIA would have invented some sort of gadget by now, wouldn't you?'

David laughed. He was spending more time in Rome now, making arrangements for the sale, and he felt relaxed there. His relationship with Bess was inching forward. Neither of them referred to the small kiss he had given her, the night after he had recovered her money for her from Ludovisi, and there had been no repeat. But she seemed willing enough to be in his company – they were together most nights he was in the city.

David's Rome visits now had a sort of triangular shape, between Bess's apartment, Gina's, where they ate almost every meal, and the Vatican. He grew to know, and to be fond of, the minute maze of streets, alleyways, passages, and corridors which made up the city state. He extended his contacts, the chief of whom was John Rich, Cardinal Archbishop of New York. As big as a bear, and as gruff when he wanted to be, and as keen on baseball as any American priest, Rich was also an authority on ivory and had a fine collection of Far Eastern, Indian, Renaissance and Gothic carvings. The two men got on very well and before long had the details of the sale sorted out.

Rich was also one of the prime movers behind Thomas's forthcoming encyclical on sex, birth control and marriage. 'Now is the time,' Rich said to anyone who would listen. 'With a Pope this popular, this active, this modern in his thinking, now is the time to update the Church in every possible way. Otherwise, fifty years from now there won't be a single Catholic left north of Mexico.'

'Don't exaggerate,' Bess had scolded him one day when the three of them met for lunch at Gina's.

'Exaggeration is a national characteristic of Americans, my dear. It's part of our charm.'

'Maybe that's why I left,' she said. 'Exaggeration can be a form of self-deception.'

Thomas planned to publish the encyclical as part of his Christmas message, but he was still taking soundings from around the world and it was as yet a closely guarded secret. Only a few people knew its details, even within the Vatican.

On one occasion, after David had finished his meetings with Cardinal Rich, he stayed in Rome an extra day. He wanted to make a tour of the antique shops, to find something for Ned's collection of fakes. Bess delighted him by asking if she could come along. 'If I'm going to collect things – I think I've got the bug – I might as well learn properly,' she said.

They went to an early mass, then started near the Piazza Colonna and worked their way through the back streets to the Via Tomacelli near the Ponte Cavour. Early on, before they had gone very far, Bess spotted a silver photograph frame in the window of a small, rather dingy shop. Enamelled in green and blue, the frame was ornate, yellowed but otherwise in good condition. David identified it as Byzantine. 'It probably came here via Venice,' he said.

'Genuine?'

'Oh yes.'

Bess bought it. 'It's a gift,' she said as they came back out of the shop and into the street. 'For Thomas,' she added, before David could ask.

He was surprised – to begin with, but not after Bess explained. 'He has no family. There's hardly anyone in the world to give him the little things we all need. I've got some photos of him when he was a cardinal, exercising his bad leg in the sea. I'll put them in the frame – he'll love it.' She looked at David. 'I've done it before, you know. Have you ever noticed his lighter? I gave him that, too.'

They walked on. David was touched, on Thomas's behalf. He had never really thought about the Holy Father's private life. Bess was almost certainly right: his Holiness would love having someone treat him like a normal, ordinary soul. The gift said a lot for Bess's understanding.

Just before lunch, in a small shop on the Lungotevere, David spotted a Karl Becker coin. 'Look,' he said to Bess, drawing her over. 'These are quite rare. Becker was a late eighteenth-century German forger of coins – he used to age his counterfeits in a metal box underneath his carriage. He'd take his brand new coins for a ride and when he came back they were old – they'd been scraped by the axle. Once you know about them, they're easy to spot. The scratch marks are much the same on each piece.'

Bess was entranced. 'I'd love to see Ned's collection,' she said.

It was, thought David, a move in his direction. Then he checked himself. Too often he forgot that he was married, and always would be in Bess's eyes. She might be an American, with American attitudes, but she was first and foremost a Catholic. Even if the Pope's reform plan succeeded, it wouldn't be for years yet. And meanwhile, even if she wanted him, David saw that her situation was very difficult. He would get nowhere if he wasn't understanding.

But her interest in Ned, that deliberately placed sentence, relaxed him, and freed him to move forward at her pace, to take each meeting as it came, letting whatever feelings were there ripen slowly in their own time. On successive visits to Rome, after his meetings with Rich, Tecce or whoever it happened to be, he and Bess found time to visit a couple of antique shops. He taught her about fakes and copies – 'Sicilian' vases showing vegetation that could not be found in Sicily, 'prehistoric' Mayan seals made in the nineteenth century, red chalk 'Renaissance' drawings on machine-made paper. And he wouldn't let her buy anything until she was certain about what sort of objects she really wanted to collect.

They found that out quite by accident. Massimo Vittrice, the man who ran Hamilton's office in Rome, had invited David to a fashion show. His wife was a designer and, he said, the show would contain some items that might interest David. David took Bess and she was entranced.

Held on the roof restaurant of the Excelsior Hotel, it was not just a cocktail party. Nor was it a simple fashion show. Before the modern fashions were shown, the Japanese company which had mounted the evening put on an exhibition of ancient silks. David and Bess, together with Vittrice and his wife, sat right next to the catwalk so they saw these rare fabrics at close quarters. The first was an eighteenth-century Chinese silk panel, showing dragons with five tails and waterfalls. Then came an Italian chasuble, embroidered with the Virgin, in blue, surrounded by the vivid gold fingers of the sun. Next came a Byzantine twill silk, showing men on horseback with falcons and lions, and sparkling as if covered in jewels. Bess could not take her eyes off the colours, and the amazingly varied textures.

The fact that silk was also a modern substance, still used all over the world to make clothes or in decoration, also had something to do with Bess's interest. For her, more than David, history came alive if it related to the present day. Silk was like the papacy, she said to David. 'Thousands of years old, yet still valuable and in daily use.'

After the show, she bought several books on silk. Then, with David's guidance, she began to buy – and acquired several small pieces: an early Sicilian example, in dark blue, gold and scarlet; a watered silk from Lucca, showing red and yellow birds; a Sarogossa silk with sapphire-coloured arabesques. Gradually, her apartment began to fill with silks in richly varied colours and textures. She loved not just to look at them, but to run her hands over the weave. She would press them against her cheek.

'You can't do that with Old Master drawings,' she teased David. 'Is that a heathen thing to say?'

But David was only too pleased her enthusiasm was developing.

Two things only marred this time for David. One was Ned's state of mind. His son still had his puzzling moods and didn't seem to be getting better. The other sour note arose in Rome itself, from David's attempt to organize the copying of the twenty-one great works which were to be sold.

Copying the paintings was no problem – the Vatican's own restoration department would do the job. If they couldn't finish by the time the pictures went on display, they could work in St Patrick's. That would add to the publicity. But the sculpture, especially Michelangelo's 'Pietà', was a different matter. Copies in the same marble were impossible: there was simply no one alive who was capable. Making casts to use as moulds was out of the question: the originals could be damaged in the process. And carving replicas in a softer stone, one that was easier to handle, would produce a coarser, disappointing result. Reluctantly, David, and Tecce, who was working with him, concluded that no copies could be made. Their confidential recommendation was shown to Thomas who, also reluctantly, approved it.

Once again the Vatican security system broke down. Two days later, the Rome newspaper *Il Messaggero* carried an article attacking this 'confidential' decision, and making it seem as if the Pope was being secretive, with something to hide. Under the headline, 'The pity of the "Pietà" ', the article argued that Pope Thomas was little short of a vandal in allowing the Michelangelo and other priceless works to go abroad 'even after it has been discovered that no copy can be made.' The article said this should have meant that all the sculptures were withdrawn from the New York auction. That they hadn't been, ran the article, meant that the Holy Father now ranked with the other 'unscrupulous' Popes in history who had 'desecrated Rome's heritage in order to aggrandize themselves.' Such a frontal attack on a reigning Pope, in a Rome newspaper, was extremely unusual. That wasn't the chief reason, however, why the *Il Messaggero* report was reprinted in newspapers around the world. The chief reason was because its author was Cardinal Ottavio Massoni.

'Did you take a fast plane, David?'

David smiled at the latest American euphemism for Concorde. Trust Rich to be up with all the current fads and fashions.

'Yes, Eminence. How else could I be here in time for breakfast? I've already had one helping of bacon and champagne, at 50,000 feet.'

Now it was the cardinal who smiled. The two of them were breakfasting at Rich's official residence on the corner of Madison Avenue and 50th Street. Afterwards, the cardinal would give David his first guided tour of St Patrick's Cathedral. Bess was flying in from Rome the same day, to approve the publicity arrangements and to help organize the display of the art. But, since there was no Concorde from Rome, she wouldn't be here for some hours yet. It was already late October and the twenty-one masterpieces were to go on show to the public in the first week of December.

The two men chatted easily over breakfast. David had brought Rich a gift, a small ivory cup, carved with monsters.

'David! How marvellous – German, seventeenth-century, by the look of it. It's not a Maucher, is it?'

David nodded. Johann Maucher was one of the top three baroque ivory carvers.

'That was most thoughtful, David. I'm greatly in your debt. If I can ever be of assistance, kindly let me know. Now shall we go across to the cathedral?'

David was impressed by St Patrick's. It may not have had the history or the *gravitas* of the major European cathedrals, but it had dignity, superb proportions, a magnificent altar and sumptuous stained glass windows. It was also busy. There was little of the hush usual in European churches. New Yorkers weren't overawed by stone and statues. David was impressed by that, too.

Later in the day he brought Bess back from the airport, to the building. His plan, which she approved, was to display the pictures and sculpture in the sanctuary and in the Lady Chapel behind the altar. These areas were surprisingly well-lit by European standards, they were well-protected from a security standpoint and the windows of the chapel and the canopy over the altar made a perfect backdrop. When David had pointed to the spot where Rich and he thought the 'Pietà' should stand, he said to Bess: 'What's the latest news of Massoni? Has Thomas taken steps to shut him up?'

'Good grief, no! How can you be a Pope like Thomas – American, democratic, open, radical – and not allow your opponents to have their say? You can't fire a cardinal, at least not for criticising you about some carvings. No, Massoni's quiet now, but he's biding his time, I'm sure. He got massive publicity from his 'Pietà' article and I guess he rather relishes being the biggest thorn in Thomas's side. He's got a following – small, since he has no territorial power base, but *Il Messaggero* will give him a platform whenever he wants it. He's not going to go away, David. Anyway, better the devil you know . . . don't you think?'

'Hmm. I'm not sure. I'd prefer it if we could shut him up at least until the big sale is safely over.'

'Well, we can't. So get used to it.' She paused. 'Get used to something else, too: you'll soon be able to get divorced.'

'What?'

'This is all hush-hush,' she whispered as they moved on around the Lady Chapel, to where David thought the Giotto should go. 'It probably won't be announced before Easter now but the main ideas of the encyclical seem set. Artificial birth control, by married couples, will be allowed. That should bring relief to millions of women in Asia and South America, not to mention Italy. And it should mean that a lot of people in the more developed countries – America especially – can come back to church and be Catholics again. Thomas will argue that more misery, more pain, more sin can be caused by having too many children than by practising birth control. Divorce too will be recognized as a fact of modern life. It won't be easy; it will take months, if not years. But for the first time, the option will be there. The Church already has the infrastructure to make it work – the tribunals which consider cases for dissolution or annulment. They will be beefed up. Massoni will hate it, lots of die-hards will. But – oh David! It's going to make *such* a difference.'

'It's marvellous,' said David. 'Wonderful.' Personally, he was delighted. But he still secretly had his doubts, wondering if Thomas wasn't moving too fast.

He showed her the rest of the cathedral. It was odd, imagining all that great classical art together in this one spot, so far from Rome. But that was Thomas's point: Raphael, Michelangelo, Leonardo da Vinci had all worked in the New York of their day. This was the natural, the obvious place to sell them.

They stood at the end of the nave looking down towards the altar and sanctuary. 'It's so *clean*, this church,' she said. 'So unlike St Peter's, which is full of curly lines, bits sticking out here and there, different coloured marbles, masses of statues. This is all straight lines and bright, clear colours. St Patrick's has much more of Thomas's personality in it than St Peter's.'

Their tour of the cathedral complete, David took Bess back in the gathering dusk to Hamilton's offices on Madison Avenue and 68th Street. Most of the publicity would be handled from there and he had arranged for her to use an office in the building whenever she wanted. He introduced her to his New York secretary, Betsy, a tall, thin girl who combined amazing energy with ferocious efficiency. 'Betsy,' he said after the small talk was over. 'I have a special job for you and it's confidential. I want a list of the twenty most successful companies in

112

America which are run by just one man. If he's a Catholic so much the better – but I am not interested in any firm where the board has a say-so on everything: I want large, successful, rich, one-man bands. Is that clear? I want the names of each of the men and their private telephone numbers. I'll expect to hear from you within a week.'

By now it was past six and the office was closing. David looked across at Bess and said: 'Back to the hotel?' They were both staying at the Stanhope, opposite the Metropolitan Museum of Art.

'Definitely,' replied Bess. 'I'd like a rest and a bath. Then you can take me out to dinner.'

'Oh?' said David. 'I thought you'd be tired after such a long flight.'

'Maybe,' she said. 'But whatever *you* think, Mr Colwyn, to *me* the Holy Father's changes in the divorce laws are very good news indeed. I, for one, feel like celebrating.' And as they descended the steps outside Hamilton's, and searched for a free taxi on Madison Avenue, she linked her arm in his.

Early December was hectic for David. The exhibition opened at St Patrick's, so he had to be in New York for that; the Israeli government finally gave the go-ahead for the sale of four Dead Sea scrolls and offered Hamilton's the business, so he had to be in Jerusalem for that; and Ned's winter term was due to finish on the fifteenth, so he had to be in England for that.

The opening of the exhibition in St Patrick's had gone splendidly, Cardinal Rich making a witty but compassionate speech which exactly suited both the mood of the occasion and the spirit of the Holy Father's plans. The lighting of the art works had been donated by one of Holly-wood's top lighting directors, an Oscar winner, and this ensured the presence of many famous film personalities. In turn that added to the newsworthiness of the occasion, and in the days after the opening the lines stretched almost the entire way around the block. A photograph of the queue, showing how it began on Fifth Avenue, snaked down 50th Street, up Madison Avenue and back along 51st Street, was taken from a helicopter and made the cover of *Newsweek*. More crowds poured in.

Naturally, Bess was in New York again for the opening. Though David had been carefully muted in his reaction to her news about Thomas's encyclical, he had been delighted to see that, for Bess herself, it was very important. Until that evening in New York, he had had no real understanding of her feeling for him. At Cardinal Rich's recommendation, they'd had their celebration at the Veau d'Or on 61st Street. It was a fairly formal place, showed no sign of *nouvelle cuisine*, tended to serve diners who preferred red to white wine, and the tables were laid out along banquettes where people sat side-by-side rather than opposite each other. Bess was therefore able to rest her hand on David's easily, unobtrusively, almost as if by chance. Their first real physical contact would have appeared to anyone watching as no more than an affectionate stroking by familiar, long-time lovers.

Inevitably the contact, innocent as it was, unlocked their tongues. And once again it was Bess who made the first moves.

She started tentatively, at a tangent. 'If I were to write a book, David, do you know what it would be about?'

He shook his head.

'Appetite.'

'Hungry – eh?'

'Not *that* appetite silly. Appetite in general. That's what first attracted me to you – your appetite for your work. And your enthusiasm for collecting. You may not realise this but you created an appetite, an enthusiasm in me – for silk. It's amazing the way something can be locked away inside and one isn't aware of it. Working for Thomas, for instance, at the Vatican, being so close to the Holy Father, I've been so busy, so engrossed, there wasn't time for anything else. But then . . . after the fair, after that business with Ludovisi . . . I guess I began to get an appetite for you too. It's funny the way appetites grow, from the tiniest beginnings.'

'Mmmmmmnn. Dare I mention my appetite for food right now?'

She dug her nails into his hand. 'Beast! I was being serious.' But she was smiling, too.

David signalled to the waiter and they ordered. He turned back to Bess. 'I can be serious too. My appetite for you rather pre-dates yours for me.' And he told her how he had called her when he had felt so low after his day out with Ned, when a man had answered the phone.

'So it was *you*, was it? I remember the call very well. We both thought it was strange. You silly mutt. I was ill, remember? That man was my doctor!'

Now, at last, he could ask her. 'But is there no man – no other man – in your life? I can't believe it.'

'It's true. There's a lot about me you don't know, David. When I was twenty-two I was engaged. Engaged, in love, and deliriously happy. His name was Nicholas. It wasn't just that he was handsome, kind and very funny.' She flashed a look at David and smiled. 'Men like that grow on trees, eh? No, he was also a great friend of my brother, Patrick. They did everything together – sailing, skiing, dating . . . When I came home from college and fell for Nick, amazingly I didn't come between them. The three of us did a whole bunch of things together. Until one night, after a storm. I had the flu and hadn't gone out. Near our home was a ford, where a little stream crossed the back road to the village. That night though there was a flash flood, and the stream turned into a torrent. Usually the road would have been closed but Nick and Paddy got there before the local police. They'd been drinking and, I expect, were driving too fast.' She looked at David, her hand on his tightening. 'The car was found submerged half a mile downstream. Nick was still in it. Patrick had been thrown out, his body tangled in a tree.' Her hands had begun to sweat, and she wiped them on her napkin. 'I was terribly upset, of course. In the normal way I would have got over it, but . . . It's over ten years ago now. The problem has always been my parents. You see, Nick was driving – his body was behind the wheel – so my mother and father always blamed him. They can't forget and won't let me forget either.' She stroked the back of David's hand with her finger. 'That's one reason why I live in Europe. I knew, in the end, that I had to get away.'

David was silent, deeply moved by her story. He reflected that it explained a lot. He was full of admiration for Bess, too, for the way she hadn't revealed her wounds immediately, as he had done. What she said raised one question in his mind. 'Did the . . . accident . . . was it that which made you find work in the Church?'

'I suppose. We were a religious family to begin with, though. Patrick once thought of becoming a priest. I'm not the mystical type, as perhaps you've noticed. But I've always been very moral. Upbringing I suppose. The selfishness and ignorance and self-righteousness in the world frighten me. We were close as a family, at least to begin with. My mother was always more in love with my father than he was with her. At least, she always thought so. I suppose that made me reticent with men, but it wasn't all. After she had me, she found out she couldn't have any more children – it would have been too dangerous. Two is plenty for lots of people but not Ma: she was, still is, an old-fashioned Catholic. She was mortified. She thought she had let down Pa. That's when she developed her habit of giving him gifts – they took the place of children. Silly things, like a hat she had seen and thought he would like. Or an unusual bottle he might want to use as a new way of promoting our liquor. She found that Fort Humbug "cannon" I told you about. Pa had his whole study filled with Ma's gifts. An early typewriter, stud boxes made of rare wood, an oar from an Indian canoe. Pa was entranced and Ma was right. Gift-giving *is* more important then people let on. If the gift is right, the person receiving it can't help but be filled with warmth.'

'But – '

'You're right. There's always a "but". It all stopped after Nick and Paddy were killed. The car was a gift.' For a moment Bess looked sad again; then she brightened. 'That's when I picked up Ma's habit. I send them gifts from time to time. Instead of letters. It means more. They didn't like it when I went away, but they're coming round a bit now.' She stroked his arm again. 'I enjoyed journalism but I have to admit now, there was always something missing. When Thomas offered me a job, it was like coming home.' She laughed. 'But the job's another reason why there've been no men lately – it *is* a bit intimidating. So when you kept trying, even though you have this screwed-up marital situation, I knew you had to be serious. And anyone who could be so persistent had to be worth a second look.' She leaned against him. 'Enough about me. Tell me about Ned.'

David laughed. Telling her about his son was easy.

'You'd like him, I think. There are three things to understand about Ned – he's crazy about American football, crazy about space, and crazy about fakes. He has no other topic of conversation and if you're not interested in those things you are, in his words, an outlaw. Still, he works hard at school and he's far from stupid. He used to be a very sunny child – great company and very funny. Not at the moment. He has his flashes but frankly I'm a bit worried.'

They talked about the difficulties any child had to face when their parents split up. Bess was very understanding.

After dinner they had taken a taxi back to the hotel but, before going in, had walked a few blocks in the cool October air. There was a shop window at the corner of 79th Street and Madison Avenue which David wanted to show Bess. It was full of silks.

'They're beautiful,' she said. 'Persian, right?'

'Yes,' he nodded. 'Your collection lacks one of these, I think. It's time I gave you a present. We'll come back when it's open.'

'It's time I gave you something, too.' She had kissed him then and again, back at the hotel, outside her room. And the following morning, when they met again in the cathedral, although she was brisk and businesslike, there was a new tenderness between them.

The next time they were together in New York, on the day of the opening, they went back to the Veau d'Or for lunch and asked for the same table. She rested her hand on his in exactly the same way. But you can never duplicate life exactly: they emerged from the restaurant to find that it was snowing.

New York was transformed. Its harsh straight lines were softened romantically and blurred by the snowflakes. Its sounds were hushed, its timetables abandoned, its pace altered, its self-assurance gone. The taxi slithered silently up Madison Avneue, throwing them against one another.

'Does Ned like the snow?' Bess asked, looking out at some people throwing snowballs.

'If he was here he would probably be asking questions like: "Does it snow on Mars?" '

She squeezed his arm. The taxi reached 79th Street and they got out. The silk shop was open this time and they went in. Bess ran her hands over several pieces of silk, pressed them to her cheek. Eventually, she chose a small lozenge that depicted a highly stylized map of the silk route itself, winding from China, across Afghanistan to Venice. It was gold, brown and red, with places picked out in patches of deep green, like pools.

Outside again in the snow they held on to each other, inching their way towards Fifth Avenue where the amber lights made it seem as if the park was coated in resin. They watched snowball fights and saw the first toboggans appear. Across the park the high buildings of the West Side faded into the murk. It seemed as if there was, for once, hardly a sound.

Because of the weather they had dinner in the hotel, then, wrapped in boots, scarves and heavy coats, went out into the snow again. They tramped the quiet streets, watched the snow settle on cars, on mailboxes, on the spindly branches of trees. They trudged over to Lexington Avenue and bought an early edition of the next day's paper, where the St Patrick's exhibition was written up. They slithered back past a school on 82nd Street where the basketball ring was topped with a perfect circle of white.

Outside her room at the hotel, David went to kiss Bess goodbye, but she stopped him. 'No,' she said softly. 'Come in.'


Next day was cold but fiercely sunny. Overnight, the city had been cleaned up. David left for Israel and then, a few days later, flew back to London to see Ned. He had been back in London only a few hours, and had yet to see his son, when he received a phone call from Sir Edgar Seton. It was a surprise. Seton was Surveyor of the Queen's pictures and his request was simple: would David go down to Windsor for lunch the following day. It was important, said Seton. David sighed. Regretfully he abandoned all hope of seeing Ned until the day after. As his driver, Patton, pulled on to the M4 in his office car, the rain slashed down in cold, cutting diagonals and David buried himself in newspaper cuttings. Sally Middleton always cut any articles about art when he was away so that he could catch up and keep himself fully informed. This morning's batch contained news of the latest development in the long-running saga about a Pieter de Hooch picture in Houston, which they claimed was real and an English art restorer claimed was a fake. Hamilton's had sold the picture to Houston, as genuine, so David was relieved to see that the restorer was backtracking a bit now. There was another interesting item: this concerned a British university which had decided to sell its unique collection of tribal art. The university had not offered the British Museum a chance to save the collection for the nation but instead had found an overseas buyer. Worse, since the collection's combined value would have necessitated obtaining government permission, permission which almost certainly would have been refused, the university had exported the thousands of items one by one, thus avoiding the need to obtain official sanction.

That was bad, David felt, a bit like the university smuggling the collection out of the country.

The Ford skimmed up the hill to Windsor Castle. The rain still fell insistently from a sky grey as the walls of the castle itself. At the gate David got out of the car and a man in a short black jacket with gold crowns on his lapels greeted him. 'Mr Colwyn? Follow me please. I'll show you to Sir Edgar's office.'

They ascended a wide oak staircase and reached a long gallery which, despite the weather, was very light: the windows must have been twelve feet high. A carpet ran the length of this gallery which, David could see, was hung with mainly English portraits of varying quality. He did not know Edgar Seton well, but the Surveyor was an authority on English miniatures and on Holbein, and David had read his books on those subjects. They had met on several occasions at exhibitions and receptions. They had once served on the same committee.

At the end of the gallery the official in the black jacket turned into an alcove and knocked at a wooden door. Seton's voice was heard faintly, 'Come in.'

He rose to meet David. He was a small, neat, tidy man with silver hair and sharp, rather beaky features. The amount of shirt cuff his suit left showing suggested that he took just a little too much care with his clothes. He came round the desk, shook hands and showed David to a sofa next to a fireplace. 'Sherry?'

David hadn't drunk sherry since university. He was struck by how similar this office was to a college room – light oak panelling, but fairly new, a biscuit-coloured carpet, burgundy curtains, safe chintzes. The pictures stood out, of course. 'Yes, I'd love a sherry,' he said.

Seton busied himself at a table.

'Veronese?' said David, looking at the picture above the mantelpiece.

'One of the perks of the job,' replied Seton, opening the sherry with a flourish. 'Yes, it's a study for his "Marriage at Cana". There's a Rubens opposite . . . and you probably recognize the Holbein behind my desk.'

David walked across. 'Superb . . .' He was genuinely impressed. 'I sometimes keep pictures we are selling in my office, but never for more than a few days. You're very lucky.'

Seton handed him the sherry and they both sat down. 'Yes, I am lucky. I'm also safe here – this is a castle after all. Doesn't security bother you people? It has always amazed me that you're not burgled more often.'

David swallowed the excellent sherry. 'Well, our clients don't really have any choice, not if they want us to sell their pictures. We have to keep them for a few days so that people who might want to buy them can look at them. We don't exactly advertise our precautions, but they're reasonably state of the art. And – ' he tapped the table between them

'– touch wood, there have been no problems so far. Not serious ones anyway.' He lifted the glass again. He hadn't been invited here to discuss security.

Seton took his cue. 'Mr Colwyn, I'm glad you could come down here. I didn't want to take the risk of being seen at your offices in St James's Square.'

David's expression didn't change. But it was a telling remark, he thought.

Seton crossed his legs. His left arm was draped elegantly along the back of the sofa. 'The truth is, it was Her Majesty who wanted me to see you. The Queen is a fine woman, Mr Colwyn, and a generous and kind employer. She also likes paintings but I think she would agree with me when I say that she is in no sense a connoisseur.' He drank his sherry. 'She is also – well, no longer as young as she was. And she is a worried woman. She believes – and here, as in all I say today, I must swear you to secrecy – she thinks that, in the past twenty years or so this nation has begun to break up. The process started with the Commonwealth, of course, but has now spread to Britain itself. She cannot say so publicly, of course – and only privately in the strictest confidence. She must not be seen to involve herself in politics. All the same, she feels – well she would like to *do* something. Something to help her subjects, help them and unite them. Bring the Commonwealth back together. The main difficulty, in her position, is what.'

Seton got to his feet, took David's sherry glass and went to the table where he refilled it. Outside, the day seemed to be brightening.

Seton returned to the sofa. 'This is where you come in, Mr Colwyn. Her Majesty has been most impressed by the activities of His Holiness the Pope. Although she has said nothing publicly, she privately applauds his decision to sell off the Vatican treasures in order to do the things he has done . . . and still plans to do. In fact, Mr Colwyn, she is so impressed that she has it in mind to sell off some of the art in the Royal Collection – the collection which belongs to her personally, rather than to the nation – and put the money to good use.' Seton paused and levelled his eyes at David. 'I must emphasize that nothing is settled yet, Mr Colwyn. Her Majesty always has to move slowly. So I repeat: she has this plan in mind, but first we must take soundings. That is why you are here today. I want your reaction.'

David said nothing. What could he say? The British Royal Collection of works of art – paintings, drawings, tapestries, furniture, sculpture – was the best private collection in the world. As a collection it was better even than the Vatican's masterpieces. It may not have had a 'Pietà' but that was about all it didn't have. The Royal Collection contained Leonardos, Bellinis, Holbeins, Titians, Breughels, Dürers, Cranachs, Raphaels – the list was immense and the quality was superb.

'Yes,' said Seton, studying David's face. 'I was stunned when the

Queen first mentioned it to me. But you'll find you get used to the idea.'

'How many works does she want to sell?'

'Ah, that is where you and I come in. I have to tell you, Mr Colwyn, that I do not exactly approve of what Her Majesty intends to do, but they aren't my pictures and, although I have some influence, in the end even I have to do as I'm told. And as part of the necessary soundings, Her Majesty would like you and me to advise her on what items she should sell and how much she might expect for them. Naturally she wishes the collection to be damaged as little as possible, but she has in mind a substantial final figure – something in the region of a hundred million, at the very least. We have to produce a list. I've already told her that, what with these other Vatican sales, many museums and galleries will be stretched for funds and so top dollars may not be available for a while.'

David had still not sorted out his exact reaction to all this. Still, some comment was required. 'I'll have to consult my colleagues,' he said, feeling rather inadequate.

'As few as possible,' replied Seton. 'And only those you trust completely. I'd like some sort of answer in – say – two weeks. If she is to go ahead, Her Majesty would like to make some sort of announcement soon. She goes on a long tour of Australia and the Caribbean in January and would like to release the news before then.'

David left Windsor in a daze, hardly noticing that the rain had stopped and that a diluted sun lurked behind the clouds. As Patton drove east, back along the M4, half-submerged in the wake of faster cars the windscreen wipers of the Ford beat rhythmically back and forth. 'Hol-bein, Dü-rer, Rem-brandt.' It was incredible, what was happening. First the Pope, then the Israelis, now the Queen . . . The car slowed as they reached the usual snarl-up where the three lanes of motorway funnelled into two near Chiswick flyover. At least it gave him time to think. He stared down at the roofs of countless houses below him. A fiercely ambitious person himself, independent to the point of stubbornness, he had never been prone to jump on whatever happened to be the current bandwagon. But he could also see that the Queen's position was rather different in the wake of the Pope's successes. This was not something she could have initiated herself. But because the Pope had done it, because he had brought about change *without* any political overtones, because his intervention had been so popular and successful, she could act now without any accusations of political interference being levelled at her. The traffic began to move more quickly along the Cromwell Road. David flipped through the catalogue of the Royal Collection which Sir Edgar had given him. Her Majesty could raise £50 million, £100 million, £500 million, just like that, depending on what she was willing to let go. The Holbeins were fantastic, the Hogarths, the Hilliards and the Frans Hals were all perfect, to name but a few. But, the more he thought about it, the more David realized that, for some unaccountable reason, he did not have the same favourable reaction to Sir Edgar's news as he had had when he first visited the Vatican. He couldn't put his finger on why: perhaps it was because he was British and the Queen proposed to sell off what he regarded was *his* heritage, or perhaps it was simply because he suspected that others in Britain would take even less kindly to the Queen's plan than he, and would seek to make trouble for Hamilton's.

The car reached Hyde Park Corner, turned down Grosvenor Place and past Buckingham Palace. David reached his office in a still uncertain state of mind, but any doubts he had – any thoughts at all in fact – were quickly dispersed by a message Sally had left on his desk. It was to call Betsy in New York. He assumed that she had some news about the autocrats, the big business bosses he had asked her to research. But it wasn't that.

Betsy sounded quite frightened on the phone. 'We've just had a visit from a real scary guy. Small and dark, hairy backs to his hands. Italian accent. He just turned up here and demanded to see you. I told him you were in London and he said to give you a message. He said for you to call off the Pope's sale. He said that if you didn't, you'd be sorry. And from the look of him, Mr Colwyn, I guess he meant it. He had Mafia written all over him.'

On Christmas Day the Queen broke with tradition. Her speech to the Commonwealth, normally pre-recorded, was made live, not from Buckingham Palace, but from Windsor Castle where she was shown surrounded by some of her magnificent art collection. And the speech itself, instead of being the usual rather bland review of the last year's royal tours, mixed with tame jokes about her immediate family, contained her bombshell. David watched her, alone in his house in Pelham Crescent. Bess was busy in Rome, his own work kept him in London, and Ned was with Sarah.

'Christmas,' said Her Majesty, 'is a time of relaxation, of looking back and looking forward. We look back to what we have accomplished in the past, and forward to what we might accomplish in the future.' Her voice was as clear as ever but had weakened with age. 'I speak to you today, not only as Queen, but as head of the Church of England. And today, at Christmas, I look across to the head of another church, the head of the Catholic Church, Pope Thomas in Rome. Like many of you, I have been heartened and impressed by what Pope Thomas has accomplished this year. With the sale of just three great works of art from the Vatican, he has managed to bring hope to the poor and needy in many parts of the world.

'Now, he plans a bigger sale. Twenty-one Vatican treasures are to be sold in New York, in order to provide a huge charitable trust fund for the relief of international poverty. In Israel the government is already planning something similar. Four Dead Sea Scrolls are to be sold, and again the money will be used to help the poor.

'Such sales are both imaginative and clearly popular. They represent, as the President of the United States, Mr Roskill, has said, a wonderful combination of compassion and business acumen.'

She paused to allow the camera time to draw back, to show more of the Windsor gallery behind her.

'Many of the pictures you see here have been in the British Royal Family's Collection for hundreds of years. Ours is one of the largest collections in the world. I have decided that some – a small number – of these works of art should now be sold and the money provided will be used to benefit some of the poorer, less fortunate Commonwealth countries and some of Britain's more ravaged inner cities. I shall be visiting several Commonwealth countries in the coming year and shall discuss with their leaders how best the money may be used. The pictures, after all, are in a sense part of all our Commonwealth, yours *and* mine.'

The rest of the speech didn't matter. Those few paragraphs of Her Majesty's Christmas message were quite enough. They made the days after Christmas a busy time for David, which was just as well. Otherwise he'd have been at a loose end. Ned had gone off with his mother and Greener, skiing in Switzerland, and as soon as Thomas's official Christmas functions were over, Bess too had gone away, back home to Louisiana. She loved her family dearly, and wanted to give them their Christmas presents in person, albeit late.

The British reaction to the Queen's news, however, confirmed David's initial doubts. Among the public her proposal was every bit as popular as Thomas's plans had been. But the art establishment in Britain, the museum directors, the dealers, the heritage organizations, were ominously quiet. David didn't like it. And he liked it even less when, during the first week of January, he was tackled openly in his club bar.

'David! Buy me a drink. You can afford it these days, with all that Vatican money sloshing around in Hamilton's.'

'Paul! Aren't you too busy to frequent bars? And what are you doing here anyway? Downing Street boring?'

Paul Clegg was an old friend of David's from university days and now a civil servant on the Prime Minister's staff.

'When I say buy me a drink, David, that's not a request, it's an order.'

'Oh yes?'

'Yes, I'm here semi-officially. I'll have a gin.'

David ordered a gin for Clegg and a whisky for himself. The other man pulled him away to a window seat. 'Cheers!' he said, sinking half his drink.

David returned the toast.

'Now, in the nicest possible way, David, the PM is not, repeat not, at all happy with this royal sale.'

'He's not the only one.' It was true. In preparation for the Queen's announcement, David had spent days at Windsor, choosing the pictures with Seton. It was a difficult time and the two men had quite a tussle over what to include. David had lost.

Clegg nodded to several club members, then turned back to David. 'This is just a friendly warning, David. Hamilton's are only doing their job, of course, and we can't blame you for that. The PM is really more angry with the Queen. This proposal of hers implies that the political approach to our problems has failed, that her government isn't doing its job properly.'

'It implies nothing of the sort.'

'Don't be naïve, David. You know the Queen and the Prime Minister don't get on. What I'm saying, so that it's crystal clear, is that you are to expect no support from the government on this sale. We are not going to make things easy for you. Quite the reverse, in fact – if any of these works look like going abroad we shall slap restrictions on them, hold them up for as long as we can.'

'Can you do that? Aren't they Her Majesty's own personal property?'

'That's never been tested. So it may mean taking Her Majesty to court over her right to export her paintings. Not an edifying prospect, I know, but the PM is so livid right now that anything is possible.'

'The Prime Minister would take on the Queen? He'd be massacred, surely. Her Majesty is vastly more popular.'

'Maybe. But he *will* challenge her, David, if this sale goes ahead.'

David drained his glass. 'I don't really know why you're telling me all this, Paul. Hamilton's can't back out now. We're committed. And, as you say, we're only doing our job.'

'I'm telling you because the PM has asked me to. He's talking to the Queen at a different level, of course, but she's as adamant in her way as he is in his. So the government is exerting its pressure wherever it can. Hence this chat.'

'But it's only chat, right? You have no real sanctions you can bring, not until the sale has taken place and pictures look like going abroad?'

'At the moment maybe. But things have a way of changing. This chat is just to let you know that the government is against the sale, on the grounds that some, perhaps all, of these pictures should be saved for the nation. Money isn't everything. There are also one or two "quid pro quos" we can offer that could hurt you. That's what I am saying.'

The room was filling up. Clegg drained his glass. 'My round next time,' he said and made for the door, nodding to others as he went.

David stared at the photograph of the Queen above the bar. Absently, he sucked some ice from his drink. Something inside him had been against the royal sale from the beginning. He felt that, slowly but steadily, he was entering a trap.

Eventually, when it seemed to David that the New Year was already quite old, Ned came back from skiing and Bess from the USA. He saw Ned first, before he returned to school. David had heard from Sarah that Ned had been a 'pain' in Switzerland – moody, contrary, silent and stand-offish. He therefore took the boy to the theatre, to a Christmas show set in the future on another planet. With Ned's passion for space David thought it might cheer him up.

During the first half, he watched his son out of the corner of his eye. He seemed to be enjoying it. At the interval over ginger beer in the foyer, David asked: 'How was Switzerland?'

'Okay.'

'Your mother says you were . . . quiet.'

'Michael Greener is not my favourite person.'

'What's wrong with him?' David was reminded how treacherous divorce was. There was nothing wrong with Michael Greener, except that he was the third side of the triangle. But David wanted to hear Ned's answer all the same.

'He's a trivet.'

'A what?'

'Come on, Dad. You're the art expert. A trivet's one of those metal things they used to stand in front of the fire in England in the eighteenth century, to keep pots warm on. In Switzerland, in the evenings, he was always standing in front of the fire, keeping his pot belly warm. And sounding off – just like a pot boils. So he's a trivet.'

These were troubled waters. Ned's description didn't fit Greener at all. For all his faults, David knew the MP to be an elegant, witty man, not self-important in any way – though he was, perhaps, a shade on the sturdy side. So what was Ned up to? Trying to protect David by pretending he didn't like Greener? Troubled waters indeed. David changed the subject.

'How's school? Looking forward to going back?'

'I suppose so. I might make the rugby fifteen this term, if the right people get crocked.'

'Ned!'

'Dead men's shoes, Dad. That's how you get on in life.'

David tried to keep from laughing. The worst of it was: Ned was right. Half-right anyway. People were drifting back into the auditorium, the interval was nearly over. It was time to broach the other subject he wanted to discuss.

'Ned, if . . . if I did what your mother has done, found someone else, I mean . . . would – would you think up a funny name for her, too?'

'Does she have a pot belly?'

'Women don't have pot bellies, Ned.'

'A squint then? Or a humpback, or webbed fingers, or a beard, or six toes on one foot, or – '

'Ned! Be serious.'

'Humpbacks are serious Dad, if you've got one.'

David laughed.

'What's her name, Dad?' Ned said softly.

David hesitated. 'Elizabeth Lisle. She's called Bess. She's a Catholic and lives in Rome. She's the Pope's press secretary – I met her handling all these sales of Vatican pictures. She's American.'

'The Vatican? That must mean she's religious.'

'Yes, she's religious, but no more than me.'

'Where does she come from in America?'

'Louisiana. Near New Orleans.'

'Are you going to marry her?'

'I don't know. I haven't known her very long.'

'Will you go and live in Rome too?'

'I haven't thought about it.'

'Does ma know about her?'

'Not really, no.'

'Am I going to meet her?'

'If you want to. Do you?'

'I'm asking the questions, Dad. What does she look like?'

'Here's a picture.'

Ned looked at the photograph David offered, without taking it from him. 'Too good-looking for you, dad. You won't keep her.'

'Thanks.'

They made their way back to their seats. To David it seemed as though the conversation had gone well enough. He had introduced the idea of Bess and his son had seemed quite amenable. Why was it then that, as the second half of the show wore on, a second half which was much funnier than the first, Ned sat very still and didn't laugh or even smile once?

Since David and Bess had not seen each other over Christmas, they decided they just had time to sneak a few days holiday, in Italy, before the St Patrick's sale. Most of the preparations had been made but it was the biggest sale David had ever handled, the biggest art auction ever held, so he commuted to Manhattan every fortnight.

Still, the two of them managed a four-day break.

They went to Lucca, Genoa, then across to Venice. It was, said David, a 'silk tour', an itinerary which followed the great Italian silk-making city-states. If Bess was to become a world authority on silk, he joked, she had to see Lucca silks in Lucca and Genoa designs in Genoa. In Lucca David bought her a fifteenth-century panel showing swooping phoenixes, the traditional Lucchese design, and a piece of sixteenth-century patterned velvet, another Lucca speciality. In Genoa they found some sixteenth-century damask with a traditional pomegranate design. And in Venice they visited the factories which still exist, and still produce world-famous silks.

From Venice they took the *vaporetto* to Burano. It was rainy and windy, so they had to sit inside, gazing out at the grey lagoon through steamy windows. 'Imagine being here in the sixteenth century,' said David, 'when Venice was at the peak of her power. Small wooden ships, no heating, no plate glass, plague every ten years, sail power only . . .'

'How romantic!'

'Do you know, fashionable women used to walk around on wooden shoes, with heels as high as ten or eleven inches – so they could be above the filth in the streets?'

'David!'

He pointed out of the window, to a small island with a wall running round it and soaked cypress trees bending in the wind. 'St Erasmo. During plagues that's where they buried all the bodies – '

'Stop it!' she said, but laughing. She cupped her hand over his mouth. He kissed her palm.

At Burano they watched crimson damask being made by small, dark-haired women with nimble fingers. In the next room a deep green silk was being hand-woven into a thick panel. 'These colours don't amount to much now,' said David, 'but once they were trade secrets. Venetian red and Verona green-earth were two of the most sought-after colours in the civilized world.'

The next room was the factory shop. 'With those brown eyes, I think green suits you better,' David told her, and ordered a roll of the Verona green-earth silk.

Bess gripped his arm. 'Oh David, what a great idea! I could make a shirt, or maybe a robe. Thank you.' They were in public so she couldn't kiss him. Instead, she just leaned her body into his.

Outside it was still raining, the wind driving the drops almost horizontally. They ran down the street, avoiding the puddles, towards the landing where the *vaporetto* stopped. They had to wait. The wind and the rain swept around them but, in the glass-walled bay, they were sheltered. Bess took out a handkerchief and wiped the rain off David's hair and forehead. He held her arm and kissed her. From here they could see the big ocean-going ships making for the Adriatic. An oil tanker, sleek and graceful despite its industrial purpose, was making towards open waters.

'I've never made love on a ship,' said Bess. 'I wonder what it's like.'

126

'It can be arranged,' said David. 'Over here!' he shouted, waving at the tanker. 'Over here! Don't go without us!'

She pulled him back, laughing. 'I'll settle for a hotel room, on the Grand Canal. Let's go to mass and then have an early dinner. I need a lot of time to thank you for the silk.'

They were staying at the Gritti Palace and because it was early February and the hotel far from full, they had the pick of rooms overlooking the Grand Canal. That night, after *involtini di Salmone* at Antico Martini, a restaurant opposite the opera house, they leaned out of their hotel window and watched the river traffic, the shifting lights and surfaces. The rich smells of cooking mingled with the damp odours of decay. The vast, dark shapes of the Palazzo Venier dei Leoni and Santa Maria della Salute on the opposite bank threw back at them the throaty roar of the *vaporetti*, the soft slapping of the water, and the more fleeting, secretive noises of half-heard conversations.

In bed Bess said: 'There's so much water here, you'd think Venice would have something in common with home – Louisiana, I mean.' She kissed David's shoulder with a smack. 'But they're quite different. Here it's . . . shapes, sounds . . . very busy . . . the water and the stones are so loud. The *language* is so loud. At home our words, our scenery – everything – is much quieter. You never *hear* the Mississippi or the swamps. You can't listen to the pepper fields.' She laid her head on David's naked chest. 'Yet it's just as sensual as Venice in its own way. When we make love, David, I always think of home now. Sex makes other things sensual, too. And not just the things, but the sound of their names. Redbud, hedgewood, pickerel, crawfish. The words sound different after – well, after . . .' She drew her finger down the flesh on David's stomach. 'Sex is like landing on water. When you first touch down on the smooth surface, it's as hard as glass. Then, as you slow down, as you relax, it gets softer, you scoop out more water, and you sink lower.'

Next day, they drove south to Rome, stopping off at Urbino. David used the opportunity to order some photocopies of documents he needed for his research into Leonardo's 'Virgin of the Rocks'. Correspondence between the Dukes of Urbino and the Malatesta in Rimini, and some other letters. It was better if he placed the order in person.

'How's it going?' asked Bess, after he had spent half an hour with the librarian in the Palazzo Ducale while she had visited the house where Raphael grew up.

'To be candid, I don't know. I've established that Leonardo spent part of his missing year in Urbino. Urbino was an independent state until 1631 when it passed to the papacy. At that time some of its treasures went to Tuscany, where the last duke's daughter was married, and some went to Rome. This makes the family papers a bit of a problem. Some of them are here and some may still be in Rome.'

'What will they tell you?'

'I don't know. Maybe they will mention inventories in which works by Leonardo are referred to. I can't prejudge, just hope.'

They arrived back in Rome in time for David to hang Bess's silks, before dinner at Gina's. The Lucca panel was mainly green and turquoise, the Genoan was red with yellow and crimson splashes. 'I must say, David Colwyn,' said Bess, squeezing his arm, which had become a favourite gesture, 'You have brought colour into my life in more ways than one.'

They had brought a small piece of Venetian silk back for Gina also, and she was delighted. In return they were treated to her best wine, a Rosso Tapino. Its fruity softness made David relaxed enough at dinner to voice his concern about Ned. He described to Bess their evening at the theatre, when he told his son about her.

She laughed. 'Too good-looking for you? I hope you don't believe that!' She cupped her hand over his mouth, just as she had done on the *vaporetto* out to Burano. Again he kissed her palm.

Then he said, 'But what do *you* think, Bess? Ned's so inconsistent. He's so moody – sometimes he just goes off on inner journeys, all by himself, when no one can get to him. But the thing I'm most worried about is this need of his to pretend. I can't expect him to be wholly in favour of a man who's gone off with his mother, but why should Ned pretend that Michael Greener is something he is not?'

'He's trying to protect you, as you said.'

'But it's out of character. For Ned, I mean. He's so realistic in all other ways. Brutally so at times. Remember that comment about "dead men's shoes"? He was right.'

She slipped her hand in his. Since their two dinners at the Veau d'Or in New York, they preferred to sit side by side in restaurants. 'If you're really worried, David, there is someone I know in London, an American psychiatrist – '

He stopped her, briefly squeezing her wrist.

'Listen to me!' she said softly. 'And don't be so old-fashioned. If Ned is disturbed by your divorce from Sarah, that's nothing to be ashamed of. He may even be heading for a depression. You'd be the last person to recognize that.'

But David shook his head. 'Ned can be so cheerful. He can't be depressed at the same time.'

'Garbage! Jokes can be just as much a defence mechanism as anything else – you know that. And what do all those moody silences mean?'

David said nothing. She squeezed his arm.

'Look, my friend's name is Tony Wilde. He's professor of psychiatry at St Matthew's Hospital, with private rooms somewhere in Upper Wimpole Street. I won't force him on you but I *can* recommend him. You'll get no mumbo-jumbo. I used to know him at Columbia – where he still teaches one week a month by the way – and if you *do* decide to go see him, give him my love.'

'And talking of love,' she said, 'let's go back to the flat. I shan't see you again until New York. The big sale.'

But David made no move.

'Bess, after the encyclical, after Thomas goes public, how long will it take do you think? For me to be divorced, I mean?'

'Well, as I understand it, as from this month you've been separated officially from Sarah for two years, so under British law you can be divorced – right?'

He nodded. 'I expect to hear from her any day now.'

'So you've already filled the first requirement. Your case can go straight to the tribunal.'

'But there's bound to be a rush of cases. It could take months. Years.'

'Mmm.' She looked thoughtful. 'If that *does* happen, I shall have to pull a few strings. I don't know about you but *I* sure can't wait that long.'

## 7

José Sandoz had not been a security guard at the Getty Museum in Malibu for very long and he had a lot to learn – not just security matters but about the layout of the gallery. It would come, though. He was a fast learner. And it was a good job for him, not too hard physically, the money was fair and, since he shared his house with four other Puerto Ricans who all had jobs and were paying for their rooms, he didn't have to spend much on his keep and always had money in his pocket.

The one problem he did have, though, was remembering the names of these damn painters. What sort of a name was Van Rijn or Breughel? Was that right even? Or Wtewael, or Cuyp? Or Caravaggio – that was one of the worst. He knew the painting, alright. It was the new one bought from the Pope. It was two rooms away, the edge of his territory. He decided to have a look at it again, to check that he had got the spelling right. It was early morning, and the museum was deserted. He walked slowly into the neighbouring room, past the Goya y Lucientes – that was a name he *could* pronounce. He entered the next gallery, longer and better lit, which contained the –

He stopped, appalled. No! Sweet Jesu, not this soon in his career at the museum! It must be an illusion – after all, no man in his right mind would do such a thing.

It was no illusion. A wild slash had been dug into the Caravaggio canvas about three quarters of the way across. It went right through the body of Christ and on past the legs of the man who was holding him. Already the canvas had begun to peel apart, exposing the wall behind. Sandoz was utterly alone. He did remember now that there had been three men in this room about a quarter of an hour before. Could it have been they? At least he would be able to give the police their description. Trembling, he reached into his pocket, took out his radio transmitter and called his chief.

Sandoz did give the police the descriptions but before the police could act upon them a report in the next day's *Los Angeles Times* pinpointed those responsible for the crime. The paper's night desk had been tipped off.

The report was headlined: 'Mafia hoods slash painting – Mars Vatican Sale', and underneath it ran, 'A painting worth more than thirty-seven million dollars by the seventeenth-century Italian master, Caravaggio, on show at the Getty Museum in Malibu, was seriously damaged yesterday by a knife cut nearly twenty-nine inches long.

'No one saw the attack on the painting but underworld sources say that rumours about such an attack have been circulating for some days. These sources claim the culprits are members of a small band of illegal Italian immigrants forced to flee Sicily some months ago, when His Holiness Pope Thomas sold the very same Caravaggio painting and with the money set up an informants' fund. This has proved so effective that many arrests have been made and numerous mobsters have had to leave the island.

'Using traditional links between Sicily and the American Mafia, these Italian mafiosi have managed to enter America and, in most cases, have been incorporated into existing mob outfits.

'Narcotics squad officers at Los Angeles Police Department say they believe Sicilians are responsible for much of the current upsurge in drug abuse in the state. There are also reports that protection rackets are in operation at two airports in California. Some officials claim that the recent crash on take-off of a small jet at Mendocino airport was the work of Sicilian underworld figures who were putting pressure on the airport management to accept their terms.

'Now, however, Mafia sources are openly admitting responsibility for the attack on the Caravaggio. This action protests the impending sale in New York of Vatican treasures, due to take place the day after tomorrow. Warnings of their opposition to such sales have already been made, they claim, and have been ignored.

'Museum staff say that the picture can be repaired but that it will take months.

'A spokesperson for the Holy See in Rome expressed horror at the attack but said that it would not affect the sale. The press officer for Hamilton's, the auction house handling the sale, who also spoke on behalf of Cardinal Rich of New York, in whose cathedral the sale will take place, said that the auction will go ahead as planned.'

This report, which was syndicated around the world, filled David with alarm. The Mafia had been very cunning, he thought. Guessing, rightly, that security at St Patrick's would be very tight, they had aimed at a softer target – and in doing so had brought home to prospective buyers of the Vatican treasures that no museum was safe from Mafia attention. The timing was diabolically perfect, too. It was too late to issue convincing reassurances, and yet, with forty-eight hours still to go, there was time for paranoia to develop and for the sale to be badly affected.

On the other hand, people are morbid as well as curious and so, despite the fact that the slashed Caravaggio was not among the pictures on show, hundreds who had not yet been to see the works of art in St Patrick's now hurried to do so.

Thomas also showed his mettle once more. When he learned of the attack, he replied: 'Mr Getty didn't make his millions without one or two setbacks. The same applies to our venture.'

Meanwhile, during the last days before the sale, David was frantically busy seeing the last few 'autocrats' on the list produced by Betsy. Her list had been fourteen strong and ranged from the boss of a drinks company in Canada, through a defence company in Washington to a shipping conglomerate in Florida. With two days to the sale to go, David had only one firm still to see, the defence giant in a Washington suburb. Like all the others on his list, it was a one-man band, in this case the brainchild of a certain Red Wilkie, a fireball of a man who was an ex-Hollywood stunt man turned tycoon. David had sent to Wilkie, as he had sent to everyone on Betsy's list, a general outline of his proposal. Then, when he visited the men in person, he would use a more tailored approach.

David was shown into an office and told by an aide that both Wilkie and his secretary were not yet back from a demonstration of some new army equipment at a proving ground in Maryland. They wouldn't be long – the helicopter was already airborne and would fly straight to the landing pad right outside the offices. Half an hour at the most. The aide handed David some coffee.

Twenty-four minutes later, the helicopter clattered into earshot and David watched from the window as it approached the large white 'H' emblazoned on the lawn outside the Wilkie offices.

When he strode in, followed now by two secretaries, Wilkie boomed at David, 'Come in, Mr Colwyn, come right on in.' He folded his six feet four inches behind his desk and offered David a cigar, waving him to a leather sofa. 'I liked your brochure. You said you'd bring some art work. Have you got it?' David took out a number of sheets of paper and photographs. He had had them produced, in strictest confidence, by some of the best graphic designers in London.

Wilkie lit a cigar and examined the papers. 'Great,' he said. 'Great. How much do you say this will cost me?'

'A hundred million, give or take.'

'A lot of money to waste on a logo.'

'Except that it's not wasted. You probably spend half that on advertising each year. What's more, whenever you want, you can sell and get your money back. Plus interest.'

Wilkie smoked his cigar. He was obviously taken with the idea. It was revealing, David thought, how many of these tycoons wanted to be more than just rich, wanted to be taken seriously as men of culture. All the businessmen on Betsy's list were Roman Catholics. In every case David had had his graphics people adapt Michelangelo's 'Pietà' to the company's logo. His idea was to tap some of the enormous profits that had been made in Wall Street and in the City of London recently, by persuading large firms to bid at the Vatican sale. He had, in his tour of the fourteen companies, pointed to three advantages. In the first place there was the enormous publicity associated with buying this or that Vatican treasure and the good cause it was associated with. Second, there was the continued publicity value of owning a great work which could go on display anywhere as free advertising for the company concerned. And third there was the prestige to be derived from use of the image in the company's logo. This was the graphic work he had brought with him.

Wilkie looked up. 'So what do you want from me?'

'Either come to the sale tomorrow night, and bid for yourself. Or give me a bid to make on your behalf. I guarantee that you won't have to pay more than is necessary.'

'How many people like me have you seen?'

'A few. About a dozen.'

'Who exactly?'

'Come tomorrow night and find out for yourself. They are all Catholics, all devout. They all run their companies as you do, by themselves. That's why I've chosen each one of you. A board would take six months to consider an idea like this. And still get it wrong.'

Wilkie chuckled. 'Too right.' He tapped ash from his cigar. 'Look, Mr Colwyn, I'm not going to give you a bid. You seem a nice enough guy but you're still new to me. But I just might come tomorrow. I've never been to one of these big deal auctions. I've got some friends in the business, though. All right if I ask them what they think of your scheme?'

'Sure, but they'll say yes, whatever they think.'

'Oh! Why's that?'

'If a company doesn't buy it, a museum almost certainly will. Dealers don't want that. Dealers profit from the movement of pictures and other art works. Once something goes into a museum it hardly ever comes out.'

'So you're saying I have to make up my own mind, uh?'

'I'm saying you always do. That's why you are on my list.'

'Why didn't you come before, give me more chance to think it over?'

'I would have done but you were always busy. That's one of the problems of being a one-man band. It's taken me weeks just to see fourteen people. Someone had to be last.'

133

Wilkie thumped his desk. 'Who else will be bidding? Give me some idea, goddammit!'

David had absolutely no intention of telling Wilkie who his rivals were. He wanted him *in* the cathedral. Once there, David was sure some of the men he had seen would be unable *not* to bid.

He gathered up his things, ready to leave. 'Let's just say, Mr Wilkie, that if you don't come tomorrow night, you just might regret it. This is, after all, a chance to break new ground. Think of it. A patron of the arts, a strong supporter of charity work *and* the pleasure and prestige of owning something that is unique and irreplaceable. There are those who might say there is something especially poignant in a weapons company, whose business is destruction, having as its mark perhaps the greatest symbol of love the world has ever known.'

Wilkie seemed to gnaw at his cigar. 'I like that, Mr Colwyn. That's good.' He looked again at the graphics David had given him, now strewn about the desk in front of him. He lifted his head. 'Okay. I'm not saying I'll bid, but you've got me hooked. I'm just wild to know who else you've got lined up. I may or may not have my cheque book with me, but I'll be there, Mr Colwyn. I'll be there.'


When David arrived at St Patrick's the next night it rather seemed to him that half of New York had turned out for the sale. Fifth Avenue between 48th Street and 52nd Street was choked with spectators, the police just managing to keep a thoroughfare open for the people actually invited so that they could be dropped by their cars at the foot of the steps. The steps themselves were also solid with bodies save for an area about twenty yards wide which, again, was kept clear by police. There were television cameras, radio reporters, arc lights galore. It was, in fact, just like a Broadway first night or the Oscars ceremony in LA. The Mafia threat had made the event more, not less, attractive.

Massoni's intervention had added spice, too. After news of the Los Angeles attack on the Caravaggio had reached Rome, the cardinal had gone into print again, in *Il Messaggero* as before. This time the headline was: 'Villains and the Vatican' and in his article Massoni castigated the Pope for tangling with the Sicilian underworld and risking the prestige and power of the papacy on a 'showbiz' venture in New York.

David had spent all day at the cathedral, checking the new security arrangements, introduced after the attack in Los Angeles. He hadn't read the article, he'd only been told about it. Massoni was not dangerous today, he decided. His attack came too late. But, sooner or later, a more controversial issue would come along and find the cardinal as its leader. *Then* Thomas might be damaged. But this was not the time for worrying about the future. He had to go back to the hotel to change into his dinner jacket. Bess was in New York but, as on other occasions, they had been too busy to see each other. They might have a light supper together later on. Much later.

Returning from the hotel, David's car edged forward, one in a long line of limousines. Finally he reached the cathedral steps, where he was recognized by a few in the crowd, who wished him luck. He was unable to dodge a cable TV reporter at the door. The woman asked him if he was nervous. 'Yes,' said David. 'Much too nervous to give interviews. Ask me after, if I'm still alive.' That got him a smile and the reporter let him go. She could, in any case, see a famous ballerina getting out of the next car and she was much redder meat.

St Patrick's vast nave was packed. David had wondered about this: he had wanted the occasion to be as exclusive as possible, but limiting the tickets to only a few hundred would have left the cathedral looking empty, which could have had a dampening effect on the whole proceedings. He had, therefore, sent out invitations to about a thousand carefully-chosen guests. In the first place he had invited some of the world's greatest living painters, from Andrew Wyeth to David Hockney to Sidney Nolan. These had been given a special showing of the pictures earlier in the day.

Hockney and Nolan were already good friends of David's but he had never met Wyeth. He found him to be warm and witty if not exactly easy. Most of them enjoyed themselves, and were pleased to have been invited.

David had decided views on fame and what it meant, or ought to mean, so he had not invited the socialites, known mainly for their ancestors and dress sense, on which Park Avenue seemed to survive. But he did invite well-known and well-regarded writers, musicians, academics, politicians, actors and actresses.

By now the almost non-stop whistling and cheering from outside the cathedral showed that recognizable faces were arriving every minute: Baryshnikov, Mehta, De Niro, Senator Kennedy, Stavros Niarchos, Gordon Getty, Leonard Bernstein. David smiled when, at about eight-thirty, Cardinal Rich arrived, glowing in his scarlet robes. He made his entrance via his limousine like all the other big names – despite the fact that his official residence had its own private entrance to the cathedral. New York is nothing if not theatre and the same may be said for the Church. As nine o'clock approached David went to stand near the rostrum. He and Rich had both decided it would be wrong to use the very fine pulpit as the place from where to conduct the auction. Instead a rostrum complete with desk and microphone stood now in the centre of the nave at the top of the steps leading to the choir. As each work came up for sale spotlights would pick it out around the walls of the church.

Most people were in their seats now and David nodded to many he knew. He had read, and believed it to be true, that several European national galleries had negotiated special funding with their government for this sale. All the Hamilton staff were in place now, the men in black tie, the women in long black dresses. For such a turnout he had given a great deal of thought to the seating. This evening might have a first-night flavour but it was a serious sale, and so the serious buyers, not necessarily the best-known names or faces, had to have the better seats. He had put the businessmen, the tycoons, where he could see them easily, and where they could see each other, near the centre aisle. Their rivalry might produce fireworks.

At about five past nine, decently late, Cardinal Rich climbed the steps to the rostrum: he was to open the proceedings. His scarlet robes gleamed in the light like a fire brick.

'Ladies and gentlemen,' he cried. 'Welcome to St Patrick's. I am not going to hold up the proceedings for long but I have two announcements you might like to hear.' As David had at the first Vatican sale, he held aloft a piece of paper. 'This is a cheque I shall be sending to His Holiness tomorrow. It represents the receipts from visitors who, in the past three months, have been to the cathedral to look at these magnificent treasures' – and he waved his robed arm majestically around the nave. 'And the amount is for . . .' Deliberately he held the cheque in two hands as if to read it for the first time, like an actor announcing the winner at an Oscar ceremony. ' . . . For one million, three hundred and fifty-five thousand, four hundred and twenty-six dollars – '

A wave of applause broke over his words, drowning whatever cents he may have been going to add. The cardinal smiled down at the upturned faces in front of him.

'And now I have a short statement which His Holiness sent me – you, us – earlier in the day.' He paused to reach into his cassock and took from it a slip of yellow telex paper. All other sounds in the cathedral died away. 'Ladies and gentlemen, I send you my blessing on this uniquely momentous occasion. The works of art to be sold this evening represent the highest artistic achievements of mankind. They include some of the most beautiful things ever produced by man. Help us transform this excellence into another form of beauty, an even purer form of love, just as our Lord's body was transformed after the Resurrection. Help us to help those who cannot always help themselves. Thomas.'

There was no applause but as Rich descended from the rostrum a buzz of anticipation swept the cathedral. The Pope's message, in its tone and brevity, had exactly primed the sale, brought people's minds back from the party atmosphere to the more serious work at hand. Not for the first time, David marvelled at the insight of his employer in Rome.

He waited for the cardinal to settle himself in the seat reserved for him in the front row. He looked across to Bess. She was standing amid the reporters, still sorting out their problems.

The cardinal was ready so David mounted the rostrum. His instincts told him that he needed to be as unlike the cardinal as possible: crisp, businesslike, ice-cool, unflamboyant. He spread his catalogue on the desk before him and surveyed the cathedral one last time, to see that his staff were where they should be. The main lights dimmed. 'Good evening on behalf of us all at Hamilton's, ladies and gentlemen. The first lot this evening is Giovanni Bellini's "Lament over the Dead Christ".' A light above the painting now came on, drawing attention to it in one of the side aisles. 'I will start the bidding at fifteen million dollars . . . fifteen million . . . who will bid fifteen million dollars . . . ?'

After the usual heart-stopping pause an arm went up in the third row and he looked down to see Sir Denis May, from the Australian National Gallery in Sydney. The bidding was on.

The sale that night was to become legendary in the art world. Just to have been there became one of the experiences to boast about in years to come. Within months copies of the catalogue, which originally had sold for $100, were changing hands for not far short of $5,000 – more if they were signed by Wyeth or Baryshnikov. It wasn't just the amounts that changed hands, it was the ferocious tussles which developed. Every item did well, even if not everybody got what they came for. The Bellini went to Tokyo, the Perugino to Washington, the Louvre landed the Poussin, the National Gallery in London got the Cranach. The Getty, undeterred by the Caravaggio assault, bought the Leonardo, for seventy-seven million dollars, and Galileo's confession. Sydney squeezed in with one of the Raphaels they were after, and the Rijksmuseum in Amsterdam paid fifty-three million dollars for the Titian, a record, like all the prices that night. But it was the Giotto, the Martin Luther excommunication deed and the 'Pietà' which produced the real contests.

David had always thought the big museums would go for the Giotto but not even he had realized how ferocious things might be. Shirikin, from the Hermitage, was in there early, as was Jakobson from the Met. Houston wanted it, so did Tokyo, Berlin and even the Italians themselves: Pini was bidding on behalf of Turin – with Fiat money David guessed. Bidding had started at twenty million dollars, rose quickly to fifty-five million dollars, by which time only Tokyo, the Hermitage, the Met and the Getty were still in. Tokyo dropped out at fifty-seven million dollars, followed by the Getty at sixty million dollars – they had already spent an enormous amount on the Leonardo and the Galileo. Given that the New Yorker Jakobson was on his home turf, and that Shirikin was a Russian, it was no surprise that the audience should be partisan. When Shirikin dropped out at sixty-five million dollars, wild cheering billowed through the cathedral and the Hermitage director, justifiably angry, stormed out. David tried to thank him over the microphone but his remarks were drowned in the general din.

The fight over the Luther manuscript was more predictable, being between two German museums, Dresden and Berlin. Until that evening, the world record for a manuscript was seven point three million dollars. In St Patrick's David *started* the bidding at seven million dollars. At twelve million dollars both galleries were beginning to hurt and instead of rising in increments of two hundred thousand dollars or three hundred thousand dollars the directors started calling out bid increases of fifty thousand dollars. David thought it unsuitable to object, especially as the bidding continued on to fifteen million dollars and then to fifteen million, five hundred thousand dollars. Eventually, after the longest battle in terms of time and *number* of bids, Dresden scraped home at fifteen million, six hundred and fifty thousand dollars. More than double the previous record.

The 'Pietà', Michelangelo's wonderful white masterwork, valued more highly than anything else on the Pope's list, was saved till last. Introducing it brought David his tensest moment. Some of the major galleries, like the Getty, the National in London, the National in Sydney, had almost certainly spent themselves out on earlier works. David was less certain that the 'Pietà' would sell than anything else on offer, simply because it was the most expensive. That was one reason why he had tried to involve commercial and industrial giants: he had foreseen this situation. Still, there were certain museums – Houston, Berlin, Osaka, Turin, Munich, Ottawa, Zurich at least – who had bid earlier on but had not yet actually *spent* anything.

The bidding started at an incredible fifty million dollars and in the event only four museums even entered the race: Houston, Ottawa, Berlin and, the dark horse, the Louvre which, with the best sculpture collection in the world, wanted this jewel. These museums did not, however, have everything to themselves. In his visits to commercial companies, David had focused on the 'Pietà' because in advertising terms, only Michelangelo's statue was simple enough, and bold enough, to make sense. And only Michelangelo, with perhaps Leonardo and Raphael, was a big enough name to ensure that any company which bought his work wouldn't then have to spend another fortune telling everyone who he was. Now, David watched to see whether his efforts would pay off.

He had noticed with satisfaction during the earlier part of the auction that the businessmen at the sale were totally caught up in the drama of it all. They had sat transfixed as the battles raged back and forth. Some of them, he guessed – he hoped – must be impatient to have a crack themselves.

He was right. No sooner had the bidding started, and the four museums announced their intention of going for the Michelangelo, a Chicago-based freight outfit, a third was George Nuttall, whose family had made biscuits for generations and the fourth was Red Wilkie, who had brought his cheque book after all.

Ninety-five million was reached soon enough but bidding then slowed, and the Canadians, the Germans, Seidl and Nuttall all gave up before one hundred million was reached. That left Houston, the Louvre, Ward and Wilkie. Wilkie went at a hundred and one, the Louvre a million later. David's money was on Houston but he was wrong. At a hundred and three million a new bidder entered: Carl Malinkrodt, who liked to say that his biotechnology firm had made him a billionaire, not overnight but over the weekend. He had been on Betsy's list but when David had seen him he had seemed totally uninterested in art. The traditional poker face, David supposed. Malinkrodt's firm also had interests in the defence business and that made him a rival of sorts to Wilkie.

Malinkrodt's intervention was superbly timed. Houston and Ward were both a little frightened by the levels they were bidding at, and the new competitor came in with such force that both sought escape as soon as possible.

But now, stung by Malinkrodt's last-minute intervention, Wilkie came *back* in! The bidding rose: a hundred and three million dollars . . . a hundred and four million dollars . . . a hundred and five million dollars . . . a hundred and six million dollars. There was not a sound in the entire cathedral save David speaking the figures.

He was staring down at Malinkrodt – it was his turn to bid.

Malinkrodt looked at the 'Pietà', back to David. Back to Michelangelo's superlative marble.

Then he shook his head.

Within moments David brought the gavel down and the 'Pietà' was sold – at a hundred and six million dollars. The applause and the cheering went on for more than a minute.

That was the end of the sale and the ordered rows of the audience quickly became a jumble as everyone rehearsed to his neighbour what he had just seen. David felt exhausted, but he knew the evening wasn't over yet. There were television interviews, triple checking the security since the Mafia threat still hung over them and the actual transfer of the works wouldn't take place until tomorrow at the earliest, and there was other tidying up to do. And after all that, a reception at the Cardinal's residence.

It was there that David finally caught up with Bess. 'The Veau d'Or will be closed at this hour. I think we'd better try further up town. What's the matter – aren't you hungry?' She looked on edge.

'Sort of,' she whispered. 'Let's go back to the hotel as soon as we decently can. There's something I can tell you only in bed.'

'Sort of,' she whispered. 'Let's go back to the hotel as soon as we decently can. There's something I can tell you only in bed.'

But it was nearly an hour before the TV crews, the all-night radio news stations, and the newspaper reporters would let them get away.

Later, David said: 'Well, what is it? What is it you can only tell me in bed?'

She lay back, stroking the inside of his leg. 'Oh that.' She grinned. 'I lied – I just wanted to get you back here. It's been ages since Rome.'

'So there's nothing you have to tell me? Bah!'

'Oh yes. I have something to tell you.' She placed her hand over his mouth, so he couldn't interrupt. 'But it doesn't need a pillow to say it on. It's not at all private – everyone will know soon enough. . . . Thomas is so delighted with the way you've handled these sales, he's decided some reward is in order.' She kissed him on the mouth. 'You're going to get a papal honour.'

David's admiration for Pope Thomas, already very high, only increased after the sale at St Patrick's. His Holiness clearly had a wider plan and it now began to emerge. He let a couple of weeks go by, to allow discussion of the St Patrick's sale to exhaust itself. During this period there were reports in the press from all over the world as the works which had changed hands in St Patrick's arrived in California, London, Tokyo, Sydney, Paris, Dresden and so on. Red Wilkie, using the graphics David had provided before the sale, announced that his company's logo would now consist of a simple outline of the 'Pietà' and that the statue itself would go on show at the firm's headquarters in Washington. In Moscow, *Pravda*, on behalf of a disappointed Shirikin, attacked the commercialism of the sale and everyone outside the communist bloc had a good laugh at that.

In the west only Italy continued to feel rather affronted by the whole exercise.

As the *New York Times* informed its readers in a special edition on the day after the sale, the pictures had netted a total of nine hundred and ten million dollars and the Italian government seemed to think the amount had been more or less stolen from it. Among the caustic comments from government spokesmen in the wake of the sale was the complaint that, as a result of the auction, one crucial piece of history – the Luther manuscript – had passed behind the Iron Curtain, for ever. But, apart from Massoni's eve-of-sale attack, the Italian government's anti-Pope stance was the only sour note to be sounded.

Then, when interest in the sale had begun to flag, Thomas announced his plans for using the money. At a special press conference, held in the Nervi audience hall, the Holy Father himself outlined what he had in mind. Of the nine hundred and ten million dollars, roughly seventy-three million dollars, or eight per cent, had to be paid to Hamilton's as commission. That left eight hundred and thirty-seven million dollars plus the one million, three hundred and fifty-five thousand dollars raised from people viewing the exhibition in St Patrick's, less one hundred thousand dollars for the copies made, producing a final total of eight hundred and thirty-eight million, two hundred and fifty-five thousand dollars. The bulk of the money – seven hundred and fifty million dollars – would, he said, be invested and the income, estimated at somewhere between thirty-seventy and eighty million dollars a year, would be used to continue with the kind of work already begun in Foligno, Sicily and the Marquesas Isles. In honour of the sale, and the part played in it by the people of New York, the fund was to be known as the St Patrick's Fund. A commission would administer the money under the direction of Cardinal Rich, who was being promoted to become joint president of Cor Unum and would reside in Rome. His place as Cardinal Archbishop of New York was being taken by Martin Naughton, a Jesuit from Idaho. Thomas also announced that several distinguished people had agreed to serve on the commission. These included Sandro Sirianni, the mayor of Foligno, the Cardinal Archbishop of Palermo, the South American Secretary General of the United Nations, who was a Catholic, the President of the Institute for Religious Works, the Vatican Bank, representatives of two Roman Catholic banks in Switzerland, Credit Lausanne and the Banque Lemann – and, finally, Mr David Colwyn, chief executive of Hamilton's of London. Mr Colwyn was also, in recognition of his work in organizing the magnificent sales which had resulted in the fund, to receive a papal knighthood, of the Order of St Sylvester.

As for the remaining eighty million-plus dollars, that, said Thomas, was to be used immediately for urgent projects still to be named. He was inviting bishops from around the world to submit proposals.

The division of the money into an immediate fund and an ongoing one was widely welcomed. Many people agreed with the Holy Father that there was an urgency in some problems that could not wait a year for the first dividends to grow.

Back in London after all the excitement, one of David's first tasks was to visit Seton at Windsor. The Queen was delighted with the success of the Vatican auction, he told David, and was more determined than ever to push ahead with her sale, despite 'one or two difficulties' David may have heard about. David agreed that he was indeed aware of the opposition to the Queen's plan.

He still had mixed feelings about the royal sale himself, but there was no going back now. With the great Vatican business such a triumph, Hamilton's board would think him crazy not to capitalize on it. Even so, David didn't much like Seton's choice of paintings to be sold. David had argued from the beginning that the pictures in the Queen's sale should not include anything by artists who had featured in the Vatican auction. Thus Her Majesty's Bellinis, Leonardos, Cranachs and Michelangelos should all be left off her list. Seton had disagreed. They were the biggest names, he said, and would fetch the biggest prices. David had also advised against including any pictures by Hilliard. Lely or Holbein. His arguments here were somewhat different. Hilliard was English, and Lely and Holbein, though foreign, had spent important parts of their lives in England and produced some of their best work there. To David this suggested that such art had special associations with Britain, and should stay there. Seton again took the opposite view. The Royal Collection was particularly strong in these artists, he said, and could best afford to lose some examples of their work.

As a result the list he produced was, to David, completely wrong.

David was still pondering its implications when he drove down to Hamble on the following Saturday to watch Ned play rugby. Clearly the right person had at last been 'crocked' and Ned had been selected in his place. It was a miserable day, wet and windy, and the cold branches of the trees which surrounded the playing field were like fine cracks in the clouds.

There wasn't a big crowd in that weather – perhaps a hundred boys and girls of the school and a dozen parents, some of whom David knew vaguely. He arrived about ten minutes before the game was due to start and so didn't have time to talk to Ned before the kick-off. They waved to each other.

David wasn't really concentrating on the game, being more wrapped up in the Queen's list, so he was taken by surprise when, after Hamble had scored, a voice suddenly spoke his name. He looked round to see a man in a sand-coloured sports jacket approaching him along the touchline. It was Kenneth Yates, Ned's housemaster.

They shook hands. 'Going well, eh?' said Yates. 'Three-nil up and only fifteen minutes gone.' Like many schoolteachers he treated adults in the same way he treated his charges and bellowed as if he was still in class.

David stamped his feet, trying to keep warm. He paid more attention to the game.

'Ned's playing well,' said Yates. 'Doing well in class, too.'

David nodded but said nothing. He knew Ned was bright and didn't much care how well he played rugby, so long as he enjoyed himself.

'I'm still worried about him though.'

David turned and stared.

'I mean it.'

'But how can you be? You just said he was doing well – '

'This is a school, Mr Colwyn, not a factory for producing Einsteins. The fact is: your son has no friends.'

The game was in the far side of the field and the noise had receded.

'That can't be true, Mr Yates. He's such an enthusiastic boy. He can't be *that* unpopular.'

'He's not unpopular. He could have all the friends he wants, but he doesn't want. And that's why I'm worried. He was in the school play at Christmas yet isn't part of the theatrical "set". He plays rugby well but doesn't mix with the "jocks". He's mad about computers but seems to find the others who are just as keen a bit of a bore.'

'Is all that so unusual?'

'Quite frankly, at his age, yes. Very unusual. We schoolmasters see a lot more than most people give us credit for, Mr Colwyn, and in my view your son is depressed.'

'What! You mean – ?'

'I mean clinically depressed, Mr Colwyn. Bad enough to need treatment from a psychiatrist.'

'No! That's idiotic, Mr Yates, surely? I don't mean to be rude but couldn't it simply be that he has a solitary nature?' Why was David being so fierce? he asked himself. The man was only saying what Bess had said. He didn't want to hear it.

'That's not the only symptom. He eats excessive amounts of chocolate, he can never get out of bed in the morning.'

'Those are symptoms of depression?'

'You can take it from me they are. Depressives often take to what psychiatrists call "comfort foods". And lying-in in the mornings is usually interpreted as an avoidance mechanism. They don't want to face the day.'

'But you just said yourself that he's doing well in class. He's just made the rugby team. That's not the behaviour of someone who is ill.'

'I'm not a doctor, Mr Colwyn, so you may find it hard to accept that I speak with authority. But I've seen a lot of pupils in my time. And I can tell you this: curiously, the fact that Ned is doing well is a bad sign. It means he's striving to keep up appearances, at all costs. It's as if he's built a dam against his feelings. He's running away from people, from emotions, and into his work.'

David was bewildered. 'Have you seen this sort of thing before?'

'Not often – but yes, once or twice.'

'And? How did it turn out? What happened?'

'In two cases the parents took my advice, brought in a specialist doctor and the children recovered. In another case nothing was done, and nothing bad happened. And in a fourth case nothing was done . . .' He paused, and looked across to Ned on the field. 'The child committed suicide.'

The two men watched the game in silence for several minutes. Then Yates held out his hand. 'I have another parent to see, so I must go. I'm glad we've had this talk. I know you're busy but I hope you'll take what I say seriously. Goodbye for now.'

David watched the rest of the game in a daze. Hamble pulled further ahead until, just after half-time, the rain got more insistent. The heavy going favoured the other side, who were bigger boys, and before the final whistle they drew level. Ned played well and David congratulated him before he returned to London. He didn't mention his conversation with the housemaster: he wasn't certain of his feelings. He had quite forgotten the Queen's list.

The next day David had to travel to Rome for the first meeting of the St Patrick's Fund Commission. This was held early on the Monday in the Secretariat of State on the second floor of the apostolic palace – in a large, square room with frescoes that began high up the walls and extended right across the ceiling. By now he was known to some of the Swiss guards in their blue uniforms and he even merited a salute as he entered the city state by way of the Sant' Anna gate.

It was good to see Rich again and this morning the bankers, some of whom he had met at the earlier meeting, when Massoni resigned, unbuttoned their reserve and made him feel more welcome. David was grateful, but it didn't deter him from making a couple of criticisms of the investment plan they presented. In particular, he considered that the fund was dangerously exposed in shipping, and his advice was that they should reduce its commitment in that area by at least half. He recommended instead investment in the rapidly expanding Australian communications industry.

Rich had thanked him for his advice but David wasn't sure it would be heeded. Admittedly, the bankers were much more experienced in the ways of the Vatican, and in Vatican politics, than he. He didn't know how much the commission he had been appointed to had real authority or was merely a rubber-stamping body for the bankers.

Later that day Thomas announced his decision concerning the applications for relief funds he had asked for from around the world. With Rich's advice, he had decided that rather than fritter the money away on a hundred small projects, he would spend it in six areas only, where substantial amounts might produce genuine and lasting improvements.

David read the press release in Bess's office late that afternoon. He went there, up behind St Peter's, since she had been too busy to see him the night before. David leafed through the release as Bess took calls from news organizations all over the world. The six projects, and the amounts involved, were:

*$20 million for the relief of poverty and the improvement of shanty towns in South America – Brazil, Peru and Ecuador.

*$10 million for the relief of poverty and other material support for Roman Catholics in Northern Ireland.

*$20 million for the relief of suffering and other material support for the Christian homeless (not just Roman Catholics) in Lebanon.

*$10 million for the relief of poverty and other material support for Nicaraguans forced to live in Honduras as exiles from the Marxist Sandinista government.

*$10 million for the relief of poverty, provision of housing and other material support for Cuban exiles living in hardship in Florida.

*$15 million to be used to help Catholics and other Christian believers who were suffering persecution in Eastern bloc countries.

At the same time Thomas announced the appointment of a number of new cardinals, in each of the six areas to receive funds: their job would be to oversee the money and make sure it was actually turned into houses, food, clothing, sewers, books, water supplies – whatever was needed.

And finally, in a surprise move, the Holy Father also announced that he was devolving some of the Church from Rome. He was, he said, instituting a Pontifical Commission for the Americas. This would have responsibility for the activities financed by the St Patrick's fund in South, Central and North America. It would also assess the implications for the Americas of his forthcoming encyclical, *Humanae dignitae* which was to be published shortly. The headquarters of this commission would be in Rio de Janeiro, which would also become the home of the Pontifical Commission Cor Unum, the Commission for Latin America and those general commissions which did not need to be in Rome – namely, the Pontifical Council for the Family, the Commission for the Laity and the Congregation for the Causes of Saints. It was his intention, said Thomas, to make Rio de Janeiro the second home of the Church, a decision which did no more than reflect the changes that had overtaken Roman Catholicism in recent years. The Cardinal Archbishop of Rio would henceforth be known as the Patriarch of the Americas. Thomas himself would visit South America to inaugurate this second home. The cost of the transfer would be borne by the St Patrick's Fund.

David had quite a wait in Bess's office. On a matter as important as this every caller wanted to speak directly to her rather than to any of her aides. She took a short break around seven, when coffee was brought in. 'How's it going down?' he asked.

She made a face. 'Difficult to be sure. Reporters who ask picky questions are often on your side over the main issues, whereas those who give you an easy ride over the phone go for you later in print.'

'But you must get *some* feel from the tone of their reactions.'

'A bit. Thomas is very popular in South America – I guess you'd expect that. Beirut, too. Obviously there's no reaction from the Eastern bloc. The two areas I'm not sure about, funnily enough, are Florida and Northern Ireland.' She stretched. 'Still, we'll know soon enough.'

The phone calls went on throughout the evening but at ten sharp Bess called it a day. She had been in her job long enough now to know that if you didn't have some kind of guillotine, being the Pope's press secretary and confidante could easily take you over completely.

David had persuaded her to accompany him to L'Eau Vive and they both squeezed into a taxi, as it was late and they were both too tired to walk. The restaurant was very full and the first person they saw as they settled at their table was the British apostolic delegate, Jasper Hale. He came over.

'What do you think of today's news?' said David. 'Bess has been on the phone to the world all day and even she's not sure.'

'That's one of the reasons I'm here,' Hale said. 'To give the Holy Father some idea of what I think the reaction to his plans will be in Britain.'

'Oh yes? What did you tell him?' David took some menus from a passing waitress.

'To expect some opposition from the British. Northern Ireland is very easily inflamed – though he doesn't need me to tell him that. Another Irish cardinal was *not* a good idea, not in my view. It merely attracts attention to the Catholic presence.'

'And why else are you here?' said David. 'You said you had more than one reason for being in Rome.'

'Ah, yes. More advice for the Pope, I'm afraid. You may know that he's reviewing the church's attitude to divorce. Any liberalization will be very popular in Britain and Ireland – and in Europe and America, come to that. But there's a rumour that a big group of bishops want to stop him. They're gaining ground, so a few of us are here to make sure the Holy Father doesn't lose his nerve.'


After Hale's bombshell, Bess and David spent a distraught night together. David would have liked to remain in Rome a few days while Bess found out what truth there was to the rumour, but he had to get back to London. The Royal sale needed attention, as did the Israeli Dead Sea Scrolls auction, now scheduled to take place in New York. The Argyll sale was due soon and there was also the more humdrum, everyday business of Hamilton's, which was still David's responsibility. It even looked as though he might be making progress again in his attempt to solve the mystery surrounding Leonardo's two 'Virgin of the Rocks'. The Urbino documents he had requested when he and Bess had visited the town had now arrived. The Rimini letters were no help, but the other papers included a hitherto unknown 1489 letter from Isabella d'Este, in Mantua, arising out of the marriage of her sister-in-law, Elisabetta Gonzaga, to Guidobaldo, duke of Urbino. The letter ran: 'Please accept this beautiful painting on the occasion of your marriage to the esteemed Guidobaldo. I have two pictures by Leonardo, one a pastel, one an oil, and I could not make up my mind which to give to

146

you. The oil I own to be the finer and it is now yours. May it give you as much pleasure as I hope your marriage to the duke will.'

David knew that when the Urbino collection had been broken up, in the seventeenth century, no picture by Leonardo had found its way either to Rome or to Florence, where everything else had gone. Several items went missing – that was known. Now, it seemed, a Leonardo had been among them. There was a meeting of the Renaissance Society soon; he would be able to present another paper.

Much as he might enjoy the private world of scholarship, however, the Vatican and Royal sales and the role he now played in the St Patrick's Fund, meant that David was becoming public property. Reading the newspapers, once a pleasure, now became a chore. He had to know how Thomas and his plans were regarded. In general, the Holy Father's decision on how to use the money he had raised met with approval. Probably the strongest objection had come from none other than Michael Greener, who had at last been promoted to Secretary of State for Northern Ireland. Sarah's civil divorce had come through – on the grounds that her marriage break-up was irretrievable – and Greener and she were to be married very soon. Following the Holy Father's announcement, Greener had made a statement in the House of Commons. He said: 'Naturally, Her Majesty's Government welcomes any aid, material or otherwise, and from whatever source. We are bound to note, however, that since in some places the Holy Father's plans are designed to help all Christians and not just Catholics, the provisions in His Holiness's Northern Ireland scheme, whereby only Catholics benefit, are provocative, to say the least.

'This is merely a comment by Her Majesty's Government, however. We have made no formal approach to the Holy See since, as I said at the beginning of this statement, we do on the whole welcome the aid.'

Other reservations had come from the American government in response to the Pope's aid to Nicaraguan exiles in Honduras. Though neither Nicaragua nor Honduras was part of the US, the State Department nonetheless regarded that part of the world as its back yard. The US Secretary of State, Erwin Friedlander, and Roskill, the President, welcomed the grant, especially as Thomas, by his grants elsewhere, had shown himself implacably opposed to the Marxism practised by the Sandinistas in Nicaragua. However, the American statement, made in response to Thomas' plans, concluded with the words: 'We shall watch the situation with interest.'

The Italians, of course, were against Thomas's plans, mainly – on this occasion – because they did not want *his* foreign policy confused with theirs, or, more likely, to overshadow it. But by this time the Italian government was so discredited in terms of aid programmes that not much attention was paid to these grumblings.

Among the British press David was interested to see that *The Econ-*

*omist* took an independent line. The paper welcomed the shift of certain departments of the Vatican to Rio. It agreed with the Holy Father that this did no more than reflect changes in the Church that had already taken place. But it was more cautious where the St Patrick's Fund was concerned. It pointed out that, throughout the 1970s, the financial dealings of the Roman Church had been disastrous. Its investments had been misappropriated, corruption had been rife. The relief of poverty was an admirable aim, said the paper, but a world leader like Thomas had to exercise caution and a wide-ranging sense of responsibility. Here, David was interested to see, the paper agreed with him, arguing that the investment profile of the St Patrick's Fund, so far as it had been revealed, was far from ideal. The article concluded by saying that the Pope might well find, a year from now, that he did not have the funds to continue what he had started and that he ought perhaps to have waited a year to ensure that the fund was performing up to expectations.

It was a good piece of journalism, David told himself. Thoughtful, unsensational, useful. Rare.

The news from Bess in Rome was vague. Either what Hale had told them was exaggerated because he wanted to stop what was afoot, or the opposition to Thomas was, for the moment, keeping a low profile. The Holy Father himself had told Bess that while representations *had* been made to him by a few bishops, it was still his intention to go ahead with the encyclical.

The Renaissance Society meeting came and went. Fortunately, it was held in Pisa on the weekend when Sarah and Greener were married. David was happy to be out of the way. His paper was a success – he called it 'The Lost Leonardo?' Bess joined him in Pisa for just one night and they had dinner with the usual Society members – Townshend from the Fogg, Shirikin from the Hermitage and so on. Bess too seemed to enjoy the company of scholars, and they themselves appreciated the odd tit-bit of Vatican gossip she was able to mix into the conversation. She also managed to find an unusual pipe for the Holy Father. 'You never know,' she told David. 'He might feel like a change from those dreadful cigarettes one day. This is a hint, from me.' They both laughed.

The break primed David nicely for the exhibition of royal pictures, at the Queen's Gallery in Buckingham Palace Road, which was to precede the royal sale. Opened by Her Majesty, it turned out to be quite an occasion.

The art establishment was there, led by Sir Christopher Bentham, director of the British Museum, and Madeleine Hall, the small, strange woman who ran the Victoria & Albert. The arts in general were represented by David Sloane, the opinionated manager of Covent Garden, Ian Coleridge, director general of the BBC, Richard Amery, the fancy publisher. Cultured business types, investment bankers and fund managers, looked sleeker than the rest, with younger, blonder wives.

David surveyed the pictures. Though he was unhappy with Seton's choice of paintings to be sold, he could still admire them as works of art. His favourite, he thought, was the small Cranach drawing of 'St George and the Dragon'.

'Good bash,' barked a voice, interrupting this reverie.

David turned to see Edward Lister, the new director of the British Heritage Preservation Trust, a man he did not know at all well. 'Thank you,' he said. 'Let me get you a drink.' He signalled to a waiter who brought champagne. 'Some fine pictures – eh?' said David generally.

Lister eyed him over the glass and didn't reply.

'Something wrong?'

'I don't know,' said Lister. 'I just thought we should have a word. We don't know each other very well – I'm new in this job, after all.' He paused. 'Look, I've been a great admirer of what the Pope's been doing – and your role in it. Very good for Britain, all that business. And I'm a banker, as perhaps you know. But – '

'But – ?' David looked at him sharply.

' – it's only fair to say that some of our members are not so happy . . .'

'What do you mean?'

Lister gazed awkwardly down into his glass. 'Well, the Pope's sale was one thing. That earthquake was such a tragedy . . . it was a master-stroke to sell the Raphael. And the other sales, too – brilliant . . . But, you know, the Pope is a law unto himself – literally – isn't he? He has his own state so he is the owner of all the art. Now this sale, the Queen's sale, is rather different – '

'Is it?' David interjected sharply. 'How? In what way? The collection is Her Majesty's own private property.'

'Yes, yes.' Lister looked uncomfortable. 'But . . . some of our members feel that the Queen doesn't really have the right to sell off these pictures. They were acquired by several monarchs, all of whom received substantial funds from the state. Even if the pictures were not in fact bought with state money, but with the royal family's private income, the state undeniably helped to keep the royal collectors in a manner which made their connoisseurship possible.'

David looked hard at Lister, trying to guess what was going on behind those grey, expressionless banker's eyes. 'Is . . . is this a warning?'

'Warning is too strong a word. I am simply saying, as politely as I can, since you are one of my hosts here, that there are some – *some* – members of the British Heritage Preservation Trust who may try to disrupt this sale. Put brutally they think the Third World should look after itself and we should hang on to what is ours.' He laid a hand on

David's arm and went on quickly. 'These are minority voices at the moment and raised only in private discussion. I cannot pretend, however, that they will not get louder, more insistent. Why am I telling you this? So that you may prepare your defence and Her Majesty will not be embarrassed. I would not like to see a battle between our trust and Buckingham Palace. No one would win.' He made to move off. 'So you see what I'm saying, Mr Colwyn. Not a warning; just putting you in the picture. I hope you don't think me impolite.' And he drifted discreetly away, back into the melée.

David let him go. He was worried and wanted to think. First the warning from Paul Clegg on behalf of the government, now this. If the BHPT ever found out that the Prime Minister was against the sale, Hamilton's would be drawn into the biggest controversy in the art world for years. He had been sharp with Lister because he had half-expected this kind of reaction all along. Damn. Nor was that all. While a rumpus involving the Queen threatened in London, a different kind of trouble loomed in New York. David also received word from his Jerusalem office that orthodox Jews from Israel had threatened to disrupt the sale of Dead Sea Scrolls authorized by the Knesset. It looked like a rough ride ahead.

The news about Thomas's trip to Beirut hit David like an ambush. He woke up one morning to find the radio and newspaper correspondents as astounded as he was. There had been no warning for him from Bess, though she had accompanied Thomas. It was to be a brief visit – two days – but in that time the Pope would meet everyone on the Christian side who mattered. He travelled late at night, arriving in the Lebanon just as dawn broke. Only after he had landed safely was the world's press alerted, by Bess's number two, back in Rome. To begin with no one could be sure whether Thomas was foolhardy, or brave. But, by the time the press caught up with him, the mythmaking was already in operation.

The Holy Father had come to see for himself how the twenty million dollars would be spent in this, the most war-torn of areas. Like that other American religious leader who had visited war zones, Cardinal Spellman, he did not arrive in flowing robes, but instead wore battle fatigues: that was a picture worth a few magazine covers at least. He saw the rubble for himself, visited Christian strongholds, met with the leaders of the various factions and discussed their aims and needs. He baptized babies born in bomb shelters, he blessed older children orphaned by the killings, he visited hospitals and clinics to comfort the wounded. He even visited an apartment block which had been shelled by Muslims only hours before and he was present when the bodies were brought out. Seeing one of the rescue workers stumble, Thomas went to help him pull the corpse from the ruins. Then, when a cry

150

went up that someone under the block was still alive, Thomas organized the digging. It took over an hour but when a seven-year-old boy, frightened and tearful though otherwise whole, was pulled out from the wreckage, the picture of His Holiness posing, smiling with the rescue team and enjoying a celebratory cigarette dominated the newscasts.

Security was tight. The Muslims would not allow such a great propaganda coup for the Christians to pass off without retaliation. The shelling of Christian areas during the night Thomas spent in Beirut was particularly heavy.

It was deep into that night when Bess called David.

'I'm sorry I couldn't tell you anything. But it was too risky – we might have been overheard on the phone.'

David was too delighted to hear her voice, and too relieved, to be churlish about that or the fact that it was one o'clock in the morning, 4.00 am in Beirut. 'Is it as bad as it sounds from all the newsreels?'

'Worse. I'm terrified and I think it was a mistake to come – and to put money into this place. It's chaos.'

'But Thomas himself is a great success. This trip was an extraordinarily brave undertaking. Some people are saying he should win the Nobel Peace Prize this year.'

'You may think so, the world may think so. Officially, *I* think so. We're all fool – '

The line had been cut then and Bess was unable to call back. David lay awake for another hour but the phone didn't ring.

Bess was wrong about Thomas's trip being a mistake. The world likes few things more than a man of peace dressed up as a warrior: there *is* a sort of contentment in action, especially if that action is vicarious. The Pope was praised for his bravery and the west, which for years had put up grudgingly with Islamic moral righteousness, relished his forthright action. His departure from Beirut was as secret as his arrival had been, and after his return to Rome, Thomas announced details of how the twenty million dollars would be spent. Essentially, he planned a fund in Beirut not unlike the one he had set up in Sicily, an informers' fund, but this time money would be paid to people who provided useful information about Muslim terrorists. Thomas had concluded, he said, that intelligence was the most important commodity in Beirut and that although certain clinics and schools would be funded the best support he could offer Christians in Lebanon was aid with information. That held out the best prospect for a just and lasting settlement.

Bess called David as soon as she returned to Rome.

'Thank God, you're safe,' he said. 'I waited up the other night but obviously you couldn't call back. And I didn't know how to reach you.'

'We were shelled! David, it was real scary – '

'Poor Bess. I felt so bloody useless, trying to give comfort on the phone, thousands of miles away.'

'But I didn't call for comfort, David. I called to tell you something very important, but we got cut off before I could say it.'

Something in her voice warned him to be prepared for bad news.

'I talked to Thomas on the flight out to Beirut. We had a long chat. Hale was right, David. Thomas *has* changed his mind on divorce. He has decided not to allow it. Oh, David! What a mess! Where does that leave *us?*'

# 8

The two brothers sat quietly, smoking and staring out to sea. Without a moon you could barely see the waves breaking on the reef but, despite the wind, you could hear them, a disembodied roar, sounding angrier than they really were. It had become a habit for Rodriguez and Pablo Portillo to sit on, late into the night after their bar had closed. They had by far the most successful drinking establishment on their stretch of the Baia de Guadiana, near the western end of Cuba, the only place for miles around where ships of any size could get in through the reef. Even sailing ships came in during the day for lunch and the brothers' famous rum cocktail, ironically dubbed a 'Battista' on the grounds that, like the island's notorious dictator, the drink 'destroys anyone in thirty days'.

The two brothers ran the bar together. Tonight had been very busy, with a lot of people in the area for President Castro's visit to the local town tomorrow to open a new agricultural research station. Only now, at two thirty in the morning, had the last customers drunk up and left. José and Sandoz had counted the money taken during the evening, paid the staff and, satisfied, were enjoying local cigars and imported brandy.

The brothers were not interested in Castro or politics. Outside the bar football and fishing were their main loves. They were discussing their plan to go looking for barracuda later in the week when suddenly Pablo, the elder of the two, a bony, slow-moving, grey-haired man, raised his head. 'Was that a boat?'

Rodriguez, younger, darker, fatter, tapped his cigar ash into an empty coffee cup. 'Not at this hour, surely.'

They both listened anxiously. The reef here was treacherous and they hated shipwrecks: shipwrecks were bad for business. They could hear nothing, only the swishing of the wind thickening the roar of the reef. The wind gusted, paused and, in that pause, they both heard it: the deep chug of an outboard motor.

'They don't seem very far out, do they?' said Pablo. 'Must be close to the reef.' The channel through the reef hereabouts was large and

153

could be clearly seen during the day. At night, however, the passage was a different matter – unless of course you had sonar which very few small-boat owners could afford.

The brothers went on smoking, expecting the engine noise to fade.

It didn't. 'You know, I think it's coming in,' said Pablo. This was odd since, apart from the danger, their bar was the only building on the bay and its lights had been put out hours ago. More, there was a fishing port only four kilometres down the coast where fuel and provisions could be found.

As both men stared into the blackness trying to locate the boat, a light suddenly flashed on and raked the beach. As it snapped off the boat's engine also died. Pablo got to his feet. 'Come on. They were lucky, getting through the reef. But they may need our help.'

Rodriguez rose also but hung back warily. 'Why didn't they keep their beam on? If they're in trouble it would have helped them land.'

'Battery trouble maybe. We'll find out soon enough. But that reminds me: we should take a light.' He went to the bar and returned with a bright red torch.

They reached the beach and to walk more easily in the sand, took off their shoes. As they trudged towards that part of the beach where the boat had flashed its light the wind whipped particles of sand into their faces. The boat, when they came to it, was visible in the moonlight and lay anchored about thirty metres off-shore. It was about twenty metres long and resembled the lifeboat of a large liner. It obviously had a powerful engine.

The brothers stood where a rubber dinghy was pulled up out of the water, and a mass of untidy, disturbed sand showed where the occupants had headed into the trees at the back of the beach.

Pablo switched on the torch. 'Hallo!' he cried. 'Anyone there? Anyone need help? Hallo?' He moved forward towards the trees, keeping his torch on. Rodriguez followed a few paces behind. When they reached the trees Pablo shouted again. He could see a path of sorts before him. 'Hallo! If you want our bar you're going in the wrong direction? Can you hear me? That's the wrong way – '

Before Pablo could finish, the torch was knocked from his hand, his arms were pinned to his side and the hard metal barrel of a gun was shoved against his neck.

'Can you hear *me*?' said a harsh voice. 'If you so much as sweat, your brains will kiss the sky.'

Luis enjoyed the road to Guane. In his job he didn't often get the chance to put his foot down. Driving for the President as likely as not meant idling the car forward in some parade or other where the chief hazard was running over the guard of honour's feet. This was different; this was motoring.

The road from Havana to the western tip of Cuba was one of the island's better highways and, early on a Sunday morning, was empty enough to enable the motorcade to speed along at one hundred kmph. There were five cars, with Luis and the President in the second. Luis, Ramon – his deputy in the front car – and Lorenzo picking up the rear, had all been on what was called a defensive driving course in Moscow. What a week that had been! Luis had never expected the Russians to drink like that! They were worse than the Spanish.

The sun shone brilliantly over his left shoulder. It had been the usual early start and they would be in Guane by nine-thirty for breakfast with the mayor. The latest road sign had said that the town was twenty-five kilometres away. After breakfast the President would be doing what he liked best, opening some technological facility. Luis knew his charge well. Castro was especially proud of Cuban medicine which had achieved miracles in reducing child mortality, in dentistry, and in basic surgery. Cuban doctors had been exported to Jamaica, Angola, Nicaragua. But the President was proud too of the way Cuban agriculture was progressing and that did not just mean the growing of tobacco. Since the collapse of the sugar industry following the President's take-over, part of it had been rebuilt, and the rest of the land had been utilized for cattle ranching, orange groves or, more recently, for rice. Cuban scientists had been particularly adept at developing new strains of rice to suit the island's conditions. It was an agricultural research station which the President was to open this morning so he was in a good mood, looking forward to the ceremony.

The motorcade swept into a gorge. This wasn't Luis' part of the island but he guessed they must now be close to the Martinez river, with the spindly mountains of the Pinar del Rio beyond the gorge. Ramon in the lead car slowed now as the road through the gorge began to twist. Luis reflected that, in his job, beautiful scenery was nearly always a security risk. He looked in the rear view mirror. The President was talking with his senior secretary, Pino. The bodyguard sat on a jump seat reading a newspaper.

They came to the end of the gorge, an area where spray from a waterfall made the road very wet. The cars slowed still further. Luis turned his head to admire the falls and so missed the explosion. He felt the blast an instant before he heard it and by then his eyes were already turning back to look ahead. Ramon had hit a mine. Luis saw the car lift off the ground, horribly mangled amid the brown smoke that almost engulfed it.

'Move!' shouted the bodyguard. 'Move!'

Easier said than done. The front car had left the road in a somersault, but then had flopped back on to the highway on its side and was blocking the way forward. Luis glanced in the rear view mirror again. There appeared to be no one behind him in the car: the President and

Pino were on the floor with the bodyguard on top of them. The other cars in the motorcade prevented an escape in that direction.

He looked ahead again. He could get round the carcass of the front car if he drove off the road and into the mud. But perhaps that was what his ambushers wanted. Still, there was no time to reflect. He had been taught in Moscow to accelerate where the natural reaction was to brake and indeed he was already picking up speed. The near side of the car slid off the road and he felt his control start to go. Almost without thinking, his right hand grabbed the lever which engaged the four-wheel drive. At exactly that moment the machine guns started, a chilling cough from somewhere up behind his head. In theory the car was bullet proof. Bullets rattled against the car, and for a moment Luis panicked as he felt the wheels slither on the mud. If he stopped now they'd all be dead. But his training took over and the car surged forward. The rear slewed round as he cleared the overturned car and pulled back on to the highway. For a moment the whole of the car's left side was exposed to the attackers. Another storm of bullets spattered against the car. Luis turned the wheel. Miraculously none of the tyres was hit and the response of the car was good. Luis picked up speed again. Guare, he saw from a sign, was fifteen kilometres away.

He reached for his radiophone and switched to the emergency frequency. The army would have a helicopter on the scene immediately. It had obviously been a serious error not to have one overhead all the time. Now, back to one hundred kmph, he allowed himself a look in the rear view mirror. It was frosted where it had been hit by machine gun bullets and on the left side it had actually been punched through by the force of the attack. Luis pressed the switch to lower the glass partition between him and the men in the back. Thankfully that still worked.

'Everyone all right?' he asked. 'Or shall I call for an ambulance?'

There was a pause, then the President said: 'No point. I'm unharmed. And poor Pino's dead.'

David reached Ned in the hospital in Southampton late on Sunday night, and before Sarah. She had been in Northern Ireland, with her new husband.

By the time she arrived, Ned was asleep, heavily sedated.

'He was very lucky,' said the doctor who had first greeted David and showed him to the ward. 'He was seen by two young scientists from the University of Reading who are studying the ecology of weirs. They were in a boat by the bank, below the weir, collecting routine water samples. Even so, they might not have seen him but for the fact that he made a mistake, or overlooked something. His trousers were firmly tucked into his boots, and held in place by a lot of stones which he meant to weight himself down with. But that trapped air in his trousers all the more securely and it was that which prevented him from sinking. We think your son jumped from one of the bridges but cracked his head on the weir as he went over – there's a nasty bruise behind his ear. Very impressive, those young zoologists,' continued the doctor. 'One ran for help while the other got the water out of your son's lungs. Between them they saved the boy's life.'

David stared at his son. He looked so helpless lying in the hospital bed, his bandaged head pathetically small on the pillows. 'Is he out of danger?'

'Physically – oh yes. I've seen far worse. How he'll be psychologically I can't say. This can't have been an accident, you know.'

'I know,' said David quietly. 'The school told me he was depressed but I didn't believe them. He seemed so – well, so cheerful when he was with me.'

'Children in broken marriages often do that, to protect the parents,' said the doctor. 'I'm not a psychiatrist but as soon as I finish my general training paediatrics is going to be my speciality.' Tactfully he left David at Ned's bedside.

When Sarah arrived, she had her new husband with her. David kissed her cheek and shook his hand.

'Would you prefer it if I waited outside?' Greener said.

Sarah answered quickly: 'Just for a few moments, Michael, please. Yes.'

'That's thoughtful of him,' said David, after Greener had gone.

'Not all politicians are ogres, you know.' She stood for a moment by the bed. Her face softened and saddened. Under her eyes, the shadows deepened. David noticed a pulse beat at her temple. 'Poor mite. What do you suppose went on inside his head, to make him do this?'

'He'll never tell us. But obviously the signs were there. You yourself said he was a "pain" in Switzerland. I blame myself. I saw one of his teachers at a rugby game: he told me Ned needed treatment. I moved too slowly. I didn't move at all. Do you know, he even weighted himself down? . . . he put stones in his pockets before he jumped.'

She sighed. 'I suppose you're right. The signs were there. But lots of parents get divorced, David, and although their children don't like it, they don't try to kill themselves either. Why us? Why Ned?'

'I *do* have the name of a psychiatrist who could treat him. I did get that far.'

'Is that necessary?'

'Well, we can't deny what Ned's done. He's bright, he's sensitive, he must have been very lonely, shuttling between you and me.'

'I know that. I just don't know whether I believe all that psychiatrists' jargon. Who is this psychiatrist anyway? Who recommended him?'

David told her Bess had.

'Tell me about her. Ned mentioned her once or twice. Isn't it a bit difficult? You being divorced legally but not in the eyes of the Church. What are you going to do?'

'I just don't know. Bess is a modern American girl, as well as a Catholic – that's why she's so good at her job. But that also makes her position . . . sensitive.'

'Can't you get your marriage – our marriage – dissolved in some way?'

David turned towards her, pleased that she was so sympathetic. 'I've thought about it, but how? There's no doubt you and I *were* married.' He looked at Ned, still sleeping. 'It was consummated. That's that.'

'But is it? I thought there were ways, if you knew the right people. In her position, Bess must know the right people. She talks to the Pope himself, for Christ's sake. David! This isn't like you. Normally, you'd exhaust every possibility to get what you want. That's how you found the Bernini, remember? And the Raphael. If you want her, and it sounds as if you do, you'll find a way. What does she say?'

'We're avoiding each other at the moment. It's too painful.'

'Well, my advice is this. Make an appointment for Ned with this psychiatrist Bess has suggested. Then find someone in authority here, a cardinal say, and try to get our marriage dissolved. I'm sure you can do it. You need a kick up the pants. Now, shall we get Michael in here?'

'Why don't we go out to the corridor? In case we wake Ned.'

Greener was sitting on a bench, quietly going through a swatch of official papers. Down the corridor his ministerial bodyguard was alert.

Greener said. 'If there's any help – '

'No,' Sarah replied. 'David thinks we should send Ned to a psychiatrist when he's recovered physically, and I think I agree. We'll stay for a few hours, Michael, so we're both here when he wakes up. There's no need for you to wait though, if you want to get back to London. You've a busy week ahead.'

Greener was relaxed and David could see what Sarah liked in him. He was on her side and was obviously very comforting.

'There's no hurry,' Greener said, 'but there *is* a canteen just down the corridor. I'll bet you're both as hungry as I am. The nurse told me Ned won't wake up for a couple of hours at least. Why don't we have a sandwich and a hot drink, then I'll go back to town and leave you two here.'

It was a sound idea and the three of them were soon installed in the hospital canteen with toast and coffee between them. The bodyguard sat at the next table. David found he warmed to Greener by the minute.

'Are you enjoying your promotion?' asked David.

'No one *enjoys* Northern Ireland,' smiled Greener. 'It's dangerous and very hard work dealing with two sides as well-entrenched as the Ulster Protestants and the IRA. But someone has to do it and I hope it will

158

mean bigger things later on.' He munched some toast. 'Your Pope's fund isn't going to help, of course.'

'Yes, I read what you said in the House about that. Weren't you a bit ungrateful? The Catholics *have* been badly treated, over the years. It's no bad thing to redress the imbalance a bit, surely?'

'I admit I may have sounded churlish,' said Greener. 'But a fund like that, in the atmosphere of Northern Ireland, becomes just another stick for one side to beat the other with. It will end badly, David. I feel it in my water.'

'And how do you feel about the Queen's sale? I've already been warned by Paul Clegg that the PM doesn't like it. What's your view?'

Greener looked at him. 'Yes – and the only reason the Prime Minister hasn't made more of a fuss is that we are behind in the opinion polls. To take on the Queen *and* the Opposition is too much, even for him. But if he can't get at Her Majesty, David, he's quite capable of hurting you instead.'

'Oh? What do you mean?'

'The Argyll sale, for instance. Young Argyll wants a seat in the Commons. The PM's promised him the next safe one – provided he transfers the sale from you to Steele's.'

Greener was right. David heard officially the next day that the Argyll family were withdrawing their commission to Hamilton's and transferring it to Steele's. He was very angry. Apart from the time and expense he and his staff had put in, which included identifying the lost Salvator Rosa, these kinds of houses coming on to the market were the chief source of Hamilton's profits in normal years. To lose one in this way was very damaging.

In the middle of all the fuss, however, and the sensational aftermath of the attempt on President Castro's life, David still found time to make two personal phone calls. One was to Anthony Wilde, the psychiatrist Bess had recommended, to fix an appointment. Ned had been very weak and frightened when he had woken up, full of anxiety and remorse. Sarah had stayed overnight at the hospital, and then had taken him home with her for a few days.

David's second call was to Jasper Hale. The apostolic delegate was delighted to hear from him and, in reply to David's request, invited him over that evening. It took a couple of whisky and sodas before David could bring the conversation round to where he wanted it, but eventually he said: 'Monsignor Hale – Jasper – I would like your help.'

Immediately Hale fell silent, ready to listen.

David explained his relationship with Bess and how the Pope's change of mind had placed him in a dilemma. He told Hale not just the facts but found that, with this man, he could also discuss his feelings. Hale, who began by simply listening, later started to scribble a few notes on a pad in front of him. 'So there it is,' David concluded. 'Unless we can find some loophole in canon law, we've had it. I'm told you are, or were, a canon lawyer. I wondered if you could help.'

For a moment Hale said nothing. Then, 'How much canon law do you know, David?'

'Very little. None.'

Hale tapped the pencil on his pad. 'Essentially there are two types of case where a marriage may be ended. I use the word "ended" advisedly. There is no divorce in the Catholic Church – and there are no "loopholes", as you put it, in cannon law. Either a marriage may be annulled, because it was invalid to start with, or it may be dissolved by the Holy Father himself for certain – very rare – reasons. There seems no reason to doubt that your marriage was perfectly valid. I take it the priest was a real priest, there were two witnesses, both you and Sarah freely entered into marriage, and understood what it all meant?'

'Yes.'

'And you have a child?'

'A boy.'

'Hmmm. So annulment is out.' He scribbled some more on his pad. 'Give me Sarah's full name, and your own. And the dates and places of birth.'

David told him.

Hale finished scribbling. 'I'll be frank. It doesn't look good. As you yourself say, you were properly married, happily married, and you consummated your marriage. Neither of you is, or has ever been, insane. I'm afraid that unless one or two very unusual circumstances apply, there is absolutely no way that, in the eyes of the Church, your marriage to Sarah can be dissolved.'

'What special circumstances are you talking about?'

'There's no point in me telling you because they might get your hopes up and in fact they're so rare as to be almost non-existent. But leave this with me for a while. I'll get back to you as soon as I can.'

As he showed David out, Hale said, 'I expect Elizabeth is as upset as you are, eh? And now she has the Castro business on top of everything. Terrible. Send her my love when you speak to her – but don't hold out any hope that I can help. I'll do my best but I can't promise.'

On the way home David bought an evening paper. Hale was right, the Castro business *had* become an additional burden on Bess. The arrest of the eight would-be assassins, charged with the murder of Castro's secretary and the attempted murder of the President himself, had been reported about a week before. Now David read that the eight had also been charged with killing two brothers, who kept a beach bar near where the raid had taken place. The two men had obviously disturbed their clandestine arrival. Inevitably, Castro was using the occasion to make anti-US propaganda, especially since it turned out that the eight had sailed in from Florida. But most people had expected that anyway.

Now, however, the *Miami Tribune* had published the results of its investigation into the affair.

The paper had good contacts among the Cuban exiles in Florida and its report centred around the activities of a construction company, Matahambre, which had been subcontracted to build twenty-seven houses under the Pope's St Patrick's Fund. The project had gone ahead smoothly and on schedule, approved all along the line. It now emerged, however, that there had been slight modifications: walls were thinner than they should have been, the yards and even the hot water tanks were smaller than the official specifications. The result was that the company had been able to skim off ten per cent of costs. A chunk of which had gone to the quantity surveyor whose job it was to ensure that exactly this sort of thing didn't happen.

Further enquiries by the paper showed that it was the Matahambre directors who had paid for the boat used by Castro's would-be assassins.

The most damning evidence, however, was the cash found on the captives themselves. The numbers on the banknotes tallied exactly with the numbers on the notes issued to a Matahambre director from two banks in Orlando ten days before the night-time invasion. As the *Tribune* itself was the first to point out, the money could have passed through a dozen hands between being withdrawn from the bank and reaching Cuba in the captives' pockets. But no one believed that it had. The reading public, and that included politicians around the world, knew what the *Tribune* knew: the link was there, direct and real, whatever a clever lawyer might make of it.

To begin with, Bess managed to keep the lid on things so far as the Holy Father was concerned. Obviously, His Holiness knew nothing of the invasion plans, she told every reporter who followed up the *Tribune*'s lead. The local funds were in the care of the cardinal whom Thomas had appointed, who had his own advisory committee made up of local church dignitaries. In the Vatican, Cardinal Rich was the man who had overall responsibility for the fund, and he too knew nothing about the affair. Bess took the line that what had happened was a regrettable but straigthforward criminal scam. There were political overtones, it was true, but there was no evidence that even the local cardinal knew anything about the 'adventure'. His recall to Rome was simply a sign that His Holiness was eager to hear for himself what had happened.

Bess also announced the Pope's view, that *if* it was proved to the Holy Father's satisfaction that the Church's funds had been misappropriated, then although the cuplrits would be sought, and prosecuted, still His Holiness's main concern was with the poor. So the financial shortfall, if there was any, would be made good from the emergency contingency fund in the Vatican.

It was an adroit move. It said in effect: the Holy Father was strong enough to take knocks without being deflected from his main aims.

And it might have worked had not Castro himself decided to go to New York to address the United Nations.

The main assembly hall was packed for the occasion, and he did not disappoint them. He strode to the lectern in his familiar fatigues, as if he'd just been fighting a bush fire. It was some time since anyone had seen him – he hardly travelled these days. His beard was greyer but every bit as bushy as they remembered. All his virility was still there.

He stood, while the applause lasted, neither smiling nor acknowledging the meeting. After it died away, he waited like a good actor for the silence to take command. He had everyone's attention.

Slowly, deliberately, he raised his right arm. His hand held a bulky sheaf of white paper. The United States ambassador to the UN turned to his deputy and whispered, 'If that's what I think it is, the shit's about to hit the fan.'

'This,' boomed Castro, his Spanish lilt big and buccaneering, 'is a contract.' He paused, slamming the document down in front of him on the lectern. 'A contract between Cuba and the United States of America.'

'No!' breathed the American ambassador. 'Please God, no.'

'This contract,' continued Castro, 'is agreement between our two countries. Despite our differences, Cuba has always allowed the United States to maintain its naval military base at Guantanamo Bay. We had no choice. Under an old – a very old – agreement, provided it paid two million dollars a year, the USA could keep its marines on Cuban soil. But for the past six months Americans and Cubans have been negotiating a new agreement.' He tapped the contract. 'To last for ten years. Under this agreement America keeps its base and in return Cuba will receive – ' and in an entirely unnecessary flourish he pulled his spectacles from his pocket and opened the contract as if to read. 'Two point four billion dollars.'

He looked up and over the top of his glasses. Suddenly he slapped the lectern with the open palm of his hand. 'Not now!' he bellowed. 'Not now! This contract remains unsigned.' Dramatically, he shoved the papers to one side so that they fell off the lectern and slumped to the floor. Press cameras clicked to capture this theatrical gesture. The more enterprising also focused on the American ambassador. He looked furious and embarrassed.

'Cuba may be a poor country by American, by western, standards. But we are an honest country.' Castro slapped the lectern again. 'We will not negotiate with liars, with murderers, with assassins. With people who give money and asylum to brigands, tawdry exiles who enjoy nothing more than midnight adventures with weapons and boats

162

and other people's money.' He glared around the hall. 'I am going back to Cuba tonight. Straight away. I would not wish to sleep in a country where murderers breed so easily, where religious leaders, so-called, mix politics with worship. But I came here today to tell Americans – the west – three things.' Again he paused. Reaching for a glass of water with one hand, he raised the other hand aloft, a single finger extended.

'One!' he bellowed. 'The United States is, as from today, given notice to quit Guantanamo Bay on 31st December next year. We want every ship, every marine, every hamburger, every American cornflake OUT! Or we shall attack American forces on Cuban soil.'

'Two! The Cuban representative to the Holy See is withdrawn. The Catholic nuncio in Havana is expelled.

'Three! Cuba's diplomatic relations with Italy are severed as from this moment. We cannot – will not – do business with a government that harbours and nourishes such reactionary forces on its soil.'

The spectacles went back into his pocket and he said more quietly, 'My secretary was killed in the attempt to murder me. You didn't know him like I did so you won't miss him as much. But I'll let you into a secret. Pino was about to leave his job with me. I had tried to stop him but he was determined. He intended to become a priest.'

At the beginning of his Presidency, James Roskill had not enjoyed the Tuesday press briefings at the White House. Many journalists were frighteningly well-informed. Also, they had a way of putting questions that riled him – and they seemed to enjoy that. However, the balance of the meetings had now changed, as the President grew more skilled and as his political successes made him more relaxed. He knew the journalists better, too, he could joke with them and he knew the simple power of referring to a bumptious pressman by his first name.

The Tuesday after the Castro performance at the UN was clear if none too warm, but Roskill liked that. As he walked to the briefing he felt confident and not a little aggressive. He knew he looked a young sixty-three, energetic but experienced, too.

As he entered the room all the journalists rose, for the office if not the man. Roskill was wearing a dark blue suit and a knitted woollen tie and in his hand he carried several sheets of paper.

As they sat the journalists muttered expectantly to one another. They knew what those papers in Roskill's hands meant. This was no routine briefing. The President was going to make a formal statement.

He placed the papers on the lectern, looked up and smiled at his audience, nodding to one or two people in particular. That old vaudeville trick never failed. 'Ladies and gentlemen,' he said and, as he did so, he raised the papers and held them high above his head, just as Castro had done at the UN. 'Ladies and gentlemen,' he now repeated. 'This is *the* contract. Yesterday, President Castro of Cuba, who is not a democratically elected leader, trashed this contract on American soil, soil that we gave to the United Nations in the hope that it would aid peace.' He took the sheets of paper, turned them, and made as if to tear them. 'No,' he said. 'No. Until the attempt on President Castro's life all that was needed on this contract was his signature and mine. It was an important contract for both countries. For the west and for peace. And it still is. For Cuba it provides aid – schools, hospitals, roads, barns, houses. There is a clause which ensures that the US will buy several million Havana cigars every year, a cause dear to my own heart.' He patted his breast pocket where the tips of two cigars peeked out. 'For the United States there is a guarantee that we shall keep our base in Guantanamo Bay well into the twenty-first century.

'President Castro trashed his copy – or maybe it was a photocopy – because he believed that the US government, in concert with a team of thugs funded by the Vatican, had attempted to kill him. That is not true. The United States government had no part in, or knowledge of, this crazy adventure, and we thoroughly deplore all such actions.

'I am also assured that the Holy Father in Rome also had no part in, or knowledge of, this fiasco. I may say that I personally regret that these Vatican funds, so worthwhile in their aim and so imaginatively raised, should be so poorly administered that they can be abused in this way. But who can doubt Pope Thomas's word? It is shameful that President Castro should accuse him in this way.'

His tone became more conversational. 'Popes – and here I speak as a Catholic – are in a difficult positon and I think we should all recognize that. They are democratically elected leaders only in the very narrowest sense: the Sacred College of Cardinals is barely a hundred strong and yet His Holiness's constituency numbers fifty million in the US alone. His moral leadership cuts across national boundaries – and that gives him access to the countries of eastern Europe which have neither the privilege of free elections nor free churches. So his moral leadership is much needed, quite as much as the funds he has raised so spectacularly. But the funds, like his authority, must never be abused. The funds, like the Pope's authority, are for charity, not politics.'

His homily over, Roskill resumed a more brusque tone and he again raised the papers. 'I shall not tear this up. The fact that the Cuban government and the American government got this far shows there is a need for cooperation. Last, and by no means least, I'll let you into a secret.' Now Roskill thumped the lectern exactly as Castro had done the day before at the UN, with the flat of his hand. 'Contract or no contract, the United States is not leaving Guantanamo Bay!'

He stepped down amid a chorus of 'Mr President, Mr President'. But that day there were no questions. Roskill turned and walked briskly out of the room. Castro may have known how to make an entry but there was none better than the President when it came to making an exit.

The press loved it. 'Roskill calls Castro's bluff,' announced the *Los Angeles Times;* 'Prez nixes Cuban' spat the *New York Post.* 'In Cuba, like it or not' yelled the *Miami Herald.* But it was perhaps the *Observer* in London which assessed the speech most thoughtfully on the following Sunday. Under the headline, 'A stoning for Castro, a sermon for the Pope', the paper's Irish columnist, Slattery Doyle, wrote: 'Amid the fuss that has followed President Roskill's tough speech last week, when he reminded the Cuban President, Fidel Castro, of a few facts of political life as seen from Washington, one important factor has been over-looked. That is why the president felt it necessary to devote a whole segment of his speech to Pope Thomas. Indeed, so different was the president's tone when referring to the Pope, that it was almost a speech within a speech. In his opening remarks, Roskill made it clear that, as all of us know, neither the US Government, nor the Vatican, was involved in the doomed adventure to butcher Castro. This was a free-lance operation – there have been similar ones before and there may well be others again. The Cubans in Florida, frankly, are a sorry bunch. All that made this operation different was the connection with the St Patrick's Fund, set up by the Pope to help the poor from the proceeds of selling Vatican art treasures.

'Why then did Roskill feel it necessary to go on and, in the nicest possible way, wearing the most expensive pair of kid gloves, warn His Holiness that his very popular policies for dealing with poverty must not go awry again? Is it because he is jealous of the Pope's successes, which have made Roskill only the second most influential Catholic in the world today?

'Or is it something else – a feeling, shared by several politicians around the world, that an active Pope, with funds and that moral authority which Roskill made so much of, could in time change the political map, making life a little more difficult, and a little less comfort-able, for the old-style network? Perhaps Roskill would like us to see Pope Thomas as an interfering busybody? For certainly the Pope is now in a position to upset the best laid plans of misers and mendacious politicians.

'This column's job is to put the right questions, invite our readers to think for themselves, not provide facile answers. So here's one more question: what would have been Roskill's attitude to Thomas, and his fund, if the assassins had succeeded and Castro, not his secretary, had been killed?'

David thought Doyle's article interesting enough to call Bess in Rome and read it over to her. They had, as she put it, renewed diplomatic relations, though they were still tense. David had told her about his visit to Hale, and Hale's reply, and that slender ray of hope was all

165

they had. But, while they were both in such emotional, and moral, turmoil, she thought it better if they didn't meet.

Bess seemed concerned at Doyle's piece.

'What really bothers me is that both Roskill and this Doyle character know that relief work, if it's done on any scale large enough to have an effect, cannot entirely ignore politics. Poverty is, after all, sometimes a *result* of political policies. Thomas knows this too. He's aware of the dangers. But can't Roskill see that if he lets them worry him he'd end up doing nothing?'

'How did Thomas take Roskill's speech?'

'Basically he's got other things on his mind. More important things. The encyclical is published next week. That will show what Thomas's main concerns are.'

Entitled *Dignitas humana*, the encyclical appeared as planned. It was a long, carefully argued document which concluded, as Bess and David knew all too well, that birth control by artificial methods was now permissible in the Catholic Church but that divorce was not. Thomas, who wrote the encyclical himself, argued that while there was no sanction for birth control in the gospels, neither was there anything which forbade it. He pointed to the obvious hardships brought on by over-population and argued that the absence of contraception was one of the factors that kept the poor poor. He reiterated that it was the duty of Catholic families to have children. There need be no limit but the way was now open, he said, for men and women to follow their own consciences and stop when they felt enough was enough.

He then went on to say that, if allowing contraception permitted parents to decide the number of children they had, then this should mean that the love which parents felt for their children should be undiluted by worries over whether they could be fed and educated. After long and painful consideration of the matter, after lengthy discussions around the world, he had concluded that the best way to ensure the greatest good for the greatest number of children was to maintain the traditional ban on divorce. Any weakening of the commitment between a man and a woman, anything that made separation more likely, impaired family life and was a psychological risk to the growing children in that marriage. Divorce, he said, was in many cases a self-indulgence on the part of parents, who needed to be reminded that their marriage was a sacrament and that their first duty was to bring up their children in God.

Reaction around the world varied enormously but again, curiously, it was Slattery Doyle, in the *Observer*, whose comments seemed to David the most penetrating. This time Doyle's article was headed: 'The Pope, the pill and politics'. It read: 'Are we now entering an age of the political Pope and if so is it a good thing? Once upon a time, of course, such questions would have been irrelevant. Until the nineteenth century,

Popes were temporal as well as spiritual rulers and exercised their earthly powers with the same courage and ruthlessness as the next man.

'But the situation now is rather different. We have, or we appear to have, a man who is willing to use his spiritual power in political ways. I am not on this occasion referring to the Holy Father's sale of Vatican art treasures to pay for charity work, but rather to his new encyclical, *Dignitas humana*.

'Now this encyclical has been in the papal works for some time. As I understand it, it was produced by the Pope himself but has been through several versions: the Holy Father's views have been changing.

'All well and good. But what bothers me, as much as the content of *Dignitas humana*, is the manner of its publication. It is hard to escape the impression that the encyclical was published last week in order to deflect the criticism of His Holiness which James Roskill, the US President, had offered the week before. I do not for an instant suggest there is anything wrong in this, but it undeniably represents a most unusual state of affairs. Traditionally the Vatican has been an institution that thought in centuries. Suddenly we have a Pope who times his spiritual announcements like any politician, so that he will get the best press.

'And what about this latest spiritual announcement? Its timing, as argued above, clearly suggests that the Holy Father expects the liberalizing of contraception to be a popular message. It is possible, nonetheless, that the Holy Father will divide the Church with this encyclical – and not in the way he might expect. It is not a document which some will like and some will hate. Rather, and more insidiously, it is a document which will have a different appeal in different parts of the world.

'Since birth control is an issue that primarily concerns the entire Third World, the encyclical will therefore be welcomed in Africa, South America, parts of Asia. Divorce, on the other hand, is an issue that concerns chiefly people in the developed west. Many of these people practice birth control already so that part of the encyclical will have no effect on them, save to remove some of the guilt. But the same people will tend to be unwilling to accept the Holy Father's continued prohibitions against divorce, and so will stray further and further from Rome.

'The end result, then, may well be that *Dignitas humana* will be much more popular in the Third World than in Europe or North America, and that, in general, it will make Catholicism more a religion of the Third World have-nots, rather than of the haves, wherever they are.'

'Which house number, sir?'

David looked at the note in his diary. 'Fifty-three, please.'

The Ford pulled in.

'I don't know how long I'll be, Pat. But wait please.'

Patton grinned. It was 6.15 now and time served after 6.30 was overtime and worth double pay. He switched off the engine and took out a book of crosswords.

David got out. He was late for his appointment with Wilde. He had learned that afternoon that another big country house was coming on to the market – Duffield Manor in Somerset – and the auction of its contents had gone to Steele's. Was it chance – or did the PM have a hand in that, too? The Chorlton family, who lived at Duffield, were staunch supporters of the Prime Minister's party so it was perfectly possible. Averne had called an emergency board meeting for next week.

He pressed the bell. Wilde came to the door himself. He was a small man, dark-haired with very blue eyes.

'Saw you on telly the other night,' he said, showing David to a seat in his study. 'You were shaking hands with the Queen. And in all the papers. You're nearly as famous as the Pope himself.' He offered David a drink.

'Whisky, please,' said David.

Wilde poured two. He added ice and water and handed one to David. 'Try that; then you can tell me why you are here.'

Wilde sat on the edge of his desk as David told him about Ned's attempted suicide and the earlier conversation he had had with the housemaster during the rugby game.

Wilde was thoughtful for a moment after David had finished. He fingered his tie – a pale pink silk.

He said, 'My first question is: are you going to send Ned to me?'

'I . . . I'm not sure.'

'What you mean is that to do so would acknowledge the problem, such as it is, to Ned and to his chums at school? Yes?'

' . . . something like that.'

'And what you would prefer is a piece of advice from me, and some reassurance perhaps, on the basis of which you yourself could help the boy without him ever going near a shrink?'

'I suppose so.'

'Would you ask a surgeon to treat Ned without seeing him?'

'Psychiatry isn't surgery.'

'But you see my point. Now look, Mr Colwyn. I'm busy, you're busy. I know that people have all sorts of idiotic ideas about psychiatry, whether it works or not, whether we head doctors aren't more mad than our patients, and so on. I don't know whether that's your view, or Ned's mother's maybe, but I'm not going to waste time finding out. Neither am I going to collude with you in some undercooked half-measures that keep your self-esteem intact but are not in Ned's best interests. There's only one simple fact you need address your mind to – and it's this: the chances are that your son will try to kill himself again within two years. If he does try again, he is more likely to succeed than fail. Now you don't have to send him to me. There are lots of doctors in this street alone. But you do have to do *something*. You can decide now, though I'd rather you talked it over with Ned; I'd rather he *wanted* to come himself, if that's what you decide to arrange. But that's the situation, as I see it.'

Later, David decided that Wilde's manner, though certainly brusque, marked him as an able doctor. In a few well-chosen sentences he had convinced David that he was a good man to treat his son. David would have to see Ned, and discuss it. But his own hesitation was gone: he would certainly try to persuade the boy to see Wilde.

He didn't go straight home. He had Patton drive him to a private view he'd been invited to attend. It was at the British Museum and celebrated the acquisitions made by the outgoing keeper of drawings, who was retiring. David was introduced to the new keeper, a woman called Jeanette Soane. A rather lugubrious lady, with heavy green eyes and red hair, she had an impressively baritone voice. After greeting David, she said: 'You don't remember, but we've actually met before. It was at the Renaissance Society meeting in Pisa. I enjoyed your paper very much – and in fact I've got a bit of information for you.'

'Oh yes?'

'Yes. You said in that paper that Isabella d'Este gave Elisabetta Gonzaga "a Leonardo" on her marriage. Have you found out any more since then?'

'No. Nothing.'

'Well, you might like to know that there are some letters of Elizabetta Gonzaga in the Vatican Archive. I stumbled across them about a week ago. I haven't read them but I've got the archive number. If you're interested, I can let you have it.'

'Interested? I'll say. Have you started here yet? Is this where I find you?'

She nodded but before she could say any more she was hauled off by the museum press officer to be introduced to someone else. David looked around for a drink but instead found himself staring straight at Jasper Hale.

'What are *you* doing here?' David asked, shaking Hale's hand. 'Oh yes. I forgot. You're a museum trustee now. By the way, there isn't any news – ?'

'Yes, there is. I only found out myself today and it's been so hectic I haven't had a chance to let you know.'

'And?'

'Well,' the monsignor's eyes twinkled. 'I'm not absolutely certain . . . but I think this little mystery could have a happy ending as well.'

David followed the Holy Father's trip to South America closely through the papers and on television. Thomas was received enthusiastically wherever he went, with thousands waiting at every turn to see him and to be blessed by him. The centre for the devolved Vatican functions was to be located in the official residence and offices of the Cardinal Archbishop of Rio and there was no little speculation in the press as to what this new organization should be called. Vatican 2 was clearly out, being too close to the shorthand title for the second Vatican council. And 'Little Vatican' was hardly respectful. Then Bess surprised everyone by announcing that, in gratitude for the twenty million dollars Thomas had ear-marked for the shanty towns and for transferring those Vatican functions which could be so transferred, the Brazilian government had given to the Church the land on which the cathedral and the archbishop's residence stood. Furthermore, it recognized this new extension of the Vatican as a separate city state just as the other Vatican was recognized in Italy. And, since the cathedral and residence were located in the Prato area of Rio, the new base of the Roman Church would be known as the Prato City State. Vatican stamps, tax and other diplomatic privileges would all be recognized at Prato.

While the European press seemed bemused by this plan, newspapers of the Third World were ecstatic. The development showed clearly the direction the Church was moving in. It gave their problems a recognition and, more, it showed that they were high up on the Church's list of priorities. The Americans, in general, regarded the new city state as an imaginative gesture; they were less hidebound than the Europeans and were inclined to watch how the new arrangements worked out in practice before condemning them. The Italians, of course, were outraged since the developments in Rio meant that there was now a potential rival to Rome as a religious centre.

For David and Bess, the Pope's South American visit came at an awkward time. As a result of Hale's researches, David was to face a tribunal in London, since the apostolic delegate had found reason to believe that his marriage could indeed be dissolved. But it was impossible for Bess to avoid the events in Rio; otherwise she would have been in London for the meeting.

The spotlight was temporarily taken off the Rio announcements when, in the same week, the eight would-be assassins of Castro went on trial in Havana. The case was heavily covered. Apart from anything else, for once it was made easy for western journalists to get visas. Photographs of the defendants in the dock showed them to be well-fed, well-dressed, and it was reported that they had no complaints about their treatment in captivity.

Meanwhile, in London, however, before David's confrontation with the tribunal, he had to face another: with Ned. David was all the more conscious that he needed to persuade his son to see Wilde because the Dead Sea Scrolls sale was coming up in New York and he would have to spend a lot of time away in the next weeks.

Since Ned had come out of hospital the school had been very helpful. At one stage, David had thought that they might refuse to have Ned back, as too much of a risk. But the headmaster was understanding, and had his own plans for dealing with Ned. Despite the fact that he was senior enough to merit his own bedroom, he was made to share with another boy who was briefed to keep an eye on Ned at all times. There was nothing secretive about this, however. It was all discussed openly.

Still, Sarah had agreed with David that expert psychiatric treatment was called for, and David said he would be the one to raise the subject with Ned.

So, while Thomas and Bess were in Rio, David travelled down to Hamble one weekend. Ned met him by the car and wanted to go for a walk. They went in the opposite direction to the weir, and tramped along what Ned said was the cross-country course. It ran through some woods where they saw one or two deer.

'How's the new arrangement working out? Is he nice, the boy you're sharing with?'

'Sure.'

'And school in general?'

'Fine.'

Ned obviously wasn't feeling very talkative. 'And how have you been keeping? Since you . . . came out of hospital, I mean?'

'I feel fine, Dad.'

They negotiated a stile. 'That master – Yates. He said you used to get depressions. Is that true?'

'I suppose so.'

'What were they like?'

'You forget to breathe.'

'What?'

'Your mind wanders, you have no control over it, you pay so much attention to it that you forget to breathe. You make little grunts. It's exhausting.'

'And . . . since hospital . . . has it been any better?'

'Yes. A bit. No.'

They were coming to the end of the wood. It was windier now. The track they were following began to curve to the right. David walked for a while in silence. Then: 'Ned, I'm worried about all this. There's a friend of mine in London. A doctor. Would you mind going to see him?'

Ned lowered his head. 'What sort of doctor?'

'A psychiatrist.'

'You think I'm mad.'

'No, of course not. But . . . these depressions . . . we have to do something about them.'

David couldn't look at his son but he sensed the way Ned scrunched up his frame, hunching his shoulders. They walked on, their footfalls matching exactly, emphasizing how alike they were. In some ways.

They came to a gate which led on to the lane back towards the school. Ned stopped. He looked down. 'If I refuse to see this . . . doctor – what happens then?'

'I don't know. Your mother and I hope you won't refuse. But we shan't force you, if that's what you mean.'

They walked on. To David the clouds reminded him of those over Windsor, the day he first saw Seton. Ominous.

'Am I mad?'

'Don't be silly, Ned. But you must have been very unhappy to do what you did. I have a feeling you won't talk to me, or to your mother. You may not think it consciously, but somewhere you probably blame us. But you might talk to this man Wilde.'

'Is that his name, Wilde? Great name for a psychiatrist.'

David looked at him. It was a typical Ned remark, to see the joke in the name.

But neither of them was smiling

They came to the edge of the school grounds. There were people in the middle distance.

'Well?'

Ned looked across at the school. 'All right, I'll see him. Anything to keep Mum and you sane.'

# 9

David ran up the steps of the archbishop's house in Westminster and rang the bell. March was offering one of its sunnier days. The door was opened by a steward who showed him into a waiting room. 'The tribunal is running a little late, Mr Colwyn,' he said. 'But they won't keep you long.'

David sat down. As usual he had brought some work with him so he didn't have to waste the time. He took a report from his briefcase and read it through. He had already looked at it briefly in his office and it did not make pleasant reading. A very rare collection of ancient weapons, known as the Rookwood Armoury, was soon to be sold – but the collection wasn't coming to Hamilton's. Once again Steele's had slipped in and, once again, the Prime Minister had clearly had a finger in the decision. The report David was holding was written by the director of Hamilton's weapons department and explained why, as in a growing number of cases, Hamilton's had lost out to Steele's. On this occasion, it appeared, Cyril Rookwood had been told – discreetly, of course – that the government would put up no objections to the export of his armoury, provided it was sold through Steele's. This made the sale particularly attractive to foreign buyers, and increased the amount of money Rookwood could expect from the sale. All this was rumour and conjecture, of course, but David had little doubt it was true. It was yet another of the 'quid pro quos' Paul Clegg had warned David about when they had met at the club.

The Prime Minister knew how to harbour a grudge and, it seemed, was determined to hurt Hamilton's to the point where they would be forced to back out of the royal sale. The board meeting called by Averne, after the Duffield Manor business, had been stormy. Although an American, Averne held no brief for the British Royal family. He believed that the PM's vendetta could seriously harm Hamilton's in the long run, and could more than off-set the boost which the royal sale was bringing. He advocated pulling out.

David, vociferously supported by Lord Afton, had disagreed. He countered by saying that the publicity which would attach to such a

173

move would be far too damaging. He admitted that the Argyll and Duffield house sales represented serious losses of Hamilton's traditional business; but once the royal sale was over, he said, it would pick up again.

Averne had insisted on pushing the matter to a vote and this had gone 8 to 7 to David. He had won again – but these attacks by Averne were getting stronger and now, after this latest report, David wasn't sure he could hold the firm on its present course.

The steward came back into the waiting room 'The tribunal will see you now, Mr Colwyn. Follow me, please.' He led the way out into the corridor and up a flight of stairs wrapped around an old-fashioned caged lift. They reached a long dingy corridor with rows of mahogany doors. The steward knocked on one and entered. He held the door for David.

Inside the sunlight streaming through the windows was so fierce it hurt David's eyes for a moment. He thanked the steward who showed him to a seat and then left the room. There were five men in front of David, none of whom he recognized.

'Good morning, Mr Colwyn,' said the man in the centre. 'I am Monsignor Desmond Waterford and I am chairman of this tribunal. As you will know, this is a somewhat unusual case, both in the way it was referred to us – through the apostolic delegate who, of course, has no jurisdiction in matrimonial matters – and, of course, in the individuals involved.'

David looked along the tribunal. It had not occurred to him that this body might not be friendly. After Jasper Hale had given David his momentous news that evening at the British Museum, he had imagined that this meeting would be a formality. Now he realized it wasn't, that Bess's closeness to the Holy Father was likely to be as much a hindrance as it was a help. There were still plenty of conservative Catholics who didn't like His Holiness having women so close to the throne of St Peter and there were even more people, David himself included, who hated string-pulling of any kind.

Bess, however, had had no such qualms. She had been just as delighted as David when he told her Hale's news on one of their transcontinental calls to Rio. Like many Americans, she did not view string-pulling as an exercise of privilege but merely as one of the ways the game was played.

The chairman went on. 'Monsignor Hale has told me the gist of your case, Mr Colwyn, and my colleagues here have all seen your file, with the personal details that you sent. Perhaps you would be good enough to tell us now, in your own words, the grounds on which your appeal to have your marriage dissolved is based.'

'Certainly.' David took his briefcase off his lap and placed it at the side of his chair. 'May I begin by saying that the information I am about

174

to give has been obtained by Monsignor Hale, who is a friend. I realize, however, that you may have to verify it.

'I am a Catholic but my wife Sarah, from whom I was civilly divorced earlier this year, is a Protestant. Sarah was born in Hawsker, north Yorkshire. It was a difficult birth and she was born a month prematurely. She was tiny – 4lb – and not expected to live. It was a winter birth – February – in a year in which there was an influenza epidemic, with the deaths of many young babies and old people. Because she was small, and in dangerously poor health, Sarah was christened immediately. However, and this is the crucial point, Monsignor Hale has discovered that because of all these circumstances the Church of England vicar who christened her decided that it was too risky to pour cold water on her forehead. Instead, he simply made the sign of the cross with holy water.'

David looked along the tribunal again. 'Monsignor Hale tells me the practice of merely applying the sign of a cross was not at all uncommon in Church of England christenings, in years when influenza was particularly high, but I understand that in the eyes of the Catholic Church a baptism is not valid unless the water has actually been poured over the head of the child. Now, in the course of his investigations on my behalf Monsignor Hale checked in Hawsker. The vicar is now dead but the organist's assistant still lives there. He remembered Sarah because she'd been such a tiny, frail child everyone in the village had been surprised she survived. It was he who told Monsignor Hale that the vicar had been so worried about her health he did not go through with a full baptism.'

David wrapped his hands together. He was more nervous than he sounded. Like on the rostrum. 'My case before you is therefore unusual but, I hope, straightforward. Since my wife was not properly baptized, our marriage was not sacramental. As a non-sacramental marriage, it is eligible for dissolution by the Pope himself in exercising what I believe is known as the Petrine privilege.'

Ten thoughful eyes stared at him. These were men who handled difficult cases every week, in which faithful Catholics wanted to extricate themselves from marriages which were no longer working. Very often they had to disappoint these people. The British tribunals had not yet started to abuse canon law, as the Americans had, by accepting pleas that people had been psychologically immature when they got married – at twenty-seven or twenty-nine even – and therefore had not 'meant' their vows.

The chairman was scribbling his notes. He finished and looked up. 'Thank you, Mr Colwyn. Very clearly put. Let me explain what happens now. We shall verify your story, and if the witnesses bear out what you say, we shall ask to see you and take your evidence again, but this time on oath. Then, your evidence and that of the witnesses is written up by this tribunal into a petition. The petition is sent to someone called a "defender of the bond", normally a canon lawyer from another diocese. If he is happy that the procedure has been properly followed and the petitioner's case is valid, the petition comes back to the bishop of this diocese, together with the "defender's" comments. The bishop reads both documents and if *he* is satisfied all is as it should be he sends the case to Rome, to the Congregation for the Doctrine of the Faith, the Holy Office as it used to be called. There the procedure is repeated. The commissioners and another "defender of the bond" examine the case. If they decide that the merits of the petitioner warrant it, they recommend a dissolution to the Holy Father. The Holy Father *personally* grants the dissolution – and here I must stress it is a favour, not a right. The Holy Father does not have to give reasons for his decision, and of course there is no appeal. Is all that clear?'

David nodded.

'Then, unless you have any questions, we need detain you no further.'

'Just one,' said David. 'How long does all this take?'

'Ah yes. Normally it would take us three to five months to reach our verdict. When it goes to Rome add another year. The Holy Father usually takes six months to make up his mind. In this case, however, Monsignor Hale has been a good friend to several members of the tribunal, Mr Colwyn, so you are lucky. Expect our reply in a month. After that, it's out of our hands.'

David left the archbishop's house fairly satisfied. Jasper Hale was an important ally. He had good contacts in Rome and was no doubt able to make useful representations on behalf of the Catholic hierarchy in Britain. If this thing came off, he told himself, he owed the apostolic delegate a favour.

When he got home Bess was in the air, travelling back from Rio, so David couldn't call her with the news of the tribunal. And next morning, before he had a chance to place his call to Rome, Sally Middleton buzzed him and said: 'Michael Callaghan on two.' He raised his eyebrows. Callaghan was press secretary at Buckingham Palace.

He lifted the receiver. 'Colwyn.'

'Ah, good. I'm glad I've got you.'

'What can I do for you?' David didn't know Callaghan well. They had met, of course, in arranging the exhibition of pictures which the Queen intended to sell. David found him rather distant and obviously capable.

'If you will forgive me for being rather blunt, Mr Colwyn, the answer to your question is: "Keep your mouth shut".'

'Eh?'

'I have just had a call from the editor of *The Times*. You will probably get one any minute. It seems they are publishing a letter tomorrow by three art professors. The letter is very critical of Her Majesty's decision to sell some of her paintings.'

'Oh no!' David's heart sank. Lister must have lost his battle. 'Are they Heritage Trust people?'

'Yes – and that's part of the reason I'm calling you. *The Times*' editor was very courteous. It seems he's running a front-page story about the background to the letter. There's been a hell of a row in the BHPT between those who want to oppose the sale and those who think that the fund will lose a lot of financial support if they attack Her Majesty. For the time being, according to *The Times*' editor, the activists have lost – but three of them have decided to go ahead on their own, as individuals.'

'What do you want me to do?'

'I'll come to that in a minute. First I want to tell you our thinking.'

'Okay, go ahead.'

'Well, Her Majesty is naturally upset at having her judgement criticized. Although she's used to it, she never gets used to it, if you see what I mean. But she is determined to go ahead with the sale. We have discussed the matter with Sir Edgar Seton, who knows the people who have written the letter, and have decided that our best course is to offer no comment for the time being. *The Times* letter will presumably spark off others and we would like to gauge the overall picture before we say anything. Her Majesty would prefer it if Hamilton's declined to comment also. What do you say?'

'We're naturally willing to cooperate in any way. But it rather depends on what the letter says. If it attacks Hamilton's as well as the Queen, the board might feel obliged to defend itself.' And that would be another opportunity for Averne to make trouble, David reflected.

'I've had the letter read over to me. It does not mention Hamilton's or even refer to you by implication. The wording is clear: forceful without being offensive, but the message is unmistakable.'

'Very well,' said David. 'If that's the case I see no problems. I'll wait for *The Times* to call and if there are any snags I'll call you back.'

'Good. Thank you. Otherwise, let's talk again tomorrow, after the letter has been published.'

Sure enough, no sooner had he put down the phone on Callaghan than it buzzed again. David didn't rate the editor of *The Times* himself, merely a reporter. But in any case the conversation didn't last long. The reporter was not persistent and David did not need to call Callaghan back.

He put his call through to Bess but she had left Rome again already, he was told, on a flying visit to Sicily with the Holy Father. They had gone in the papal helicopter and would be back that evening, but very late. He left a message that he would call the next day. Then he called

Anthony Wilde and told him Ned had agreed to treatment. They fixed the first appointment for a week later.

Next morning, when David picked up *The Times*, he saw that the front page article was headed: 'Art Experts Attack Royal Sale.' It, and the letter inside, was a fairly straight-forward account of what he already knew from his conversation with Callaghan. David was quoted, but only in passing, saying that the sale would go ahead as planned.

The interesting development, however, came not in *The Times* but in other papers. Inevitably the rest of Fleet Street had picked up *The Times* story, and the reaction David liked most was emblazoned across the front of the *Daily Express*.

'HOW DARE THEY!' ran the banner, and underneath, 'Three eggheads in shock attack on the Queen!'

David didn't much care for the language used by the popular papers but he hoped their sense of outrage would be widely shared.

He had a meeting that morning at the British Museum – he was seeing Jeanette Soane about the Elisabetta Gonzaga letters in the Vatican – but as soon as he got to the office after lunch he called Callaghan. The press secretary was phlegmatic. 'My instincts still tell me to do very little. There are plenty of people who support Her Majesty in this and presumably some of them are writing to *The Times* even as we speak. If this controversy remains simply a letters' wrangle in *The Times*, it will eventually fizzle out. The main thing is not to make matters worse by overreacting. Agreed?'

'Ye-e-es,' said David doubtfully. 'I still have to hedge my bets in case anyone attacks Hamilton's. After all, the heritage lobby has been building for years. This could be the issue the activists have been waiting for. Especially as they must know the government is not exactly your ally. Anyway, we obviously should keep in touch.'

Almost immediately the phone buzzed again. 'Bess! Am I glad to hear you! How was Sicily? Come to that, how was Rio?'

'Rio was fantastic. I found Thomas some lovely Portuguese tiles for his bathroom. Yellow and white – very papal. Sicily was fantastic. I even managed to find the most fantastic piece of black patterned velvet. But it's even more fantastic to be back here in my little apartment.'

'I know what you mean.'

'Tell me your news.'

At last he could tell her about Hale's discovery and the tribunal.

'Oh David! That's wonderful. I feel ten foot taller. Are you going to come to Rome so we can celebrate?'

'Soon – but I don't know just when. We're having a bit of bother with the Queen's sale today. Three professors have attacked her in the press.'

'Yes, I know. Some of the Italian papers have already been on to me for our reaction.'

'That was quick. What are you saying?'

'Nothing. No comment. That we are flattered your Queen is emulating Thomas and that we hope the sale will go well. But we don't want to get involved in an internal British matter.'

'I've had a bad feeling about this sale ever since the beginning. I never felt the same about Thomas's ideas.'

'One piece of advice, David darling. Don't just sit back and wait for the story to develop. See if you can take it forward yourself, with some new angle. If you keep the press reporting, you delay their thinking. Delay it long enough and something else often happens to take their minds off you completely.'

'Thanks for the advice – but enough about me. When am I going to hear all about Rio?'

'As soon as you get your body out here. So much happened it will last through several plates of Gina's pasta. At the moment though, we're rather worried by what's coming out at the trial in Cuba. It doesn't look good and if I'm difficult to get hold of, it'll be because I'm trying to talk to our contacts in Havana.'

After David hung up, he thought over what Bess had said, about not sitting back and waiting for the attack on the Queen to develop. What could he do?

He went to the window and stared down at St James's Square. On the steps of the London Library he recognized two famous authors chatting together. He noticed that one gave the other some change which the man then put in a parking meter. The simple action gave David an idea. That was it! Yes, it might work. Otherwise things might get out of hand. He went to the phone.

'Callaghan.'

'David Colwyn, at Hamilton's.'

'Oh yes. Problems?'

'No. Not really. I wondered if you were free for a drink tonight. I've had a thought.'

'Let's see. No, there's nothing I can't get out of. This can't be done on the telephone?'

'No.'

'Very well then, any time after six thirty.'

'Good, let's say Booth's at six forty-five.'


Douglas Kirkhill was angry. He was a big Ulsterman, raw and fiery. His red hair seemed to shoot out of his head and the veins on his cheeks made it seem as though his face had been polished with a red glaze. This morning he was actually more than angry; he was close to tears.

He parked his big black Ford in the bay provided for him and stepped out into the rain. He didn't bother with his raincoat on the car's back seat but immediately marched across the yard to a pair of double white doors over which a blue sign announced: 'Kirkhill construction.'

'May!' he called to his startled secretary. 'Tell Michael Molyneux I want to see him.'

Molyneux was the union shop steward at Kirkhill's and when he hurriedly arrived at his boss's door he found, to his great surprise, that the man had a glass of whisky in his hand.

'Sit down, Michael. Have a drink.'

Molyneux didn't like the look of this. Kirkhill was a fair boss, and he never touched the whisky before seven in the evening. That was how he had made the firm such a success. Kirkhill's built houses, roads, even bridges and hospitals, and they always delivered on time and within their budget. Molyneux poured a small whisky and sat down. He looked around. The office was like the man: solid and unflashy. A modern desk, a table for meetings, a photograph of his wife, now dead, and his boy, also dead, killed by the I R A, stupid bastards, when they had blown up a restaurant by mistake. The office of a man who had no home life, who lived for his work and spent most of his days away from it on building sites all over the six counties.

Kirkhill looked at him. A phone sounded in the outer office. Almost as Kirkhill spoke Molyneux knew what was coming and closed his eyes.

'We've lost another tender. The bridge, the new one across the Bann at Coleraine,' said Kirkhill. 'That makes four in the last seven weeks.'

'Who . . . who got it this time?'

Kirkhill glared at him. 'Foley's. Again.' Foley's was a relatively new firm. A Catholic firm. 'And for the same reason.'

'Money?'

The boss nodded. 'I was told their tender undercut ours by *thirteen* per cent. The materials have to be same. The labour. I doubt if their office costs, or transport are even as good as ours.' He poured more whisky down his throat. 'But since that damn fund of the Pope's, they can get their money cheaper. That's what screws us. It's so unfair!'

The two men sat opposite each other, gloomily staring at the rain which rattled against Kirkhill's office window. The boss had been increasingly morose of late, and Molyneux had grown used to sitting with him, until he had talked himself out. He had never known him this bad so early in the day.

'There was a time, Michael, when a Protestant firm would have got these contracts, whatever the figure on the tender. That was unfair, too – you know I think that. But now it's gone the other way. It's the Catholics who get all the breaks.'

Molyneux nodded. The boss didn't need to convince him.

Kirkhill breathed out loudly and lifted himself to his feet. He lumbered to the window and looked down, throuh the rain at: the machinery, the supplies, the small architect's office he was so proud of. He went to pour himself another whisky but then thought better of it. Instead he turned and pointed the bottle at Molyneux. 'Four tenders, Michael, four lost in seven weeks. That leaves only one that's anywhere near happening. That cinema in Larne. It comes up the week after next.' He put the bottle back in the cupboard. 'If we don't get that, I'm going to have to start laying off men.'

However worried the Holy Father and Bess might feel about events in Cuba, in Beirut success followed success. The Christian security forces there found that as a result of the St Patrick's Fund the quality of their information began to improve dramatically. Several telling arrests were made, and three huge discoveries of weapons and ammunition, forcing the Muslim paramilitary to backtrack. The clinics and camps set up by the St Patrick's Fund also struggled to life.

David had his secretary clip anything in the newspapers about fund activity. He was in no way responsible for the uses to which the money was put, but soon the first dividends would be declared and he needed to keep in touch.

In general, David was feeling fairly buoyant. Ned was seeing Wilde; he himself was to receive his papal honour soon and when he went to Rome for that he would take Ned, so the great meeting between his son and Bess would finally take place; he had been to see the tribunal again – they thought he had a case and had taken his evidence on oath. Also, David's idea to deflect criticism of the Queen's sale appeared to be working.

It had been planned during his drink at Booth's with Callaghan. Together David and the Queen's press secretary made a formidable pair, well able to twist a few aristocratic arms, and within a week David was ready to make an announcement. It made the front page of the serious papers and showed that Bess had been right: by thinking up a scheme to move the story on, the papers were obliged to report developments, rather than merely sit back and criticize.

'Other collectors,' ran the subhead in *The Daily Telegraph*, 'follow the Queen's example and sell art to help the poor'. The text continued: 'Hamilton's, the Fine Art Auctioneers, announced last night that several British collectors, impressed by the Queen's decision to sell part of the royal collection in order to raise funds for international relief, have lent her their support by donating paintings of their own which will be added to the sale.

'The collectors include Lord Haddon, who will sell his Breughel, "Peasants skating", Mr David Berry, chairman of IMI, who is putting up Canaletto's "Torcello", in the family for generations, Sir Frank Richter, the publisher, who will send his small Rembrandt etching, "The Lesson", to the sale, and the Earl of Stow, who is to make available the famous "Bull Fight" by Goya, now on loan to the National Gallery of Wales.

'This remarkable show of support for the Queen's proposal comes only days after three professors of art attacked Her Majesty's sale as being against the national interest. Mr Michael Callaghan, the Queen's press secretary, last night welcomed the news. He said, 'These donations show, I believe, what support Her Majesty has in the country.'

David had personal reasons to be gratified with the story. He knew that he had impressed Callaghan both with the idea itself and with the way in which he had subsequently carried it out.

Letters about the sale still appeared in *The Times* but, since Hamiltons' announcement, the Queen's critics had lost a lot of force. Or had seemed to.

Charlie Winter sat in his pale blue Pontiac on the New York street and lightly touched the gun under his jacket. He was definitely nervous. He often was at this stage of an operation. His partner, Harry Weizack, sat next to him, not speaking. For the past three days, acting on a tip-off for which they had paid good money, and would have to shell out a great deal more if this stakeout came to anything, they had been following three men. The tip-off said the men were heroin dealers and were about to take delivery of a bulk order with a street value of seven million dollars. Charlie and Harry, special investigators of the US Customs branch, had picked them up at Kennedy airport three days before, where two of them had met the third off a Lufthansa flight from Frankfurt.

The tip-off had identified the incoming passenger from a glass observation booth in the arrivals hall (where he had received the first instalment of his pay). The two men who met the passenger had escorted him to a van and before the van entered the mid-town tunnel, the customs' department computer in the World Trade Centre in Lower Manhattan had identified it as being registered in the name of a New Jersey meat company suspected of being part-owned by the Cicognani family, one of the five mob families of New York. By the time the van had turned south on Lexington Avenue, Charlie had three other cars in support: only with a 'box' of four cars could customs be sure of tailing the van without being spotted.

For seventy-two hours the van had been discreetly followed. It was possible that the man who had been met at Kennedy was the supplier. He had been identified by the customs' officer at the airport as Hellmut Ewald, of German nationality, but was not known to Interpol or German police, nor was he included in the customs' computer. At a guess he had arrived 'clean' – his 'merchandise' had probably been smuggled in some days before, from a different country, and was now being stored

182

secretly. The men meeting him were almost certainly link men, go-betweens who took the risks on behalf of the Cicognani family.

Charlie and Harry had settled down to a long wait. They knew, from previous experience, that the German would want to ensure he wasn't being followed, or lured into a trap. He would want to see the colour of the Cicognani money. He would want to know about security.

He had checked into the Grammercy Square Hotel, in the name on the passport he had used. He had gone to the movies and eaten at a brasserie uptown on 54th Street. He had been picked up by the van twice and taken to two separate addresses, one at Mercer Street in Soho and another at 18th Street just off Broadway. Then, this Sunday morning, he had been picked up a third time, very early, and brought here to Rotier Street in Queen's. Charlie hoped something was going to happen now. He was getting impatient.

The van was parked outside a toy shop. Being Sunday, the shop was closed. One of the mob men waited in the van while the other had gone inside with Ewald.

Suddenly, as Charlie was imagining the breakfast he was missing at home, the door to the shop opened and the other mob man came out. He pinned the door wide and then went to open the back of the van.

'Looks like they're making a move,' said Harry.

'Stand by,' whispered Charlie into his microphone. 'Suspects may be loading what we are loooking for into their van.'

The man reappeared at the doorway, this time carrying two cardboard cartons. The other man got down from the driver's seat, went round to the back and climbed in so that he could stack the cartons. Then the first man went back inside the shop while the driver lit a cigarette.

Charlie reached for his binoculars in the glove compartment. When the man came out a second time he could see that there was red overpainting on the cartons but his arm obscured the lettering.

He waited for the man to come out again. This time Charlie breathed out heavily. 'Shit, Harry, this could be it. You know what's supposed to be in those cartons? Olive oil. Since when have toy shops sold olive oil?'

He picked up his radio. 'Okay you guys, we're going in. There's some cartons being loaded that look too juicy to pass up. Pete, you there?'

'Charlie!'

'Pull over to Roosevelt Avenue and block their exit – but not till I say.'

'Right.'

'Jimmy?'

'Here.'

'There'll be a back entrance to the shop somewhere, probably an alley off Parsons Boulevard. Find it and cover.'

'You got it.'

'Rocco!'

'Yes?'

'Cover us in case it gets dirty.'

'We'll be there. I can see you from here.'

'Okay then. Anybody not ready or not clear about what to do?'

Silence.

'Good luck then. Let's go!'

Charlie and Harry drove quietly up Union Street, arriving abreast of the shop just after one of the men had disappeared back inside. As Charlie braked and pulled the Pontiac over so that the van's way forward was blocked, Harry – who already had his window down – was aiming his gun at the driver.

It took the driver maybe two seconds to realize what was happening, but that was enough. By now Rocco's car was visible twenty yards down the street and Charlie had his gun on the driver as well. The man put up no resistance.

But then the door to the toy shop banged shut and bolts could be heard being slid into place. The men inside had seen them. Shit! thought Charlie, now things could get really nasty. He didn't want a shoot-out without being able to alert the neighbourhood, it wasn't good publicity for the Customs Department. Still, it looked as if he had no choice.

'Harry!' he yelled and grabbed both him and the driver and bundled them behind the van, out of sight of the toy shop and fairly safe if shooting started. It also gave them a chance to search the driver. Amazingly he wasn't armed – they found his gun under his seat in the van. Harry handcuffed him to the driving wheel so he and Charlie were free to go after the others.

As it happened, though, it wasn't on Union Street that the shooting started. Before Charlie or Harry had worked out how to tackle the front of the shop, gunfire was heard at the back.

Charlie motioned down the street for Rocco to take charge as he and Harry approached the front of the shop. He looked in through the window, past shelves of dolls and plastic aircraft. The shop looked empty. Using the barrel of his gun he smashed the glass in the door while Harry lay flat behind the brickwork.

Nothing.

He reached in and slid back the bolt, careful not to snag his skin on the jagged glass. He swung the door open.

Still nothing.

Harry got to his feet and together they entered the shop. The first room, the shop proper, looked well-stocked but dusty, as though it hadn't been open for a while. That figured. Charlie next stepped through a narrow passageway to a small backroom. There he froze, seeing movement beyond the window. 'Harry!' he whispered and pointed.

'Right with you.' Harry flattened himself against the wall where the door would open, his gun pointed at head height towards whoever came through the back door.

They stood on either side and Charlie signalled for Harry to pull it open. Outside it was sunny. There was no one to be seen. Charlie began to sweat: he hadn't been this close in a tangle for months and he didn't like it. He had to move, though. Those earlier shots would have brought people onto the streets and they were all now at risk.

He inched through the door. As he did so, he noticed a shadow to the left behind the wooden casing around some pipes. He decided that commonsense was the better part of valour.

'There are two of us,' he said loudly. 'We know you are behind those pipes. You may get one of us but never two. And your buddy is handcuffed to your van. You can't get away.'

He was sweating again. He had made his voice sound more confident than he felt.

'Sir?'

At first Charlie thought the voice was Harry's. The he realized it came from outside. From behind the pipes. 'Jimmy?'

'Yes, sir, it's me.'

'Christ, I nearly killed you.'

'You nearly bought it yourself.'

'What happened?'

'We got them. One injured – in the arm and chest – and the German gave himself up.'

'Holy shit. No kidding. Wow!'

'This way – ' and Jimmy led them back through a small yard to an alley. There, Jimmy's junior partner stood guard over Ewald and the injured mobster. Also, as Charlie had feared, a group of local residents stood watching at the far end of the alley.

'Have you sent for an ambulance?'

'Yessir.'

The operation was quickly tidied up. The ambulance arrived, the crowd was dispersed and Charlie and Harry drove away with Ewald in their car, the van driver going with Jimmy. But not before they had opened the cartons. For a moment Charlie thought that they had made a dreadful mistake – each carton really did contain bottles of olive oil. Only when all the bottles were taken out of one and it remained curiously heavy, did he realize that it must have a false bottom. Slitting the cardboard with his knife, Charlie found what he'd been looking for: a good kilo of white powder trickled out when he turned the carton over. And there were thirty cartons.

Later that night, after Charlie had paid off the final instalment to his informant, the interrogations began. One interesting discovery was quickly made. Both the New York men were illegal immigrants. From Sicily.

'How many anti-Popes have there been?'

'Ned! I don't think that's a very suitable question. Not now.'

There was an amused silence around the table at Gina's. They had all been nervous about this meeting: David, Bess, Ned. David knew that his son's many questions were a sign of nerves, and he also knew that if Ned had not liked Bess, he would have lapsed into silence.

They were celebrating David's investiture into the Order of St Sylvester which had taken place that morning. It was the first time David and Bess had met since Thomas had changed his mind on divorce. The news was better now, though: the tribunal in London had considered the evidence, the 'Defender of the Bond' had assessed it and the petition, favourable to David's case, was now with the Bishop. If he agreed then it would soon go to Rome as the next stage.

'When was the Great Schism, then?' Ned insisted. 'Didn't some Popes rule from Avignon and some from Rome?'

It was Bess who answered. 'I haven't a clue, Ned. History was never my strong suit. I deal in the present. Now, if you want a look at the papal computer tomorrow, then *that's* something I *do* know about.'

'What can it do?'

'What *can't* it do? The phone numbers of every bishop in the world, the nature and location of all modern miracles – with our assessment of them, a worldwide list of all prominent Catholics who have told us that, when they die, they will bequeath their estates to the Church, estimates of who listens in to the Vatican radio, assessments of the religious beliefs of world leaders, the location of every site said to hold a piece of the Holy Cross and other relics . . .'

'Are there miracles, still?'

'Oh, yes. You'd be surprised. Come tomorrow and find out.'

Ned looked at his father.

David smiled and said: 'Fine by me. You two will have to go alone, though. I've got to spend the morning in the Archive, chasing Leonardo.'

'Is it a date, then?' asked Bess. Ned nodded straight away.

David relaxed. Ned would not have agreed to accompany Bess, all by himself, it he were not ready. It was a good sign. David was buoyed up, too, by the conversation he'd had with Wilde on the day before he and Ned had flown to Rome for the investiture.

'I'm getting some good stuff,' Wilde had said when David rang for a progress report.

'Good stuff? What do you mean?'

'Sorry. I mean Ned's beginning to talk much more freely in our sessions. I don't intend to be specific, he has to be able to trust my discretion, but I *can* tell you he's saying more, and with more feeling.'

'May I know in general what you've been discussing?'

'The future.'

'Isn't that unusual?'

'Very. Most psychiatrists concentrate on the past, on the circumstances that have brought the patient into their care. I prefer to get my patients thinking about the future – its pleasures, its possibilities – as soon as I can. The technique has its risks: if people see their future as bleak the effect can be depressing. But if it works, recovery can be quite rapid.'

'And with Ned?'

'Two things. He seems to have frightened himself with his suicide attempt. That sometimes happens. The chief effect, clinically, is to make his sleep very disturbed. Fears always surface in the dark, in bed. I have therefore prescribed a mild sedative and told the school: naturally his housemaster will keep the tablets, not Ned. But you yourself should keep some with you at home, for when he is with you.'

'How long will they be needed?'

'Not too long. The tablets are as mild as I can make them and Ned is not to use them as an excuse for sleeping in in the mornings. I've told his school and I'm telling you. Sleeping in is a bad sign and should be stopped.'

'Whatever you say. You said there were two things.'

'Yes. In our talks about the future, I have found that Ned has a secret passion. He hasn't told you or his mother because he thinks you will disapprove.'

'No! We're not the disapproving types – surely.'

'You're both ambitious for Ned. You want him to go to university, for instance.'

'Is that unusual – or bad?'

'Maybe not, but that's not how Ned sees it.'

'Are you saying he doesn't want to go to university? It's early days yet, he's got a lot of time to make up his mind. Does he want to do something else? Has he told you that?'

'Frankly, yes. And I sense that he'd like me to pass it on. Although he's genuinely interested in fakes, his real interest is in gold. He loves gilded things, gold jewellery, gold objects from history, those wonderful Sienese paintings with gold backgrounds, gold bookbindings, ormolu. You'd be surprised how much reading he has done, how much he knows. Anyway, rather than go to university and study an academic subject, he wants to be a craftsman. He wants to be apprenticed to a goldsmith.'

David had been surprised and flummoxed. It had never crossed his mind that Ned might not want to go to university. He examined his feelings. Was he disappointed? To be honest, he supposed he was. He had always imagined his son at university. He realized that part of his feeling arose because the children of his friends all seemed to be going to college these days. He had assumed Ned would want the same. On the other hand, was it really so terrible that Ned should want to be a craftsman? After all, David knew plenty of picture restorers, enamellers, jewellers and, yes, gold and silversmiths – and he found them a calming breed, men and women who got quiet but very positive satisfactions from their work. The more he thought about it, the more he realized that such a career suited Ned's personality. And his son would be following him into the arts – he had always wanted that.

'What should I do?' he asked Wilde.

'Face it. Discuss it with him. Tell him how you feel. How *do* you feel?'

'Surprised. Part of me is disappointed, but I can see it makes a kind of sense for Ned.'

'Good. We're really making progress now. Let me know how your talks with him go. He'll give me his version but I'd also like to hear yours.'

Now, at lunch in Gina's, David had yet to raise the subject with Ned. He wanted to do so as naturally as possible, and hadn't yet worked out just how. At that moment Gina approached their table and spoke to Bess. The signorina was wanted on the telephone. Bess got up and went to the back of the bar, where the phone was. She was gone some time. When she returned she sat down, fiddled in her bag, then drew David to one side. 'Here are the keys to the flat. Take Ned there after lunch and I'll see you later. I'm just going to slip away, I don't want to spoil the party.'

'What's wrong? Why are you going? *Where* are you going?'

'The office, where else?'

'How long will you be? Ned will be disappointed. I'm disappointed.'

'I don't know how long. Maybe quite long. Please apologise to Ned. But I must go.'

Quickly she cupped her hand over David's mouth so he could kiss her palm.

'You haven't said what's wrong. Is it bad? You look worried.'

'I *am* worried. For Thomas's sake. We've just heard from the Archbishop of Havana. In spite of Thomas's intercession those eight assassins were executed this morning.'

When Jack Silver, the Mayor of New York, heard about Charlie Winter's heroin bust his first reaction was to visit the custom's men in the World Trade Centre. Then he called a press conference in City Hall. He strode into the room and started speaking almost before he had reached the microphone. He was a small man, with rich black hair, wide eyes and a mouth that was big in every sense. His family were in the tailoring business but you wouldn't have guessed it from his generally sloppy manner of dressing.

He spoke quickly, 'I'm sorry to call you guys here at short notice, I know you like to have a lie-in after the weekend.' The waiting reporters laughed politely – it was a joke they had heard more than twice before. 'But I'm pleased about something and I'm on fire about something. I guess I'm wild too. You could even describe me as pissed-off. And you guys know how I like to let go.'

They did indeed. Silver had got where he was by letting go. He was a professional at indignation, a master at being the outraged and innocent victim. It was no bad thing either, in its way. In fact, it was an astute political skill. People – voters – have feelings. Sometimes they have strong feelings. They don't always *want* their political representatives to see both sides of an issue. Sometimes they want to be shown that their prejudices are shared and respectable enough to be said out loud. This is what Silver saw himself as: a mouthpiece.

'What am I pleased about? I'm going to tell you. What am I steamed up about? I'll get to that later. I'm pleased, very pleased, with our boys in customs. Eleven million dollars worth of heroin isn't peanuts. Maybe that's five hundred kids here in New York who won't end up as junk. Maybe more. Those guys in customs, Charlie Winter and his fellow officers, deserve a big slap on the back. They took some risks but it worked out. I've written their boss, the Secretary of the Budget, and recommended a bonus. I have a copy of the letter here. The city is going to honour them, too, and I want you people in the press to push it. There's enough bad news in your goddamn rags – like pictures of my ugly mug – so here's some good news for a change.

'Now, what am I steamed up about? Well, it will take a little longer to explain so if you need to change the tape in your recorder, or you want to go to the john, do it now.'

Silver paused and grinned. He knew he was good copy. It was the best way of getting his message into the goddamn rags untampered with.

'What I'm steamed up about is that two of these darned heroin dealers turn out to be illegal immigrants. We pay enough in goddamn taxes to stop this sort of thing but still it goes on. And I'm hopping crazy, I'm melting with rage that these two pushers are illegal Sicilian immigrants. Let me remind you of the last time some illegal Sicilian immigrants made headlines in this country. It was a few days before the great sale of Vatican treasures here in New York, at St Patrick's Cathedral. A painting, a priceless old master as you may recall, was slashed at the Getty Museum in California. The Mafia did that because they wanted to get back at the Pope, they wanted revenge because his fund in Sicily had proved so effective. Then there was that business at

Oakland airport. What seemed like an accidental fire in a warehouse and a failure of the runway lights, just as a 727 was landing, turned out to be part of a protection racket. The 727 left the runway, killing thirty-six. No one was ever caught, but the word was that Sicilian immigrants, illegal Sicilian immigrants who had left Italy because of the Pope's fund, were responsible for that too and got some hefty payoffs from Oakland airport authority so it wouldn't happen again.

'Now, I've always been a great fan of Pope Thomas, and not just because he's an American. What he's been doing, selling off those pictures and putting the money into charity work is really neat.' Silver spread his arms. 'Oh I was a great fan. Until last night. This morning, now, I'm *still* a fan – but part of me is fuming. And that's what I want to tell you about. Last night, very late, I went down to customs to congratulate those guys. And what do I find? I find that these two Sicilians, one of whom is in hospital at your expense and mine, one of whom is in prison at your expense and mine, have also been forced to leave Sicily because of the Pope's fund.'

The reporters sat up. So far it had been amusing, a typical Silver-tongued speech. Now he was getting to the gold.

'As I say, I think the Holy Father is a fine man. I'm Jewish and Jews and Catholics have had their differences in the past. But this issue has nothing to do with that. What I'm steamed up about is that, when you come right down to it, as a result of the Pope's fund in Sicily, a bunch of Sicilian gangsters, a gang, or two gangs more likely, have come to America. Illegally. And here they have been indulging in what they know best: crime.'

He thumped the table. 'And that's not good enough! We have too much of the home-grown variety to need any assistance from outside.' He lowered his voice. 'Of course, I'm not saying His Holiness is to blame. But blame isn't the issue. The Holy Father never intended the Caravaggio painting to be slashed in L A. But it was. He never intended Fidel Castro to be attacked. But he was. He never intended those Florida bums to invade Cuba. But they did. He never intended them to be executed. But they were. He never intended airplanes flying into Oakland to be put at risk. But they were. And I'm sure he never intended his Sicilian fund to help boost heroin smuggling in New York.' He had been building up gradually through all this. Now he was shouting again. 'But it did!'

Now Silver changed tack again. He smiled. 'You boys and girls in the media are always telling us we live in a global village, an ever-smaller world in which we are all ever-more-closely related, where what happens in one place produces effects someplace else. Well, for once maybe you and me see eye-to-eye. Politicians know that. That's one of the reasons we move slowly when you people are always urging us to go faster. In any change there are effects no one can foresee. So people get hurt, often quite innocent people!' He pointed a stubby finger at them. 'I think that is what's happening here . . . I think that the Pope, for all his goodness, for all his imagination, for all his compassion, is naive.'

He held up eight fingers, knowing it would make a good picture for the next day's editions. 'So far the Holy Father's schemes have succeeded – or appear to have succeeded – in eight places. In Sicily, in Foligno, in the Marquesas Isles, in South America and in Nicaragua, in Beirut and Northern Ireland and, for all we know, behind the Iron Curtain.' He took away one hand entirely. 'But there have been three hitches also. Unintended effects. So far, I suppose, that's OK. But if anything else were to go wrong . . . well, we're all watching. You simply cannot inject money of the kind now at the Pope's disposal into the world and *not* cause ripples. That's the way the world is. Elected politicians know that.

'Now, we are going to have to pay, you and I, for those Sicilians captured on Sunday. We shall have to pay while they are being held in custody. We shall have to pay for the trial and, if they are convicted, we shall have to pay to keep them in prison until they can be deported. Can we even risk deporting them? If what we hear is true they wouldn't spend long in Italy. They immigrated here illegally once – so what's to stop them doing it again?' He looked around the room. 'I'm sorry if I've gone on too long. But I wanted you all to know the way I feel. Because I guess a lot of people in this city will be feeling the same'

By itself the Silver speech would have been bad enough. But the executions in Cuba, which Silver had referred to, complicated the Pope's situation still further. That evening Bess was summoned to the papal apartments for an emergency dinner with Thomas. It was a quiet, intimate meal: the only other guests were Thomas's two secretaries and Cardinal Rich.

Bess found Thomas perplexed by Silver's attack. He played with his soup, a chicken consommé. 'Surely a politician like Silver, an experienced man, knows that we have to take risks in whatever we do?'

'Yes,' said Rich. 'He said as much. But Silver isn't in the business of making well-considered, diplomatic moves. He's an American, a New Yorker. They pride themselves on saying what they are feeling, even if what they are feeling will change in ten minutes. You should know that, Sir, being American.'

Thomas looked thoughtful. 'Maybe I've been in Europe too long.' He turned back to Rich. 'The Fund? You are still happy with the way it's going?'

Rich was firm. 'Oh yes. This is not the time to lose our nerve. Silver was right when he said that you cannot administer the sort of money we now have without encountering problems. Charity work of any size is bound to look political. David Colwyn told me at his investiture that the British government is far from happy with their Queen, who as you know is following your example. They see her action as implicitly critical of their achievements. So there will always be that kind of risk. More serious, I think, is the danger that where so much money is concerned you will always tend to get corruption. That's not a political issue, it's a moral one and, in my view, far more damaging. The corruption behind the Cuban raid, for instance, did us much more damage than the raid itself.'

Thomas had been listening intently. Now he turned to Bess. 'Elizabeth, what do you think? Should we reply to Silver?'

The wine was sparse at papal meals and Bess was making hers last. 'I think we should reply – but discreetly and intelligently. I think we should take account of what Silver says without making a song and dance about it. I'm not sure I agree wholeheartedly with his Eminence here. I think the executions in Cuba have done us a great deal of harm, especially coming so close in time to the arrests of those Sicilians in New York. We couldn't know that this particular coincidence would happen but I suspect that, in politics, they happen all the time.'

A couple of nuns arrived to take away the soup plates. A bowl of spaghetti was placed at the centre of the table and the water and wine glasses were refilled.

'Go on, my dear. How should we respond discreetly and intelligently?' Thomas always seemed so much taller sitting down. He had a very long body.

'I'm coming to that but first let me make one other comment. The American presidential election is coming up in November. Roskill, a Roman Catholic, is going for a second term, and his Democratic opponent, the black senator from Louisiana, Oliver Fairbrother, is a baptist. So the first thing to bear in mind is that Catholicism is already an issue in the campaign. That's why I think we should respond to Silver – because the difficulties won't go away and we mustn't be seen to avoid them. Our response, though, is something else again.'

She had their complete attention. The spaghetti grew cold on the table between them. 'First, we should use the fact that the Vatican and the United States have certain things in common, the most powerful of which is a hatred of communism. The Holy See has taken the view for many years that the Church in the Eastern Bloc is staffed by KGB agents masquerading as priests. We have evidence of that and in consequence for almost as long we have funded private religious observation. With the St Patrick's money we have been able to step up our support, which is now substantial, especially in Czechoslovakia, Hungary and Rumania. Yet so far we have published very little about our achievements. Can't we bring them on to the front burner? Some successes would go down very well in the United States.'

Thomas was nodding approvingly. He turned to Rich. 'Well, Eminence? What do you think?'

'Next to a plate of pasta, I think Miss Lisle's is the most nourishing suggestion of the entire evening.'

They all smiled and the spaghetti was at last served.

Rich spoke as they helped themselves. 'Our researches are nearly complete, Holiness. We are nearly ready in Hungary and in Rumania to appoint two "*in petto*" – secret – cardinals. As a first measure you might announce that fact, that we have two men in place, even though we cannot name them. That would show we are making progress and would stress how difficult it is to work in communist countries.'

'Well, that's a start,' said Thomas. 'Perhaps we could discuss the matter of the cardinals tomorrow. We need to be certain that admitting their presence doesn't endanger their work, of course.'

Rich nodded.

Thomas turned back to Bess. 'An excellent suggestion, my dear. Anything else?'

'Yes,' she said. 'Oh yes. I haven't mentioned it before because I was waiting for the timing to be right. But now I think it is. I think you should visit America.'

# 10

Michael Molyneux stared at his boss. Kirkhill had sought him out on a building site in the Dundonald suburb of Belfast where they were just finishing a cinema renovation. Kirkhill had taken off his tie and held it in his hand. His waistcoat, under his jacket, was unbuttoned. His shirt neck was open revealing a few wisps of red-grey hair.

Molyneux frowned. 'Tell me again, Douglas. I don't believe it.'

Kirkhill waved his tie in an exhausted fashion. 'We were beaten. By Foley's, yet again. I cut where I could. I even cheated on a few things – I was determined to win this one. But it's the cheap money they're getting! Being Catholics they can do it, with this new fund of the Pope's. On a four million pound contract they undercut us by one hundred and ten thousand pounds. That's a lot of money.'

'Did you try to buy anyone a drink?'

Kirkhill stuffed the tie in his jacket pocket. 'Of course! I'm one of the bribe barons of Belfast, Michael, you know that. But Foley's did too – and they had a hundred thousand more to play with.'

The two men stood staring at the ground between them.

'Douglas?'

'Michael.'

'I remember what you said last time.'

'Hmm.'

'You said that if we didn't get this one we'd have to start laying men off.'

'Yes,' Kirkhill breathed. 'That's what I said.'

'Is it still true?'

A long pause. 'It is still true, Michael. I'm sorry.'

Another pause, even longer this time. Then Molyneux said: 'How many?'

Douglas looked his old friend in the eye. His blue eyes were sad. 'Fifty, Michael. Fifty men. Maybe more.'

Molyneux rocked on his feet. Fifty men meant fifty families affected, maybe as many as a hundred children. Jobs weren't easy to get in Ulster. Moving wasn't easy either, no one wanted to live here so you couldn't sell your house, even if you owned it. The union man was suddenly very angry. He knocked the boss's chest with the knuckle of his forefinger. 'I'm not having this, Douglas. I'm not having it, I tell you. You leave this to me.'

Thomas's American tour, when it was announced, was an immediate hit. The simultaneous announcement of two Iron Curtain cardinals *in petto*, which is the Vatican's terminology for 'secret', went down very well in the west. Also, Bess had a stroke of luck. Unexpectedly, the Chinese government finally recognized Thomas's choice as Bishop of Peking. China's three million Catholics had often had their own leaders, hitherto approved by the government but not by the Vatican. Thomas, thus, had succeeded where no one else had before. In fact, this was the result of a classic piece of *realpolitik* behind the scenes, for the Jesuits had offered to expand their teaching in the country *without* including religious instruction, at least until pupils were sixteen and old enough to decide for themselves. The offer was a simple *quid pro quo* which Thomas thought worth it. The money for these new schools was to come from the next year's St Patrick's Fund which would be administered locally through the Cardinal Archbishop in Hong Kong. Not even Jack Silver could possibly argue with the merit of providing education in poor rural areas.

A further reason why Thomas's visit caught the imagination of the American people was Bess's idea that Thomas should visit his small home town of Fort Wingate, Nebraska, before he went to Washington or any of the big cities. It put politicians where they belonged, at the back of the queue. Not that politics would be at the back for long. Thomas was scheduled to meet both presidential candidates, Roskill and Fairbrother and Mayor Silver too, come to that.

Bess was therefore gearing up for one of her particularly busy times and David's life was getting hectic again, too. The Dead Sea Scrolls sale was close and, in fact, they found they would both be in New York at the same time.

But they would probably be too busy to see much of each other. They therefore sneaked as many weekends as they could together, either in Rome or in London. It was on one of Bess's rare trips to England that she brought David the best news of all. The Holy Office had received his petition from the Archbishop of Westminster. They were over two hurdles; two more to go.

The car pulled out of Llandovery and they had their first glimpse of the River Towy. This part of Wales, due north of Swansea, began to get very heathery. For the umpteenth time, Ned squirmed in his seat. 'Can't you tell me yet where we're going?'

'No,' said David. 'I want it to be a surprise.'

It was a couple of weekends after Bess's visit to London, which had gone very well, so far as David's domestic arrangements were concerned. Bess and Ned now enjoyed each other enormously. But David was in a quandary so far as his Leonardo research was concerned. He had drawn a blank in the Vatican Archives: the letters of Elisabetta Gonzaga contained no further reference to Leonardo, either as a painter, engineer or inventor. Still, Ned's wellbeing was much more important than solving the Leonardo mystery and that was why they were in Wales now.

At Llanwarda they turned right, climbing steadily past Talley. They could see a village ahead, grey slate roofs with white chimneys. 'I think we've arrived,' said David.

Ned sat up but looked mystified. 'Where are we?'

'Two minutes and all will be revealed.' David had with him a small card with directions on it. He studied it again now. Before they entered the village they turned right, towards Cilycwm then, after a few hundred yards, left, then right again almost immediately on a road that headed into some hills. After a quarter of a mile the road stopped at a gate with a brand new green-and-white sign which read: 'PUMPSAINT GOLD MINE'.

Ned stared at the sign, then at his father.

David smiled. 'Dr Wilde said you were interested in this sort of thing. This is the only commercial gold mine operating in Britain. It reopened this year, for the first time since the 1930s. The head of Hamilton's gold and silver department arranged this visit. We are expected.'

Ned's eyes were as wide as the Towy. But all he said was 'Fantastic!'

The next three hours were a dream for Ned. David found them fascinating, too. They were shown the full workings of the mine – the drilling, the purification of the ore, the security arrangements, the finished product, smooth, shiny and bright yellow. Afterwards however, both knew that on the drive home there was some serious talking to do.

David waited until they were back on the Brecon and Abergavenny road out of Llandovery. Then he said, 'What made you so interested in gold in the first place?'

'You did, Dad.'

'What?'

'Yes. You probably don't remember but about eighteen months ago you took me to the Worshipful Company of Goldsmiths, in London.'

David did remember.

'You took me because they have there a collection of faked and forged hall-marks – forged punches, forged casts, remember?'

His father did indeed.

'You were right, it was very interesting. You know I've always liked fakes. But I found gold even more interesting.'

'Why?' It wasn't an aggressive question. David just wanted to know.

'Forgeries, I suppose, are interesting because of their imperfections. It's the little things that give the game away. On the other hand, gold is so perfect. You can see why all the ancients worshipped it. And it *looks* so marvellous. I'm not interested in gold as bullion, Dad, but in what you can do with it, in making beautiful things out of it. I know you want me to go to some egg-head university but, honestly, I'd much rather become an apprentice to a goldsmith.'

'But are you sure you want to start so early?'

'Yes. You've got to put in years and years of work before you can ever be any good. I read in a book that Benvenuto Cellini produced his famous salt cellar when he was forty-three but he'd been working in gold since he was nineteen.'

David was impressed. Ned had done his homework.

'You seem to know a lot already.'

'A bit. But there are a lot more books I want to get, exhibitions I want to see – gold coins, South American gold objects made by the Incas, Sienese painting, French eighteenth-century furniture.'

'Where does one go to learn to become a goldsmith?'

Ned looked hopefully at his father. 'There are colleges in London, then you work at one of the jewellers in London, Amsterdam, Paris or New York. A good goldsmith has to master dozens of techniques. But you can't be a great one without some flair for design too.'

His father looked across. 'And?'

'Who knows, Dad? I've done some designs at school but – well, I've never shown anybody.'

'Hmm. I'd better have a look, when we get back to Hamble.'

It was left at that, for the moment. They drove on and crossed the Severn Bridge on to the M4. As they achieved the smooth expanses of the motorway, Ned went to sleep. David kept turning the matter over in his head. And as time went on and the miles passed, and he began to get used to the idea of Ned as a craftsman, another thought from earlier in the day crept back into his mind.

The manager of the gold mine had described, in passing, the way gold and certain other colours had been singled out in the contracts of old masters as very large items of expense when pictures were commissioned. David knew that painters in Renaissance times bought their pigments already made up from druggists known, in Italy, as *speziali*. They had their own guild. The guilds had their written records, minutes etc. It was just possible that, since he had drawn a blank with Elisabetta Gonzaga's correspondence, the records of the Urbino Guild of *Speziali* might contain some mention of Leonardo, when he had ordered gold or some other precious pigment. It was a long shot but, so far as he knew, virgin territory and therefore worth a try.

*

The helicopter flew at about four-hundred feet. Cardinal Mario Pimental could see its shadow streaking across the Yuscaran scrub below. He looked down at the toy trees and occasional cows and tried to work out once again whether he found Honduras beautiful, barren or both. Tegucigalpa, not the easiest capital city in the world to pronounce, was a dump, hardly a city in the European sense at all and Pimental was a good Portuguese, educated at the Lateran University in Rome. Give him a Mediterranean city – Barcelona, Naples, Genoa – any day. Still, as a cardinal appointed to the sacred college by Thomas, he had not been able to refuse the assignment as the man in charge of the St Patrick's Fund in this area. He had first met Thomas in Argentina and shared his idealism. They had had many adventures together in the Far East when they were younger and the Holy Father probably thought he still retained his appetite for the remote, just as he himself did. And Pimental was good at the job, too, though he would rather have been in Europe. After the Cuban fiasco, Thomas had tightened up the whole operation, and all expenditures had to be personally sanctioned by the relevant cardinal. Further projects could only proceed one stage at a time with a visit from the cardinal in between.

That was why Pimental was in Honduras now. A small township was being built near the border with Nicaragua, to house exiles from that troubled country. Thomas was aware that these people occasionally mounted raids into Nicaragua and he was adamant that Vatican funds were only to be used for peaceful purposes: it was Pimental's job to ensure that what was built matched in cost exactly the funds provided. Nicaragua was a Marxist state, godless despite the presence of one or two renegade priests in the government, and the Vatican could therefore support the exiles with a clear conscience, so long as its resistance did not extend to the provision of arms.

So far the money provided had been spent on a dirt road, which the helicopter was overflying now, on electric power, a massive pump for water, some trucks and telephone lines. The exiles were still living in tents but if, as a result of Pimental's visit today, it turned out that all their figures added up, then the go-ahead would be given for prefabricated houses to be built. This was, therefore, an important visit by the cardinal.

'How much further?' he shouted to the pilot, above the rattle.

The pilot looked at his watch. 'Thirteen minutes. We follow this road as far as the river, then hop across some mountains which the road has to skirt, rejoin the road and we're there.'

Pimental looked ahead. The yellow strip of road unravelled before them like a long thin shoelace. Up ahead he could see the river. There was no real expanse of water, just a dry, stony bed waiting for the occasional flash flood. As he stared, however, he saw something glint. It didn't look like water.

'What's that?' he shouted, pointing.

The pilot leaned forward, then lifted his binoculars. 'Looks like an accident at the river.'

'Can we help?'

The pilot looked at his watch doubtfully. 'We'll be late.'

Pimental tapped the pilot's arm. 'Let's have a closer look. If we're half an hour late it's not the end of the world.'

As they descended and drew close they could see that a truck was overturned, half in and half out of the river bed. A car, an enormous, battered American model from the era of black and white films had smashed into it and, amazingly, the truck had come off worse. The sun glinted off the metalwork and the windscreens. There had been a fire, the blackened smudge on the bonnet of the car was clearly visible from the air. Two men were kneeling over a third, laid out on the ground. A fourth man was waving a yellow shirt wildly, trying to attract the helicopter's attention.

The river bed itself was the flattest terrain, so the pilot put the helicopter down there. Pimental got out and motioned for him to follow. 'You know some first aid?'

The pilot nodded, retrieved a box from the back of the cockpit, and followed the cardinal.

The man who had been waving came towards them, pointing to a dry way across the mud of the river bed. When he saw the red cardinal's piping on Pimental's soutane, he dropped to one knee. Pimental automatically held his ring out to be kissed but he looked at the same time to where the man was lying near the overturned truck. 'Is he still alive?' he asked.

'Alive, Eminence,' said the man. Then, instead of kissing the ring, he suddenly grabbed Pimental's hand and, rising swiftly to his feet, pulled the cardinal's arm behind his back. 'Alive, Eminence,' he repeated, jabbing a pistol into his back. 'And if you want to stay that way you will do exactly what I tell you!'

Pimental, his arm twisted agonizingly up between his shoulders, watched as the apparently injured man now leaped to his feet and the other two with him seized small machine guns from the car and trained them on the pilot.

For a moment the whole scene froze. Then the man behind Pimental yelled: 'Cesare! The helicopter!'

The third man ran to the machine. He stopped, reached into his shirt and took out a green-black grenade about the size of an avocado. He slipped out the pin and rolled the grenade under the helicopter, behind the cockpit, where the fuel tanks were. He ran and was well into safety as, seconds later, the helicopter was blown to pieces, first in a hard shattering of glass and metal and then a softer billowing as a red and yellow ball of flame and a sooty black feather of smoke followed it into the sky.

Pimental felt himself shoved forward. 'To the jeep!' yelled the voice behind his back.

He was pushed past the 'accident' and back along the road. After about a hundred yards they turned off the road on to a track. The pilot was being shoved in much the same way behind him. The two other men followed at a distance, covering everybody with the machine guns, just in case.

A quarter of a mile down the track, they came to a couple of jeeps cunningly concealed in the scrub and guarded by a fifth man. Pimental was roped to the front seat of one jeep, the pilot to the other. Both had sub-machine guns at their necks.

The jeeps started back down the track to the road, and turned along it towards the river. They saw no one. The inactivity wouldn't last, however. The cardinal would soon be overdue at his destination and the feather of black smoke rising from what was left of the helicopter now reached a hundred feet or more into the heavens.

When the jeeps reached the river they turned upstream, transferred to the sand, and picked up speed. No one spoke for about fifteen minutes. Then, with the river bed becoming narrower and rockier, the jeeps turned back to the bank where a track came down to meet it. This led uphill through some dense trees. There was some argument as to which route to take when they came to a fork but the man who had twisted Pimental's arm was clearly the leader, and prevailed. They took the more southerly route and eventually began to descend a long slope into a forest. The driver switched off the engine and coasted. In the silence they could hear if they were being followed. Behind them all was still. The descent, Pimental thought, was like sinking in a submarine in a leaf green sea.

Then they came to a ridge where the trees thinned and, two hundred feet below them, the cardinal could see a green fertile valley with the white and brown buildings of a small town.

The leader addressed Pimental directly. 'Jalapa,' he said. 'Welcome to Nicaragua, Eminence.'

Bess sat at her desk and prayed that the phone wouldn't ring for at least five minutes. It hadn't stopped all day and she was badly in need of a break. The time was already eleven-thirty and there was no hope of bed yet.

She wasn't in her own office but in the special operations room set up in the apostolic palace to handle Pimental's kidnap. The room was on the second floor, in the secretariat of state. Since Massoni's resignation, Thomas had acted as his own Secretary of State. The room was small but had a high ceiling, tall windows with lace curtains, and was hung

with ancient maps. Someone had once collected cartographical curiosi-
ties – maps of places like Friesland and the island of California, which
never existed.

One of Bess's assistants was with her, plus Rich's secretary, since the
Fund was obviously involved, and Ramon Lucientes, the Holy Father's
Mexican secretary, who was in charge of this emergency. From time to
time Thomas himself had looked in. Bess had instructions to inform
him the minute there was any development. They were waiting now
for the latest demands of the Nicaraguans.

The Sandinistas had been clever. For a day after the helicopter's
charred remains had been found, they had allowed everyone to think
that the cardinal and pilot had been killed in an accidental plane crash.
The Vatican had received a lot of sympathy and His Holiness, through
Bess, had announced a memorial mass to be held in St Peter's. Pimental
had been a close friend and Thomas was deeply upset.

Then, in a dramatic move in Managua, the Nicaraguan capital, the
Sandinistas summoned foreign reporters to a press conference at the
Camino Real hotel. There, to everyone's astonishment, they produced
Pimental, alive, apparently well, but under armed guard.

The cardinal made a short speech, saying he was well looked after,
though naturally somewhat tired. No one in the Nicaraguan government had spoken with him and, so far as he was concerned, no kidnap
demands had been made. He seemed genuinely perplexed. Then the
Nicaraguan Foreign Secretary marched in.

Miguel Almirante was a small man with pale skin, dark hair and
sharp, jerky eyes. Speaking rapidly, he announced that forty-three
people had been killed in and around Jalapa in recent weeks by snipers
and night raiders. Most of these raiders, he said, came from the settlement known locally as Nueve Managua – his soldiers laughed grimly
– which was being supported by Vatican funds and had been about to
receive a visit by Cardinal Pimental. The settlement was anathema to
the Nicaraguan government, said Almirante. It was not on Nicaraguan
soil but was being used as a safe base from which guerrillas could attack
across the border. Almirante said he hoped the cardinal would contact
the Pope while he was in Nicaragua and discuss what might be done
to prevent the funding of such attacks.

These tactics were designed, of course, to get the world's attention.
And indeed, the Nicaraguan gambit paid off dramatically: world press
coverage was phenomenal.

Thomas, his instincts still sound, responded promptly and forth-
rightly. He condemned the Sandinistas, praised the courage of Pimental
and the pilot and refused to negotiate with Managua while hostages
were being held. He delivered the speech himself, and his firm stance
had won him many admirers.

The Sandinistas' response, carefully calculated, was brutal. The

Vatican had until midnight (Nicaraguan time) to agree to disperse the Nueve Managua settlement. If Thomas failed Pimental would be executed as a *quid pro quo* for the forty-three Nicaraguans killed around Jalapa by snipers and raiders. Thomas had promised no deal. Managua was eight hours behind Rome: there were eight and a half hours still to go.

Bess was exhausted but she had at least the strength to call David. 'Today has been bloody, darling, and there's worse to come, I'm sure. I sometimes wish I'd let you stop that tanker in Venice – and we could have sailed away on it.'

'You'd soon have got bored.'

'Yes, I know. I couldn't give all this up really. How's Ned?'

'Better than ever. Making friends at last. The shrink gets more optimistic by the week. He always asks after you – Ned, I mean.'

'Well, when we all settle down, we must have a holiday together. What do you say?'

'Can't come soon enough, so far as I am concerned.'

They hung up, each feeling wretchedly distant from the other, and aware of the tragic backdrop to their conversation.

In Rome the night wore on. Midnight, one, two, three, three thirty. Seven thirty in Central America. A nun in white brought soup, sandwiches, coffee, wine. Rich's secretary stood up and stretched. 'Why don't they call?' he muttered.

As if to answer his question, the phone rang. Lucientes took the call. But it was Thomas himself, on his internal line, calling down from his private apartment upstairs, to check that they had all been fed and were in reasonable spirits. He said he was going to try to sleep for an hour. Everybody settled down again.

Four o'clock. Four thirty, four forty-five. The sandwiches were finished, the coffee flask empty. No one wanted the wine that was left. It was nearly nine in Central America.

Finally, a few minutes after five, the phone did ring. But only once before Lucientes lifted the receiver. There was a hissing down the line: it was an international call.

'Managua here,' said a voice in Spanish.

'I hear you well.'

'Who is that?'

Lucientes gave his name.

'Is the Holy Father with you?'

'No, he is upstairs sleeping. Give me your message. I will pass it to him immediately.'

'The price is ten million dollars.'

'What?'

'Ten million dollars. You have a fund – yes – a special fund. You send some of it to Honduras – ten million – for houses. You say. We

202

want the same for Nicaragua. To build houses also, equipment for factories, for farms. Tell the Holy Father that we shall not harm his friend the cardinal if he agrees to give us this money within one week. I will call in an hour. You must give me your answer then.'

Thomas was woken and was in the operations room in less than fifteen minutes. He wore a white shirt, black trousers, slippers, no skull cap. But he was as impressive as ever, thought Bess, though his limp, at this moment of crisis, was especially pronounced. He was smoking. Nuns, typically calm and immaculate, brought fresh coffee and hot rolls.

'I suppose it's good news that they've changed their demands,' said Rich's secretary. 'Maybe it shows they never intended to kill – '

Thomas cut him off. 'We've been had.'

'What do you mean?'

Bess was puzzled too.

Thomas gulped some coffee. 'I've a shrewd idea our Sandinista friends intended this all along. They must have guessed we would not negotiate while they were holding a hostage. They also knew that if they *started* by asking us for money, they would look very bad. This way they've been much cleverer.' He limped to the window and looked out on a deserted St Peter's Square. 'Having made a set of ideological demands, which we haven't met, they now reduce them to merely financial ones. People take ideologies more seriously than money and so, if we continue to hold out, it is *we* who are made to look bad. . . . You know, I have to admire their thinking. The way they set their demand at exactly the amount we put into Honduras has a symmetry about it, an internal fairness that makes it very difficult for us.'

'You're not thinking of paying them are you?' It was Rich's secretary. He stared at the Pope.

'Yes. We have to. These aren't ordinary kidnappers. They think of themselves as soldiers, idealists, trying to raise money for their country. They mean what they say. We may not like their politics but there it is. They won't haggle over cash: they want the same as we put into Honduras.'

He looked at his watch, then at Lucientes 'They will be calling in . . . twenty-four minutes. I'm going to get some more sleep. When they come through, tell them we accept.'


The Vatican's deal with the Sandinistas produced a mixed reaction around the world. Hardliners disapproved of any move which gave comfort to kidnappers, whoever they were. On the other hand, though Nicaragua was now officially Marxist, many people there were in fact still deeply religious Catholics. The Nicaraguan government's handling of the whole business was extremely distasteful to such people and there were demonstrations in Managua and a mass was held in Pimental's honour.

Once the cardinal was safe in Rome, Thomas announced that the new town project on the Honduras-Nicaraguan border would continue to be built as planned, but that the town now had a name. It was to be called Pimental.

Somewhere a clock chimed the hour. It was too dark for Michael Molyneux to read his watch. He counted the strokes: three o'clock. The others should be arriving any minute. He was craving for a cigarette but it was too dangerous. He couldn't risk being seen. A light breeze swept his hair, the only sound save for his breathing. As leader he had to be here first but he was very nervous and, now that it came to it, more than a little frightened.

He heard footsteps approaching on the pavement and moved back behind the wall. But the footsteps were of only one person and they went on past, up the road. No, when they came they would come in pairs.

It was a pity the operation had to be so large – three sets of two men, plus himself, making seven in all. But they mustn't get caught and it was safer this way. There were council houses nearby: any sound they made might carry that far. God, he so badly wanted a cigarette. But he didn't dare risk it. Instead he reached into his pocket for some chocolate and slid a square of it into his mouth. Amazing how it warmed his insides.

More steps. Surely this was the first two men. There couldn't be *that* many people around in Belfast at three in the morning. He strained his ears against the wind: were there two pairs of feet?

*Yes.*

On cue the sound of the steps stopped and, after a few moments, squelching could be heard as they stepped off the pavement and onto the grass. He still didn't move; they would know where to go. They were guards. He caught glimpses of faces as, close now, they separated and moved in different directions.

Another three minutes then more steps, two more figures separating in the dark.

Only two more to come – but they had the equipment. He bit into the last of the chocolate. The wind hissed about his ears – what was that? Yes, two sets of steps. Slower, more deliberate than the others. As they should be. More uneven. Again the steps stopped. Again there was a pause. This time he stepped out from behind the wall and whispered, 'Over here!'

They followed him. Ten yards. Twenty. He found the door. Still no one spoke as the two who had been last to arrive put down the drums they were carrying and made a back for him. For a big man Molyneux was surprisingly light on his feet. He stepped on to a knee, then climbed to a shoulder. He stood so that his head was above the edge of the wall. It was breezier here, perfect conditions. And there was more light; he could detect the glow of the city to the east. Swiftly, he hauled himself on to the top of the wall and sat. This was the tricky part – dropping down the other side without making a sound. He jumped.

Jeesus! There was a deep puddle, and a distinctive sucking sound broke the silence as he landed. He stood in the mud, listening.

Nothing.

He let another minute go by and then eased back the bolts of the gate and pulled the door inwards. The two men outside manoeuvred the drums through. A fourth man slipped out of the dark and came in with them. He was to guard the gate. A fifth man would be watching the gate on the outside. The two others watched from further away, in case the police should choose tonight to pay one of their visits. There was no nightwatchman at this yard and the police, Molyneux knew, prowled around every few days.

Inside, the floor of the timber yard was mostly concreted over, so to maintain silence they now pulled large woollen socks over their shoes. Sounds travelled on the wind. Molyneux reminded his men the housing estate wasn't far away.

Taking one of the drums, he whispered: 'I'll deal with the offices as planned; you do the timber.'

The yard was conveniently arranged for what they had in mind. The offices and warehouse, containing the most valuable materials, were in the middle, entirely ringed by stores of raw timber, half-made-up doors, staircases, kitchen units, window frames and so on. Even the offices themselves were made largely of wood.

But it wasn't easy to slop petrol over walls and timber stacks without making a noise and the job took longer than they had anticipated. Molyneux's two helpers went right around the edge of the yard, dousing most heavily the section near the gate where the fire would start. Molyneux himself doused the wooden office walls. It took fifteen minutes, though it felt much, much longer. Then the three of them returned to the gate, where the guard joined them. They slid back the bolts and all except Molyneux and one other man melted quietly away into the darkness of the city.

'Ready?' Molyneux whispered. For reply a stick was handed to him, one end wrapped in rag. The smell gave away the fact that the rag was soaked in petrol. They had to move quickly now, before their handiwork could evaporate into the night sky.

He ran again to the office building, holding the stick. He took a lighter from his pocket and flicked it. It flared and went out in the breeze. Damn. He tried again. The lighter flared and went out once more. He tried a third time, getting nervous. This time the rag caught and burst into flame. Quickly he laid it against a wooden wall he had well doused and which still reeked of petrol. Then he ran.

The other man was waiting. As soon as he had seen Molyneux's stick in flames he had lit his own. He stood now, as Molyneux ran past him to the gate, then tossed his torch into a pile of narrow wooden timbers which had been fully soaked in petrol. Then he too ran.

Out through the gate, they pulled the socks from their shoes. Then away. The others had already vanished.

The flames caught immediately on the timber. The offices, which were made from harder wood, took a little longer. The paintwork caught first, then the wood underneath began to smoulder. In three minutes the fire had taken hold and the first orange-white fingers of flame began to poke above the walls of the yard. In six minutes the fire was out of control. It was another three minutes before a milkman on his way to work spotted the glow. It took him two more minutes to find a phone and another six for the first fire engine to arrive.

By then it was too late to save anything. And by then Michael Molyneux and the others were a long way from Foley's.


'. . . Hans Holbein did charity work. Lorenzo Lotto and Vincenzo Catena left money in their wills for the sons of poor painters. Veronese helped out his friend Schiavone, even the great Titian himself tried to get work put in the way of *his* friend, the architect Sansovino. Hogarth was a governor of the Foundling Hospital in London. I therefore conclude, Mr President, that painters and other artists have historically been as concerned with the relief of suffering and the alleviation of poverty as any group of people. And so I can see nothing odd, nothing unusual, nothing unpalatable in Her Majesty's desire to sell some of her collection in order to help the world's poor. In fact, quite the contrary. I believe this is as noble a purpose for art as the original impulse which created these works. Mr President, I beg to oppose.'

With a flourish, David picked his notes from the wooden box in front of him, and flopped back on the bench behind. Lusty applause broke out all around, spiced with cries of 'Shame'.

He had been in two minds whether to accept the invitation to take part in this debate. Ever since the 1930s when the undergraduates had voted *not* to fight for king and country, the Oxford Union Debating Society had attracted more than its fair share of publicity. It was, without doubt, a curious institution. A small room crowded with young men and women, clever above everything else, all tucked up in white tie and tails, who – when they had the floor – were as pompous as they were self-confident, as wet as they were witty. And yet it was undeniable that, over the years, the undergraduates who held office in the Union very often went on to become prominent politicians or government officers. The Union, despite its anachronisms, despite its ridiculous rituals, or perhaps because of them, still retained its appeal.

The motion this evening was: 'This House believes that the Royal Collection should remain royal.' David had found himself in a dilemma when the invitation had arrived and not a little irritated. On the one hand he was drawn to the debate. But he was also irritated, because the debate's choice of motion showed that, as he had feared, the indignation felt by some people at the Queen's sale would just not go away.

David was opposing the motion, of course, with Sir Edgar Seton. Proposing was Walter Haffner, of Cambridge, one of the three professors who had originally written to *The Times,* and Euan Metcalfe, a Tory backbencher who was widely regarded as voicing the Prime Minister's views. Metcalfe was an art dealer as well as an M P.

The professor had opened the debate and, though a university man himself, he clearly had no experience of the Oxford Union for his contribution was too earnest, too pedantic, too moral in tone. Oxford wanted its erudition heavily larded with wit. On the other hand Seton had been an even worse disaster. His jokes had been feeble and he had hectored the audience, claiming in so many words that the Queen could do as she pleased and the sale was no one else's business. He had offered no intellectual arguments, had not treated the national heritage issue, and had made no one laugh.

Metcalfe was different again, and a great success. He was clearly a professional. He had a fund of stories, largely irrelevant to the debate but very funny, and had even David helpless with laughter at one point. Metcalfe also felt very strongly on the issue and this came across. He had the sense, however, to wrap his feeling in a simple – but forceful – argument, concentrating by way of demonstration on just one of the pictures in the royal sale, a Claude which had arrived in Britain after being seized when an eighteenth-century French warship sailing from Italy to France was intercepted and captured. The captain of the vessel had given the Claude to his monarch, Metcalfe said. 'But we should not forget that the captain himself was paid in part out of public taxes,' he went on. 'It was public taxes that helped capture the Claude, so we all own a little piece of it. Indeed,' said Metcalfe, 'if the Claude were to fetch say five million pounds at the sale, which would not be unusual these days, then I suggest that, with fifty-seven million people in Britain today, we each have about a ninepenny share in the Claude. And I can tell this house,' he wound up amid smiles, 'I want to keep my ninepence right here in Britain.'

His was a hard act to follow but David had some experience of appearing in public. He was an auctioneer, after all, and it was as an auction that he treated the debate. Metcalfe had left his notes on the box which acted as a lectern at the union. David leaned across picked them up and held them aloft. With his other hand he reached into the pocket of his dress trousers and, with a deliberate flourish, took from it his gavel. A cheer went up.

'What!' he shouted above the cheers, '*What* am I bid for this manuscript? I can't claim it's in good condition. The jokes are medieval, the sentiments are Victorian, the paper is cheap but you would only expect that from its previous owner.' They were at least laughing, Metcalfe included. 'Do I hear a *sou*? A *sequin*, an *ecu*, a *scudo*?'

'How about a sovereign?'

It was Metcalfe, his quickness earning him further applause.

'Bought in!' David yelled above the laughter, dropping the papers on the lectern in front of him. At least he had shown that his side had a sense of humour. From then on he had their attention. He made no other attempt to be as funny as Metcalfe, but he kept his argument light. His main thesis had been provided by Bess, it was an account of the plans of earlier Popes to sell off the Vatican treasures and why they hadn't succeeded. His aim was to show that throughout history conservative forces in matters of art were as narrow-minded as the Queen's critics were now being.

It was fun, the speech went over well, and he sat now, chatting to Metcalfe, as the votes were counted. David wanted to win this vote. He knew the union was a small place and unimportant. He knew that the debate was judged strictly on the merits of the arguments, not on the audience's own convictions and thus its result would be no gauge of public feeling. Even so, he wanted to win. His attention wandered from what Metcalfe was saying. He had never imagined Seton would speak so badly. Strange.

The union president got to his feet. He was a small, rather chubby man, already going bald though he was barely twenty-two. But he had a big voice, which he clearly liked the sound of. 'Ladies and gentlemen,' he barked. 'I will remind you of the motion: That this House believes the Royal Collection should remain royal. And the result is: for the Ayes – 112; for the Noes – 103.'

David's heart sank. They had lost.

The first inkling David had that the Dead Sea Scrolls sale might present real problems came when he received a visit, in London, from the CIA officer attached to the American Embassy in Grosvenor Square. To begin with the man seemed interested in the exact route which the scrolls were taking on their journey from Jerusalem to New York. Given the scrolls' religious importance, the CIA believed it was at least possible that one or other terrorist group would try to hijack them. But then the conversation moved on to three employees of Hamilton's who the man clearly regarded as security risks. One was an Iranian, another was a young French woman who had been born in the Lebanon and the third was an American girl with an Egyptian boyfriend. David knew little of his staff's private lives, but he resisted the CIA man's suggestion that these three individuals be put on other duties, away from the Manhattan offices, until the sale was over. Apart from the fact that there was really nowhere he could send them, he refused to believe any of them was a security risk.

'But that makes no sense, Mr Colwyn. If seemingly innocent people were not occasionally more than they seemed, there would be no such thing as terrorism.'

'Yes, I understand. But these are people who have worked here for years. They've been trusted before and they can be trusted now.'

'Can they? Have you ever sold anything of this religious significance before?'

'No, but – '

'That's my point. These scrolls are so important – forget the monetary value for a moment – that the situation is unique. If a terrorist group got their hands on them their bargaining power would be unique also.'

David saw the American's point. He promised he would think carefully about the people concerned but he would like firm evidence that, besides having Middle East connections, they were actually involved with illegal groups. He owed them that, at least.

The CIA man promised that as soon as they discovered anything concrete, David would be the first to know.

After he had gone, David felt uneasy. He could do without trouble over this Israeli auction. The royal sale was being difficult enough. The debate at the Oxford Union had received more publicity than he'd expected and Haffner, the Cambridge don, had written again to *The Times*. The issue simply refused to go away.

The government, too, was still putting pressure on Hamilton's. When, in an unprecedented move, the Victoria & Albert Museum had decided to 'de-access' – ie sell off – some of the less distinguished pieces which it kept out of sight in its basement, once again the business had gone to Steele's. Even though these pieces were less distinguished in a museum sense, they still included some very fine works of art – paintings, furniture, Far Eastern jewellery and sculpture. Art worth millions. It was a blow to Hamilton's prestige that the firm could ill afford.

On the other hand, the long queues outside the Queen's gallery in Buckingham Palace Road testified to the popularity, among ordinary people, of Her Majesty's decision. Thousands went to the gallery every day and paid two pounds to see the works on display. No figures had yet been released but David reckoned the money raised had to be significant. He hoped the palace would announce the figures soon: in his view the sale could do with some good publicity.

In the meantime Ned, thank God, seemed to be pulling round really well. His metalwork designs were very promising. David had looked through them when they had got back from the trip to the gold mine in Wales. They ranged from jugs to medals, from cuff links to brooches, from nut crackers to bells, and included a brooch based on Bess's name in convoluted filigree. Because of the cost of working in solid gold, David had said Ned must start by learning the techniques for laying on gold leaf. In any case, that was something that could be done at school – he could decorate woodwork, leatherwork and pottery produced in the school's workshops. Ned had been delighted and the pair had a date to visit together a forthcoming exhibition of gilt bookbindings at the British Museum. And, in addition, Tony Wilde was talking about terminating Ned's treatment.

David's meeting with the CIA was followed within a week by one with a man who said he was from the Israeli Embassy in London, though David suspected he was from Mossad, the Israeli security service. 'I see from your confidential report to our government,' the Israeli said, 'that you expect the sale of the scrolls to fetch anything from ten million dollars to fifty million dollars. Can't you be more specific?'

'No. I'm sorry. Even those figures are guesses. With the Raphaels and Titians we sold for His Holiness we at least had something to go on – masterpieces we had auctioned earlier on. But nothing of this age and religious significance has ever come on to the market before.'

The Israeli shrugged. 'The CIA, as I believe you know, are worried that one or other of the terrorist groups might try to steal these scrolls. That's not our worry. Our worry is that Orthodox Jews, militant right-wingers, will intervene in the sale. They oppose the disposal of any part of Israel's heritage. They didn't fight for 2,000 years to get Israel back, they say, just to sell off bits now. And there are a lot of Jews in New York, Mr Colwyn. Many of them are orthodox and some of them can be very tough. I'm here to tell you that I think we can contain them. But – and this is an important "but" – it will be of great benefit to the Israeli government if we can announce very soon what we are going to do with the money. That will take the wind out of the orthodox sails, so to speak. Now, if you were able, as with His Holiness the Pope, to advance us some of the money beforehand you would be doing us all a very great favour.'

David had foreseen this. Indeed, he was a little surprised the Israelis hadn't asked for cash up-front before now.

'I will do what I can,' he said. 'But quite frankly this particular market is so uncertain that one of the possibilities we have to consider is that the auction receives no bids at all. Personally I don't for a minute believe that will happen. Nevertheless, the Pope's sales have involved known commodities for which there was a known demand. The sale of the Dead Sea Scrolls involves neither. Even if I can get an advance through my board, I doubt whether it would be more than five million dollars.

That's a lot of money for a manuscript but it's not that much in political terms. I wonder if the social programmes you could put into effect with that amount of money would really steal the thunder of determined Orthodox Jews.'

'Clearly put,' said the man from the embassy. 'But my government's instructions are clear, too. We must ask for an advance before the sale. I repeat: your main problem will come from Orthodox Jews and, in my government's judgement, an advance sum will help defuse that opposition.'

The board meeting which considered the Israeli request was very stormy. Probably, David reflected afterwards, he had mishandled it. He opened the discussion, describing his visit from the CIA and from the Israeli embassy. He put the arguments of the Israeli government and explained his own views. As soon as he had finished Sam Averne weighed in. He was ferociously *against* giving the Israelis any advance money at all. He used David's own arguments, and, reversing what he had said at earlier board meetings, threw in a reason of his own: 'Anyway, we are old-fashioned auctioneers, not bankers.'

David had a shrewd idea that Averne was motivated, among other things, by old-fashioned anti-Semitism but he couldn't say so.

What Averne's fierce attack did do, however, was to make it appear that Averne and David were on different sides. In fact David had simply put both sides of the argument fairly to the board but, by opposing the advance to the Israelis so strongly, Averne made it seem as if David was equally strongly in favour. So, when it came to a vote at the end of the discussion, and the board decided that it would not advance any money at all to the Israeli government, the impression to everyone present was that, for the first time, David Colwyn had lost a vote to Sam Averne.

The Israeli at the embassy was phlegmatic when David called him to tell him the bad news. 'Well, Mr Colwyn, we shall have to do what we can to make sure the sale goes off well. All I can say is that by this decision you people have made my job harder. A lot harder.'

The black car moved at walking pace along the Crumlin Road. A thin grey drizzle was falling. The flowers were the only spot of colour: they nearly submerged the car, there were so many of them. Only the driver had any idea of the intensity of the fire at Foley's. The remains of Donny Kelleher, the new night watchman who had burned to death, weighed but a few pounds, there was so little of them left. The coffin behind was mainly for show, for it was largely empty. A grisly thought. The driver could feel the difference in the way the hearse steered.

Behind the car several hundred mourners stretched back, their numbers swollen by the sense of outrage sparked the night before by a report in the Belfast *Telegraph*. The article had stated that Kelleher's death had not been accidental. According to a confidential report prepared by the fire brigade the fire at Foley's had been arson. Worse, again according to the *Telegraph*, it was rumoured that the fire had been started by Protestant rivals of Foley's in the construction business. They hadn't meant to kill Kelleher, it was said, because they didn't know he was there. But he was dead all the same. Catholic firms in Ulster had been having it good lately, thanks to the low interest loans they enjoyed as a result of the St Patrick's Fund money, and the Protestant firms were obviously hurting.

The driver turned the wheel and the car swung into St Brendan's cemetery. Kelleher's widow and relatives had only learned about the arson theory the day before, so there had been no chance to change the church which was obviously now going to be far too small for the crowd that had turned out. In no time it was full, with a hundred more outside.

The service was short and the sermon was not especially fiery or sentimental, at least not by Belfast standards. Nor was the priest particularly political. Afterwards, however, when the coffin was carried outside to the grave, the mourners noticed three men in long raincoats and dark glasses slip through the mass of people and position themselves on either side of the slit in the earth. Kelleher's widow, a small dark woman with a pinched, angry mouth, stood at one end of the grave flanked by her grown-up children. As the coffin was lowered into the ground and the priest's voice was the only sound, each of the men in raincoats donned a black beret. The coffin reached the bottom and was laid gently on the soil. From under their coats the three men took pistols. Kelleher, in view of recent events, was to be awarded a military funeral, I R A-style.

The low murmur of the priest's voice was still the only sound. Moments later he finished and stepped back and raised his head. He may not have been political but he was Irish and knew what was coming.

The three pistols were raised and aimed solemnly to the sky. The angry widow swelled with bitter pride as three shots rang out in unison three times across the graves of the churchyard and echoed off the walls of the council houses nearby.

'Mary, mother of Jesus,' whispered the driver, who was standing by the hearse, sharing a cigarette with one of the men who would cover over the grave when everyone had left. 'There's going to be trouble now.'

'This is a Maioli binding, Dad.'

David leaned over the cabinet in the British Museum. 'What on earth does Maioli mean?'

'It's the Latin version for Mathieu. Thomas Mathieu was secretary to

Catherine de' Medici in the sixteenth century. He had a great library and his books are famous for their bindings. They had speckled gold dots all over them. See?'

David was impressed with Ned's knowledge.

The boy pulled his father across the room. 'Now this is a fanfare binding, dad. The gold is tooled in designs based on the figure "8", with a space left blank in the middle for the family's coat of arms. These are slightly later.'

'I don't like those as much.'

'No, nor me.'

David looked down at his son. 'When am I going to see something *you've* made?'

'Soon. But have a look over here. This is an English binding, by Edwards of Halifax. See what they've done here . . . there are two books. One is closed properly, and all you can see at the edge of the book is a solid mass of gold leaf. Now, the next book has the leaves splayed out . . .'

David looked and was delighted. On the leaf edges of this other book could be seen a coloured illustration that was painted as if under the gold.

'Neat, eh? You can only see that illustration when the edges are splayed out. Otherwise it's hidden. They had a passion for secrets in those days.'

'They certainly did. I've run up against a few secrets myself, in the past few days.'

'What do you mean?'

'With my Leonardo research. I've been looking through the guild records for *speziali* and apothecaries in Urbino, to see if there's any mention of Leonardo buying colours there.'

'No luck?'

'No. The Vatican sent me a whole microfiche of the documents but, so far, nothing. Any ideas?'

'Where did Leonardo die?'

'Cloux, near Amboise in France. Why?'

'It's just that when people die things get written down. You told me that. It's after people die, you said, that the auction houses contact their heirs, to see whether anything is going to be sold off. Maybe the same happened with Leonardo. If there are any lost documents maybe they are not in Urbino or Rome, but in France.'

'Hmm. Interesting but doubtful. Now, while I remember, as I'm going to be away in New York for a few weeks, I want to make it up to you when I get back. Is there anything else you'd like to do, any other exhibition you want to see, come May or June?'

Ned was looking at another binding. 'Well, there is one exhibition I'd like to see, but it's in term time and it means going to Paris. On the other hand, if you're going to Amboise, you could take me along and we could stop off on the way.'

'What's the exhibition?'

'Russian icons, at the Louvre. In about a month.'

'What have they got to do with gold?'

'Dad! They have gold leaf halos and backgrounds with unusual patterns stamped on them. The stamps are different from anything else and I want to be able to copy them. What do you think?'

'Sounds like a good trip *if* I need to go to Amboise, of which I am very doubtful.'

David was wrong, however. The more he thought about Ned's comment on Leonardo, the more it seemed to him that the fate of the great man's papers after his death was a possible source for him to follow. From books, David discovered that the majority of Leonardo's belongings, when he died in 1519, had passed to a friend, Francesco Melzi, who had taken them all back to his native Milan. Melzi had made an attempt to catalogue them but, when *he* died, his son Orazio had dumped them in an attic, regarding them as no more than trifles. Later they had been found and, through one series of adventures or another, dispersed around Europe. Much had been lost and what remained was spread between Milan, Madrid, Paris and London.

Though there were many original writings by Leonardo in these several museums, David reckoned they must all have been gone over thoroughly by scholars already. He decided, therefore, to start at the house in which Leonardo had died. It was a museum now and there might be some clue there to guide him towards one line of inquiry or another. If the dates fitted and he was back from New York in time, then he and Ned could kill two birds with one stone and visit Amboise *and* the icon exhibition on the same visit.

But first there was the Dead Sea Scrolls sale to get out of the way. Sam Averne had been throwing his weight around since he had won the board vote and at the final board meeting before David left for New York, he made another attack on the Israelis, asking if this was really the kind of business Hamilton's needed. His contacts in New York had told him there might be 'bad trouble' and he wondered aloud whether the firm shouldn't, even at this late date, pull out. He had also got hold of figures from inside Hamilton's which confirmed what David had known for some time, that business in Italy was down by over twenty per cent as a knock-on effect of the Italian government's opposition. Averne said: 'I also hear on the grapevine that the British government is thinking of amending the law on the export of works of art. At present, as we all know, if someone wants to export a painting or a piece of sculpture, or anything else which is regarded as of national importance, it can be held up for several months, to give the nation time to raise the money to purchase the item itself. My information is that the government is thinking of extending the time-lag, to two years.'

'But – ' the Earl of Afton tried to interrupt but Averne stormed on.

'I know. They may not get it through parliament. But if they do it will have a very depressing effect on the auction market here. Foreign buyers may simply not bother to bid for items if they know that anything worthwhile is going to be held up for so long. The government may be considering this measure as a way of preventing the sale of the Royal Collection, but they must be aware that it will have a wider impact. Hamilton's won't be very popular – with anyone.'

'But it's against their own interests to hit the auction business. We are a source of foreign currency.' Afton spoke at last.

'True. But the Prime Minister bears grudges. He's getting at the Queen through us.'

It was the first time David felt that the Earl's support for him had begun to falter. If the government *did* bring in the measure Averne described – and he, David, had heard nothing of it – then the situation was certainly serious. But damn Averne all the same.

The Earl spoke again. 'Sam, I don't see that we can withdraw from the Dead Sea Scrolls sale. It might look like anti-Semitic discrimination on our part and that I won't have. Nor, as I have said on countless occasions, can we withdraw from the Queen's sale. It would be professional suicide. We have to bear in mind the deep affection in which the Queen is held in this country. The Prime Minister represents one point of view, and he has more sanctions at his disposal than anyone else, but masses of people up and down the country vastly prefer Her Majesty to Her Majesty's government. If it were to get out that we had backed down for political or nakedly commercial reasons, we could suffer badly, very badly indeed. Nor should we forget that David's approach has earned the company enormous sums in commission. We have had the best year we have ever had.'

It was a long speech for the Earl and he sipped some water. 'On the other hand, we don't want to provoke the Prime Minister needlessly. For me, that means we should see these sales through and then call it a day. Should any other major institution approach us about selling off its art for charitable purposes, we should, I think, decline gracefully. I didn't agree with Sam before but I think I do now: it's time to lower our profile.'

There was no vote that day. The upshot was that the two major sales were going ahead. The lead David had given was being followed. At the same time, David was under no illusions. Averne, all of a sudden, was making the running. It was no secret he wanted David's job and, equally important, wanted to remove the nerve centre of Hamilton's to New York. The worst of it was, David could do little to stop Averne at the moment – he had to devote all his energies to New York. If that failed his position in the company could be in serious jeopardy. How quickly circumstances change, he thought. Only a few weeks ago he had received a papal honour for his success in organizing major auctions – now this.

It was a comfort to have Bess to talk to on such occasions, even if she was a thousand miles away. When he called her this time, however, to tell her about Averne's latest onslaught and to work out when they would meet up in America, he sensed she was itchy, impatient.

'Bess! You're not listening to me. Here I am, crying on your shoulder, telling you my troubles and your mind's somewhere else. Don't!'

She snorted. 'It's not that. I *do* sympathize. I guess you feel about this Averne character like I feel about Massoni. It's . . . it's just that I think my good news outweighs your bad news and I can't wait to tell you . . . Oh David! The Holy Office have approved your case! You'll be hearing officially in a day or two. Isn't it marvellous? Now only Thomas has to say yes and we can get married!'

# PART THREE

# 11

The little girl, all in yellow, waited alone at the foot of the aeroplane steps. In her hands she clutched a bunch of flowers that matched her dress. Nervously, she turned and looked round for her mother, who was part of the reception committee standing on the concrete apron behind her. But her mother motioned for her daughter to turn back and stand up straight. This was an honour that would come only once in a young girl's life.

The engines of the plane had stopped before the staircase had been rolled into position. Now the door at the top of the steps was opened and, after a short delay, Thomas appeared. He waved to the welcoming crowd and descended the steps to the little girl. This had been Bess's idea. For this, Thomas's first visit to his native America as Pope, so many people had wanted to welcome him – the mayor of Fort Wingate, his home town, the local cardinal, the local Oklahoma senators, the apostolic delegate in Washington – that it had been decided none of them would. Instead, what better symbol of the country than an ordinary person, an unknown, and a child as well?

All eyes focused on the girl now as she curtsied to Thomas and stiffly stuck up her arm holding the flowers. A hundred press cameras clicked. Thomas smiled and, while taking the flowers, kissed the top of the young girl's head. Relieved of her honour at last, she turned and ran back to her mother. Like everyone else, Thomas laughed at this and the cameras clicked again. He turned to Bess, who was standing behind him with her own camera, to keep an unofficial record for Thomas for his private use. He passed her the flowers and gave her a broad wink. It was a good start.

The idea of a Pope beginning his visit in smalltown America may have seemed odd at first, but Americans are both deeply democratic and sentimental, and the story of the local boy who had made it to the top in the spiritual world was as romantic as any Broadway fable. For the next few days no American could pick up a newspaper, or turn on the television, without seeing Thomas either fishing in the river he had fished in as a boy, eating candy in the candy store on Mainstreet, celebrating mass in the tiny local Catholic church, lunching at the orphanage he had been brought up in, attending a barn dance in the evening, or opening a clinic named after himself. He shook hands with just about everybody in the town and all of them were given souvenirs. As a boy Thomas had sketched the town and still had the drawing. Bess had prints made and then Thomas signed each one. They were a great success.

By the time he arrived in Washington, Thomas was a superstar. This was America and there was no other word for him. The trip to Fort Wingate had made him much more than a world leader or a religious symbol. He was now a legend. His presence, not just on American soil, but his backtracking to his roots had brought home vividly to Americans what no amount of publicity from Rome, or political activity, or religious promulgation, could do: *he was one of them*. He liked fishing and baseball and candy. Jefferson was his favourite president. He had a soft spot for the Miami Dolphins. He told one reporter the things he most missed in Rome were blueberry muffins. Americans had heard often enough that any one of them could be president. Now, seeing Thomas wade in Battle River, fishing instinctively where the best pools were, the nation realized that any American could become Pope, too. He was not God, as one humorous columnist put it, but it was a damn close thing.

Roskill and his advisers had quickly realized how well the Holy Father's visit was going and as a result the President had insisted on helicoptering out to Andrews Air-force base himself, to meet Thomas when he arrived in Washington. At one stage the plan had been for Roskill to receive the Pope on the White House lawn as he received many heads of state. But the Pope now called for something less routine.

As Thomas's green and red Alitalia jet taxied to a stop in front of him, Roskill, hatless, headed up an impressive list of dignitaries: the Secretary of State, the Washington cardinal, the Speaker of the Congress, the Chief Justice, the apostolic delegate and Oliver Fairbrother, the Democratic candidate in the forthcoming presidential election.

The group looked orderly enough but few knew that behind the scenes there had been waged an almighty battle of protocol. Thomas and Roskill, both being heads of state, should therefore meet on an equal footing. But Roskill was also a Catholic, which made Thomas, in theory at least, the President's senior. The President, as a dutiful Catholic, should kneel and kiss the papal ring. Roskill himself wasn't sure what to do about this. The election campaign was almost upon them and if he *did* kiss the ring he would annoy all the non-Catholic voters in America, among whom there were plenty of critics on the lookout for a papist conspiracy. If he did *not* kiss the ring, on the other hand, he would annoy all the Catholics who had helped put him into office and whose unswerving support he needed soon in his fight to be returned for a second term.

It was Thomas himself who suggested a solution to the President's dilemma. As he stepped on to the ground, Thomas revived an old papal custom. He got down on his knees, leaned forward, put his hands on the tarmac in front of him and, on this, the first stage of his visit to official America, kissed the ground. In doing so he bowed before all Americans, not just the President, and an appreciative roar went up from the watching crowds. Then, after Thomas had been helped to his feet, Roskill approached and, bending but not kneeling, he kissed the ring – and a potentially awkward moment passed off without a hitch.

Thomas and Roskill spent a few moments in private conversation, while the press took photographs. Most people were surprised at how tall Thomas was, topping the President by a good three inches. He was also more tanned. Then Roskill turned and led His Holiness, limping quite noticeably, to the line of waiting dignitaries.

Thomas's visit to Washington was quite unlike his stay in Fort Wingate but that was no bad thing. There was a White House reception, a visit to Congress, he opened a hospital and two schools, visited Georgetown University and the Pentagon and also took part in a radio phone-in programme during which time ordinary Americans, not all of them Catholics, were able to put questions directly to him in a manner never contemplated before.

If the planning that had gone into this visit had been Bess's mainly, Thomas carried out his part with equal brilliance. Whether it was in the Capitol Building, a hospital in a poor area, or on radio, he had the happy knack of cheering everyone up and offending no one. When he was asked over the air what he most disliked about America, he quickly replied: 'It's too far from Rome.' But when someone asked him whether he missed not having a wife, his reply was both serious and frank. 'I'm an orphan so I have never had what most people would call a family life. Some people would call the Church a family but that's not what the questioner means. I *do* feel lonely from time to time, or perhaps solitary would be a better word. I miss the companionship that a loving wife would provide. But all life is a trade-off. You can't have everything, and you'll never be happy if you think you can. Knowing what to settle for is the great secret.'

It was common sense, plus a bit more, and it came from the Pope. People loved it.

Having worked so hard in setting up the tour, Bess found that, thanks to Thomas's virtuoso performances, she had little more to do. And the first chance she got she put in a call to David, now in New York.

He sounded tired. 'It looks like a big demonstration is going to be mounted to try to stop the sale. It could turn ugly.'

'Why? What's happening?'

'What *isn't* happening? The building already has about twenty people outside all day long, with banners and placards saying things like "Save our Scrolls". They shout abuse at everybody who comes in or out. There have already been two Jewish associations in New York calling for the sale to be cancelled.'

'Don't they want to support relief work?'

'Yes. But they want the Israeli government to find some other way. They say this sale risks the scrolls passing out of Jewish hands, which would be scandalous.'

'What now?'

'The scrolls actually arrive tomorrow. Obviously we can't put them on display. So we've had to contact all potential buyers individually and arrange for them to come here one by one. Security has also been a problem, but I think we've licked that.'

'What are you doing?'

'I hope this phone's not bugged . . . what I've done is call in a favour that Cardinal Rich owed me. Although he's not here in New York any more he still carries some weight. We're going to store the scrolls in St Patrick's Cathedral.'

'Is that a good idea? Doesn't strike me as very secure.'

'Not normally. But I don't think ultra-orthodox Jews would raid a church, do you? And there's a vault that's pretty easy to keep guarded.'

'When shall I see you?'

'The way things are at the moment, any day of the week, so long as it's between one a.m. in the morning, when I finish work, and one fifteen, when I fall into bed.'

They hung up. David loosened his tie. It had been good to talk to Bess. Even her phone calls made him feel relaxed. This Dead Sea Scrolls sale was a real pain. They would have been better off selling the damned things in London.


The Oval Office was smaller than Bess had expected. It was the first time she had been in the famous room and now, as the press photographers finished their work, taking pictures of the Pope and President together before they got down to a session of private talks, she looked about her. The garden beyond the window was superb: that lush April green reminded her of what she always forgot – Washington was part of the south.

It was the day after Thomas's triumphal entry into Washington. The dinner, the night before, had been a muted affair but enjoyable enough. None of the President's many showbusiness friends had been invited to entertain the guests: the White House chief of protocol had decided that wasn't suitable for a religious leader. Instead a small orchestra had played Vivaldi and Mozart. Bess knew that Thomas's real preference was for jazz.

But today the work proper started. The last of the pressmen were being ushered away by two young men in military uniforms and Roskill turned to the Pope and motioned him to a seat at one side of the table. As Thomas moved around, Roskill added: 'Your tour sure seems to be going well. You must be pleased.'

'Oh, but I am!' cried Thomas. 'Very pleased. And it's mostly due to Elizabeth Lisle here. She's a great organizer.'

They sat down. There were four people on either side of the table. With Thomas and Bess there were Annibale Sarni, the apostolic delegate to Washington, and John Rich. Roskill had Erwin Friedlander, *his* Secretary of State, Lowell Wade, the American ambassador in Rome, and Cranham Hope, a political advisor and speech writer. So far as Bess remembered he was also a specialist on Pacific affairs. She wondered why his presence was necessary.

She soon found out. As soon as the Oval Office was cleared of all but these eight most trusted advisors, the President's manner changed. He had made his political capital out of welcoming the Pope; he had aligned himself with a successful tour and that was enough. Now politics proper began.

'Holiness, we have not always seen eye to eye in the past, you and I, and I hope that our talks today will ensure that such misunderstandings do not happen again.'

The tone was so abrupt that Thomas's head jerked upwards warily. Roskill didn't notice or, if he did, it didn't make any difference. 'You see Cranham Hope here besides me. Cran has just returned from a fact-finding mission on my behalf to the Philippine Islands in southeast Asia.'

Bess stiffened in her seat. What was coming next?

The President poured himself some water. 'Now the Philippines are going to pose us a few problems in the next months. They, like us, have an election. My problem is this: at the moment the islands are run by this man Sebbio – not to everyone's taste but he has been on our side since Cory Aquino was voted out and he lets the United States keep its naval and air-force bases in his country, bases that we consider vital. At the same time, his opponent in the elections is a guy so left-wing that were he to win he would pursue policies almost certainly against the interests of the US. Probably within a few months, the Philippines would be asking us to remove our bases. I cannot allow that to happen.'

Thomas seemed about to interrupt but Roskill steamrollered on.

'Now Cran tells me that the local vote is very evenly divided. At present our guesstimate is that a swing of only three per cent either way will make all the difference. As you will be aware, Holiness, the

Philippines are overwhelmingly Catholic. Your cardinals and bishops hold a lot of power. Both sides in the election badly need their support, their endorsement. Cran tells me the bishops are already meeting, sounding out opinion among themselves and will make a joint pronouncement about three weeks before the election. And Cran's best advice is that the Church will side with the left-wing opposition.'

Roskill slapped the table with the flat of his hand. 'Damn them! Don't they realize that the remoter islands are crawling with lefty guerrillas? People just waiting for encouragement! If we let in a regime that is bound to be anti-American, it could be a disaster. I want you to stop it!'

There was silence in the room. Bess could see what was happening. This approach had been planned by Roskill all along. After the warmth and the glitter of the previous day this tough, sharp-shock tactic was calculated to throw Thomas off balance.

Thomas let the silence swell, till it filled the room. Only then did he address the President. 'Mr Roskill, the Holy See does not have much by way of land or raw materials. We are not a large state in the conventional sense. In fact, land-wise we are the smallest there is. You, on the other hand, are one of the biggest, in some senses *the* biggest. No one, therefore, least of all me, can stop you flexing your muscles if that's what you want. Your presidency has been no different from your predecessors' on that score.'

Now it was Roskill's turn to bridle. The meeting was hotting up.

'But a Pope – any Pope – ' Thomas continued, 'has two advantages you do not. Firstly, and obviously, he has roughly two thousand years of history to look back on. Two thousand years of *successful* government. And so a Pope is not always impressed by the day-to-day problems that other leaders seem bothered by. Seen in the sweep of history they often don't amount to a row of beans. Secondly, and perhaps less obviously, Popes in the modern world are the only leaders whose authority goes *across* frontiers. The Philippines are an excellent example of what I mean. I could, as you say, give instructions that the bishops support President Sebbio. There is no guarantee that they would obey me completely or that the people would vote the way their bishops tell them. But in this case probably enough would take notice to win the day for Sebbio. The question is: is it a worthy use of the Church's power? Mr President, aren't you falling into the same trap as all the European powers – the British, the Dutch, the French – have fallen into in recent years? In Egypt, in Nigeria, in Uganda, in Zimbabwe, in Mozambique even. In each case the communist spectre was raised when what actually happened was that those countries became, not communist but nationalist, non-aligned. Angola, Nicaragua and Aden were different again. They *did* become Marxist but, as in Vietnam, they became more virulently so because the western powers fought so hard to prevent them. Most countries just want to be left alone, Mr President. The Philippines might be one of them.'

This time it was Roskill who tried to interrupt but Thomas waved him down. 'If I were the leader of a big state, Mr President, an economic rival or a military ally, you would not have spoken to me as you have just done. Oh, you would make plain your views. But you would never ask something of me without offering me something in return.'

Thomas paused but no one else seemed disposed to speak now. Bess marvelled at the Holy Father's performance. His talk of the two thousand year sweep of history had put in his place a President who had been in power somewhat over three years and might not have more than a few weeks to go.

But Thomas hadn't finished. He was American enough to know when to press an advantage. 'I will do as you ask, Mr President. It has been in my mind now for several weeks to bring what influence I have to bear on the bishops in the Philippines. I will not ask you for anything in return – for the moment. But I shall, I shall . . . As sure as elections are lost, not won, there will come a time when you can perform a similar service for me. Now, what is the next thing on our agenda?'

But nothing else in the morning's talks came close to that encounter in terms of excitement for the aides around the table. Roskill may have got what he wanted but no one was in any doubt that the President had been bested by the Pontiff.

All was smiles again as the meeting broke up, an hour and a half later. But the President's expression, to those who knew him, was forced. Having been shown up by Thomas in front of his aides, he was seething inside. And, like many a successful politician, Roskill knew how to harbour a grudge. Someday, as sure as elections were lost, not won, the Pope would be made to pay for what he had done that morning.

David's car turned off Park Avenue into 71st Street – and stopped. There was no way the car could reach Hamilton's offices. A blue police barrier closed the road. Further down the block he could see a mass of people, mainly dressed in black, and all carrying placards or banners. He left the car, walked around the barrier and made his way towards the crowd. As he had guessed, the black coats belonged to Orthodox Jews. No one seemed to recognize him as he threaded his way through all the people but as he turned into the building several voices called out anti-Hamilton slogans.

The commissionaire saluted. 'Good morning, sir!' A policeman stood next to him.

'Any problems?' David asked.

'Not so far, sir,' said the commissionaire. 'They've made no attempt to enter the building. But there's four security guys standing by, just in case. This officer is here more as a witness than anything else.'

David nodded to the policeman and smiled. 'Let me know straight away if there's any change.'

'Yessir,' said the commissionaire smartly, clearly enjoying all the drama.

As soon as he reached his office, David told Betsy, 'Get me Eldon. I want him down here as soon as possible.' Eldon Fitzpatrick ran the antiquities department of Hamilton's in New York. When he arrived, David came straight to the point. 'This demonstration against the scrolls might fizzle out. And even if it gets worse and the press picks it up – and I'm sure they will – the publicity could still work either way. It could help the sale, but it could just as well harm it. Now how many people do you think are in the market to buy the scrolls?'

'I thought you'd ask that,' said Fitzpatrick, taking a file from under his arm. 'By my reckoning, not more than twenty-two worldwide. That includes institutions like Harvard, who want one for their Semitic Museum; it includes the British Museum, Texas University, Tokyo Museum and the six private collectors whose names you know. And then, of course, there's the Vatican. It could well be their turn to *buy* through us.'

David nodded. 'Are all twenty-two coming to the sale?'

'Five aren't. Shrive and Kappler have retained dealers to bid. I'm not sure who but my guess would be Fine and Loewe. Johnson and Tribe are going to bid over the phone. Cressey I don't know about – you know how secretive he is. Also, I hear he's not very well.'

'So, we're fairly well-covered.'

Fitzpatrick nodded. 'Yes, and I don't think they'll be put off by the publicity. There's a lot of talk about the preservation of national heritages all over the world now. These people are used to the arguments. Either they agree with them, in which case they don't buy, or they disagree, in which case no amount of demonstrating will put them off. The sale itself is all-ticket of course so we shouldn't have too many problems there.'

Mollified, but still a little apprehensive, David let Fitzpatrick get back to work. Most likely the sale would go well and the protesters would fade away after. But you could never be too careful. He noticed a light flashing on his phone: an incoming call.

'Yes?'

'It's Lord Afton from London,' said Betsy.

David looked at his watch: 8.45 a.m. in New York meant it was 1.45 p.m. in London. The noble lord should have been at lunch.

'It must be important, sir, to keep you from your club.'

'I'm *at* my club, dammit! Bad news, I'm afraid. There's not much you can do, David my boy, but I thought you ought to hear it from us, rather than anywhere else.'

'Hear what? What's happened now?'

225

'It's the buggers who want to stop the Queen's sale. During the night they daubed huge slogans all over the walls of Buckingham Palace Garden in Constitution Hill. Enormous letters in orange paint, saying things like "Don't flog the Fragonards" and "Cranachs not Corgies". There's even one which says "Dürer before Diana". The police are doing what they can to scrub the paint off, but it's too late really. I'm afraid it'll be all over the evening papers. Not to mention the bloody television.'

So many people in New York wanted His Holiness to visit their school, open their hospital, top out some housing project, address this or that meeting, like the United Nations, that there was little time set aside for worship. To cope with the demands on him, the Holy Father hit on the idea of celebrating the first mass of the day in St Patrick's, at 5.30 a.m. It was an arrangement Bess could not have improved upon.

In the first place there were no other appointments fixed for such an hour. Second, America was such a hardworking, puritanical country that early morning meetings of almost any kind were regarded as a virtue, and the very idea of such an early mass succeeded in attracting even greater interest in such a hardworking and devout Pope.

It was a marvellous morning when Thomas led the papal party on the short walk from the New York Cardinal's residence, where he was staying, to St Patrick's. Away from the cathedral, the streets were deserted, the air was cool and clear and the sun had the city almost to itself. It swept down the cross streets and spilled into the broad avenues with a sensual force that was blinding. Thomas could have used the corridor that linked the Cardinal's residence with St Patrick's but, on such a morning, he preferred the fresh air route.

Despite the hour, around St Patrick's there was a crush of some two to three thousand people. It was, after all, the only chance Roman Catholic New Yorkers would have to worship with His Holiness. There were cheers and shouts as Thomas approached the steps of the cathedral. John Rich was in the papal entourage but his successor as Archibishop of New York, Cardinal Naughton, now waited at the great bronze doors to welcome everybody. There were banks of television cameras and rows of press photographers, all impressed with the Holy Father, and themselves, for getting up so early. Thomas waved and slowly mounted the steps. The cameras followed: another advantage of the early mass was that it would be the lead story on all the breakfast TV shows across America.

Inside the packed cathedral Thomas paused while Cardinal Naughton pointed out various features, the dimensions of the building, its grandeur and majesty. Then together the two men made their slow way to the altar.

For the devout, the high point of the service was the chance it offered a few of the faithful to receive the sacraments from His Holiness himself. With such a large congregation, it needed several priests to administer the eucharist. But Thomas took his part, in the centre of the cathedral, and the lucky ones were to remember it all their lives.

Yet that wasn't what made the headlines later; it was Thomas's sermon. St Patrick's has a magnificent pulpit in carved white stone. It was the perfect setting for the announcement.

'Friends,' Thomas began after he had climbed the short spiral staircase and gazed out over the faces turned to him. 'We are today in a magnificent cathedral. We can be grateful, and give thanks to God that St Patrick's Cathedral is without doubt the most beautiful building on what is, equally certainly, the most striking thoroughfare in the world. I mean, of course, Fifth Avenue. We can give thanks for the marvellous rose window behind you. We can give thanks for the outstandingly fine organ which provides us with timeless music of the ages, making this spot a refuge from the noise and the chaos that threaten us all. But these attractions, wonderful as they are, are still not the features which set this great House of God apart from others in the United States.' Thomas pointed to his left and raised his voice. 'Here in St Patrick's are found the blessed shrines of *two* saints. On your left the shrine of St John Neumann.' Thomas now swept his outstretched arm in a wide arc to the other side of the nave. 'And here is the shrine of St Elizabeth Ann Seton, the very first American-born saint.'

He paused and beamed down at the faces of the congregation.

'Friends, I have some glad news for you this morning. A piece of Christian news that will cause great rejoicing.' The congregation stirred, not knowing what to expect.

'In Rome, though it will soon move to Rio, there is part of the Vatican known as the Congregation for the Causes of Saints, the job of the Congregation is to examine the evidence in these cases where individuals are to be considered for canonization, whether or not they should be regarded as saints. It is a serious task, and can take much time – years, in a few cases, centuries.' He paused again, enjoying himself. 'But, from time to time, the Congregation reaches a conclusion. And I can reveal to you today that the Congregation recently *did* reach a conclusion. I have considered the Congregation's recommendation and approved it. So you who have come to celebrate mass here this morning shall be the first to know that we have a new saint, that he is American and that he is – ' Another pause for effect. Overhead was heard the faint roar of an early jet from La Guardia ' – Peter Knaths who, as some of you will recall, was a missionary in the old west, the wild west. He rescued a number of outlaws, converted native Indians to Christianity and performed two acknowledged miracles. In one he caused the Holy Virgin to appear before a murderer who at that moment was free, with another man wrongly convicted. The murderer subsequently gave himself up, saving the life of the other man. In the second miracle a sheriff who was mortally wounded was held from death by a similar visitation. St Peter Knaths thus today becomes America's third saint. His relics are in New Mexico and that is where his shrine shall be.'

As Thomas finished, and before he could bless the congregation, there was an instinctive reaction on the part of some people to applaud. But many of those present didn't know whether a church was the appropriate place for applause. The result was that a few people applauded, and one or two cheered, but then quickly fell silent.

Thomas laughed at their confusion. 'It's good news. I think just this once we *ought* to cheer.'

And *that* was the shot the news bulletins carried all day: Thomas laughing as he led the congregation in the cheering. If anything could have enhanced the high esteem he was now held in, this was it. In New York, the news completely overshadowed everything else that day. It overshadowed the daubings on the walls of Buckingham Palace Garden, it overshadowed the news of the growing bitterness in Northern Ireland, and it completely overshadowed an article on the Op-Ed page of the *New York Times* by a leading Jewish scholar.


Not that David missed the article. He groaned when he opened *The Times* that morning. He was breakfasting by himself in the hotel and so allowed himself to swear out loud. The article was entitled 'Why we are going to court over the scrolls' and was written by a rabbi from Jerusalem, a man who was a recent immigrant to Israel from New York. The piece followed what was for David a familiar line of reasoning – namely that the scrolls did not belong to the government of Israel and therefore could not be sold by them. The scrolls dated from a time before the state of Israel, as now constituted, ever existed. If they belonged anywhere, the rabbi argued, they should be in the safekeeping of the Jewish religious establishment. But such artefacts, he concluded, could never be 'owned', only held in trust for everyone – not only Jews but people of all religions.

David noted that the rabbi affected a high moral tone throughout his article, yet made no reference to the point of the sale, the high moral purpose to which the money raised would be put. But it was the article's final paragraph that caused him to hurry to the phone. The paragraph read: 'These arguments seem to us persuasive. So persuasive that today, on behalf of the Hasidic Biblical Archaeology Society, I am prepared to petition the New York District Court to have the sale stopped and these items withdrawn. I am convinced we can prevent this barbaric auction taking place.'

David made three calls. The first was to Norman Praeger, Hamilton's attorney. Had he seen the morning paper? Yes, said Praeger and he was already in touch with the court, to find out where exactly the hearing would take place, and at what time.

'Why didn't they give us decent warning? There's hardly time to prepare a defence.'

'This is New York, David. They don't have to let us know – that's up to the court. Presumably they filed their case at the close of business yesterday, pleading urgency in view of the sale date being so close. In the circumstances their article in the paper *was* an early warning.'

Next, David called the Israeli consul to find out what line his government was taking. The attaché was phlegmatic. The arguments were familiar, he said, the organization was an extreme one, in so far as it was an organization at all and only consisted of the rabbi and one or two others. It certainly did not represent either Israeli public opinion or the general legal view in Jerusalem. He was having telexed from Jerusalem the results of a recent opinion poll which showed that most Israelis thought the sale a good thing. He would be in court with his own legal advisor.

Somewhat relieved, David placed his third call, to Eldon Fitzpatrick at his home. He too had read the piece. 'I know what you are going to ask me to do,' he said as soon as he recognized David's voice. 'Make twenty-two phone calls, right?'

'Correct,' said David. 'Reassure everybody who might be a buyer that the sale will go ahead, that we are fighting the court action, that the Israeli government is fighting it with us and that the Hasidic Archaeology whatsit is a two-man, two-bit extremist operation. And make sure that all those who haven't yet viewed the scrolls see them today. Okay?'

David then went to his office – there were more demonstrators today, no doubt as a result of *The Times* piece, but they were quieter, better behaved, since the focus of attention, temporarily, had shifted to the courts. Praeger came through an hour later to say that the case had been set for eleven thirty a.m. before Judge Fielding, who had a reputation for being rather anti-establishment and was himself Jewish. Praeger didn't know how to read him.

David talked to London. The Buckingham Palace daubings were making news. Worse, new trustees had been appointed to the National Gallery and the National Galleries of Scotland. They included two board members from Steele's – but none from Hamilton's.

At eleven Praeger came into David's office and they both travelled down to the court in Lower Manhattan together. As David had expected, the press, alerted by *The Times* piece, was there in force. The attaché, a small, thick-set man, with a high forehead, looked very relaxed, smiled a lot and shook hands with David. 'It was good of you to come, Mr Colwyn. But I'm sure there'll be no bother.'

David wished he could be so sure.

The rabbi who had written *The Times* article was a burly man with a

229

sharp nose and a pair of piercing eyes. Recognizing David, he nodded, none too politely. His lawyer knew Praeger and they exchanged formal greetings.

The case started ten minutes late, by which time David was getting jumpy. The court was an unassuming room, lacking the pomposity of a British court. David and Praeger, having no standing in the case as simply the agents for the sale, sat in a neutral part of the courtroom, among the general public.

The judge, surprisingly young by British standards, had quick, blue eyes and a wide mouth. His copy of the *New York Times* was open at the Op-Ed page. He took out a large book and his pen and said, 'Okay, who'll start?'

Mordechai Sheinman, the lawyer colleague of the rabbi who had written *The Times* piece, stood up and put the case. It was, essentially, the same as that advanced in *The Times*. He argued that antiquities discovered in the ground belong, not to any individual, but to the state – and that meant every citizen, not simply the government of the day. He claimed further that this was even more true in the case of the scrolls since, as they were documents of purely religious significance, if they belonged to anyone in Israel, it was not to the government but to the Chief Rabbi.

Although Sheinman finished without advancing any new points, he made the case seem far more reasonable than the rabbi had in the newspaper and David became seriously apprehensive.

Then the attorney for the Israeli government rose. Lawrence Kohler was a tall man with lanky silver hair and a voice full of warm, generous vowels. 'I have three points only, Judge, and I needn't take too much time over it.' He smiled. 'First I shall seek to show that the Hasidic Biblical Archaeology Society is not representative of Israeli public opinion on this matter – therefore they do not have the moral authority they claim. Second, I shall seek to show that the Israeli government *does* own the scrolls, and therefore may sell them if it so wishes. And third, I shall seek to show, though you may deem it inappropriate, that religious authorities in Israel have no objection to this sale.

'Now to the details of my first point.' Kohler held up a telex. 'This came in from Israel, Your Honour, earlier today, from Jerusalem.' There was a rustle of interest in the public part of the court. 'It gives the results of an opinion poll conducted in the past few days by a very reputable organization, totally independent, I might say, of the government. The poll shows the results of two questions put to the Israeli people.' The attorney pulled his spectacles from his jacket pocket and put them on. 'The first question asked was: "Do you approve of the sale of some of the Dead Sea Scrolls in order to provide funds to help building projects in Gaza, Galilee, the West Bank and South Africa?" Seventy-eight per cent of those asked said they approved, ten per cent disapproved and twelve per cent didn't know. In other words, Your Honour, far from being outraged, as is claimed in this morning's *New York Times*, and as my learned colleague has just argued in this court, Israeli public opinion overwhelmingly supports this sale.

'Now to the second question. This time people were asked: "Do you think the sale of certain Dead Sea Scrolls marks a significant loss to the religious and archaeological heritage of this country?" To this question seventeen per cent said it *was* a loss, sixty-seven per cent said it wasn't and the don't knows stood at sixteen per cent.' Kohler polished his spectacles with a handkerchief. 'Clearly, Your Honour, there is no deep sense of loss in Israel that these relics are being sold. People know that there are many scrolls and that by no means all of them are being sold . . .

'I turn now to a separate piece of paper.' He held what looked like another telex above his head. 'This too came in from Israel this morning. It is a joint statement from the Minister of the Interior and from the Minister in charge of archaeological work in Israel. The statement reads: "Under Israeli law, any archaeological find, whether of religious significance or not, is the property, first, of the state of Israel and, second, if the state is not interested, of the owner of the land on which the discovery is made, provided he or she is an Israeli citizen and resident." The Minister of the Interior adds a postscript of his own, Your Honour. It reads: "Permission to excavate or cover over any site must be obtained from me. Although I consult with the relevant religious authorities where appropriate, I retain full authority in such matters." '

Kohler handed both telexes up to the judge. Then he raised yet a third piece of paper. 'Finally, Your Honour, I have one more statement for the court, this time from the office of the Chief Rabbi in Jerusalem.'

David looked across to the Israeli consul with admiration. Either he had anticipated these troubles or he had worked damned hard that morning.

The lawyer continued, 'The Chief Rabbi says: "I welcome the opportunity to comment on the sale of archaeological material found in the caves at Qumran, known popularly as the Dead Sea Scrolls, in New York. These materials are clearly of great importance in the history of Israel and, equally clearly, it would be very wrong to dispose of the majority. But that is not the plan. We should remember, too, that the importance in documents of this kind resides less in the materials themselves than in the information they contain. Since these particular documents have been studied now for several years, and their contents published and therefore preserved for all time we see no reason why the sale should not proceed. Indeed, for religious relics to perform such an excellent service for humankind is to be applauded." '

Kohler put down the paper slowly and took his time removing his spectacles. There was no sound in the courtroom. 'It is my contention,

Your Honour, that the Hasidic Biblical Archaeology Society came here this morning more for the sake of publicity than with any real hope of stopping this sale. As I trust I have shown, the sale is legal. The HBAS is *not* representative of any substantial body of opinion and it is wrong on matters of law. I therefore contend that the sale should be allowed to proceed – and I go further. In giving your judgement I ask that the Hasidic Biblical Archaeology Society be instructed to pay all costs.'

David tensed. Kohler seemed to have forgotten that the judge was a conservative man, Jewish and would not welcome an attack on the HBAS. As if to confirm his fears, he saw the judge frowning to himself as he finished making his notes. Eventually, he looked up and nodded to the rival attorney. 'Do you want to come back on any of that, Mr Sheinman?'

Sheinman stood. 'We do not seek publicity, Your Honour, as I'm sure you realize. We seek only to have the sale stopped. I would add this: the sale, however legal it may look in the eyes of my learned colleague, sets a dangerous precedent. The world, if it has any claim to civilization at all, ought not to be blinded by statistics and opinion polls. The right place for the artefacts of a nation's cultural heritage is in that nation. There it can inspire future generations. Without a sense of historical continuity, civilization, religion, mean nothing.'

Clever, David thought as Sheinman sat down. Whereas their side had hit the judge with facts, the other side had appealed to his emotions and sense of pride in his religious feelings.

'I will retire to consider my judgement.' Everyone rose.

Outside the courtroom no one said much. The Israeli consul still looked relaxed. Kohler was already reading the papers of another case. But David was nervous.

An usher beckoned them back in and the judge reappeared. The two attorneys stood and approached the bench.

'Gentlemen,' said the judge, 'I cannot see any reason to stop the sale. Whether the Israeli government's actions are popular or not is no concern of this court. My concern is only whether the sellers have the legal right to sell what is on offer. I see no reason to disbelieve a minister of the Israeli government when he takes the trouble to contact the court from thousands of miles away. The appeal to have the sale stopped is therefore dismissed and all costs are to be borne by the plaintiff.'

Immediately, before anyone could say anything, he rose and strode out through his private door.

David went to shake the attorney's hand. Now that they had won, the Israeli consul looked no more relaxed than he had throughout the entire proceedings. He was delighted, he said, to have no costs to meet. David grinned. As they came out of the courtroom, however, the rabbi-scholar, the man who had written *The Times* article, approached David.

'All smiles – eh Mr Colwyn? Well, let me tell you, we're not finished yet. This was a peaceful attempt to get the sale stopped. Since the court wouldn't listen to us, we'll have to try something else. That means Hamilton's itself comes under attack. Believe me, sir, by the time we've finished with you this will have cost you far more than it cost us today.'

One thing to be said for Quentin's, the restaurant on the Upper West Side where Bess and David finally managed to have dinner together that night, was that if your reservation was for nine o'clock that was exactly when you were shown to your table. It was one of the few places in Manhattan where the *maître de table* didn't abuse his position.

David had not had a good day. After the tribulations of the court battle, he'd had to face the New York correspondents of the British press who wanted his reactions to the Buckingham Palace graffiti. Then he had to worry about the threat that the HBAS would now attack Hamilton's. All this, he told himself, was a long way from the usual sheltered life of a fine arts enthusiast.

But if he was exhausted, Bess looked stunning. She was wearing a black silk dress, edged in purple piping, like a monsignor's cassock.

'I don't know which to admire more, the Pope's tour or your dress . . . How was the White House?'

'Wonderful. I'd like to live there.' She laughed, then became serious. 'But it might easily have been a disaster.' She told him about Roskill's attempt to bully Thomas and how His Holiness had turned the tables. 'You know it's amazing – all these other countries have foreign ministries and so on, with hundreds of people working out policy options, and yet a guy like Roskill still comes to us for help. Little us, with barely a dozen foreign diplomats. The Catholic Church really is the only truly international country, if you see what I mean.'

A waiter brought a menu.

'You all leave New York tomorrow?'

She nodded. 'Forty-eight hours in Chicago, then Boston for two nights. Back to Rome from there. And you?'

'The scrolls' sale is the day after tomorrow. A day clearing up, then back to London. Any news from Thomas, by the way – about the marriage dissolution, I mean?'

'No.'

'If only he'd get a move on. Doesn't he realize you want to have children?'

'You know, I'm not so sure I do any more.'

'What?'

'It's true. I know it's my duty as a Catholic – but there are other duties, too. Thomas and I, we're both Americans and you must have noticed something about Americans, David. We have large appetites, for everything. We pay lip service to family life but actually for most of us it now comes second to our jobs. A good companion – lover, spouse

233

– plus a good job. But the job comes first. That's the American way to happiness these days. I don't disagree. I'm doing a job I think is important. I think Thomas is no ordinary Pope, that what he's trying to do with the St Patrick's Fund especially will be remembered and may just change the world a little bit. I don't want to sound priggish but I reckon the work I do is more important than having babies. Have you thought, David darling, that maybe this is God's way of telling me what to do?

'Which raises another awkward question. When Thomas gives us the go-ahead, and we get married, what then? I enjoy my job, so I couldn't give it up and live in London, and you wouldn't give up what you do, would you? So we'd have the kind of life we have now, only we'd be called married.'

The waiter took their orders.

David turned back to her. 'You sound as if you don't much relish the idea of marriage any more.'

'Bah! Men! Always apocalyptic. I'm just raising the problems. Someone has to.' She reached across the table and cupped her hand over his mouth, so he could kiss it. 'I love you very much, you silly man. But look at me; I'm not classic housewife material, am I? We should be thinking ahead, David, that's all I'm saying, not just waiting on Thomas's word. Think of it, you in London during the week, me in Rome. Then long weekends in either city, together. It doesn't sound bad to me and will probably help keep the marriage fresher than a good many others. We can work hard in the week, and love hard at weekends.'

'The idea is growing on me.'

'I'll say this for you, you're flexible.' She stroked his cheek. Then her face darkened. 'I only wish they were like you in Northern Ireland.'

'Why? What do you mean?'

'We've had a scary report from our apostolic delegate in Dublin. It seems the IRA are planning a major offensive in the north.'

'I hate to sound cynical, Bess, but what else is new?'

'This is. It won't be just another sectarian attack, you see. I don't know if you followed the story, but a night watchman was burned to death in Ulster some weeks ago, after the warehouse he was guarding had been set fire to. The night watchman's firm was Catholic and word has it that the arsonists were from a rival Protestant firm. But the Royal Ulster Constabulary has made no arrests, even though it seems pretty clear who did it. So, inevitably perhaps, the IRA will think up a little "justice" of its own.'

'Bloody awful, I agree. But, I repeat, nothing new in that.'

'Except that the attack happened in the first place because the Catholic firm was getting support from the St Patrick's Fund. The Catholics, God knows, have had a rough deal in Northern Ireland and the fund seemed a great way of helping them. But now I guess the fund is helping to put Protestant firms out of business. It looks like a third time the St Patrick's Fund will have backfired. Thomas is riding high now. But if a full-scale sectarian tit-for-tat develops in Belfast things can change very quickly.'

Yes, thought David, reflecting also on his own precarious position in Hamilton's, they certainly can. What he said was: 'Have you been to the Metropolitan Museum yet? The Giotto they bought has a room all to itself.'

'No, I haven't,' replied Bess. 'The only other free half hour I've had, I managed to sneak off and buy some jazz records for Thomas. There's a great music shop on 42nd Street. But when we were in Washington we saw Red Wilkie's helicopter at Andrew's Air-force Base. It has an outline of the "Pietà" on each side. Looked a bit incongruous to say the least. I gather he's going to install the original sculpture in the atrium of his new headquarters in central Washington. It should be quite a draw. We were also told that he plans to rename "Wilkie Defence" and the new name is "Pietà Products". I can't say I like it, but at least it shows that the Holy Father's approach is working better over here than in Italy.'

'Still problems with the Romans? What news of Massoni?'

'He's still writing his column in *Il Messaggero*. It doesn't make world news all the time, but the Romans love it. He just bitches on about everything Thomas does.'

'What sort of thing does he say?'

'His latest attack is on the canonization of Peter Knaths. I tell you, Thomas doesn't see him as a problem but I think Massoni is acquiring power through his column. They'll never have media religious leaders in Italy like we get here in America, but Massoni is becoming a sort of Roman equivalent. *Il Messaggero's* circulation is climbing steadily and it seems to be due almost wholly to Massoni.'

'Is it just the Romans who go for him? What about the Sicilians, for example?'

'Oh, they're on our side, of course. But, elsewhere in Italy, I don't know, David, there'll always be some people who like to knock whoever's at the top of the tree.' The food arrived. Bess helped herself to more wine. 'Look, do we have to spoil our dinner? Isn't there something nice we can talk about? What news of Ned?'

'Ah!' cried David. 'I had nearly forgotten. I've got something for you.' He reached into his pocket and took out a small box. 'It's a gift – but not from me. Ned gave it to me, for you, just before I left to come here.'

Bess put down her fork and took the box from David. Inside was a crush of white tissue paper. She took it out and unwrapped it. Inside

235

the paper was a brooch, a mass of gold wire, intertwined in complicated arabesques.

'Ned's now a goldsmith,' said David. He reached across and set it down on the tablecloth. They could both see, entwined in the mass of loops and coils, the name 'BESS' faintly distinguishable.

The limousine eased forward through a thicket of bodies. A posse of blue-coated police forced back the angry crowd. The car was about thirty yards from the main entrance of Hamilton's on 71st Street but it might just as easily have been thirty miles. An egg, not the first, smashed against the windscreen, and a low cheer went up from the people on the sidewalk.

'You all right, Mike?' said David, anxiously.

'Yeah,' growled the driver. 'It'll take more than that to stop me, Mr Colwyn. I was in Vietnam.'

David gazed back through the car windows at the distorted faces, shouting and spitting at him. It was a big contrast from the smiles outside the first Vatican sale, when the 'Madonna of Foligno' had been on offer. Admittedly, David had expected trouble after the court case and the warning he had received, but nothing as bad as this. He had spent most of the day checking with the police and his security people that there would be adequate protection for all those who wished to attend the sale, and had been able to dash back to his hotel to change only an hour before the gavel was supposed to fall. Now it looked as though he would be late for his own auction, the first time that had ever happened in all his years on the rostrum.

But the limo at last reached the main doorway. Here the police held the protesters back. David had advised all the big potential buyers to enter by the side door, but he thought it would look cowardly if it got out that he, as chief executive, had failed to brave the crowds. The Israeli consul had felt the same. David only hoped he was already safely inside.

Two of Hamilton's own security men came out to the car and opened the door for him. As he stood on the kerb they positioned themselves either side. A roar went up from the crowd, banners were waved in his face, screams yelled in his direction. Lights flashed in a mini electrical storm as press photographers recorded the occasion.

But David made it safely inside. He thanked the security men as the second set of double doors leading into Hamilton's closed behind him, shutting out most of the noise. It was exactly eight o'clock. He rushed to his office to comb his hair and pick up his marked catalogue, then dashed down to the auction hall, on the mezzanine floor.

When he arrived he was surprised, but gratified, to see that the hall was full to overflowing. Clearly some people *liked* a bit of danger; the stormy publicity had done no harm at all, at least not to attendance.

*

David mounted the rostrum and smiled down at the many faces he knew. He opened his catalogue and set his gavel down. 'Good evening, everyone. Welcome to our sale.' From now on, his intention was to proceed as if everything was absolutely normal. He glanced around the room to check that his assistants were all in place. He turned to the head porter who nodded gravely: the lots were ready to be displayed.

'As you know, ladies and gentlemen, there are four lots for your consideration tonight, four scrolls from the Dead Sea caves at Qumran, all of immense historical and religious importance and all put up for sale by the Israeli government which wishes to make charitable use of the funds so raised. Once again, therefore, this is not a simple commercial transaction tonight. It is something far more important, and I hope you will reflect that – in the energy of your bidding.'

He flattened the pages of his catalogue.

'Lot one is the Hodayoth Scroll, known as 1QH, and which consists of eighteen columns dating from the first century AD.' David looked down at his notes, though this was largely for effect as he well knew what he was going to say. 'I will start the bidding at six million. Six million dollars – any more, any more?'

Again the terrifying dead seconds while he struggled to keep a look of relaxed confidence on his face. But then a dealer, Muffy Ward, on the telephone and in touch with David Tribe, a Texan private collector, raised her hand. The evening was off.

To begin with, the sale went marvellously well. The Hodayoth Scroll fetched seventeen million dollars, bought by David Tribe; the Apocryphal Psalms, lot two, also went to Texas, to the university at Austin, for nineteen million dollars; and the War Rule, nineteen columns describing the perpetual struggle between good and evil, fetched nineteen million dollars also but went to Tokyo Museum.

David now turned to lot four. 'The last lot, ladies and gentlemen, is the Genesis Apocryphon, known technically as 1QapGen, an Aramaic paraphrase of the Genesis story with many supplementary embellishments. The scroll itself dates from the first century BC but the composition perhaps goes back to the second century BC. I shall start the bidding at ten million dollars.'

In no time it was at eighteen, with three people in the bidding: Michael Manasseh, a private collector from Los Angeles, Leonard Mayer of the Semitic Museum at Harvard, and Raymond Snowden, a private New York antiquities dealer.

At that point, however, David noticed a commotion at the door at the back of the room and the captain of the security guards, who was supposed to be on duty down at the main entrance, forced his way in. He marched down the centre aisle towards the rostrum looking grave.

David stopped the bidding and leaned forward. A buzz swept the room as the two men became locked in a whispered exchange. David

237

straightened his back. 'Ladies and gentlemen, it was perhaps inevitable that we wouldn't get through tonight without *some* slight bother. I have just been informed by my chief of security that the Hasidic Biblical Archaeology Society which, as you know, has been demonstrating at the front of the building, has set fire to part of the ground floor – now there's no need to panic,' he reassured them as people started scrambling to their feet. 'I understand that the danger is not serious and the fire department *have* been informed.' He raised his voice still more. 'I should say that we anticipated something like this and we have reserved a room at the Westbury Hotel around the corner on Madison Avenue and 68th Street. Champagne and canapés are available there now, ladies and gentlemen, and the sale will continue in one hour. Please leave quietly by the door to your left where you see a Hamilton's commissionaire in dark blue. He will lead you to the Westbury by a side route. I repeat, the danger is not serious, there is no need to panic and the sale will continue at the Westbury Hotel in an hour.'

Though he sounded calm, David was furious. He had pleaded with the police to keep the demonstrators on the other side of the street. Still, the situation could have been worse. He discovered, when he went to investigate, that someone had thrown a small firebomb through a window into a ground floor room where back numbers of auction catalogues were kept. The shiny, heavy paper of the catalogues had burned slowly and harmlessly, but with a lot of smoke and that had set the alarm system off immediately.

But the publicity the fire brought, for Hamilton's and for the HBAS, and the danger it threatened for all the well-heeled people at the auction, were far from harmless. David put all this firmly from his mind. The evening wasn't over: there was one scroll still to sell. He left the security chief and a captain from the fire department in charge of the Hamilton building, satisfied that all was as well as could be expected, then walked briskly round to 68th Street.

When he arrived at the hotel he was relieved to see that most people had come across from the other building. They seemed not to be too badly affected by what had happened: in fact they looked quite cheerful. The champagne and canapés were being served as promised and, as David arrived, someone shouted: 'Here he is! Come on, Colwyn, let's get going. It's cold in here without a fire.' But the man was laughing, enjoying the unexpectedness of it all.

There was no rostrum at the Westbury, just a raised platform and a lectern. No matter. The chairs for the bidders were more comfortable than at Hamilton's. David climbed on to the platform, reached down and took a glass of champagne from one of the hotel staff holding a tray. As he tossed it back a low ironic cheer went up from the others in the room. David looked to his left: there was the head porter holding the Genesis Apocryphon as if nothing had happened. The other scrolls were safely at his side, too. David winked and they both smiled at each other. He opened his catalogue and a silence descended on the room.

'The Genesis Apocryphon, then. The bidding stands at eighteen million dollars – with you sir.' He nodded to Leonard Mayer, then blandly surveyed the room. 'Any more?'

And with that unflamboyant remark the bidding restarted. And, perhaps because people in the room now shared a special camaraderie, they seemed unaffected by what had gone before. Manasseh dropped out at twenty-two million dollars and at twenty-five million dollars Mayer, very reluctantly, gave in too. Raymond Snowden got it for twenty-six million dollars.

The New York dealer approached David. Briefly they spoke together, then David addressed the room. 'Ladies and gentlemen, before you go, I have been asked by Mr Snowden here to announce that he was bidding on behalf of the Vatican Secret Archive which has therefore acquired the oldest manuscript relating to the bible.'

# 12

David arrived back in London completely exhausted. In the sense that it had raised eighty-one million dollars and that meant a commission for Hamilton's of sixteen point two million dollars, the Dead Sea Scrolls' sale had gone well. But the cumulative effect of the court case, the demonstrations and the fire had drained him. And, coming as it did at the same time as the daubings on the walls of Buckingham Palace, it meant that Hamilton's featured in some rough press coverage on both sides of the Atlantic.

At the regular board meeting which took place shortly after David returned, the Earl of Afton congratulated him on earning Hamilton's such a handsome commission. But the Earl seemed muted. Averne now openly proposed that the firm should withdraw from the Queen's sale, giving as his reasons the bad publicity which had attended the scrolls sale and the fierce opposition that continued to rumble on in Britain about the royal pictures. The Earl still maintained that Hamilton's could not withdraw but, it seemed to David, with less and less conviction.

It was with some relief, therefore, that David travelled to Paris with Ned at half term for their weekend together in the Loire and at the Louvre.

At Paris airport they hired a car. The plan was to spend Saturday in the Loire, at Cloux and Amboise, for David's benefit, and then to travel into Paris on Sunday and visit the Louvre on Monday, for Ned's.

They found Leonardo's château at Cloux a rather sombre building. It gave David no new ideas of where to look for Leonardo documents, nowhere that had not been covered by countless scholars before. Dispirited, but trying for Ned's sake not to show it, he travelled back to Paris.

The Louvre visit was altogether more successful. In the first place, they almost immediately bumped into Ed Townshend, David's friend and sparring partner in the Renaissance Society, the American who was a curator at the Fogg Museum at Harvard.

'Ed! I might have expected to see Jean-Claude Sapper here, since he's the curator, or Ivan Shirikin, since his museum has the best collection of icons in the world, but why are you here? It's not your field, is it?'

Townshend shook his hand. 'No, it's not my field but I'm an exhibition junkie.' He turned and pointed. 'That's Jean-Claude down there, talking to the bald man with the double chin. He, incidentally, is the reason we shan't be seeing much of Shirikin any more. Dear old Ivan has been kicked upstairs, "promoted" to run art tours in the motherland. The bald guy's got his job at the Hermitage. He's called Dorzhiev.'

David would have liked to introduce Ned to Jean-Claude Sapper but the curator was obviously busy with Shirikin's successor. So David and Ned and Townshend toured the icons together.

'This sort of stuff isn't your field either, is it?' the American asked David.

'No. Ned here is interested in gold, what can be done with it, how its appearance varies according to the craftsmen who work with it. He wants to be a goldsmith. There aren't many icons in Britain and no really good ones. So we're here to see one kind of gold work we can't see at home. Now, come on, Ed. You're outnumbered by the Colwyns – why *are* you here? In Paris I mean.'

'To visit the Bibliothèque Nationale, what else? I'm researching a book on great rivals in art, to see what effect their rivalry had on their work. You know, people like Domenichino and Lanfranco, Algardi and Bernini, Leonardo and Michelangelo. People who were contemporaries but couldn't stand each other. The BN has some important documents I need.'

'Are you getting much?'

'It's early days yet but there's a lot of material. I need to research who the artists' friends were, too. In the Bernini documents, for example, there isn't much about Algardi. But in the documents of Bernini's friends, there's plenty on how he felt about his rival. And vice versa with Algardi. I'm hoping it'll cause quite a stir.'

Before he could say more a figure approached them. It was Jean-Claude Sapper. 'Edward! David! How marvellous to see you both. Why didn't you let me know you were coming? And what are you doing here anyway? Neither of you has ever so much as mentioned icons to me before.'

Townshend explained why they were all there and introduced Ned to Sapper. Then Townshend said, 'What's happened to Dorzhiev?'

Sapper grimaced. *'Eh bien!* Washing his hands. I have to take him to lunch. I must say our little dinners at the Renaissance Society aren't going to be quite so cosy any more. He's nowhere near as *sympathetique* as Shirikin. Knows his business though, so I suppose I shouldn't complain. I'd invite you along but I've got some press people coming and the chairman of the trustees, so you see my problem.' He made to leave. 'Sorry this had to be so short. Oh yes, and before I go, we've just made the most wonderful acquisition: if you have time you must see it. It's a Titian that turned up out of nowhere. There's no doubt that it's authentic but we haven't been able to trace it back any further than the early eighteenth century. We've just put it up with all the other Italian paintings – do have a look.' And he dashed off down the gallery.

The three of them debated whether to take Sapper's advice or to go straight to lunch. The Louvre is a big place and it was a long walk from the icon exhibition to the Italian rooms. But in the end Ned prevailed upon them to go.

The Titian was superb and showed Hercules at the Crossroads. It had been cleaned and its reds and crimsons glowed like fire, its skin tones a mysterious mixture of cream, pink and brown, giving a hint of mortality to the divine warrior.

David wandered on beyond the new Titian, past the huge Veroneses, past the Louvre's own version of the 'Virgin of the Rocks', and stood before a picture he was not so familiar with. It was a portrait of John the Baptist by Giovanni Antonio Boltraffio, a not very good Milanese painter who was a follower of Leonardo. Suddenly, as he looked at the picture, a thought struck him. Boltraffio was a follower of Leonardo. At Cloux he remembered seeing a print of a portrait by the same artist, a likeness of Francesco Melzi, the very man who had inherited Leonardo's documents. The original, if he remembered correctly, was in Bern. But that didn't matter. What mattered was that Boltraffio was a friend both of Leonardo and of Melzi. If Townshend was right then it might pay David to look at Boltraffio's papers, if there were any, to see what reference they made to Leonardo. Maybe Boltraffio actually took possession of some of da Vinci's papers. It was a long shot, but if he drew a blank with Boltraffio there were other friends of Leonardo whom he could check out. That was a very promising line of research. Much cheered, he offered to buy Townshend and Ned lunch.

A week after his return from America to Rome His Holiness announced at one of his regular audiences that he had recommended the bishops of the Philippine Islands in the Pacific to support President Sebbio in the forthcoming elections. This drew fire from some quarters but was quickly welcomed by President Roskill. Other western leaders said nothing publicly but their silence was taken to signify approval.

None knew that, at the very moment the Holy Father was making his speech about the Philippine bishops, Nicaraguan troops were secretly moving light artillery and flame-throwing equipment up near the border with Honduras to the west of Jalapa. Tired of the constant harrassment of its townships within striking distance of Pimental, the Nicaraguan government had resolved to take out the new town once and for all.

Two days later, the attack began, at midnight. Two thousand infantry troops moved up during the afternoon, using the available rivers. Heavier artillery was drawn up to the north of Ocotal and west of El Jicaro from where Pimental was just in range. The attack time had been chosen for the Americans' 'benefit' as much as anything. It was then two a.m. in Washington when the government's reaction would be slowest. The heavy artillery opened up first, bombarding the area for thirty minutes. A helicopter attack immediately followed: six helicopter gunships went in low and dropped firebombs on the town, concentrating on areas not destroyed by the bombardment. At about half past one, local time, the infantry attacked, with orders to take no prisoners but to confiscate all weapons and ammunition found. Three hours later some infantry were caught by the first American-backed Honduran airforce planes, but by daylight the great majority of the infantry had slipped back across the border. Although some planes scored lucky hits, the Nicaraguans suffered hardly any serious casualties and managed to shoot down one Honduran aircraft.

At the press conference summoned the next morning, the Nicaraguan government displayed a cache brought back from Pimental of no fewer than 2,750 rifles, 5,000 grenades, three million rounds of ammunition, 50 mortars, 200 landmines, and 200 pistols. There was no doubt that the discovery was genuine: some of the armaments were still in their packing cases, stamped 'Baltimore'. They proved convincingly that Pimental was not the peaceful settlement it was supposed to be.

At the conference, the Nicaraguan foreign minister made a statement: 'This proves conclusively that the reactionary forces of the west, American capitalism combining with Roman Catholicism, intend to destroy Nicaragua. We have always maintained that Pimental, built with Vatican money, was not the refuge it was depicted but rather a loaded gun aimed at the heart of this small nation. Today the world can see that we in Nicaragua do not exaggerate. But we now have those weapons. We have the guns and the ammunition, the grenades and the mortars. And Pimental has been reduced to rubble. I do not rejoice in loss of life. But we have shown today that we shall do whatever we have to do to protect ourselves, whether our enemies be capitalists, Catholics, or both.'

Roskill had been raised from his bed that morning at five past three. He was very angry. Entering the command room, he fired off a number of orders, sending US military support to the area, ships offshore, every piece of American muscle he had at his disposal for just such an emergency. For an hour and a half he watched developments, by which time he knew that there was nothing he could do. The Nicaraguans had gone in, hit Pimental hard, then gone away again. He dared not order American forces to follow them.

Coffee was served but it wasn't enough. Whisky was brought. Roskill grew calmer.

'Cran! Cran – where are you?'

'Here,' said Cranham Hope quietly.

Roskill eyed him thoughtfully. 'Now, Cran – what the hell are we going to do about this Thomas guy? I guess he didn't mean to, but he's sure landed us in it.'

'Right now,' said Hope, 'we do nothing.'

'Don't tell me that, Cran. This fund of his – he's like a kid with a new toy. Between you and me, Cran, he needs teaching a lesson.'

'Nossir.'

'*Cran!* Why not, goddammit?'

'Mr President, think, sir.' Cran held up his hand with three fingers extended. 'Number one, he is the most popular person on the planet, yourself not excluded. Second, he came out on your side over the Philippines – and you accepted his support. If you turn on him now not only will you look inconsistent but mean-spirited and disloyal.' He lowered his voice. 'And there's a third reason for you to stay off the Pope's back. The best one yet.'

Roskill stared at Hope. 'I don't like your tone. There's something I haven't been told.'

'Yes, there is. All that hardware the Nics found at Pimental wasn't the Pope's doing. It wasn't paid for with his money – all that really did go on building.'

Roskill stared at Hope. His hand gripped his whisky glass. He waited, his gaze raking Hope's face.

'You guessed it, boss. *We* put the guns there. Every last one of them was paid for out of CIA funds.'

The following Saturday David saw Ned off on the Belfast shuttle from Heathrow. The boy was to spend the weekend with his mother and stepfather in Ulster. Then David himself caught a flight for Rome. There was a St Patrick's Fund meeting on the Monday morning and it was to be his first proper Roman weekend with Bess for some time. He was looking forward to it.

He went straight from the airport to Gina's for a late lunch, where Bess was waiting. She looked strained and the campari on the table in front of her was untouched. David kissed her, waved to Gina and settled into a chair. The sun was fierce and the shade offered by the umbrella was not really cool. He had brought her a gift, a piece of Lyon silk, but now was not the time to give it to her. 'What is it?' he said. 'What's wrong?'

She gulped her Campari. 'Everything – or it feels like everything.'

Gina brought David's favourite beer. They exchanged greetings, but Gina, sensing Bess's fragile mood, went back inside the cafe.

'Come on,' said David, 'tell me. You're upset.'

She nodded. 'It started with this damned Nicaraguan thing. Obviously it wasn't the St Patrick's Fund that paid for those guns. According to our source it was the CIA – Roskill, or his people. We can't prove it, of course, but Thomas is certain it's true. And it all happened only the day after he'd gone public on the Philippine Islands. It makes him appear not only political but a lackey of Roskill's as well.'

'Don't worry,' said David. 'It'll blow over. Thomas is still very popular.'

'It might – if that were all.'

'What do you mean? What else is there?'

'What else *isn't* there? Why do you think I look so tired?'

'Tell me.'

For her reply she placed two forks and a knife in a row on the tablecloth in front of her. She played with the first fork. 'The Syrians are massing their troops in the Bekaa valley, ready for a push on Beirut. Our contacts there tell us they particularly intend to hit the St Patrick's Fund projects, as retaliation for what the fund did to their informants. Whatever happens, we shall take the blame. Thomas knew the fund there would be a risk – it was the biggest risk he took – but he hoped to buy time for a negotiated settlement.' David went to interrupt but Bess picked up the second fork and waved him down with it. '*La Repubblica*, one of the papers here in Rome, has been leaked a copy of a confidential Vatican report which shows that visitors to the city state have dropped by seventeen per cent in the last months – since the treasures were sold off. The decline is also true of Rome in general. There *are* other explanations: the Alitalia strike meant that fewer people had holidays in Italy, and the weather was bad. But the figures suit Thomas's critics, especially those in the Italian government and Massoni. And of course ordinary Italians benefit greatly from having the Church here. They want the Vatican to keep growing in popularity, so the figures will harm the pontiff not only in Rome but throughout Italy.'

She held up the third piece of cutlery. 'Third, you'll find out officially on Monday, at the fund meeting, but I can tell you now. The first year's income from the fund is due to be paid out in a month and Thomas has been helping vet new applications for relief.' She swigged her drink again. 'Oh David! Thomas has been so upset by the Nicaraguan business, he's having a problem seeing straight. You remember that dam which burst, about a month ago, in Vietnam? The Thu Bon river near Dong An. It killed seven hundred people when the water flooded a mine and drowned all the workers – remember?'

David nodded.

'Well, Thomas wants to send some St Patrick's money to help them. I can't make him see how it would antagonize the Americans. I tell him his popularity in America could disappear overnight. *He* says yes, he agrees, but he'll only be able to get away with things which are unpopular now, when he is at the peak of his popularity. He also thinks it will help on his coming trip to China. Oh darling, it's such a mess. The Americans aren't ready for charity in Vietnam; the wound's too raw still. And will be for some time yet . . .'

She finished her campari, tossed her hair back the way he liked, made a visible effort to relax. 'Let's eat,' she said, looking round for Gina. 'That's how good you are for me, David. This is the first time I've felt like eating in days.'

That night, in her flat high up among the gables above the Via dei Banchi Vecchi, they made love especially tenderly. And slowly. David sensed, correctly, that Bess needed to be removed for a time from where and what she was. He gave as well as he could give.

Next morning, they rose early for mass. Afterwards, while Bess went to buy the Sunday papers, David prepared an elaborate English breakfast – eggs, toast, bacon and tomatoes, with fresh coffee and juice newly squeezed from blood oranges. It was ready when she got back.

'Read it out to me,' he said as she came in the door. He helped her to some eggs.

'Oh, God! I'll translate as best I can. "The number of visitors to the Vatican has plummeted since the Holy Father sold off a number of Renaissance masterpieces some months ago. According to an official report, so far secret, the number of visitors paying to explore the Vatican museums has dropped by a mammoth seventeen per cent, down from two point two million the last time an official record was taken, to 1,822,000 now. This has resulted in a loss of income to the Vatican of" – let me convert the lire – "one million, one hundred and twenty thousand pounds."

' "A Vatican spokeswoman said yesterday that there were many reasons which might account for the fall in attendance which was not, in any case, seen in Vatican circles as worrying. She declined to speculate on what those reasons might be. A spokesman for the mayor of Rome, however, was more forthcoming. He described the report's conclusions, if true, as a disaster. For the Vatican and for Rome! He said the decline in visitors has already cost Rome a lot. 'The Pope is a very popular man, right across the world,' said the spokesman. 'But he has always maintained a special relationship with the people of Rome who not only revere him but look to him for leadership and for policies which maintain the city as a traditional centre for pilgrims and tourists.' "

'Then there are interviews with local Romans – shopkeepers, restaurateurs, taxi drivers – exactly the sort of people most affected financially by a slump in tourism. Naturally, they're all critical.'

Though Bess had been relaxed when she woke up, David now saw the tired look return.

'Tell you what,' he said. 'It's a glorious day outside and I've never seen you in a bikini. Why don't we go to Port' Ercole for the day, find a hotel for lunch, and have a swim in the sea?'

'But – '

'No. You can be as busy as you like while I'm in the fund meeting tomorrow. But today, forget the Vatican. Come on, put yourself first for once. Now where do you keep your bikinis?'

In order to stop him ransacking her cupboards, Bess had to find her swimming costume herself. Then David, sensing that he was doing exactly the right thing, bundled her into her car and they set off for Port' Ercole. Lots of other Romans seemed to have the same idea so they didn't reach the hotel he had in mind until twelve forty-five. It was on a cliff with a wonderful view of the Argentario peninsula. They had a quick swim before lunch, a beautiful shellfish barbecue over which they took their time, and there was more swimming in the afternoon. They had an early supper in the port – shellfish again – then made for Rome, arriving late, just on midnight. Gina's was still open and David felt like a brandy. Neither of them wanted to end the day. He had held off giving her the Lyon silk: now he did so.

Eventually, about twelve thirty, they wished Gina goodnight and strolled back down the street to Bess's apartment. As they approached, a man got out of a car and walked towards them. David tensed.

'Mr Colwyn?' said a very English voice.

'Yes,' answered David, still wary. 'Who are you? What is it you want?'

'Stanbury, sir. Edward Stanbury, second secretary at the embassy here. We've been trying to contact you all day.'

'Oh yes? Nothing wrong is there?'

'I'm afraid there is, sir. Earlier today the IRA attacked Ardglass Manor which, as you surely know, is the residence of the Secretary of State for Northern Ireland. The minister escaped, sir, but I am afraid his wife – your ex-wife, sir – caught the full blast.'

Ned was safe. The children's annex at Ardglass Manor was in a wing to itself, to keep the noise away from the minister's study. David asked Bess to explain his absence to the St Patrick's Fund Committee and caught the first plane to London. By then Ned had been helicoptered back to his school, at his own request, where he was recovering. By then, too, the details of the attack had been fleshed out. Also its motive.

It had been a mortar attack, mounted from – of all places – a nearby churchyard. The church, it turned out, contained the entrance to a seventeenth-century secret passage which exited in a cave a quarter of a mile away. Locals had known about the passage but, for some reason, the security men had not been told. The cave was outside the security ring drawn up around Ardglass, but the churchyard was within range, as the tragedy proved.

247

It was, however, the motive for the attack that chilled David. It wasn't just a random attack on a British minister. The IRA had delivered an 'official' statement by telephone to the Irish *Times* in Dublin late on Sunday night. Using a special code word to prove his identity, the telephone spokesman said the attack was in retaliation for 'The cowardly way in which Protestant construction firms in Northern Ireland have responded with arson and murder to simple commercial competition on the part of Catholic building firms in the area.' It was a clear reference to the fire in Belfast when the nightwatchman had been burned to death. And to the St Patrick's Fund.

Ned, when David reached him, was well enough, considering the circumstances. The school were not pressing him to attend classes, but he still shared a room with the same boy they had chosen to help him through the worst of his depression. Everyone was conscious that the episode could trigger Ned's illness all over again, but the headmaster judged – quite rightly in David's view – that Ned needed *some* familiar routine to his life.

When David arrived, around lunchtime on Monday, he found Ned not in his study but in the school workshop, alone save for an assistant master. He was sitting at a high bench with a mass of gold wire in front of him. David could see that Ned had been crying but, when he arrived, the boy seemed absorbed in what he was doing. Clearly working with his hands gave him comfort.

David stood by his son and put his arm around him. Ned, still seated on his workbench, leaned into his father. After a moment, David felt Ned's body shake with silent sobs. For minutes, father and son remained there, unmoving, unwatched.

At length, David murmured gently, 'The school say you may come home if you like, or you can remain here and I'll stay in the town. It's up to you.'

Ned reached into his pocket for a handkerchief. He didn't have one: David gave him his. Ned wiped his eyes and blew his nose. 'I'd feel lonely in London, Dad. Can you stay here?'

'Sure,' David said quietly. 'I've already booked into the George Hotel, so I can see you every day.'

Outside the weather was fine so they decided to go for a walk. Across the playing fields, into the woods, then towards the river. David wasn't so sure that this was a good idea but Ned seemed to know where he was going so his father said nothing. They walked for two hours that afternoon and went without lunch. At first David thought his son should get something to eat but then he realized Ned was trying to tire himself out, so he could sleep. They parted around four with Ned already in bed. David left the hotel phone number with the housemaster and went back to the George. His own way of coping with grief was much the same as Ned's: busy-ness. He called Sally at the office for his messages and then spent a couple of hours on the phone, catching up, before he got through to Bess in Italy. It was good to have her to talk to and this made him realize how alone Ned was. He had no brothers or sisters to share his feelings with, and no one like Bess.

In his room in the George on that Monday night David tried to gauge his own reaction to Sarah's killing. He tried to put some order into his feelings. It took him quite a while to admit to himself that he didn't actually have many. He was sorry for Sarah, that was true enough. But he felt no panic about what he was going to do without her. His main thoughts concerned the effect her death would have on Ned. He would need to call Dr Wilde tomorrow to find out what reaction to expect.

David also admitted to himself, cautiously at first, that if his first thought had been for Ned, his second had been that he was now free to marry Bess – whatever the Holy Father said. It was a disgraceful reaction, he told himself, and he put it out of his mind, reflecting, as he got undressed, how quickly a relationship dies. That was what made him saddest, in fact. That his feelings about Sarah's death were no stronger.

Lying in bed he had a third reaction. Perhaps he was hypersensitive, since he worked for the St Patrick's Fund himself, but he knew that sooner or later other people would make the connection he had already made. That Sarah's death had been, however indirectly, provoked by the fund. The fund had helped to create the conditions under which Foley's flourished at the expense of Protestant firms. You couldn't blame Thomas: the link was indirect and the fund had done a great deal of good in the province. But you could say that Thomas was indirectly responsible for Sarah's death, just as you could say that David was too, since he helped administer the fund himself. The news from Nicaragua, the slump in Vatican attendances, and now this murder in Northern Ireland were all bad blows for Thomas, ammunition for his enemies. If Bess was right and the Syrians did mount an attack on Beirut soon, that might be another area where the pontiff would come under fire. It was ironic – worse, it was tragic – that Thomas should face such a prospect so soon after his triumphant tour in America . . . David fell asleep.

Next day Ned seemed more subdued. David was worried. He'd called Anthony Wilde but the psychiatrist was away on holiday. This time Ned and David went for a ride. They drove up on to Salisbury Plain, about three quarters of an hour away, where it was windswept and the sky was vaster. Ned's eyes had taken on a staring quality which perturbed David. 'Are you sure you want to stay at school, Ned? Wouldn't you rather go abroad somewhere?'

'No.'

That's how it was all day. A one-sided conversation.

David didn't want to leave his son after their drive but there were things he had to do. Everyone was being very understanding in his London office but David *was* chief executive. He couldn't just stop working. It was a busy time, too: mid July. The season was winding down and there was a lot to get out of the way before the summer arrived. For one thing, in the wake of the Dead Sea Scrolls' sale, opposition to the royal sale had intensified in Britain. It had, in fact, passed into the public's general consciousness. Everyone in Britain knew the sale was coming in the autumn, and everyone English knew there was vigorous opposition to it. That opposition showed itself in a variety of ways. For example, with the arrival of summer a new crop of T-shirts made its appearance. They depicted details of paintings the Queen intended to auction with, underneath them, the words: 'Don't sell me!'

David stayed at the George until Sarah's funeral, which was on Friday in her home village of Kingsparish in Somerset, where her mother still lived. David and Ned drove down together. It was a bleak day of rain and wind as if the English summer was already over. With Ned's heavy silence next to him, David needed to fill the car with sound. He switched on the radio and turned it to an all-news channel. As they swept down the M4, it soon became clear that the Syrian push in Lebanon had finally started. The fighting was heavy.

David had always got on well with Sarah's mother, who felt her daughter had treated him badly. And she adored Ned. So that part of the day was comforting. But Greener was there and that was more awkward. He was swathed in bandages from the blast.

Still, watching the coffin being lowered into the ground, all four of them, David, Ned, Sarah's mother and Greener, found a sense of community in their sorrow. David held one of Ned's hands, Sarah's mother held the other.

In the car on the way back to London Ned said: 'Do you believe in God, Dad?'

'Yes.'

'I don't.'

'Go on.'

'I talked about it a lot with mother. We couldn't see the point.'

They drove on in silence.

Then Ned said, 'I don't believe in religion. It doesn't tell you things. It doesn't help you to understand things.'

'But at least you enjoyed meeting the Pope.'

'That was great. But all that money the Pope gives away, dad. The fund thing you work for. It's terrific and you've got to do it, but it's bound to go wrong.'

'How can you be so sure?'

'Charity can't replace politics, Dad.'

'You think that's what the Holy Father is trying to do?'

'I reckon he's aiming too high. Charity should help twos or threes, little groups of people who can't help themselves, like the disabled, say, or the blind.'

'What about the poor?'

'Difficult. They're not really a group. They're different in each place where there's poverty. Can I have a Coke, Dad? I'm thirsty.'

They stopped at a garage shop. David bought the Coke, filled the car with petrol, and they drove on.

David wasn't sure, when he reflected on this exchange, what it added up to. But it made him uneasy. Ned was obviously grieving for his mother but, that apart, he had decided views about Thomas and his schemes, had probably discussed them in class at school. He, David, had been given a glimpse of how the rest of the world might see the Holy Father's activities. Not for the first time, it occurred to him that Thomas's programme was complicated and its effects were fearfully unpredictable. Massoni's had been right about that. After he had dropped Ned off at his school he called Bess from the hotel. He couldn't get through at first but, around nine, ten in Rome, he tracked her down to Gina's.

'How was the funeral?' she asked.

'As grim as funerals always are. But Ned stood up well. Amazing how resilient children are – more than adults at times, I think. We had an interesting chat in the car on the way back. Just as amazing what goes on in young minds. But forget all that for the moment; what's your news from Beirut? Is it as bad as the BBC says it is?'

'Well, I don't know what the BBC's saying but it's bad, darling, very bad. The Syrian attack was savage, and around lunchtime the Israelis joined in. Two Israeli planes have been shot down and seven Syrian Migs. I'm told there are burning armoured personnel carriers every-where – and the Christians really took a battering: heavy artillery, rockets, strafing from planes – you wouldn't believe the smoke and the rubble. And – this is the worst from our point of view – a very careful destruction of all the clinics and the camps that Thomas had built months ago.'

'How's he taking it?'

She sighed heavily. David could hear Gina shouting orders in the background. 'Part of him knows that what's beginning to be said in some quarters has some truth to it – that he is, in a sense, responsible for all the things that have gone wrong lately.' Her voice changed. 'Yet the biggest part is still the old Holy Father, the crusader, the American who believes that what he's doing is right and who's determined to fight for it.

'Ironically, we've had two pieces of good news today. The China trip has finally been agreed. He's going there in November – while the American election is on as a matter of fact. Even more exciting, you remember Thomas created a new cardinal *in petto*, in secret, some time ago? In Eastern Europe.'

'Yes, yes I do.'

'We now have a secret report from Hungary. The number of people receiving mass has nearly doubled in the past year. Apparently Thomas's appointment of the cardinal really sparked something. An enormous underground movement seems to be growing and the authorities are furious.'

'That's good to hear. So what now?'

'Thomas is giving a general audience next week. He will announce the China agreement, and the developments behind the Iron Curtain. And then, despite what I have been telling him, he is determined to go forward with this Vietnam offer.'

'You mean the flood relief?'

'Right. He's sending ten million dollars, David. Ten million. The Americans won't buy it. He's going to destroy all the fruits of that marvellous tour. Think what Massoni will make of that in his newspaper column. And you haven't heard the worst yet!'

'What's that?'

'I was at a reception at the Villa Stritch the other night. That's where all the senior Americans attached to the Vatican live. One of the curial priests there, who works in the Secretariat of State, had heard the rumours about the Vietnam gift. And he reminded me of something I had forgotten. Dong An, where the dam and the mine are, is not fifty miles from Da Nang. Does that ring any bells?'

'No. Should it?'

'If you were an American it might. Da Nang is where Roskill's son was killed in the Vietnam war. Thomas is going to help the people who killed the President's son.'

Thomas delivered his statement, about Russia, China and the Vietnam flood relief, just as Bess said he would. The Wednesday audience was packed, the Nervi hall brimming with pilgrims. Scores of children, the lame and the sick were brought to him for his blessing. This included a party of blind schoolgirls from Brazil, from a special school in Rio. When they arrived, late, there were no seats left so His Holiness had them brought to the stage where they were allowed to sit at his feet while he made his speech and afterwards prayed with them.

His speech that day, the vivid words he used to describe the plight of secret Catholics in the Eastern Bloc – he called them the 'Invisible Vatican' – was, for those present, a moving experience. But for the American journalists in the Nervi hall, his speech had a rather different impact, and one that Bess had accurately foreseen.

The *Chicago Sun-Times* headed its report: 'Cash for the Cong: Pope's Bad Taste Gift'. The *New York Daily News* went further, with 'Pope Tom, the Saigon Sugardaddy'. Bess was in despair. She felt she had let the Holy Father down. She should have argued more convincingly for him not to make the Vietnam gift. But it was too late now.

Roskill was the man she most feared and he offered no reaction until the following Saturday, when he made one of his regular radio broadcasts from his Camp David retreat. Then, in the course of a rambling tour around foreign affairs, he said: 'One world leader whose foreign policy is attracting a lot of attention at the moment is Pope Thomas. Since he has held high office, His Holiness has changed the face of contemporary diplomacy. Some of his actions have been of great benefit to mankind. The hope, and material assistance he has given to many of the world's victims has been an inspiration to us all. But even the Pope, as I am sure His Holiness would be the first to admit, cannot do everything. Neither is he, in secular matters, always infallible. We have seen already that his interventions in Florida, Northern Ireland, Honduras and Nicaragua have produced side-effects that have been – well, unfortunate is a generous word for them.

'But it is a more recent initiative that I wish to talk about today. I refer to His Holiness's decision, revealed last Wednesday, to send ten million dollars for the relief of distress recently caused by the collapse of a large hydroelectric dam in Vietnam. Now, I'm not a hard man and can sympathize, as all Americans can sympathize, with hardship wherever it occurs, and no matter who the victims are. At the same time we have a wise tradition here in the United States which teaches us to look after our friends and our friends' interests. Likewise, we expect our friends to look after us and to remember our interests and take them into account. And I am bound to say that this gift to Vietnam does not seem to me to be the act of a friend. There are many Americans alive who fought in Vietnam and who still bear the scars of the wounds they received. And there are many, I count myself among this number, who lost loved ones in the years of war there and whose sense of loss will never be erased. This whole nation, this great nation, still hurts from the trauma of that time.

'I cannot believe that His Holiness Pope Thomas intended to hurt and humiliate the American people by this action. But I say this: we *are* hurt, we *are* humiliated. We wish our friends to stand by us, just as we would wish to stand by them. And I conclude with this thought for His Holiness: by all means pursue your charity work . . . but maybe you should bring that charity just a little nearer home.'

Outside America, however, the Pope's gift was seen in a very different light, as evidence that Thomas really was intent on helping the afflicted, of whatever religion. Given the one-time French presence in Indo-China, there were those who suspected Thomas of trying to stimulate a religious revival in Vietnam, as he was doing in the Eastern

Bloc. But in general the money was seen as an immensely practical way of solving a serious problem.

David read Roskill's speech in Monday's *International Herald Tribune* in Rome. Ned himself had suggested that, after two weeks at the George, his father have a weekend away. He gave David a packet for Bess. 'It's a new brooch. I . . . I never got a chance to give mum hers . . . so I unwound the gold wire and remade it for Bess.'

David was touched. He had been in two minds about whether to leave his son. But Wilde, now back from holiday, had offered to visit Ned and it was the weekend of the school play so there was plenty for the boy to get involved in.

David wanted to be in Rome not only to see Bess, and to discuss their own changed circumstances in the light of Sarah's death, but also to spend some more time in the archive. If he didn't keep at it, he would never solve the damn Leonardo mystery.

As was their habit, they had dinner at Gina's. A crowd was watching the television in the back of the bar, leaving them to themselves. Bess was wearing a green silk shirt made up from the roll David had bought her in Burano.

Before he could raise the subject of marriage, Bess got in first. 'What do you think of these?' She held up her wrists to reveal a pair of gold cufflinks.

'Very pretty,' said David, a trifle impatiently. 'A gift? From your mother?'

'No. There's more to these than meets the eyes.' She leaned forward comspiratorially. 'After the Pimental business, we've all been issued with anti-kidnap devices. Minute radio transmitters. These are mine.'

David was impressed, appalled and amused in about equal measure. He could see it was a prudent move but was worried that Bess should be considered a target. And he was amused that the whole business, serious though it was, appealed to her love of gadgets.

He fingered the links. He certainly couldn't tell that they were anything other than genuine jewellery. But his impatience was still there.

'Darling . . . Bess . . . I don't want to talk about horrible things, like kidnaps . . . I want to say . . . I want to say that we don't have to wait for Thomas now,' David said. 'With Sarah dead, I'm free to remarry.'

Bess rested her chin in her hand. She looked at David with such tenderness he felt a slight pinching at the back of his eyes, as if he was going to cry.

'Are you certain, darling, that you want to rush from one marriage to another?'

'I'm not rushing. Sarah's been gone years, really. I felt sad at the funeral, Bess, but I cannot honestly say I was devastated. Is that an awful thing to say?'

'No,' she said softly, placing her hand over his. 'You were doing your grieving ages ago, when I first met you, remember? Don't feel guilty, David. You've nothing to feel guilty for.'

'You will, then? Marry me, I mean?'

She gripped his hand and closed her eyes. When she opened them again, all doubts were gone. 'I *will* marry you, darling. I love you – I guess things won't be easy, with our jobs and all, but if you're willing to give it a try, then so am I. And what's more, I'm sure Thomas will marry us.' She gripped his hand tighter. 'But I can't marry you yet. Not until all this business between Thomas and Roskill blows over. So much is happening – Russia, the China trip, the new Holy City in Rio. He needs me, David. He needs me even more than you do.'

David frowned. 'But that needn't change after we are married. If I work in London and you work in Rome, and we meet up for the weekends, I think it could work very well.'

'Yes, it could. And it will. But not just now. I'm not saying I won't marry you, David – just that I can't this very minute. Is that so terrible? Nothing's going to change. Please don't ask me to go against what I instinctively feel is right. Please.'

That was how they had left it. There was also the matter of children. They had mentioned it once, in New York. How did Bess feel now? David wondered. It was something to be discussed on another occasion.

At first David felt hurt by Bess's response. However, the ferocious tenderness with which she made love to him that night soon dispelled any doubts he might have had. Bess could not lie with her body. He had awakened in her a sensuality of which she was more and more aware – and more and more determined to satisfy. As David's hands and lips gently scored her skin, this way and that, Bess whispered the memories of her childhood which his touch evoked. Spanish moss. Magnolia. Cocodrie. Bocage.

Next morning it was such a lovely day he walked from Bess's flat, across the Tiber, to the Vatican Archive. The archive was a wonderful place to work. He had been given a desk in a small room, stacked high with manuscripts. There was no view, but the Roman sunshine streamed in through the window carrying with it the noises of birds, airplanes, traffic. It *sounded* like a view. The Boltraffio file was, of course, less voluminous than the Leonardo ones but still, there were many documents: contracts, odd bits of drawings, letters from patrons. David settled to his task, making a careful note of all persons mentioned in the papers. There were other sources to try if Boltraffio proved a dead end.

The Vatican Secret Archive was only open in the mornings so, around twelve thirty, David made preparations to leave. He went to the librarian to hand back the file and to request some photocopying. The librarian was not at his desk so he waited. Suddenly he noticed, across the room, two figures seated together. With a shock he realized one of them was Rome's foremost newspaper columnist, the cadaverous Cardinal Massoni himself. With him was Diego Giunta, the head archivist, who was holding a piece of paper and speaking in rapid Italian. The pair hadn't noticed David. He heard the word '*Papa*' several times and several references to '*i lettere segreti*', the secret letters. David recalled that Giunta was writing the official life story of the previous Pope, Pius XIII. Presumably he had discovered some unpublished letters. David smiled to himself. Though he was no fan of Giunta's, still less of Massoni's, he well understood the excitement of the scholar who has made such a discovery.

The librarian came back and David explained which documents he wanted photocopied and sent to London. Bess had a business lunch that day so he planned to eat alone. He left the Vatican by the Porta Sant' Anna, turned left and walked to the Piazza del Risorgimento. Just off the piazza was a little trattoria he had once stumbled across where they deep-fried fresh anchovies as part of their antipasti. He had never forgotten the taste and went there now.

The restaurant was quiet and, more to the point in view of the high Roman sun, cool. David made his way to the back of the restaurant where he could read, as well as eat, in peace. He had with him I. B. Hart's book, *The World of Leonardo da Vinci*. If Boltraffio failed him, he wanted to be ready to pick up with other friends or, thinking of Townshend, who had given him the idea, enemies of the great man. He settled to his book and the anchovies. He had plenty of time. Bess would run him to the airport later and perhaps they could carry on their discussion about what they should do now that Sarah was dead.

Enjoying his book, David lingered over his veal, and ordered a second cup of coffee. By the time he paid his bill the restaurant was beginning to empty. On his way out, he noticed the vivid scarlet piping of a cardinal's soutane. He looked across – it was Massoni again. But his companion this time was not Giunta but a Slavic-looking man with jowls and hardly any hair. David vaguely thought he'd seen the man before, but couldn't place him. Perhaps he was Massoni's newspaper editor.

In the afternoon he paid a visit to Hamilton's Rome gallery. Massimo Vittrice welcomed him but had no news. No good news anyway. There was no shortage of bad news. The Italian government had decided to go into the art market itself. Faced with the export of Vatican works, the government had given instructions that any good Italian art that came on to the market in other countries it would seek to buy back. Several agents had been commissioned, among them Steele's in London. But not Hamilton's.

The firm was still being discriminated against, both in Britain and Italy. There were those on the board, Averne of course among them, who thought the Holy Father should be asked to compensate Hamilton's for this loss of business. David didn't agree – his view was that Hamilton's had done very well out of the Vatican sales. They couldn't complain now. Still, it meant that, on this, as on almost every issue, Sam Averne and he were on different sides.

On his way back to Bess's flat where he was to meet her and pick up his luggage, David bought an English newspaper. In the taxi he read that on the previous day, the British Prime Minister had referred to Sarah Greener's assassination in a party political broadcast. In placing blame he hadn't mentioned Pope Thomas by name but his meaning was clear enough. Speaking on behalf of his government, the Prime Minister had described its achievements in Northern Ireland – new roads, new schools, a new reservoir. Then he had added: 'Some people seem to think of Northern Ireland as a depressed area, like Sicily or Vietnam. Those of us who know the province recognise that to be unholy rubbish.'

On their way to the airport David read the speech to Bess. 'Coming from a Prime Minister whose party has made a mess of the Irish question for decades, I think that's a bit rich,' she said. 'Still, for once we've had some good news at our end, today, thank God. The "Invisible Vatican" in Hungary appears to be flourishing. Reports are coming in which show a growing demand for religious services across many rural areas. The authorities are desperately searching for our secret cardinal. They haven't found him yet, though. Nor will they.'

Bess's conversation turned to the China trip. 'That's Thomas's next great adventure and I have to be sure that nothing goes wrong.' She was driving and swung the car on to the *annulare*, Rome's ring road. 'An advance party is going out in October to check the Holy Father's itinerary and to see for themselves all the places he'll be visiting on the tour. Besides mainland China, we shall be going to Hong Kong and Taiwan – '

'Bess!' cried David, interrupting her. 'We have to talk. About us. Are you avoiding it?'

She manoeuvred the car into the fast lane. 'Of course not. But let's not get heavy and emotional all the time, honey. We have so little time together – let's enjoy it.'

David's earlier reservations returned. But he said nothing. It was no use insisting with Bess. He sat back and looked out at Rome's sun-baked suburbs.

They reached the airport in what seemed like a few minutes. She pulled the car to a halt underneath the 'Departures' sign, leaned over and kissed him. 'Give my love to Ned and tell him he has to look after you. Because his father can't have what he wants immediately, he thinks he's never going to. And that's nonsense.' She kissed him again. 'Come back soon. I'm missing you already.'

257

He got out, and lifted his bag from the back seat.

'I forgot, I've got something for you,' she said, as he stooped to wave goodbye.

'What is it?'

'The official report on the first year of the St Patrick's Fund investments. A draft for you to comment on before publication. It's appalling, darling. I only hope Massoni hasn't got hold of a copy yet. I didn't really forget it, I just left it till now. Read it when you're on the plane. It's really bad.'

As Bess had said, the report was bad. It was worse than bad, it was a disaster. The bland wording of the chairman's opening statement was bad enough: 'The fund has performed below expectations. The investments in high technology have been especially disappointing, with the computer market, at the moment, apparently saturated. But shipping and airlines are all underperforming and our holdings in these areas have barely kept pace with inflation.'

You could say that again, thought David, as he glanced at the figures on the next pages. When this news got out Thomas was going to come under even more pressure. Especially if Massoni got his hands on it. Neither he nor the Romans had liked the sale of the treasures and this would confirm all their worst prejudices.

The following day, back in London, David looked more closely at the figures, making a few notes on a pad at his side. He was in his office and it was by now the last week of the season. Only two minor sales – of portrait miniatures and stained glass – remained before the staff ran for the beaches of Europe. What he had on his desk was not the financial report that would eventually be published. He had a much fuller account, showing among other details the dates on which shares had been bought and sold. After five minutes he tore his page of notes off its pad and got to his feet. Sally Middleton wasn't in her room, so he left her a note: 'Gone to London Library, back in an hour.' He took the Vatican report with him and walked across the square to the Library. A wind swept down King Street, deep yellow clouds gathered. He loved the London Library, the best club in London, with the best staff of any library he had ever come across. Inside he went down to the basement, where the newspapers were kept. He had the place to himself, and he was there for more than an hour, nearer two. He went back over the previous months, checking company news, share prices and the dates on the fund document. Once he found the pattern, and he knew what to look out for, his job became much easier.

But his horror only grew. He walked back across St James's Square feeling as stormy as the day around him. If he was right, and he was pretty sure he was, the St Patrick's Fund had not merely failed – it had been made to fail deliberately.

# 13

August arrived. In Italy Thomas left for Castel Gandolfo, south of Rome in the Alban Hills. Massoni kept up his sniping in *Il Messaggero*, attacking the Holy Father's 'Invisible Vatican' programme as 'provocative' and the China trip as 'supping with the devil'. But so far he didn't seem to have got hold of any advance information about the St Patrick's Fund report.

In America the election race was beginning to heat up. According to the opinion polls, Roskill was ahead but Fairbrother was well supported and gaining ground.

In Brazil, meanwhile, one of the party of blind schoolgirls who had sat on the stage with Thomas at the audience in the Nervi hall, had slowly begun to see again. Juliana Caratinga, now nine, had been blind since she was three when some paint had been spilled into her eyes. It was quite possible that her eyes had somehow now recovered from the paint in a perfectly natural course of events. But that wasn't how many people thought of it. That wasn't how the young girl thought of it herself. To her and to many others, her recovery was a miracle, a miracle performed by the Holy Father that day in the Nervi hall when Thomas had touched and blessed all the girls from Rio and sat them on the stage with him. Juliana's school was in the Olaria section of Rio, not so far from where Thomas had set up the devolved Vatican in the Prato and it was fast becoming a shrine.

Thomas had not encouraged this: he wasn't in favour of cults, especially those which concerned living people, but there wasn't much he could do about it in Rome. Bess was less negative about the development than Thomas. She kept an open mind concerning the causes, natural or supernatural, that had cured Juliana Caratinga. But the episode undeniably showed how differently the Holy Father was viewed in the west and in the Third World.

In England David was thankful for the peace of August. There were no auctions, many of the galleries were closed, the dealers already on the beaches of Sottogrande or Castiglione della Pescaia. Most relaxing of all, Sam Averne was away on Long Island until the Memorial Day weekend in September.

Ned had come home from school still feeling very low but Anthony Wilde remained convinced that he was on the mend. 'Take him away somewhere you can spend a lot of time together. Get his mind off home – England, school, his mother's world – for as long as you can. Do things with him but also give him his own space.'

David's plan was for them to spend three weeks in Rome with Bess. They could all explore the city, and go out to the beach whenever they felt like it, while he – David – could spend a few days in the Vatican Archive.

But first, David put on paper his suspicions about how the St Patrick's Fund investments had been made to fail. He was now convinced of this: the pattern recurred too frequently for anything else to explain it. Shares had been bought in companies well after they had begun to sink, even after warning notices had appeared in the press. Other shares had been sold while they were still rising. In some circumstances that might be good business, but the fund managers had been getting off the roll far too early for it to make sense. One question remained: who was masterminding the operation? It wasn't clear from the document David had. The fund was managed on a day-to-day basis by two Swiss banks with close Vatican connections, but David knew nothing about them. His plan was to show the report to Bess and, if she agreed, give it directly to Thomas on his return from Castel Gandolfo at the end of the summer. That way only the minimum number of people need know of his discovery.

As soon as he and Ned arrived in Rome he gave Bess his confidential report. She was so disturbed by it that she decided to pass it on to Thomas immediately. Until he reacted there was nothing else either of them could do.

For the first few days in Rome Bess looked after Ned while David visited the Vatican Archive. As always, he enjoyed himself enormously, so much so that he half-wished he could have the academic life permanently. Then, at least, Sam Averne would be off his back. It was only a half-wish, though. He loved the auction business, and he knew that he would find life as a full-time academic irksome.

Boltraffio didn't produce what he'd hoped for. He turned to another of Leonardo's aides, Marco d'Oggioni. Like Boltraffio, he had worked in da Vinci's studio in Milan and just might have taken possession of some papers belonging to the master. The file on d'Oggioni was as thick as that for Boltraffio and so for nearly a week David happily ploughed through his papers.

At the end of that time, though, Bess and Ned were growing weary of the hot, sticky Roman days. Together they had visited the Central Institute for Restoration where Ned had been able to see picture frames and antique furniture being re-gilded. Bess took him to the archive, near where his father was working, and where the Vatican's great collection of books is kept, so that he could study the bindings, many of them decorated with the most sumptuous gilt tooling.

The three of them now decided to take a complete break – and headed for Sicily, to a place none of them had ever been, Agrigento on the south coast, looking out towards Africa. They found a small hotel just outside the town, at Porto Empedocle, from where they could see the many Greek temples halfway up the hills which overlooked the sea. They found a quiet beach just along the coast towards San Leone and went there most days, lazing in the sun and flopping into the water to cool off when the heat became too much. There was only one good restaurant in the town, overlooking the port, so they went there every night. They read, ate ice cream, didn't make it to the Greek temples, didn't take any boat rides to the off-shore islands, and didn't bother with English language newspapers. Bess could have scoured the island for Sicilian silk but didn't get round to that either. They did notice that there appeared to be a slight resurgence of Mafia activity on the island – there were a couple of articles about it in the local Sicilian press and Bess cut them out, intending to show them to Thomas later. They went to mass.

In the evenings they systematically worked their way through the Sicilian specialities on the menu – *maccheroncini*, swordfish, *cannolichi*, *ruote*, and a white wine from the slopes of Mount Etna. After dinner each night they went for the same walk, out towards the end of the jetty. The stars seemed very close this far down Europe. There was also constant movement out at sea. David had no idea there was so much traffic off the coast of Sicily. They would watch the lights of ships steaming by and imagine who was on board and where they were headed.

One evening they were strolling back from the jetty, past the fashionable end of the port, where the bigger yachts overnighted, when suddenly Bess stopped. 'Look!' she said, pointing.

The others followed the direction of her arm.

'Jeesus!' said Ned. On the side of one enormous yacht was painted a name and a black silhouette they knew all too well: the 'Pietà'.

'It must be Wilkie's boat,' said David. 'That's just the kind of thing he'd do.'

Just then, as if to confirm David's supposition, Wilkie himself came on deck. David and the others made to hurry off, but they were too late. 'Colwyn! Is that you? Hey – that's really something. What are you doing here?' He answered his own question. 'Having a vacation, I guess, just like me. Don't run away, come aboard, have a drink. I've got something to show you.'

They were caught, unable to escape without being rude. A crewman appeared and slid a gangplank between the stern of the boat and the jetty. Ned went first and the others followed.

'Come below,' said Wilkie after David had introduced the others. 'It's air-conditioned and cooler.' And so, regretfully, they foresook the warm, sensual night outside, the stars and the breeze, for the clammy interior. Wilkie fixed them all drinks at a flashy brass and mahogany bar in the saloon. Then said, 'I suppose you noticed that I've renamed the boat? Neat, eh? There's more than that up my sleeve, though. You'd better just come along with me. Have I got something to show you.' He led the way forward to a cabin that was obviously his office. Here he reached into a wide, shallow map drawer and took out a series of designs. 'What do you think of these?'

David stared. So did Bess and Ned.

They were architectural drawings of Michelangelo's 'Pietà' set in several different, recognizably American scenes. There was the 'Pietà' outside the Pentagon, outside the White House, near the ice rink at Rockerfeller Centre in New York, with San Francisco's Golden Gate Bridge in the immediate background, as part of the Bel Air Hotel complex in Beverly Hills, as part of the waterfront in Chicago, in the main hall of Caesar's Palace hotel in Las Vegas.

'What *is* all this?' David asked, knowing the answer. Bess was silent.

'My plan's to get the "Pietà" maximum exposure. I need eventually to find a permanent home for it. I don't think my own office building in Washington is the right place, after all. Not enough people can see it. So, I'm planning to send it on tour – three months in each of these sites. Then, wherever it looks best will be its permanent resting place.'

'But . . . Caesar's Palace . . . is a casino.' Bess was appalled.

'Sure. You don't think that's suitable? I think the more unusual the better. Millions of people will see it in Caesar's Palace. It'll stand out more there than in some museum.'

'It'll stand out anywhere.' Bess couldn't believe the drawings. She did believe them.

'You don't like them, do you?' Wilkie's voice had an edge to it. 'Too bad.' He collected them up and slid them back into their drawer. 'Sorry if my crude ways offend you but *I* think it's a good idea and *I* own the damn stuff. I can do what I like with it.' He led the way back to the main saloon, where the drinks still waited. 'Here, you'd better have these,' he said gruffly. 'I've got to see the captain.' And he disappeared.

Soon afterwards a crewman approached them and said, 'Mr Wilkie sure hopes you'll forgive him but he's had to call America and just can't leave the wireless room. Maybe I could see you good people ashore.'

And so, not twenty minutes after they had stepped aboard, David and Bess and Ned found themselves back on the jetty walking quickly away from Wilkie's yacht. Bess was beside herself with anger. 'Showing the "Pietà" outside the Pentagon, indeed, or in a Las Vegas casino . . . I'd like to sink Wilkie's boat. Right now.'

Next morning they carefully examined the harbour from the hotel before they ventured out and were relieved to see that Wilkie must have set sail during the night. For the rest of the week the weather continued hot, and a little *Etna bianco* at lunch each day ensured that they all, Ned included, fell asleep for a short while each afternoon. Then they swam, or went out on hired bicycles along the coast. In the early evenings they went to church. At night, after Ned had gone to bed, Bess and David lay together, looking out to sea. Their room had a private balcony from which the view was stupendous. The light was out and they could see the stars.

'What are you thinking?' said David during one of their silences on their last night.

'That this place is subversive.'

'What?'

'It's so peaceful here, so quiet. I think I like it.'

'What's so subversive about that?'

'Because I shouldn't like it. I like work, really. And I like movement, action, change, speed. When I was a girl I loved cycling. I biked everywhere.' She turned to David and rested her head on his chest, placing his hand on her thigh the way she liked it. 'One evening I'd been out somewhere and left it very late. It was getting dark and I had no lights on my bike. They were strict in those days about lights on bikes. I was with Patrick and we decided to race home. I was in the lead – and going very fast. But it was getting dark and a bit scary. A car came up behind me but didn't overtake, just kept me in its headlights. All sorts of horrible thoughts went through my head and I didn't dare look round. Boy, was I scared! I peddled harder. Then, after what seemed ages, the car pulled alongside – and I saw it was a police car! Part of me was relieved: it wasn't what I thought it was. But the policeman shouted for me to pull over, so I got worried all over again about not having any lights. I stopped and he stopped and I said, "I'm sorry, sir, I know it's getting late and I was hurrying like mad to get home before it's really dark. I know I don't have any lights." He looked at me and grinned. "Don't worry about that, kid," he said. "That don't bother us none. We just thought you'd like to know – you were breaking the speed limit back there!" ' Gently, Bess bit into David's flesh. 'I like to be doing things, David, you know that. I like racing around. A place like this makes me doubt the whole direction of my life.' She turned to him and touched his arm lightly. 'Do something to me now, darling.' She grinned. 'Let's have some action.'

Next morning was Sunday. They couldn't make the drive back from Agrigento to Rome in a day so they planned to spend the night at Messina, catch an early ferry next morning to Reggio di Calabria and drive the seven hundred kilometres nonstop next day. They ate that night at Pippo Nunnari's, the best of Messina's restaurants. Monday morning they made an early start and had breakfast on the ferry. David had grabbed an English language newspaper on the stand in the port. It was the previous day's *Observer*. He didn't look at it until they had settled with their brioches and coffee, by which time the boat was already out of the harbour. But when he opened the paper he knew at once that his holiday was over. Sir Edgar Seton had disappeared.

The story was headed: 'Queen's art expert looted Nazi pictures, bugged politicians.' During the Second World War Seton had worked in the Allied Monuments and Fine Arts Commission, whose job it had been to recover art works looted by the Nazis. According to the newspaper, on three separate occasions Seton had recovered looted paintings – a Rubens, a Poussin, a pair of El Grecos – but, instead of returning them to their rightful owners, had passed them secretly to the Russians. Much more damaging, after the war Seton had worked in collaboration with another art expert, one Philip Lloyd, who had opened a gallery in Old Bond Street. In the course of his job as Surveyor of the Queen's pictures, Seton had come across many prominent people interested in art. These he had referred to Lloyd, and with help from the Russian embassy in London, Lloyd had fitted bugging devices into the frames of any pictures he sold to important politicians.

The scheme didn't always work. But often usefully compromising or informative conversations were conducted in rooms where these pictures hung. The *Observer* reporters had visited the homes of three unsuspecting politicians, together with an electronics expert and found bugs hidden in the frames of the pictures, or else in the wood, when they were painted on panel.

By far the most damaging part of the story was the fact that both this Lloyd and Sir Edgar Seton had disappeared.

Buckingham Palace had refused to comment, so the story ran, and said it would not do so until Seton reappeared and had the chance to defend himself against the charges. But by the time the *Observer* went to press on the Saturday evening, he had been missing for four days. Suspicions were growing that Lloyd and he had skipped the country for Russia.

David passed the paper to Bess. The scandal didn't include him in any way, but he couldn't help feeling involved. After all, the royal sale was now only weeks away. How would that be affected? He reminded himself that Hamilton's had held on in the face of the attempts to stop the Dead Sea Scrolls sale, but he wasn't sure he could count on that again.

He decided he had to get back quickly. At Reggio he phoned Sally Middleton, made some other calls and then decided to aim not for

Rome but Naples, which was nearer and where he and Ned could catch a plane later that day.

He arrived back in London not a moment too soon. Two days after the *Observer* story, the *Guardian* carried one noting that each of the international art conferences Seton had attended in the past five years – in places like Siena, Antwerp, Munich or Vienna – had also been attended by Sergei Litsov, Keeper of Paintings at the Pushkin Museum in Moscow and also the brother of Gregor Litsov, now known to be a high-ranking official in the Soviet security services. Was this how Seton maintained secret contact? the paper speculated.

As before, Buckingham Palace refused to comment. But the chief effect of this discovery was that no one now believed that Seton would turn up again. It therefore made front page news when he did so.

The Russians stage-managed his reappearance in the most brazen manner. An exhibition of Sienese painting had been scheduled in Leningrad for some time and, when it opened a few days later, a prominent guest at the reception was Sir Edgar Seton. He gave no interviews, and was very clearly 'accompanied' by two bodyguards, but the Russians were proud of their propaganda coup and if they didn't allow interviews, they positively encouraged photographs. The picture of Seton sipping a vodka while talking to the wife of the curator of the museum, was in every paper. David also noticed, in the background, the new director of the Hermitage, Dorzhiev, the bald, jowly man who had been pointed out to him by Ed Townshend, that day in the Louvre. David had seen him somewhere else, and recently, but he couldn't pin down the occasion.

Two days after Seton's appearance in Russia, David was summoned not to Windsor, not to Buckingham Palace, but to the Lord Chamberlain's office in St James's Palace. It was so close to his own offices he walked.

The Lord Chamberlain was a small man, superbly groomed, balding a little and tough as a torpedo. He showed David into his office himself and came straight to the point. 'Her Majesty has decided the sale cannot go forward as planned.'

David had half-anticipated the news, but was still shocked. For a moment he couldn't think what to say.

'We shall of course reimburse you for whatever you have already had to spend. But, in the circumstances, you must appreciate that the sale is unthinkable.'

'Aren't you playing into Seton's hands? If you abandon the sale, won't Her Majesty look needlessly foolish?'

'Yes, Mr Colwyn, perhaps. We doubt if Seton planned this all along, just in order to embarrass Her Majesty. Presumably he fled because he was flushed out by the *Observer*. But whatever the reason, the result is much the same: Her Majesty *is* embarrassed.' He lit a cheroot and offered David one. David declined. 'But this Seton debacle isn't the Palace's only reason for cancelling the sale. The British Heritage Preservation Trust have made it very clear to us that they intend to go to court to prevent it. Normally such groups don't have the sort of funds to risk an expensive court case, but there are some wealthy people in the BHPT who have now said they will support the legal action financially. Her Majesty feels that, coming on top of the Seton business, and continuing government opposition, she should not now proceed. I am very sorry for the inconvenience you have been caused and, yes, we do realize this will make the Palace look irresolute. However, it is better for us to grin and bear it. All I ask is that if Sir Edgar wrote anything for the catalogue, you let me have it. His material might be innocuous but it could embarrass us further.'

The announcement from the Palace came later that day. By then David had recovered enough to tell Sally and the firm's press department to go home and he, too, went missing. (He had dinner, alone, in his club.) He knew he couldn't stop the newspapers printing more or less what they wanted, but if no one with authority to speak could be found, coverage would be that much less.

Next day it seemed that David's low-profile policy had paid off. All the papers concentrated on the embarrassment caused to the Queen by Seton's disappearance and, secondarily, on the discreet jubilation among the heritage lobby. There was also passing reference to the Pope, comparing the success of his sales with the fiasco of the royal one.

Thomas, in any case, was also back in the news, and in the wrong way.

*Repubblica* was first with the story that the St Patrick's Fund had underperformed disastrously. The Holy Father had never been as popular in Rome as elsewhere and the financial news did nothing to change this. But what chilled David more than anything was a report he spotted in the Naples paper, *Il Mattino*, two days later. The Holy Father was far more popular in the south of Italy, given the success of the Vizzini fund in Sicily and the papers there were thus more sympathetic. The article, which must have been leaked to the paper by someone either on Bess's staff, or in Thomas's household, had the headline: 'Vatican Fund: Failure or sabotage?'

It read: 'Sources in the Vatican suggest that there is more to the failure of the St Patrick's Fund than meets the eye. Besides the official report, due to be released next week, we understand there is also circulating a private commentary on the investment activity of the fund, written by one of the members of the commission set up to administer it. Details are not to hand but it would appear that this report, by comparing the dates of market movements and the dates when the fund sold or acquired certain shares, concludes that the fund was made to underperform deliberately. This evidence has been sent to the Holy Father but no action has yet been taken.

'The investment strategy of the Fund, although overseen by the Institute for Religious Works, was actually run on a day-to-day basis by two Swiss banks, Credit Lausanne and Banque Leman. One of the directors of the Banque Leman is Dott. Aldo Massoni, brother of Cardinal Massoni who resigned some months ago as Secretary of State in protest at the Holy Father's decision to sell off the Vatican treasures to create the St Patrick's Fund.'

David stared at the article. Neither he nor Bess had known of the Massoni/Banque Leman link. Did it mean that the Cardinal had actually prevailed on his brother to help the fund fail, because he disagreed with Thomas? Was that why the Cardinal had not written about the fund's failure? Because it was too close to home? Thomas would surely have to act now to prevent Massoni doing any more damage?

Before David even had a chance to discuss it with Bess, however, there was another bolt from the blue. A report in the *New York Times* alleged that the victims of the Vietnam dam disaster were still waiting for relief, still in the makeshift homes they had moved to after the disaster, and the dam itself was still in ruins. Furthermore, two officials appointed to administer the Vatican fund had absconded, taking the money with them.

Given that James Roskill, now in the middle of his presidential campaign, had had a son killed in Vietnam, the media eagerly awaited his response to the latest news. It came in a televised press conference at the White House. A journalist from the *Los Angeles Times* put the question everyone wanted to ask. 'Mr President, a report in the *New York Times* suggests that the money sent by His Holiness the Pope to the Vietnam flood victims has been drained away in some other direction, perhaps stolen. What's your reaction to that?'

The President took his time answering. He composed his features into a sad frown. These signs said he was a reasonable man, and a compassionate one. 'First, I am of course angry that the poor and needy should have lost out yet again. It's disgraceful. But I think the episode shows something more, something more important. As I have said before, I am a great admirer of the Holy Father. But this episode, like others in the recent past, merely confirms that the world is a complicated place. It's full of people you cannot trust. Governments you cannot trust, bureaucrats you cannot trust – in Great Britain they have discovered royal advisors you cannot trust,' he added with a snort. 'Many of us were against the Pope's plan to send money to Vietnam in the first place. He disregarded our views and went ahead. Now the plan has backfired, just like some of his other plans have backfired. I think this merely shows that attempts to eliminate poverty in the world, to move forward to peace, if these efforts are to succeed at all, they should be undertaken by legitimate world leaders backed up by the careful research that can only be provided by a professional diplomatic corps. I guess the Holy Father, for all his undoubted virtues, is meddling in things he knows little about. He's an amateur. A rich amateur, maybe. But an amateur nevertheless.'

The press loved rivals – and who better than two of the most powerful men in the world? Roskill's words bore on the presidential race, too. Though there were those in America who agreed with him about the Vietnam episode, most Americans reckoned he was playing with fire, taking on the Pope so publicly this close to an election.

'Pressure from the President, I see,' said David, bending down and kissing Bess. It was the Saturday after Roskill's press conference, and David had arrived in Rome for his first weekend with her since Sicily. He planned another stint in the Vatican Archives. 'How's Thomas taking it?' As usual they met at Gina's in the Via dei Banchi Vecchi. He waved to Gina and ordered a whisky.

Bess shrugged. 'He's okay. You can't win them all, David, and the balance sheet is better than you might think. We've had our setbacks here in Rome, in Vietnam and in Northern Ireland, but our plans are a great success in South America, where Thomas is now regarded as a saint, in Sicily, in the Pacific, in Eastern Europe. And it's a draw in Central America and Beirut. That's not so bad – a better score than the foreign policies of America or Britain can claim, anyway.'

'You don't think Thomas is beginning to lose the propaganda war? Roskill seems to be gaining more attention.'

'Our standing rises and falls, David. My office can have *some* effect but it's limited by what the Holy Father wishes to do. We had a setback in Vietnam – fair enough, we acknowledge that. But when the China trip comes off, Thomas will be hugely popular all over again.'

'What about here in Rome? There isn't a fund meeting for another month. What do you hear?'

'Your report stirred up everyone, as you must know. And, indirectly, exposed the Massoni/Banque Leman link. But Thomas cannot fire Massoni, since he doesn't really have a proper job any more. He could appoint him to a far-off post but Massoni would just refuse to go. But at least I hear that Banque Leman is to be replaced as soon as possible. Of course, that'll be front page news, too, when it gets out.'

'And the fund?'

'Thomas is determined not to lose momentum – there's so much to do – so for this year he's making up the shortfall out of capital. Now that you have found *why* the Fund is underperforming, he thinks the fund will build up again in this coming year. So he's willing to top up the forty-five million dollars dividend to the seventy-five million dollars it should have been.'

'And spend it on?'

'Two programmes. The first is the Invisible Vatican in the Eastern Bloc. We've earmarked thirty-five million dollars for that – to pay the salaries of the secret clergy there; and for an underground newspaper, a version of the *Osservatore Romano*.'

'Isn't that playing with fire?'

'Of course! But how else can you combat communism? With diplomacy? Roskill's wrong there. Look at what happened in Poland. The trade union movement shook them up far more than any diplomacy.'

'And the other forty million dollars?'

'Ah, now there I'm worried. That's where we may be heading for trouble. Four million dollars are to go to each of ten cities around the world with deprived inner areas, where there has been racial violence or riots in the past months. Marseille in France, Amritsar in the Punjab, Bogota in Colombia, Naples, Algiers, Santiago, Liverpool, Soweto Manila, and Detroit in the United States.'

'Hmm. And Detroit is Roskill's home town. I see what you mean.'

Bess nodded glumly. 'By giving Detroit this aid Thomas is not only putting it on a par with Third World cities, an insult in itself, he's also saying that Roskill's policies still leave his own home town in need of outside help.'

'But he can't deny that Detroit *has* had trouble.'

'Yes, but that isn't the point. However deserving Detroit may be, the fact of the matter is that this thing between Roskill and Thomas is getting personal.'


David drew another blank in the Secret Archive. The file on d'Oggioni was as uninteresting as that on Boltraffio. Leonardo had had a sizeable entourage, David knew, but there was only one other assistant whose name was known with any certainty. This was one Giacomo Salai, an unwholesome character, a liar and a thief who became only a third-rate artist. David decided to check Salai's file on his next trip, but not with any real expectation of success. He returned to London.

There he found Sam Averne back from his Long Island holiday and at first sight a changed man. He oozed friendliness, referred hardly at all to the failure of the Queen's sale, and stayed out of the way until the first board meeting of the new season.

But at the board meeting all was explained. At the end of it, under any other business, Averne announced that during the summer he had spent a long weekend at Newport, Rhode Island, with Mrs Isobel Miller, head of the Miller clan which owned Cleveland Ore Inc and whose collection of French Impressionist paintings was one of the best in the world outside a museum. Her late Monets alone, it was said, were worth sixty million dollars. Averne had persuaded her to sell, through Hamilton's. Her only son had died tragically about a year before and she wanted to set up a medical foundation in his name, devoted to combatting the disease that had killed him.

A buzz went round the boardroom but Averne held up his hand. 'Mr Chairman, that's not all. In August it was also my privilege to be a guest at the home of John Iridopoulous, the Greek shipping magnate. His house in Palm Beach, as you surely know, contains some of the greatest Old Master drawings in private hands. Rembrandt's "Judas", Tiepolo's "Apollo", Veronese's silverpoint study for "Rebecca at the Well" among them. This information should go no further than this room but I guess it's no great secret that world shipping has suffered a slump – and Iridopoulous is forced to sell.

'And finally – ' The board members gasped. Averne had more? ' – and finally, I was approached in Long Island by Gordon Flaxman, son of the late actor. The son does not share his father's passion for art and would like to auction the pictures with us. George Flaxman did not have a large collection but he did have four jewels: Turner's water-colour of Westminster Bridge, a Monet view of the same subject, one of Van Gogh's views of the bridge at Arles – it seems Flaxman had a thing about bridges – and a Cezanne watercolour, a self portrait. Mr Chairman, I have asked the relevant expert departments and, all toge-ther, I estimate that these three collections should bring in at least eighty-eight million dollars. The commission on each sale will be the full ten per cent so it's easy for the board to work out our share.'

He sat back smiling as an appreciative buzz broke out. The Earl of Afton brought the meeting to order. 'Sam, that's wonderful news, especially at this moment, when we're still recovering from the Queen's decision not to sell her paintings. We must announce this at once. The board is in your debt – you may be sure of that.' He paused. Discreet applause broke out. Afton nodded. 'Well, I think that closes the meeting. Until next month.'

Afton and David walked back to their offices together. 'Come in a second, David, please,' said the chairman as they reached his door. He closed it behind them and they both sat down. 'Well, what do you make of that?' he asked, fishing out a cigar.

'It's wonderful news,' said David ungrudgingly. 'Great news. Sam's hardly had time to get brown this summer. He was working too hard.'

'He wants your job.'

'I know. Everyone knows that.'

'What are you going to do?'

'Do? I'm not going to *do* anything. Sam can't run this company as well as I can, you know that. Just because he's found three collections doesn't mean he should automatically take over. God, how quickly people forget. Just because the royal sale didn't come off, and through no fault of mine, I'm suddenly under threat. I thought that at least I might count on you.'

270

'David!' the Earl said gently. 'You will always have my support. But there is a reason why I asked you in here today. Look at me.'

David stared at the Earl.

'Notice anything?'

'No. No. Should I?'

'Hmm. I'm losing weight. It'll start to show soon. I'm ill, my boy. At my age you can guess what's wrong. You're the first to know, naturally, just as you're the first to hear what I'm going to say now. I shall resign at the end of the year. I plan to announce it at next month's board meeting.'

'Oh no! I'm so sorry – '

'Don't be. I've had a good run for my money. I'd have told you first anyway, of course, but I mightn't have told you today if it hadn't been for Sam's little show in there.'

'Why? What difference does that make?'

'Look, David, Averne wants more than your job. He wants to transfer the main activity of Hamilton's to New York. With me out of the way your position on the board is much weaker. You have your enemies there and Sam is their leader. Once they find out I'm going they'll hang on and bide their time until the new year. Therefore, my advice to you is to provoke a boardroom battle with Averne *now*, something you can win on. But you have to get to him before or at the next board meeting. If you beat him, then I can announce my resignation and make a recommendation that you be chairman as well as chief executive. That would settle things. But you have to find an issue and find it quickly.'

David went back to his office, his mind in a whirl. The Earl was asking a lot, expecting him to come up with a plan in so short a time. David had no doubt, though, that the Earl's analysis of Averne's intentions, and his strength, was accurate. He stood at his office window and looked at the October day outside. He had often worried about Ned's career. But until now he had never really worried about his own.

Bess was right about the reaction to Thomas's plan in Detroit. Far from welcoming the Holy Father's gift, many people in the city were angry at having their city lumped in with 'Third World Dumps', as one newspaper called them. It didn't help that anti-Detroit jokes increased on American television. The baseball team, for instance, was derisively entered for the 'Third World Series' and so on. The city's pride was easily injured.

But the Americans were not the only ones incensed. The Russians, stung by the thirty-five million dollars earmarked for the Invisible Vatican in Hungary and other Iron Curtain countries, issued a statement through *Pravda* which, strangely, echoed Roskill's earlier remarks. It accused the Pope of amateur meddling in world affairs, in the internal politics of other countries, and described him as irresponsible and subversive.

That, of course, only gained Thomas more support in the west. Two days later, however, a further announcement was made through *Pravda* headed: 'Subversive cardinal killed, resisting arrest.' It read: 'Hungarian police this morning tried to arrest Constantin Kharkov, aged 61, near Kaposvar, a hundred miles south of Budapest. A religious fanatic and subversive, Kharkov is understood to be the secret cardinal created by Pope Thomas to lead the underground church in Hungary.

'Kharkov was discovered at five a.m., sleeping in the basement of a school on the outskirts of Kaposvar. He resisted the arresting officer, and tried to flee. He was injured in the abdomen and died soon after his arrival in hospital.

'The shooting comes after weeks of civil disobedience in the region, where Sunday strikes have been common, schools have been used as illegal meeting places, and tuition in schools has been tampered with.'

By a sad irony, the news of Kharkov's murder increased the Holy Father's prestige around the world. Religious movements in the Soviet Bloc wouldn't stop because one of their leaders had been killed and in fact his death only served to show how seriously the authorities in Budapest and Moscow took the threat he represented. In many people's eyes the Church, the Catholic Church of Rome, was the only power on earth doing anything about the evil of communism.

Thomas himself, however, was distressed. Kharkov had not been a close friend but the two men had met several times and the Holy Father had developed an enormous respect for him. How his identity had been discovered was a mystery. A special mass was held for the dead cardinal in St Peter's.

Thomas then announced that a clear line of authority had been established when the underground movement had first been set up. This very danger had been foreseen, and so the leadership of the Invisible Vatican now automatically passed to the next in line, as did the *'in petto'* title of Cardinal. This was a new imaginative touch – a cardinalate given to the position, not to the man – and it was popular, too.

The following weekend, as part of his campaigning in the presidential race, Roskill went home to Detroit. On the Sunday night he was to address a mass meeting of party faithful in the open air at the football stadium. His staff let it be known in advance that he would use the opportunity to make a major speech, a speech which might change the course of the campaign. In consequence all the networks were there and most of the serious foreign press.

It was a warm night, unseasonally so, with a soft breeze that carried the tang of the lake with it. For an hour, from seven to eight, the arriving crowd was entertained by some of Roskill's friends from showbiz –

singers, comedians, actors and actresses who gave fund-raising homilies. There were no jokes about the Third World.

Just after eight the lights of the stadium were dimmed. A solitary bright beam came on, highlighting the lectern on the stage. The crowd hushed. Then a loud but disembodied voice came over the speaker system: 'Ladies and Gentlemen, the President of the United States of America . . . born and raised in Detroit . . . James Roskill.'

As the last two words were spoken Roskill himself stepped quietly out of the shadow and into the light. This was a local boy back among his friends. Back home and no different, an ordinary American, no less unassuming than when he went away to become President. Cheering broke out spontaneously and swelled. Roskill raised both arms to acknowledge the ovation. The lights came back on and as he turned to face each section of the crowd a louder cheer swept in a slow wave around the stadium.

The cheering lasted for close on four minutes. Then, as Roskill shuffled his papers and the lights around the stadium went down again, the noise subsided. Roskill took out his spectacles and put them on. The noise died away completely.

He didn't speak. Roskill knew exactly the value of keeping his listeners waiting. Then he folded the papers in front of him and put them away. This was to be no set speech, dry and careful. He showed that in his very first words.

'It's damn good to be back. I'd forgotten what the lake smelled like.' He paused. 'Despite all the knocking some folks give it, I *like* Detroit!' Cheering filled the stadium again. This was going to be one of Roskill's combative speeches. This is what his audience liked, what they had come to hear. He let the noise die away completely before leaning forward again to speak into the microphone.

'We meet tonight four million dollars richer. Four million. Four million to be spent in the city helping the victims of the recent racial troubles and those who live in poor areas. Now I'm a practical politician and I'm not dumb enough to look a gift horse in the mouth. Four million dollars is four million dollars. Provided it gets spent to benefit the public and isn't skimmed off into some very private pockets, then I say to the Holy Father, thank you. Thank you very much.

'But, like you friends here tonight, I am from Detroit. Like you I love this city and I'm somewhat puzzled by the Pope's gesture. I'm surprised that we come so high up on his list of relief priorities. Until now I hadn't thought of us as one of the world's major problem areas. Yes, we have our local difficulties – who doesn't? But, I must confess, I did not think of us as the Manila of Michigan, or the Amritsar of America. And nor did you my friends, I'll bet. I had never imagined Bogota as one of the great industrial foundries of the world, as Detroit is . . . Like you, to me it came as a bit of a shock. A great shock! I had never

273

imagined that, in the midst of America, in the midst of plenty, there was this desert called Detroit. I had never imagined us as the Vatican's poor relation . . . And so, before coming here tonight, I did some research. I wanted to find out just how beat-up Detroit is, how badly it compares with other cities. And I needed, of course, somewhere to compare it with. Somewhere that doesn't merit the Holy Father's attention as this city does . . . So my friends, which city did I choose? I chose Rome'

Roskill paused, knowing that a murmur of interest would rustle round the stadium. Then he went on. 'What did I find? Let me treat you to some figures, some official statistics. Let's start with unemployment, everyone makes so much of that these days. In Detroit unemployment is running at nine per cent. That's too high, but what is it in Rome? In Rome, friends, it's eleven per cent. Now let's ask about child mortality, since that's supposed to be a guide as to how healthy a society is. Here in Detroit child mortality runs at about nine deaths per thousand population, as against eleven per thousand in the US as a whole. But what's the figure for Rome? Eighteen, my friends, eighteen. Double what it is here.

'Now let's ask about standard of living. In Detroit ninety-five per cent of people have telephones – and in Rome the figure, friends, is seventy per cent.

'There's more, so keep listening, keep listening good, as my mother used to say. The number of doctors in Detroit is forty-seven per one hundred thousand people. In Rome? Twenty-seven. In Detroit the number of children in care, because their parents are for some reason unfit to look after them, is two per one hundred thousand of the population. In Rome? Seven.

'Now let's look at crime. Burglaries in Detroit ran last year at about thirty-seven per one hundred thousand of the population. The figure in Rome? Fifty-three. Crimes of violence in Detroit rose last year by four per cent; in Rome they rose by seven per cent, nearly double.

'Finally, I can tell you friends that we, here in Detroit, spend one hundred and nineteen dollars and fifty cents *each* per year on welfare, helping out the less fortunate people of the city. What do they spend in Rome? Not even fifty dollars a head, friends. The official figure in Rome is forty-six dollars exactly.'

Roskill's figures were biased, of course. He had chosen only those which showed Detroit to advantage. He had mentioned for example only the *rise* in crimes of violence, not the absolute levels, which were much higher in Detroit than in Rome. He had mentioned nothing that showed the extent of racial discrimination in Detroit. But it was the emotion of the speech that interested the crowd, not the facts.

'Now, like you friends, I am suspicious of statistics. We all know that you can prove anything with figures. These figures I have given you are probably no more illuminating than any others. But – ' he paused for effect – 'but, if they prove anything, they prove what you and I have always known. That Detroit is a damned fine town, a city as wonderful as any in America – and a damned sight better than a good many others. We may not have been around as long as Rome . . . but this city of Detroit is just as fine a place to live as anywhere *now!*'

Roskill paused as the applause rose around him. Then, after a few seconds, he leant forward on the lectern. Utterly relaxed, he was totally in command of the crowd. The sight of his shoulders, hunched now above the lectern, showed he was about to become more confidential in his tone. Silence fell. Everyone knew that Roskill was always at his most biting when he got confidential.

'We live in unusual times,' he half-whispered. 'We have unusual problems, *terrible* problems – nuclear war, terrorism, communism . . . We have the old problems, too, of starvation, military aggression, ignorance and – yes – poverty. And we also have the mass media to make sure we none of us forget these problems.

'Mercifully, as a result of all that, with God's help we have created sophisticated governments whose job it is to try to solve these problems. Sometimes they succeed, sometimes they fail, but they keep on trying.'

He removed his spectacles and started to polish them with his handkerchief. 'In addition to all this we now have an unusual Pope. Pope Thomas is, as Popes go, unusual. I think we can all agree on that.' He smiled and the expectant hush in the stadium deepened. His audience knew that when Roskill smiled the worst was yet to come. 'Thomas is American, friends, so perhaps we should expect him to be unusual. We Americans like to think that there *is* something special about us, with our open system of government, which means that anyone, even I, can become President.'

The sound of one hundred thousand people chuckling to themselves rose above the stadium. But now the President stood up straight and suddenly became very serious.

'Pope Thomas has tried some very unusual techniques in world diplomacy in the last months. I was an early supporter. If any one man can be said to have tried to change the world, it is he. When he announced that he was going to sell off the Vatican treasures and devote the proceeds to good causes, that, I thought, was a damned good American idea. But then, when the projects he wished to support became clear, I, along with several other world leaders, was obliged to question his judgement. You will recall the fiasco of the Cuban invasion. Then there was the expensive farce of the Nicaraguan kidnap which gave the Marxist government there the pretext to raid the new town of Pimental, with the result that many died. As a result of Pope Thomas's policies we have seen the wife of the British minister for Northern Ireland murdered. We have seen interference, and more deaths, in the Middle East.'

Roskill had been gradually raising his voice as he paraded his grievances. Now he shouted: 'But Thomas's most telling failure, and, in my view, his most ill-considered intervention, was the aid he sent to Vietnam. I deplored it at the time – as I'm sure you did, friends. Now, with the latest revelations that those funds have been skimmed off by cheapskate Vietnamese bureaucrats, I can only say, as much in sorrow as in anger, "I told you so!" ' Roskill's face now took on a fiercer look. 'This latest plan by the Holy Father, however, is the last straw. I know you will forgive me, folks, if I speak plainly. As an American and a Catholic, I say: "Enough is enough, Thomas!" By all means let us have an unusual and compassionate Pope. Let him involve himself in charity – yes! But not – never – in politics. Today's world is too complicated, too dangerous, too interdependent for gestures that catch the eye but have not been properly thought through.

'Friends, I bring you some fresh news tonight, news which unfortunately bears out what I say. You'll have noticed that I haven't yet made any reference to the Holy Father's activities in the Soviet Bloc. Since I think I may claim to be as anti-communist as anyone, you might well expect me to welcome what the Pope has been doing . . . And yet, what is the end result of this scheme? Well now, you all know that Cardinal Kharkov has been brutally murdered, and you may say that that is the price the Church has to be willing to pay for taking risks . . . But friends, I have been talking to our ambassador in Beijing and he tells me that the Holy Father, who had been hoping to visit the People's Republic of China in November, will not now be going. The invitation to him has been withdrawn. And the invitation has been withdrawn, friends, because the Chinese do not wish the Holy Father to begin the kind of activities in China which he has set up in Hungary and Rumania. They are, or were, prepared to make agreements with the Vatican in which benefits went to both sides. But they are not prepared to entertain a Pope who may, to judge from his behaviour elsewhere, actively undermine their authority over their own people. Accordingly, our ambassador was informed that the invitation to the Holy Father has been revoked!'

There was absolute silence in the stadium. Roskill was winding up now. It had been a good meeting. Now was the time to finish with a bang. 'Friends . . . when I came here tonight, like you, I was burning with anger at the humiliation Detroit has been made to suffer in the past few days. I was therefore determined to set the record straight, and I hope I have done just that. But I haven't quite finished. I want to say two more things. I say first that the Holy Father, for all his virtues, has in truth become like a medieval alchemist in reverse. Far from taking base metal and turning it into gold, he has taken a number of beautiful, sublime art treasures and he has turned them, or the money raised by their sale, into the basest of metals – international corruption, insecurity, deceit, and danger. And I say second that I am a Catholic and I make no bones about that fact. But the truth, as I see it, is more important. As a political leader I have always stayed out of religious matters and so I now say this to the Holy Father, to Pope Thomas. There's no place in the modern world for a political Pope. Either he should stay out of politics – or he should resign!'

# 14

David learned of Roskill's speech early the next morning, when he saw the lead headline in *The Times*. Immediately, he dialled Bess's number in Rome.

'I've never seen Thomas so angry!' Bess's voice was shaking. 'One minute Roskill's sucking up to the Holy Father, actually asking for his help in the Philippines – and the next minute this. He's looking for votes, of course. All the same, I could shoot the snake.'

'What will Thomas do?'

'Do? Nothing. Popes don't resign. At least, not since the middle ages. Can you imagine, *La Repubblica* here actually ran a story today on Popes who have resigned, plus a sidebar on the replacement candidate who might be elected if there was a conclave tomorrow? Needless to say, Massoni came top.'

'What's happening to the China trip?'

'Wasn't that nice? Well, we're still going to Hong Kong, Taiwan – and we've had an invite this morning from the Philippines. So it's business more or less as usual. Thomas will carry on as before. This will all blow over, and David, with any luck Roskill will lose the election. And it's not all black for Thomas – don't forget there are some extraordinary things happening in Rio.'

It was true, David had to concede. Juliana Caratinga could now see again perfectly well, a fact which was revered throughout the entire country as a miracle. The spot in her school playground where she had first regained her sight was now a shrine. A local sculptor had made a likeness of the girl leaving, in the manner of Buddhist sculptures, a local priest to add the eyes. The shrine was visited by hundreds every day and the number was growing, as was the number of reported miracles performed on the spot. Juliana herself travelled Brazil, attending services and speaking of Thomas's powers.

'I'll see you on Friday, then.' David was due in Rome for a fund meeting.

'Of course, darling. Gina's as usual. And don't worry about us. The unexpected is bound to happen.'

Cardinal John Rich craned sideways in the back seat of his taxi to look at the New York skyline rising high like an enormous, old-fashioned key above the FDR Drive and the glittering East River. Despite his years as cardinal in Manhattan, the rawness of New York was still as attractive as ever, as natural a force there as were the Atlantic gales off his native Galway. Whenever his work in the Secretariat of State brought him here he loved it.

He had arrived the day before, from Rome, and was leaving now for Detroit to begin negotiations for the St Patrick's Fund cash to be brought to the city. He had been able to break the journey and spend one night in New York. He had an interesting meeting with some acquaintances in Wall Street, at the Securities and Exchange Commission. They had agreed to carry out an inquiry on his behalf. Discreetly. Using their contacts in Switzerland. The rest of the time he had spent with friends. They had taken him to a reception at the Metropolitan Museum where he had been able to see Giotto's 'Stefaneschi Tryptich' in its new home, then they had gone downtown, to the Colonna, for dinner. A marvellous evening.

The cab mounted the Triboro bridge and slowed for the toll barrier. He looked at his watch: five past seven. He was in perfect shape for the eight am La Guardia flight to Detroit. The taxi joined the line at the toll. The driver at the front did not have the correct change so the line moved slowly. Rich picked up his *New York Times* and followed the election campaign news. Since Roskill's attack on the Holy Father, the Cardinal was hardly a fan. He searched the paper in vain for a rebuttal from the black Democrat, Oliver Fairbrother. But he was steering clear of the fight between the President and the Pope.

Roskill's speech had complicated the Cardinal's Detroit visit and Rich was by no means certain how to handle it. The local archbishop had seemed curt when Rich called to arrange a meeting. Obviously the archbishop was under his own local pressures, and for him to accept the money on behalf of the city of Detroit put him in what was, at the moment, a very unpopular camp. Still, it would all blow over. Rich was invigorated. He had never known church work be so invigorating.

The cab inched forward. He looked up. There were two cars in front. Suddenly the window darkened and he saw figures surround his vehicle. All four doors were snatched open, and on either side of the cardinal, a stocky, armed figure forced his way in. In front another man leapt into the passenger seat and pointed a gun into the driver's kidneys.

'Get out!' he hissed. 'Or you'll die in your own shit!'

As fast as he could the driver scrambled out. A fourth man got in behind the wheel. By now the cars in front had cleared the toll. With perfect timing the taxi screeched off through the barrier without stopping or paying, and on to the turnpike beyond. Already the cardinal's wrists had been handcuffed together behind his back, his skull cap had been ripped from his head, and a wide strip of sticking plaster drawn over his lips. He kept very still. He could feel the hard barrel of a gun against his ribs.

The cab sped along the elevated section of the freeway. At the first exit it left the highway, made a right turn, travelled three blocks into Queen's, made another right turn into a dead-end road where a white van was parked. Nobody spoke. The driver pulled up behind the van. The man sitting next to him got out, opened the vehicle's rear doors and the cardinal was manhandled out of the cab and into the van. Two men got in with him, the doors were closed, and then he felt the van move off. He couldn't see out. Very quickly he became disorientated and had no idea where they were heading. For about forty-five minutes them twisted and turned, stopped and started. Eventually, Rich felt the van head down a steep incline, which presumably led into the basement of a building. The engine was switched off and doors opened. Sure enough, he was in an underground car park. He was led through one, two, three doors, all of them rusted grey in colour, ending up in a small room with a steel bed, a bucket and a square of tiny, bottle-glass windows high in one wall, showing that the room was for the most part underground. And still, impressively and alarmingly, no one had spoken.

But now a fifth man appeared. Like the others he was small but thickset. A gold cross hung on a chain around his neck. When he spoke it was with an accent, either Spanish or Italian. 'Know what the biggest ransom ever paid is?' He stood close to John Rich. There were gold teeth at the side of his mouth.

The cardinal shook his head.

'Twelve million dollars. Think you're worth it?'

Again, the cardinal shook his head.

'You better be. Or you're dead.'

For once David heard the news before the press did. Bess called from Rome. 'Twelve million dollars! Can you imagine it? Slap in the middle of New York, in broad daylight, too. I don't know whether Thomas can stand the strain. Coming on top of everything else . . .'

'Hang on, Bess. I'll be in Rome tomorrow.'

'Bless you, darling. This is one of those times when I wish we'd jumped aboard that ship in Venice. I feel – well, I feel *wrong* about this one. The kidnapper who made the demand was apparently very coarse and insulting. It's not at all like the Nicaraguan situation. Incidentally, we are sending Cardinal Pimental since he's been through it all himself. We've told the kidnappers, whoever they are, to contact him at the archbishop's residence in New York. I just pray Roskill will leave us alone while we try to sort it out.'

It was a forlorn hope.

While Pimental was actually in the air aboard an Alitalia flight from Rome to New York, the US President issued a statement in which he said that the kidnapping, though it was of a priest travelling on a Vatican passport, was an internal American matter and would therefore be handled by the FBI. Since, however, the kidnappers had made contact via the archbishop's residence on the corner of 50th street and Madison Avenue, the director of the FBI in New York, Frederick Brodie, whom Roskill had put in charge, had to station his men there. By the time Pimental landed at JFK airport Brodie already had his men in position.

The 747 pulled into gate fifty-six at the International Arrivals Terminal and the captain shut down the engines. The door swung open and the immigration officials came on board. Two of them conferred with the chief steward who, after a moment, pointed forward, to row B in the first-class compartment. The immigration officials stepped across.

'Cardinal Pimental?'

He nodded.

'I am sorry, Father, but I have orders to deny you entry into the United States. You are going to have to leave, on the first available – '

'What? Why? But I am here to help with the kidnap – '

'I am sorry, Father. I know why you are here. But here is my legal authority . . .' and the man took a document from inside his jacket. 'It is signed by the Secretary of State in the Justice Department. I'm telling you, Your Eminence, you can't come into this country.'

Pimental swayed, as if from a body blow. He fought for time to think. 'At least let me call the archbishop's residence. You owe me that courtesy.'

'My orders are to escort you to the VIP lounge and have someone wait with you until this aircraft is ready to return to Italy, when you will be put back on it. Now come with me, please.' The man smiled and said more gently. 'There are phones in the VIP lounge, sir.'

The passengers in the first-class compartment stared mutely at this confrontation. In the back of the aircraft, the other passengers – ignorant of the reason – grew impatient at the delay. But now Pimental took a small bag from under the seat and said, 'How shall I reclaim my other luggage?'

'Give me your baggage tag, Eminence. I shall arrange it.'

The three men, the immigration officials and the cardinal left the aircraft. As they walked, Pimental addressed the man who seemed the more senior of the officials, 'You say the Secretary of State Justice Minister himself authorized this. What are his grounds? Does he realize what he's doing?'

'I'm sorry, Eminence. My orders are not to discuss anything with you. Just to put you back on the plane you came on. I'm sorry.'

They walked on in silence to the VIP lounge. From there Pimental called the residence and was put straight through to Naughton, the archbishop.

When the archbishop found out what had happened he was shocked. Roskill was really playing rough.

'You will tell His Holiness?'

'Of course, Eminence,' said the archbishop. 'Right away. No doubt he will have to consider retaliatory diplomatic action. If there is any comfort I can give . . .'

'Thank you, but no. After my experiences in Nicaragua I should have learned to expect the – the unusual. See you in Rome, Eminence. At L'Eau Vive perhaps.'

After two and a half hours the senior immigration man returned, carrying the cardinal's single piece of luggage and escorted him back on to the aircraft. By then press and TV cameras were in position.

And so, later that day, before Pimental was very far out back across the Atlantic, pictures of him being escorted on to the Alitalia flight, having been barred entry into the USA, led all the news bulletins.

What the media didn't yet know was how badly the treatment of Pimental was affecting the relations between Archbishop Naughton in New York and Brodie of the FBI. Both men were aware of the ill feeling between their respective superiors. But Brodie, despite his name, was not a religious man and he had arrived at the residence determined to stamp his own authority on the situation. All the phones were tapped, even the archbishop's private line. Brodie established himself in the archbishop's office, where a direct line was set up to the White House. It was Brodie who decided when and where to brief the press. No one, not even the archbishop, was allowed to leave the residence without an FBI escort. The kidnappers had said they would deal only with the Pope's representative and that was the single thing that prevented Brodie from taking over completely.

At the first press conference, given later that day, Brodie was robust in defence of the way Cardinal Pimental had been barred entry. 'We naturally sympathize with the difficult situation in which the Archbishop of New York and the Holy Father find themselves. But there's just one point I would like to make in this press briefing, which will explain the FBI's position in this matter and also address the kidnappers, in case they are watching.

'The Justice Department's reason for not allowing Cardinal Pimental to enter the country is that the kidnappers – and now I speak directly to them – have said they will deal only with the Vatican. Now, in our view, this crime occurred in the first place only because Cardinal Pimental was kidnapped in Nicaragua and was released after a ransom had been paid. The Vatican claims it sent him here because, on account of that experience, he would now make an excellent negotiator. To us, however, it seems that his presence here might signal to the kidnappers that the Vatican is ready to surrender yet again. And, I have to tell you, there will be no surrender in this case.

'I have to tell you also that the taxi in which the abduction of Cardinal Rich took place has now been found. It has been tested for fingerprints, and one set belongs to an individual whose prints were last found at Oakland airport in Oregon – that's right, we believe this gang of kidnappers is the same as the gang of illegal immigrants from Sicily who caused an airsmash at Oakland in an effort to extort money from the airport authorities there. The President, therefore, feels very strongly that this case should be handled by the FBI – and I agree with him. This is not just a case of kidnapping: these men are wanted for other crimes too. The kidnappers can talk to Naughton, but they will have to *deal* with me.'

The first call came later that night. A man asked for Archbishop Naughton and then, almost immediately, Rich's voice was heard. 'This is John Rich, speaking on tape. You will be trying to trace this call so my message has to be brief. I am treated as well as can be expected. The price is twelve million dollars. The next call, tomorrow, will be to Rome, the Vatican. You will know who it is: he will use the code: Punta Raisi. The answer must be yes or no. No in-betweens.' The line went dead.

'Shit!' said Brodie. 'They're trying to sidestep us. Time I called the President.'

The President's orders were clear, if dangerously unorthodox. 'Don't alert the Vatican. Don't let Naughton contact Rome. Keep it in America. Those bastards blew up an American plane on American soil – they're not going to get round us by talking to the Europeans. Keep everyone in the dark.'

Brodie raised his eyebrows, but did as he was told. He even slept in the archbishop's office. A coffee machine joined the telephone taps near the window. No one was allowed in or out of the residence.

All next day Bess called Naughton every hour, on Thomas's behalf, but was never put through. At about half past three in the afternoon, Rome time, a Vatican operator took a call from someone calling himself Punta Raisi but he hung up, thinking the man was a crank.

By dinner time in Rome, when Bess still had nothing to report, Thomas decided to call the President. Bess placed the call for Thomas and was quickly put through to Cranham Hope. The President was with his Chief of Staff at the Pentagon and could not be disturbed. But Hope said he would call back in an hour or so.

Bess wondered whether it was true or the President was just being difficult.

An hour later, almost to the minute, the phone in Thomas's private study began to flash. Bess took the call, recognized Hope's voice, and handed the receiver to Thomas. 'Mr President, thank you for calling back.' There were no pleasantries. Thomas smoked as he talked. 'That's right, no news. That's why I called you. As your advisors must have told you, the longer a kidnap goes on with no news, the bleaker the situation. I want to try a change of tack. Yes, I realize it is an internal US matter. You have made your view on that perfectly clear. But what I am saying is that your approach obviously isn't working – hear me out, Mr President, please.'

Thomas took a deep breath, pulled on his cigarette. 'You may recall that when I toured America some time go you asked a favour of me regarding the Philippine Islands. I obliged. I also said there would come a time when you could return the favour. That time has now come. I would like you to let me play this kidnap my way. We need to re-establish contact. If you are right and the kidnappers are Sicilian, maybe we can contact their friends or relatives on the island and bring them into the negotiations. It's worth a try, surely. So that is the favour I ask, Mr President. That you step back, pull Mr Brodie off the case, and leave it to me.'

Bess watched Thomas as he listened to the President's reply. The Holy Father's hand gripped the receiver tightly. Gently, he scratched the side of his nose with his other hand. His eyes seemed to focus on an area somewhere in front of his shoes. He bit his lower lip. The cigarette burned, unsmoked in his fingers. Then, very slowly, without saying anything, he lowered the receiver. Bess could hear the President's voice still coming from the earpiece until, gently but firmly, Thomas placed it back in its cradle. The Holy Father got to his feet and went to the window. The *tufo*, the sound of the Rome traffic, seemed especially loud tonight.

Bess tried to make it easy for him. 'He'd forgotten his promise, I suppose?'

Thomas turned back. 'Oh no, he remembered all right. But he said he wasn't keeping his promise. He said the election was too close to let a – and then he blasphemed – Pope interfere again. Then he laughed and said I could hear his confession after it was all over. I don't know what else he said. I put the phone down before he had finished.'

Four thousand miles away, Roskill was barking down the direct line to the archbishop's residence in New York. 'That Pope hung up on me! D'ya hear that Brod? The man hung up! No one hangs up on me! Nofuckingbody! Anyway, that settles it. If there's any comeback I can always say he refused to cooperate.'

Brodie grinned into the phone. He enjoyed a fight, especially when he knew in advance he was on the winning side. He put the phone down and ordered some dinner. The archbishop's residence wasn't too far from Daniel's Deli on 49th and Lex so he sent out for some pastrami and pickles and a six pack of Miller light. Then he settled down to wait. The FBI was good at that.

It was another twenty-eight hours before there was any news. And then it didn't come over the phone. There were no more telephone calls from the kidnappers in the matter of John Rich. Just before dawn the next night a motorist in the Park Avenue tunnel between 40th Street and 31st Street noticed what looked like a bundle of rags laid out along the edge of the driveway. At first he took it to be a tramp, trying to keep warm in the October nights. But the tunnel was too dangerous for that, surely. He slowed, and saw the tiny patch of white collar at the man's throat. An avid reader of newspapers and magazines, the driver braked to a halt. He had a dreadful feeling he had stumbled on the fringe of an historic event. He was right. With a curiously excited shudder, he recognized the dirty, mutilated and dead face of Cardinal John Rich.

David was already in Rome when the news of Rich's death came through. He was with Bess, lunching at Gina's when she was called to the phone. From where he was sitting he couldn't hear what was said, but he could see the change that came over her face.

She came back to the table physically altered by the news, and close to tears. 'I'm frightened, David. This battle betwen Roskill and Thomas has become very personal, very bitter. And it has cost John Rich his life.'

David said nothing, but put his hand over hers across the table. She was again wearing the green shirt made from the Venetian silk he had bought her. He hoped it wasn't always going to bring her bad luck.

'Thomas was so close to John Rich. He had an anti-kidnap device – sewn into the lining of his skull cap. It must have been dislodged.' She sighed. 'Thomas will be shattered.' For a moment she seemed lost in a private memory. David too was shocked. He had liked John Rich.

'Thomas has been changed by Roskill, you know,' said Bess. 'He never intended they should fight, it's just developed that way. But Thomas will never be the same again. And I reckon he'll blame Roskill personally for Rich's death.' She moved her other hand so that David's was held between both of hers. 'I'm worried what might happen now.'

David said softly, 'Roskill might lose a lot of support, don't forget, for messing up the kidnap. It could damage his campaign.'

A waiter brought the pasta they had ordered but Bess no longer felt like eating. 'The way things are, David,' she said after the waiter had gone, 'I don't think Thomas will wait long enough to see how Roskill's standing is affected. We're meeting this afternoon, officially to consider Cardinal Rich's funeral. But I'll bet Thomas will sound us out on his next move against the President.'

'Next move? What do you mean?'

'I don't want to say. It's too frightening. A couple of nights ago he and Roskill had a very ugly telephone conversation. And just after he'd put the receiver down Thomas muttered something. I only half heard and I didn't like it. But I've an idea it may crop up again this afternoon.'

'But what is it? What are you talking about?'

Bess shook her head and would not be budged. Later David drove her to the Porta Sant' Anna in the Vatican, for her meeting. Then he went back to the flat and, after reading for half an hour or so, fell asleep.

He fell asleep feeling sorry for Bess and not a little guilty. The fact was that, before the appalling news about Rich had come through, he had had a very exciting morning in the Secret Archive. The file of Giacomo Salai, the most unprepossessing of Leonardo's assistants, had in the end proved the most productive. Buried within it had been a scrap of paper which, though innocuous enough in itself, stood out, given David's line of interest. On the paper was a small drawing. It didn't look much, it showed a woman's head. She had heavy eyelids and looked down. She appeared contented and sad at the same time. This was exactly the pose of the Virgin in both the Paris and a London 'Virgin of the Rocks'. But what also drew David's attention was a small outline of a spoon alongside. Leonardo had occasionally done this to represent amounts of pigment to be used – he had designed his own measuring spoon. The figures next to the spoon therefore represented the proportions of various colours. Scribbled alongside the spoon was the word 'carne' – flesh – and a set of figures. What made David sweat with excitement was that the writing was back-to-front, mirror writing, and apparently in da Vinci's hand. What he had, so it seemed to him, was a new da Vinci sketch, albeit small and crude, and – possibly more important – the master's formula for the flesh tones of the Virgin in the 'Virgin of the Rocks'. What was doubly exciting was that David knew the Paris and London versions of the painting differed markedly in their flesh tones. If he was right, and this was a page of Leonardo's notebooks that had got caught up with Salai's things, then he might just be able to settle the origins of the two paintings once and for all. And there was more. An archivist had noted on the Salai file that other Salai documents were located, not in the Secret Archive, but in the library of the Montaforno family in the Palazzo Montaforno in Rome. The Montafornos had been a Milanese family who during the Renaissance had provided the Church with a Pope and several cardinals. They had presumably been patrons of Salai. David would have to check their archives.

This was the excitement that had tired him. Bess's distress also had an effect and David's sleep was troubled. He dreamed a vivid tale about a painting which kept changing. To begin with it represented the bridge Ned had jumped from, only in the dream the river flowed not with water, but with molten lava from an underwater volcano. Then the bridge disappeared and he saw Roskill in a pulpit, floating in the river of lava and preaching. Suddenly Sam Averne came drifting down the lava on one of Leonardo da Vinci's inventions which turned into a helicopter and flew away. The helicopter flew right by him, its blades making a knocking sound which grew louder and louder until they woke him and he realized that Bess was banging on the door: she did not have her key.

Immediately he was awake. When he let her in he could see that she had been crying. He took her coat and put his arm around her shoulders. 'Bess, darling, what is it? What's happened?'

She turned and put her arms around his waist, pressing the side of her head to his chest. He could smell her hair and tears. 'Oh David, it's awful. I can't get to Thomas any more. I've never seen him so angry. He's gone all quiet inside. I don't know what to do. He won't take any advice, just says his mind is made up.'

'Made up? What do you mean? Made up about what?'

'We hardly discussed the funeral. He's obsessed with Roskill. Do you know what the kidnappers are saying? They're saying it's Roskill's fault that poor John Rich died. They're saying Roskill kept us in the dark about the fact that they wanted to deal with us here in Rome. Apparently, they told the FBI man in New York they were going to call us here – they even gave him a code so we could warn our switchboard to put the call through quickly. But Roskill wanted to keep the negotiating in the USA so badly he forbade the FBI man to let anybody tell us. He's denying it now, of course, but the call really did come through – we checked with the switchboard. And as the operator wasn't prepared, he didn't recognize the code so he just hung up.' The tears started again. 'It's wicked.'

David hugged her. 'At least if this is true, Roskill's wrecked his election chances. So what is it Thomas is going to do? What *can* he do?'

'The worst thing possible. At least for a Catholic. He's going to excommunicate him.'

Thomas did not stop at excommunication. Besides releasing the momentous news, the Vatican Press Office also, unusually, revealed the Holy Father's reasons. It explained how, on the night before Rich's body had been found, the President and the Holy Father had talked on the telephone. The Vatican statement explained that the President had blasphemed at the Pope and then, in the Holy Father's view, had deliberately withheld crucial information which could have saved Rich's life. Instead, Roskill had put politics ahead of humanitarian, Christian compassion. The press communique concluded that James Roskill had forfeited the right to receive the blessed sacraments of the Catholic

287

Church. The excommunication was designed, as was all excommunication, to bring the offender back to God's ways.

Naturally, all eyes turned to Roskill. But, as had happened once
before, after Thomas announced relief for the Vietnamese dam victims,
the President suddenly became inaccessible. He avoided press conferences and cancelled several meetings of his campaign tour.

Around the world many people, especially in non-Christian countries, were puzzled by Thomas's action in excommunicating Roskill.
Others vaguely approved. Excommunication implied a judgement on
the American President which no one else was able to make. Many had
not been happy with the way the President seemed to have handled
the kidnap. There was a difference between resolve and foolhardiness.
Anyone could be implacable: negotiations, on the other hand, involved
judgement and Roskill hadn't shown any. John Rich had been on a
mission to help the victims of bigotry, and Roskill had sacrificed him
with hardly a thought.

Those who disapproved of what Thomas had done came mainly
from Europe and America, where politicians were accustomed to being
treated with respect. Many Americans, who privately may have thought
Roskill's handling of the kidnap rather swaggering, nonetheless could
not stomach foreign condemnation, especially from such an anachron-
istic source as the Vatican.

In one city above all others there was unanimous opposition to what
Thomas had done: Rome itself. The Italian government, never a friend
of Thomas's, knew it didn't matter that the Pope was himself American:
in America the Pope *was* Italy, and sooner or later, American public
opinion would turn against Italy for what the Holy Father had done.
And yet he was a Pope who spent almost as much time on his travels
as he did in their city, and whose foreign policy was much better known
than the government's. It was too much.

The Italian parliament debated Thomas's action in an emergency
motion, and deplored it officially in a vote in which the only opposition
came, ironically, from the Communists. That in turn made headlines
in America, that only the communists in Italy appeared to support the
Pope.

Massoni weighed in, of course. His column, syndicated around the
world, was headlined: 'Excommunicate me!' He wrote that, not for the
first time, he agreed with the actions of the US President and not
with those of the Pope. Admittedly on this occasion the President's
judgement had ended in tragedy: that was very sad but it was not a
sin. Massoni then went on to ask Thomas where His Holiness thought
sin started. The Bible, he reminded Thomas, said that one could sin in
one's heart. He concluded: 'Since I agree with what the US President,
James Roskill, has done, then in a sense, if he has sinned, I too have
sinned. Indeed, I have committed the same sin. Will His Holiness

therefore now excommunicate me and the thousands and thousands who agree with me? Has he the strength, the will, the support, the authority? And if he won't excommunicate me, why then did he excommunicate the President?'

Thomas ignored him.

The news from the White House, when it came, was a surprise. There was no speech. In fact, there was no formal announcement of any kind. There was no need: Roskill knew how to make an impact. Instead, on the Friday of that week, journalists who were following Roskill on the campaign trail were given his last itinerary before the election on the following Tuesday. Distracting them completely from the question of the kidnapper's telephone call, this showed an item for the Sunday which read: six-thirty a.m.: Celebration of Holy Mass, Washington, Georgetown Cathedral.

This was sensational. As an excommunicated Catholic, Roskill was not eligible to receive the sacraments, and therefore was planning deliberately to defy the power of the Pope. More, having checked with their religious affairs correspondents, reporters were able to write that any priest administering the sacraments to an excommunicated person automatically excommunicated himself. So who would administer the sacraments at the cathedral? The White House would not help, and the mystery deepened when it was found that Georgetown Cathedral was in fact locked and the archbishop had left hurriedly for an undisclosed destination. Nor could the apostolic delegate help. He was as much in the dark as anyone.

The world was therefore held in suspense for more than twenty-four hours. No one really minded; they enjoyed licking their lips.

Even more so as Saturday wore on. For that morning in America was published the latest Gallup poll on Americans' voting intentions. It too was sensational. It showed – for Roskill: forty-point-five per cent; for Fairbrother: thirty-eight-point-five per cent.

The important thing was that the poll had been taken *after* Thomas's excommunication of Roskill and, when compared with previous polls, showed that the gap between the candidates had narrowed. The election was wide open. According to the pollsters, the excommunication had only reinforced Republicans in their support for Roskill. Right wing Democrats, on the other hand, had swung in sizeable numbers away from him.

The White House refused to comment on the Gallup figures. 'The only poll that matters is the real one on Tuesday' said a spokesman.

Back in Washington, the television cameras arrived at the Cathedral that Saturday night, in readiness for the morning. To the technician's surprise, they found the cathedral *still* locked. Consultation with the White House produced the information that the Catholic archbishop of Washington, anxious not to take sides in the dispute, had closed the cathedral and had disappeared, with instructions to his staff to disperse also. However, said the White House, the President still intended to celebrate mass there, whether the cathedral was open or closed. Either inside the church, or outside it. And so, during the night a weird, spindly monster began to grow in front of the cathedral as first scaffolding, and then cameras and lights were erected, like the precipitate in some magical concoction.

It was during the early hours, also, that someone in the press learned the identity of the priest who was to administer the mass. 'Just got a call from the bureau in Rome,' a sound man told anyone who would listen. 'It's six hours ahead there so they're up already. It seems there's some rebel Italian who's flown over here secretly. They got his name from the Alitalia passenger name list. I've never heard of him. Name like Mossoni, or Massoni maybe.'

Thomas didn't see the worldwide television transmission of Roskill's arrival at the cathedral. At eleven o'clock that Sunday morning – five o'clock in Washington – the Holy Father and his entourage left Leonardo da Vinci airport aboard Alitalia's papal 747, bound for Hong Kong, Taiwan and the Philippine Islands. Thomas had news of the 'mass' patched through to him via the jumbo's radio but he missed the extraordinary scenes outside Georgetown Cathedral.

He and Bess had learned about Massoni's part in the Roskill service only hours before the newsmen outside Georgetown Cathedral. Deep in their last minute arrangements for the Far East trip, Thomas, Bess and O'Rourke had considered whether any action was needed to counter Massoni's participation but had decided against it. He could stew in his own juice.

What Thomas and his entourage missed was the sight of a pitch-black freezing cold Washington morning, that gave the curious event a certain intimacy. During the early hours the camera crews and reporters had been joined by several thousand onlookers, Catholics and non-Catholics alike. The cathedral was still locked. They waited, intrigued by what would happen when Roskill arrived. Police kept the roadway outside the cathedral clear and the steps leading up to the main door.

Massoni was the first to arrive. His tall, cadaverous form emerged from a black limousine just before six-thirty. He had with him another priest whom few in the crowd recognized but who was identified easily enough by the Italian commentating for R A I, the Italian state network. It was Fr Diego Giunta, keeper of the Secret Archive in the Vatican. The two men gathered their long black coats and mounted the steps. As the cameras trained on him, Massoni tried the door to the cathedral. It remained obdurately locked. He signalled to Giunta. The priest immediately turned and went to the boot of the limousine. The two men had come prepared: Giunta took from the car what the more

290

knowledgeable onlookers soon recognized as a portable altar, the kind used in missionary work or indeed by the Pope himself on his many travels.

A breathless reporter for CBS news described the scene: 'The two priests are now erecting the altar on the top step of the cathedral. It's about waist-high, about four feet long and two deep, with what looks like a red baize undercloth, and a white, lace-edged top cloth which they are draping over it now. I can see a simple brass – or perhaps it's a gold – cross, which they are placing in the middle . . . and I do believe they've brought some fresh flowers, irises by the look of it. Now, despite the cold – it's three below here in the nation's capital – the two priests have taken off their coats. Underneath they wear white surplices, again lace-fringed, and gold-threaded stoles. . . . I guess religious services have been held in some pretty odd places – mountain tops in Vietnam, submarines, space shuttles and so on – but the steps of Georgetown Cathedral, in the freezing cold, must surely be one of the most bizarre ever.

'But now, I see headlights in the distance. Is this the President and First Lady arriving?'

It was. The presidential limousine, preceded by a police car, slid into the light provided by the TV stations. The President's bodyguard was first to emerge, then Roskill himself. He was dressed in a dark blue overcoat and wrapped in a large red scarf against the cold. His breath floated in front of him, white in the night, black when seen against the TV lights. His wife, Martha, in ample furs, followed him. Together they mounted a few steps and then stopped a few paces down from the altar, so that the crowd, and the TV cameras, could see Massoni and Giunta as well as the presidential couple.

Out of the night the familiar figure of Cranham Hope, the President's political aide, appeared at Massoni's side. He was holding a microphone. 'One, two . . . one, two . . .' He knew perfectly well it was working, but the affair mustn't look too stage-managed. 'Ladies and gentlemen, may I have your attention please. The President has asked me to say that he will make a statement after the service but could you please not interrupt or make any noise until then, so that he and his wife may celebrate mass in peace. Thank you.' And he faded back into the dark.

For the benefit of non-Catholics most of the networks had on hand someone to explain the service for them and to stress the significance of the religious event that was now taking place. Roskill who, like Bess before him, realized how much the American psyche equated early mornings with virtue, had also ensured that the mass was a long one. The sight of him and his wife standing throughout it was bound to be impressive. Massoni spoke quietly and in Latin, so there was a lot of in-filling to do on the part of the commentators before the presidential couple were called forward to kneel before the altar. As they did so several reporters noted that the heel of Roskill's right shoe was worn away at one point. Every great man should have his weaknesses.

At length, but not before the TV commentators had made much of the presidential couple's forebearance in the freezing cold, the service ended. Roskill and his wife shook hands with Massoni and Giunta and turned to face the crowd. The microphones and the cameras closed in. 'It's cold and Martha, the cardinal here and Father Giunta are all badly in need of some black coffee back at the White House – so I'll keep this as short as I can. As you know, His Holiness Pope Thomas a few days ago administered what Catholics have to consider the worst punishment that can befall a human being: excommunication, exclusion from the Church, the right to worship and the right to receive the symbols of man's awesome relationship with God. And yet, just now as you saw, on the steps of this cathedral that had been barred to me, I received the sacraments from Cardinal Ottavio Massoni, a former secretary of state at the Vatican, and himself a candidate for Pope in the last conclave. Some explanation is needed as to how these two apparently irreconcilable events could occur.

'I have, in the past hours and days, taken expert advice on this matter. And my research has produced a surprising conclusion. It is that a number of leading churchmen – at the moment obviously I cannot say who – a number of leading churchmen seriously question the authority of Pope Thomas. Discoveries are being hinted at in Rome that cast doubts on his authority. Rather than plunge the Holy Mother Church into a damaging controversy, these leading churchmen tell me that they intend to press for His Holiness's resignation as soon as he returns from his visit to the Far East. My advisors further tell me that, as there seems to be an undeniable element of personal spite in my excommunication, the divine spirit has clearly abandoned Pope Thomas and his resignation ought now to be a matter of course. He should recognize this himself – and go.

'In these highly unusual circumstances, I understand I am free to regard myself as *not* excommunicated and therefore eligible for the sacraments.

'That is the end of my statement so far as this morning's mass is concerned. I am now going to have breakfast with my family and with Cardinal Massoni and Father Giunta. But before I go I would like to add one thing. If Americans do not like me, or the country we have under my leadership, they are free – entirely free – to fire me from the job this very Tuesday. That would be excommunication by a fair process and I do not shirk it.' Roskill smiled his avuncular, craggy grin. 'You know, the irony is: under my administration we have increased the percentage of children in religious schools by between two and three points. And yet I get excommunicated.' He shook his head. 'Crazy!

'But I'm American and I'm fighting back. I call upon Thomas to follow the path of his distinguished predecessor, Boniface – and resign!'

Questions rained in from all sides as Roskill shepherded Martha back into the limousine. But the reporters knew it was hopeless. Roskill's exits were as good as his entries.

Roskill's jibe about excommunication and the voters was clever and did not go unnoticed. As the CBS correspondent pointed out, he had tied Thomas's fortunes to his own. The election was now not only a verdict on Roskill. In a sense it was a verdict on Thomas, too.

David watched in dismay. He was staying at the George in Hamble. He had been invited to a craft show at the school that Sunday afternoon and, not wanting to miss the broadcast, had overnighted at the hotel to save driving down in the morning, when the Washington mass was being televised.

The school craft show was going to be a bit of a squeeze. He was leaving for Rome that evening. The all-important board meeting was now barely ten days away and if he could tie up the Leonardo attribution it would be a major coup and ought to be more than enough to keep Sam Averne at bay. The Montafornos had been most accommodating, and had agreed immediately to let him use their archive. Bess wasn't in Rome, of course, she was already in the air, bound for the Far East. But he would be using her apartment. He wondered how Thomas and Bess were. They would have missed Roskill's mass and would hear about it only second hand. He would have liked to be the one who briefed them. They could have answered his questions, too. Like what Roskill had meant about Thomas's authority being doubted.

He switched off the television and put on his jacket. It was nearly one o'clock, just time for the George's traditional roast beef lunch before he went to the school. Ned had turned down the offer of a hotel meal, saying he hadn't quite finished one of the works he was putting on display and needed every available minute. But he had pressed David to be there in time for the opening, at two-fifteen, which was being performed by the headmaster's wife.

In fact, David was there with minutes to spare. The exhibition was being held in a large hall but parents were directed first to a smaller room where chairs were set out in rows. When he saw his father Ned dashed over: 'Thanks for coming, Dad, and being on time. I'm still finishing something. See you later – okay?'

Ned was gone as quickly as he arrived.

Schools are not auction houses. Although the show was scheduled to start at two-fifteen, the headmaster's wife didn't appear until gone two-thirty. No one else seemed to mind but David was already itchy. He had to be at Heathrow by six, which meant leaving the school at four-thirty to be safe. Eventually, however, Susan McAllister, the headmaster's wife, climbed on to the platform and beamed down at the parents. She had a voice bigger than her body. 'Ladies and gentlemen, it's my pleasant job to open the proceedings today and traditionally that is done by awarding the prize for the winning entry in this, the school's craft fair. And the fact is that in this year's competition one entry stands out above everything else. It is, in our view, of professional standard already. And when I explain its background to you, I hope that you will see how imaginative the idea behind the project is.' She paused. 'Ned Colwyn?'

David was flabbergasted to hear his son called forward. He had won the craft prize? With something that was already of professional standard? Fantastic!

Ned was on stage now. 'Hold them both up,' said the head's wife. Ned held aloft two silver spoons.

'Now,' said Mrs McAllister, 'this is where, I hope, the fun starts. One of these spoons is original. It is what is known as a Puritan spoon, dating from the seventeenth century and it was loaned to us from the local museum. The other, which I may say I find indistinguishable from the original, was made by Ned Colwyn here in our workshops. You may well ask what the school is doing breeding forgers but of course the copying of masterpieces is one of the historic methods of teaching students. And in this case there is an added bonus. Sitting in the audience today is Ned's father, David Colwyn, the experienced auctioneer some of you may have seen on television recently. I understand that, for many years, Ned and his father have shared an interest in forgeries and his father, Ned says, has taught him a lot. The question now to be asked is: has the son outstripped the father? This is what we thought was imaginative about Ned's approach. He's throwing down this challenge to Mr Colwyn, to see whether, in front of everybody here today, he can tell his son's work from something that is more than three hundred years old.'

Heads turned towards David. Well, he thought, this is something I've really landed myself in. He smiled, stood up and, amid scattered applause, walked to the platform. He smiled at Ned and took the spoons from him. Puritan spoons are fairly plain, with notched ends. He turned them over in his hands while all eyes remained fixed on him.

He had to admit it, the workmanship was excellent. His admiration for Ned soared. He held one in one hand, one in the other. That told him which was the real spoon. Ned had overlooked the fact that real Puritan spoons were exceptionally heavy. The spoon in David's right hand was distinctly lighter than that in his left. He took a quick decision, handed the spoons back to Ned, but addressed himself to Susan McAllister. 'I am ashamed to say that I seem to have bred a master forger. I'm afraid I haven't a clue. They both look identical to me.'

Applause and laughter followed his words as he shook Ned's hand. Above the clatter, the headmaster's wife said: 'And that, I think, opens the craft exhibition. Don't anyone tell the police about Ned. He can start making money next!'

It was a good-humoured start to the day. David was taken round by Mrs McAllister. 'Sorry to do that to you,' she said. 'But thanks for being a good sport.'

'Thank you for giving Ned the prize. You know, I wasn't sure he should be a goldsmith when he first mentioned it. I always wanted him to go to university. Giving him the prize today will boost his confidence. And mine.'

She smiled. 'I'm so glad. In fact though, as I said, he won easily. Now, I must go and say hello to some other people. Excuse me.'

David strolled round the hall. Mrs McAllister was indeed right, and it wasn't just a proud father's view: Ned was in a class by himself, so far as Hamble school was concerned anyway. He said as much when he caught up with Ned at his stand.

'Did you really not know which spoon was which?'

'No,' David lied. 'D'you think I lied?'

'It's just that you once told me how heavy Puritan spoons are. I couldn't get the density right in the school workshop. I was afraid you'd be able to tell easily.'

'Hmm,' said David noncommittally. 'The workmanship was excellent. You're very good. We'll have to start thinking where to send you soon.' He lightened his tone. 'I only hope I can afford it.'

'Well, you're better off as from this week.'

'Huh? What's that supposed to mean?'

'I saw Dr Wilde last week. He told me to tell you that you can stop sending him those cheques. He doesn't want to see me any more. He thinks I'm all right.'

Next day, Monday, the day before the American presidential election, Thomas spent in Hong Kong. He attended a service there, but the main purpose of his visit to the British colony was to hold a day-long meeting with the bishops of South East Asia to discuss their worries, particularly the fate of the Church in mainland China. This meant he was able to avoid the press for most of the day. However, at the airport that evening, just before the papal entourage left for Taiwan, Bess felt she had to make some kind of reply, on Thomas's behalf, to the calls Roskill had made for the Holy Father's resignation.

The conference room, normally the VIP lounge, was crowded. This was the kind of story that could be hurried along by media intervention and the journalists were as ever eager to make mischief under the guise of reporting events. Bess addressed the press corps with a prepared statement. 'We are now leaving for Taiwan, after a successful meeting, here in Hong Kong, of the South East Asian bishops, where many things of importance to the future of the Church were settled. A new approach is to be made to the Chinese government in Beijing and the Thai government is to allow Catholic missionaries to work in the country to help with the reception of refugees from Khmer Kampuchea. The government of the Marquesas Isles, in the Pacific, have invited the Holy Father to visit them, to inspect reconstruction work after the terrible tidal wave which, some time ago, devastated much of their territory. He has agreed, but a date is yet to be settled. The government of South Korea has accepted an offer from the Holy Father to set up a Catholic University in the country, at the Vatican's expense under the St Patrick's Fund. The institution will be run by the Jesuit order and will eventually accommodate three thousand students.

'From all this, ladies and gentlemen, you will see that the Holy Father, far from considering resigning, as has been suggested in some quarters, is as busy as ever trying to use the Holy Spirit for the betterment of the human condition, wherever it is needed. The Catholic Church is an international entity. The Holy Father feels that, in order to preserve that unique quality, he can never allow himself to be aligned too closely with one block of countries, one set of narrow interests. That is why he was in Rome yesterday, Hong Kong today and he will be visiting in the coming months many Pacific Islands, Israel, South America, Canada.

'President Roskill has his political aims, and he has only two terms of office at most to fulfill them. Besides being a uniquely international office, the position of pontiff is also unusual in that it allows a man, guided by the Holy Spirit, to devote his lifetime's effort in the directions where that effort is most needed. Despite setbacks, the many successes of the Holy Father's policies show that the directions he has identified are indeed deserving of his, and our, attention. But that work is far from finished. We are leaving now to continue it. Thank you.'

Bess, O'Rourke and Thomas had laboured long hours over that statement. O'Rourke had been in favour of the blandest mishmash, but Thomas and Bess had wanted something much tougher. In the end they had listened to O'Rourke and toned down earlier versions, avoiding comments on the 'discoveries' in Rome that Roskill had referred to. They would be attended to, whatever they were, on the Pope's return. But still they had kept in Thomas's firm intention to continue in office, and to continue working in the same way.

And so, on the morning of the American vote, the *New York Daily News* was able to lead with: 'Pope to Prez: I'll not resign'. And, in smaller type: 'I'm in this job for life.' The *Boston Globe* said: 'Pope works on, despite calls for his resignation.' And, further down: 'Looks forward to a lifetime of effort, helping the poor.' The *Straits Times* in Singapore had a somewhat different perspective. Its headline ran: 'Vatican cash for South East Asia' with the subheading: 'New help for Kampuchea refugees, a college for Korea.' But the election was not taking place in the Far East.

In America the voters in the north and east faced steady rain. In the south and west it was its usual sunny, self-satisfied self. Roskill and Fairbrother voted early, accompanied by their wives and their respective press packs. Both were asked on camera what they thought of the Pope's statement of the day before.

Fairbrother said: 'I wish the Pope well. He is giving Catholics a sense of dignity. But right now I am more concerned that the voters of America will excommunicate James Roskill.'

Roskill said: 'I have only one thing to add to what I said outside that locked cathedral on Sunday morning. It is this: If I am elected again today, as I expect to be, I shall not need a lifetime to accomplish what I think is wrong with this country. Another four years will be enough.'

And, as ever, the unexpected played its part. Shortly after Roskill returned to the White House, after voting, news came through that a US helicopter had crashed in Honduras. There was no suggestion that the 'copter had been fired at, but the crash had taken place very early that morning, in the dark, in what the Pentagon called 'difficult terrain'. All the three-men crew were killed. Nothing overt was said in reference to Thomas's projects. But at the back of everyone's minds was the thought that the Nicaraguans were now more active thanks to the pontiff's policies in the area, which had backfired. Roskill made a fuss of sending the men's families his goodwill. He telephoned wives or mothers and called the men 'heroes'. Later on, but well before the polling booths closed, tapes of the phone calls were released to TV and radio stations.

The *New York Times* Business Section also revealed that day the sensational news that Red Wilkie had decided to sell the 'Pietà' by Michelangelo, which he had bought at the great Vatican sale. Wilkie was quoted as saying that, as an American, as the chief executive of an American company, he could not be seen to tolerate an attack on a US president of the kind made by Pope Thomas. A board meeting had been called and the decision taken that, with the company holding a valuable piece of art so strongly identified with the Vatican, the board believed it now had no choice but to divest itself of the sculpture, and would also be changing its company logo. With no apparent sense of irony Wilkie said he intended to sell the 'Pietà' through Steele's. His encounter with David and Bess in Sicily had clearly riled him.

One place where the election was watched especially keenly was in Rome, where Roskill's call for Thomas's resignation had been greeted with undisguised joy in many quarters. The President had refused to name 'leading churchmen' who questioned Thomas's authority and there was no shortage of speculation in the Rome press as to who they

297

might be. In general two groups were favoured: the northern Italian cardinals, from wealthy commercial cities which had the same political interests as Roskill, and the traditional Roman families who had provided cardinals and Popes for generations: they had been against Thomas since the great sale of treasures. No one seemed to know what the 'discoveries' that the President had referred to were.

For David, working alone in Rome, America's election day was one of mixed fortunes. In the morning he continued to make his way through the Giacomo Salai file in the Palazzo Montaforno. The previous day had been one of orientation, finding the way the file was organized. Now he looked through the documents themselves. About eleven o'clock he came to a slip of yellowed paper with a red chalk drawing on it. It showed a young man with a head of tight curls. Someone had pinned to it a typed note. Translated from the Italian, it read: 'Giacomo Salai: self-portrait.' Except that it wasn't. David was immediately convinced of that. Clearly the family which had had this drawing in their possession had been told time and again, probably by second-rate scholars, that this was a drawing by a third-rate artist. But the hair was too detailed, the profile too well-drawn, the shading showed too much attention to detail for it to be by Salai. Moreover, David knew another drawing similar to it: 'Neptune' in the Royal Library in Windsor. He knew it because it had been one of Leonardo's drawings on Seton's list for the Queen to sell. The image of Seton, with the new director of the Hermitage, Dorzhiev, flashed into his mind. Wasn't he an expert on Leonardo's style? David would now have to get some other authority to authenticate this new drawing, someone in the west. When should he tell the Montafornos? As soon as possible, he judged. If they wanted to sell, then obviously they would certainly welcome having it authenticated. If *both* things checked out – if they did want to sell and it really was a Leonardo – then his position at Hamilton's was safe. The drawing mightn't be worth the millions that Averne's American collections were, but its discovery showed that David still had the magic touch. A Leonardo drawing was worth ten million at least. The waverers on the board would stick with him. He *must* prevail on the Montafornos to sell and he *must* get the drawing authenticated as soon as possible. As he left the palazzo that day, he inquired when Prince Alberto Montaforno would be home. He was the head of the family. David was told the prince would be back the next day: he was in Milan on business. A meeting was arranged for six.

David headed for Gina's in good spirits. If the prince would sell, then perhaps Michael Stone at the National Gallery in Washington would fly over at the end of the week. Hamilton's would pay and he was the highest ranking Leonardo scholar in the west. His good spirits didn't last. That evening's paper in Rome carried the news of Wilkie's proposed sale of the 'Pietà', through Steele's. David felt sick. Now his job really *was* on the line. Even if the Montafornos chose to sell, and even if the picture *was* a Leonardo, it might not be enough. Even if he had really solved the Paris/London battle over the 'Virgin of the Rocks' attribution, it still might not be enough. Although it brought Hamilton's prestige to have an imaginative scholar on its board, that was an academic matter which didn't show directly on the balance sheet.

He spoke to Bess later and that helped. But she was depressed, too. 'No one is interested any more in what Thomas is *doing*. All they want is his reaction to Roskill's latest outburst. It's sickening.'

'But what about Massoni? Thomas has to do something about him now, surely?'

'You bet. He's finally seen the light. He's going to strip him of his cardinalate. It hasn't been done for years – we're checking just when. It's a lengthy process but we are going to announce it as soon as we get back. We have certain information about him that will force him out.'

'Whose idea was it, for Massoni to say mass, I mean?'

'Roskill's, after someone on the White House staff had shown him a translation of Massoni's article entitled "Excommunicate me!" '

'Hmm. Everything will be so much easier for Thomas if Roskill loses the election.'

'You're not kidding. Look, darling, I have to go. I'll talk to you as soon as I can. Pray for us. You know, I think for the first time ever I shall pray for something bad to happen to someone, that Roskill loses.'

'Don't do that.'

'What do you mean?'

'Pray instead that Fairbrother wins.'

The election was a cliffhanger, at least to begin with. Since exit polls had been outlawed, for the effect they had on other parts of the United States which were behind in time and had yet to vote, the first results didn't come in until around ten p.m. eastern time, already three o'clock in the morning in London and four in the rest of Europe.

David spent the early part of the evening in the flat hanging some new silks Bess had bought. There was a Florentine damask patterned in gold pomegranates, and a Lyon silk zig-zagged in silver and framed in red lacquer. Looking around the apartment, he saw now that there were photographs of himself here and there, though nothing yet of the two of them together. And there was a drawing of a saddle Bess had told him about. It was an invention of her father's: it was safer, he claimed, than anything else on the market. But that wasn't the main point. Bess and her parents had grown closer in recent months and that gladdened him: she was settling, more content. She needed action less, he thought, reminding himself of their conversation in Sicily. Bess had always been brave; with her background, her personality, her job, her particular form of solitariness, it had been necessary. Now it was less so.

Later, he watched developments on television at Gina's. She gave him a table where he could see the screen. It was the first time he had joined the TV watchers at the back of the bar, but it was more fun than being alone in Bess's apartment.

The first states to be declared put Fairbrother ahead. He took two of the industrial east coast Democratic states, while Roskill took a more rural southern state. Analysis of the vote put Roskill at forty-six point five and Fairbrother at forty-four per cent. As usual the 'don't knows' would make up their minds at the last minute but the gap between the two candidates stood at only two point five per cent.

By eleven in Washington, five a.m. in Rome, Roskill was leading by twelve states to Fairbrother's five but the results were still going mainly according to tradition. David was still there in Gina's having the first of what would be several breakfasts. The result mattered to Thomas, to Bess and therefore to him. Gina was there. She had been to bed but was up already. There were four others in the bar. Around five-thirty everyone was waiting for the Idaho result. The polls all showed that, this time round, Idaho was a crucial state. Heavily agricultural, it had always been safe for the Republicans. But Roskill's economic policies, which had hurt Idaho farmers, had changed the alignment of the state in unpredictable ways. Pre-election polls had shown Fairbrother's support as less than a percentage point behind Roskill: Fairbrother *could* do it, right in the Republican heartlands.

The screen was showing an interview scene in Georgia. A local senator was discussing what had happened in that state, traditionally Democratic. Suddenly, at the foot of the screen, a line flashed up, and kept flashing: 'Roskill holds Idaho.' 'Roskill holds Idaho.'

And that seemed to start the rot. By one a.m. in Washington Roskill's lead had increased to seventeen to six. Half an hour later it was twenty-five to six and Fairbrother seemed stuck. At two twenty-nine, eight twenty-nine in Rome, Fairbrother conceded defeat. The final tally, not in until much later that day, was: Roskill: forty-one states; Fairbrother: ten. And in votes: Roskill fifty-nine point six percent, Fairbrother: thirty-nine point one percent. It wasn't a landslide exactly but it was more than convincing, especially as the polls had got it wrong.

Shortly afterwards the markets opened in London and they, like Wall Street later on, surged ahead as business breathed easily again. Roskill was to address the American nation later that evening on TV, in a special post-election broadcast. By then, however, his actions had already answered one of the questions everyone was dying to ask: would his feud with the Holy Father continue? As soon as he was shaved and dressed, after three hours sleep only, the first thing he and Martha did was to drive to Georgetown Cathedral and attend mass. This time it was open and the Bishop of Washington led the proceedings. Something had changed.

David took a break from Gina's after his meeting with Prince Alberto Montaforno. He felt like celebrating so he went back that night to the small restaurant just off the Piazza del Risorgimento, where they deep fried the anchovies, the place where he'd spotted Massoni. He had reason to celebrate, despite Roskill's depressing victory in the election. The prince *would* sell but only if the drawing really was a Leonardo. So David had tried a call to Michael Stone in Washington where, to his delight, he was told that Stone was already in Europe, in Milan, working in the Brera Museum and staying at the Hotel Principe e Savoia. He was in the shower when David phoned but called back soon after. Astounded at David's news, he said he could be in Rome on Friday night.

So, before the weekend was out, with two days to spare before the board meeting, David would know whether or not he had something to fight Sam Averne with.

# 15

The 747 seemed to race on for ever without rising, its huge wings swooping endlessly between the fringes of palm trees that lined the runway. Then, at the last minute, the floor of the aircraft sloped up and the shoreline of the Philippines became visible below.

Underneath the flightdeck, in what would normally be the first-class compartment, Thomas had his office. Above, behind the captain and flight crew, the aircraft was converted so that the Holy Father could sleep comfortably in a large bed. The rest of the contingent, and the press, were in the back. As the seat belt warning sign was switched off, a stewardess brought Thomas some *Pellegrino* water. Bess strolled forward, leaning to counteract the upward slope of the aircraft. She flopped into a seat besides him.

'Tired?'

He nodded. 'Flat out, very nearly. Perhaps for once I'll be able to sleep on one of these things.' He smiled. 'You must be exhausted, too. I suppose when you are married you won't be able to work these long hours?'

She shot him a furious glance. 'I haven't let you down yet, have I?'

He laughed. 'What would I do without you, Elizabeth? You're the only one who ever talks back at me. It's as if *we* are married.' They both laughed.

'Here, have some water.' He offered her his glass.

She swallowed what was left in one gulp. 'So, what's your verdict on the tour?'

Thomas stiffened. 'You know as well as I do. It started well, but got progressively worse. The conference in Hong Kong was a great step forward. The college in Korea will attract many students and the refugee work in Thailand, though not very newsworthy these days, is still important. The Taiwan bishops are faithful, but I fear that, in consequence maybe, we will have a problem opening up China.'

'And the Philippines?'

Thomas bit his lower lip. The visit had been an outward success but they both knew there was far more to it than met the TV camera's eye.

'And to think Roskill persuaded me to help Sebbio back to power! Dear Lord.'

A huge banquet had been hosted for Thomas in Manila by President Sebbio himself. Since Thomas had instructed the bishops to support him, Sebbio was, in effect, God's choice for many voters, so he could not but greet the Holy Father sumptuously. But as a politician Sebbio knew that the power of the Church could be as easily turned against him and he was consequently about to begin a discreet anti-Church programme throughout the islands under his control. Religious education in schools was to be downgraded, the Jesuit university was to be closed, the Catholic bank was to be nationalized, the number of bishops was to be limited, their privileges reduced. None of it was official yet but the local archbishop had already been warned.

Bess signalled to the stewardess for more water. 'Now that Roskill's back for a second term, we can expect the flak to fly even faster. How do you want to play it?'

Thomas grimaced and lit a cigarette. 'I must say I hadn't counted on all this when I was elected. But I can't shirk it. I've got to sort out this Massoni business.' Thomas shifted in his seat and took the water which the stewardess brought. 'But we must hold on, Elizabeth, to what we have been doing. The world doesn't revolve around Washington, or Rome, come to that. We shouldn't always be worried by our critics. We should remember instead that at least half the world is on our side. I'm sorry our enemies have to include Roskill – but there it is.'

He gave her the water. 'My dear, I think I *will* try to get some sleep now. Why don't you do the same? It's a long flight; there'll be plenty of time to eat and talk later. We'll think better after some sleep.'

They both got to their feet. Bess went back to the main cabin and Thomas retired upstairs. He didn't undress but simply lay on the bed. Nonetheless he was quickly asleep, a deep but troubled slumber.

The aircraft was not a regular flight. Because of the security risk at airports, the 747 was carrying extra fuel tanks, and so didn't have to land between the Philippine Islands and Rome. It did, however, have to change crew, since it was in the air more than the maximum limit allowed. Shortly after the second crew had taken over, five hundred miles east of Sri Lanka, Thomas was woken. As he emerged from his sleep he was puzzled. It was not O'Rourke waking him, nor his valet.

'I'm the first officer, Holiness. The captain would like a word. On the flight deck.'

This was unusual, surely. Thomas rubbed his eyes. He wasn't a man to stand on his dignity, but he was used to people coming to him.

'Won't it wait, my son? Does it have to be now?'

'Yes, Holy Father. It is urgent, I think.'

'Urgent? Hmm. If it is urgent then maybe you should fetch – '

'Excuse me, Holy Father. The captain requests you come alone. It is a delicate matter.'

'The aircraft . . . it is . . . safe?'

'Oh yes. Perfectly safe. It's not that. Please come.'

'Very well. Let me use the washroom please.'

The first officer hadn't moved when he came out, and led him forward on to the flight deck. Thomas's limp was very pronounced. The captain, seated on the left, waved Thomas to the other seat. 'Holiness, please.'

The first officer backed away, closing the door behind him. Thomas looked around. Outside the clouds below were getting dark in a rush of browns, yellows and reds. He noticed that the engineer was also absent.

He glanced at the dials and levers, the pulsing lights. Awkwardly, because of his leg, he manoeuvred himself into the co-pilot's seat. 'Well, what *is* all this? Why do you need to see me so urgently? And why the secrecy? Is somebody ill?'

'Much more serious than that, Holiness.'

'Well, stop prevaricating. What's the matter? What is wrong?'

'Rome has refused landing permission.'

'What! Why? What for?'

'They don't have to give reasons, Holiness. But they do say there will be a personal message for you very shortly. That's why my first officer was so insistent on having you come to the flight deck. Whatever it is should be coming through any minute.'

Thomas stared at the remains of the sun. A golden sliver of cloud pointed like a dagger straight ahead. Towards Rome.

Rome. Refused permission to land! This was Massoni's doing, he knew it. And the airport closure meant he had the support of the Italian government.

'You can speak to the main cabin below from here, right?' Thomas asked the captain.

The captain nodded.

'Then could you ask for Elizabeth Lisle and Patrick O'Rourke to come here, please.'

The captain passed on the request. The Holy Father sat immobile, oblivious as the last shards of daylight left the sky. He lit a cigarette. There was a knock and Bess and O'Rourke entered. They were surprised to see the white figure of Thomas in the co-pilot's seat. 'Close the door behind you,' said Thomas and, when Bess had seated herself in the engineer's place, he told them of the latest development.

For a moment they said nothing, thinking. When Bess did speak it was not to the Holy Father but to the captain. 'We have to get to Rome. Can't we chance it? Just ignore their ban and put the plane down?'

The captain shook his head. 'No pilot disobeys the orders of air traffic control. If one ever did, no flight would be safe again. But that's not the point. If we approach within twenty-five miles of the airport they will be within their rights to block the runways with aircraft.'

'What about other airports? This is an Italian aircraft! They can't stop us from entering Italy.'

'No. They'll let us in. But they want to stop us from going into Rome, or anywhere near it. I'm sure they'll clarify that when they call back.'

Bess looked at her watch. 'What time is it in Rome?'

'Six here is nine o'clock in the morning in Rome – ah, here comes the call.' The captain motioned for Thomas and Bess to put on the headsets attached to their seats. There was no set for O'Rourke.

'Hallo! Hallo!' said a voice. 'Rome calling AZV 001. Are you receiving?'

'AZV 001,' said the captain. 'We hear you, we hear you.'

'Just a moment, AZV 001. Stand by, please.'

The line went dead. The captain raised his hand to signal they should remain quiet. Thomas drew on his cigarette. Then another voice spoke.

'Thomas? Thomas? Can you hear me? Thomas?'

'Ottavio!' Thomas barked the name as he recognized Massoni's voice. 'Where are you? What's happening? What is this nonsense about the aircraft being refused landing permission?'

'I'm in the Vatican, Thomas. In the offices of the Vatican radio. On the hill. It is of course the government who have refused you permission to land.'

'Then why are you calling me?'

And why are you calling the Holy Father by his Christian name? thought Bess.

'To let you know, Thomas, that later today the sacred college will meet.'

'What? Who called it? It can't. I'm thousands of miles away.'

'Yes.' Massoni let the silent implication hang between them. After an interval, he added: 'A letter has been found.'

'What do you mean? Talk sense, Eminence. What sort of letter?'

'Diego Giunta found a letter, researching his biography of Pius XIII. In it he appoints Cardinal Salvin as his successor.'

'Rubbish, Massoni. No one has used that method of choosing a Pope since the earliest times. And Salvin is dead.'

This was obviously the discovery Roskill had referred to.

'That doesn't change things. Your election was uncanonical.'

'It's disgraceful! The letter could be a forgery – who says it's genuine anyway? Your duty is to wait till I – '

'It's not a forgery, Thomas. It's genuine. And canon law is quite clear. A Pope may appoint his successor. The fact that no one has for hundreds of years does not rob the method of its validity. You yourself chose to revive an old custom regarding your name. No: your election was uncanonical.'

'I won't have it! You are flouting the law, Ottavio, and you know it. What you are trying to do is wrong.'

There was silence at the other end of the line. As Bess listened, shaking with alarm, she realized that, yes, Massoni knew full well that the whole exercise was dishonest, but he was going ahead anyway. It didn't much matter whether the letter was a forgery or not, and it probably wasn't. It was just convenient. Had it not been there, they would have found something else. Massoni was speaking again. 'Thomas, the sacred college, or those of it who can be assembled in time, meets later this morning – in about three hours from now. Either you will have resigned by then, in which case we shall proceed to the election of a new Pope. Or we shall decide on the validity of your election. If we decide that it was uncanonical – and I need hardly add that such is the view of nearly every cardinal I have spoken to in the last thirty-six hours – then we shall say so, and *then* proceed to elect a new Pope. That Pope will be in Rome and canonically elected. If you persist in calling yourself Pope after that, you will be in heresy and will be deemed, from Rome, as the anti-Pope. Not an enviable situation but, for many of us, preferable to what we have had to endure lately.'

'Does the Italian government realize it is breaking the law in barring me? Under the terms of the Lateran Pacts all Popes were to be allowed freedom of movement.'

'Yes, Thomas, but I am afraid the Italian government has two answers to that. In the first place, they consider you abrogated the Lateran Pacts with your sales of Vatican treasures. Second, since you are no longer Pope, the Lateran Pacts do not apply anyway. You must have realized, Thomas, that this move has the support of the Italian government – you are deeply unpopular with them – and of the Americans – you don't need me to tell you what Roskill thinks of your policies. They will recognize the new Pope immediately and, I think I can be sure in saying, many of the other western states will follow suit pretty quickly.'

'All sewn up, eh?'

'You can't keep travelling, Thomas. The heart of the Catholic church is in Rome. You pay the price, otherwise. As you see.'

'Ottavio? Are you proud of what you are doing? Do you think it is God's will?'

'Look what your sense of God's will has got us: a divided church.'

'No, Ottavio. We are a controversial church – but in the best sense, because we are working for change. Change is always unpleasant for some.'

'It is the poor who usually suffer when the world changes.'

'Reactionary propaganda, Ottavio. A businessman's credo. You only have to ask the poor whether they want change. If they didn't, it would never happen.'

'Are you going to resign, Thomas? Please.'

'And leave the field free for the forces of reaction, Ottavio? No. No. We are judged by our works. I am happy to be judged by mine, Ottavio. And you?'

Massoni ignored the challenge. 'I don't expect the conclave to take long, Thomas. I will call you back in a few hours. You had better get some sleep.' The line went dead.

For a while Thomas sat quietly in the co-pilot's seat, an incongruous sight in his white robes, skull cap, and earphones. His cigarette had gone out. Neither the captain nor Bess dared speak. Even O'Rourke had heard enough to know what was happening. At length the Holy Father took the headset off and rose to leave the flightdeck. 'Who do you think they will elect, Elizabeth?'

But it was a rhetorical question. They both knew the answer.

Even very busy people have many quiet, lonely moments, brought on as often as not by the enforced idleness associated with modern travel. But for Bess nothing compared with that long night over the Indian Ocean. For a couple of hours she went back to the main cabin: Thomas would want to be alone. She discussed their predicament with O'Rourke – he was distraught – and then she pretended to sleep – otherwise the rest of the contingent would have been able to tell from her face that something was wrong. After that she wandered forward again, ready to be with the Holy Father whenever he needed her. She tried to work at her papers but, knowing what she knew now, it was hard.

After about three hours Thomas appeared down the stairway. His face was grey. Together they ate a sandwich and drank a small glass of red wine. She had never seen him so drained. O'Rourke was in the back of the plane.

Thomas caught her looking at him. 'What is it, my dear?'

'Sometimes, Holiness, I wish you were an ordinary man, a regular boss. Then I could put my arms around you, and hug you.'

He smiled, sadly. 'And there are times, I can tell you, when I wish I was an ordinary man, too. One makes choices, of course. But at this particular moment, Elizabeth, I envy you the marriage ahead of you.'

She was reminded of something that had long been at the back of her mind. 'I've been meaning to ask you, Holiness, that petition, from David Colwyn, for the dissolution of his marriage – if there hadn't been the accident, if his wife hadn't died, would you . . . would you have granted the dissolution?'

For a moment a look of pain clouded Thomas's face but then he said, firmly, 'No.'

'Why not?'

'There was nothing in canon law to forbid it. But canon law, even Catholic canon law, is not written in stone. The case took advantage of a loophole and a rather absurd loophole at that. There are times when the technicalities of the law aren't enough – one has to consider the intention behind the law. And obviously the intention was never that. There was another reason, too – '

But just then the co-pilot appeared again and beckoned. Together Bess and Thomas mounted the stairs to the flight deck. Thomas clambered into the co-pilot's seat and put on the headphones. As before Bess listened in from the engineer's place.

'Hallo? Hallo? Thomas? Ottavio here.'

'Yes.'

'Have you changed your mind?'

'Tell me your news first.'

'The college has met. A Pope has been elected. The announcement is being kept confidential, since it is so unusual, until after this conversation. To allow you one more chance to resign. Will you, Thomas?'

'Tell me, Ottavio, who has been elected?'

A pause. 'I have, Thomas.'

Thomas said nothing.

'Only because I am old, Thomas. I won't last long, then they can try someone else.'

'*I* am Pope, Ottavio.'

Now there was silence at the other end. Then, 'Thomas, the announcement about the uncanonical election of yourself, and the news of my elevation, will be released later today. Since you will not stand down, you know what must happen. Henceforth you are to be regarded as Anti-Pope and, as such, the Italian government will in no way sanction your presence on the Italian mainland. They also point out that you are travelling in an Alitalia aircraft, the property of the Italian state and they wish to repossess it. If your captain is listening, as I assume he is, then I say to him that you will be granted permission to land in Palermo, which is the only Italian airport outside the mainland that will take 747s. You, Thomas, will be allowed to stay in Palermo for forty-eight hours, during which time you must make your own arrangements for your future. Your personal belongings will be sent on to you. Now Thomas, both I and the Italian government would like your assurance that you accept these arrangements.'

Thomas was slumped in his seat. Bess was crying. After a pause, Thomas, not remembering where he was, nodded.

'He accepts, sir,' said the pilot with unconscious irony. 'The Holy Father is nodding.'

'Very well. Will you now please change course for Palermo. A specially chartered aircraft will meet you there. I'm told you are about five hours flying time from Sicily. I will speak to you again before you land.

After the official announcements have been made.' Again the line went dead.

For a while longer Thomas stared in front, and into the night, while behind him the tears ran down Bess's cheeks and would not stop. The instrument lights were low on the flight deck, little specks, as if the stars were here inside. The glow, reflected on the undersides of their faces, gave everyone a surreal look, sallow and pale. From time to time the captain reached forward to turn a switch, or adjust a dial. But the aircraft kept steady, burrowing deeper and deeper into the night. Thomas sat very still and, now and then, Bess wondered whether he had fallen asleep. What was the other reason, she wondered, why he would not have allowed David's dissolution? She might never find out. Lights winked at the ends of the aircraft's wings, their reflection flashing off the instruments in front of her.

Minutes passed. An hour. A stewardess brought coffee. Thomas sipped his but still didn't speak. Bess lost count of the cigarettes he smoked. Sometimes there were lights below them but mostly it was just black. The engines, sensed through their vibration rather than heard, turned on and on. The massive aeroplane hurtled above the earth in a smooth, clean path, cutting a line across the sky like a razor on the skin before the blood flows.

Thomas stirred. He turned and, incredibly, through the cold tears that still stuck to the corners of her eyes, Bess could see he was smiling. It was a small smile, a sly grin as much as anything. He patted the instruments in front of him. 'He's slipped up, Elizabeth. Massoni's overlooked one thing. The good Lord hasn't abandoned us entirely.' He patted the 747's instruments a second time. 'He's delivered this monster into our hands. Massoni thinks he can have it all his own way. He's wrong.' Thomas made for the door out of the flightdeck. His movements were awkward; his leg was hurting again. 'Come on, Bess. Stop crying. There's work to do!'

David had intended to spend the rest of his time in Rome at the Central Institute for Restoration while he waited for Michael Stone. They were familiar there with Renaissance pigments and, he hoped, would agree to examine the Leonardo formula he had found in the Vatican Archive, to see whether it pointed towards the 'Virgin of the Rocks' in Paris or London. But the news from the Vatican overtook everything. For a long moment the entire western world held its breath.

Now lacking the will to visit the CIR, or the inclination to wait in Bess's apartment, he installed himself in Gina's, in front of the television like half the neighbourhood. Roskill, who had obviously been given some inkling of what was afoot, responded quickly to the news. Within hours the United States officially recognized the new Pope, just as Massoni had predicted. In Gina's, meanwhile, as elsewhere in Italy and around the world, they watched their televisions for news of Thomas's arrival in Sicily.

And it soon became apparent that, whether or not he had had any choice in the matter, it had been a grave mistake for Massoni to send Thomas to Palermo. Thomas, in that dark night, had eventually realized that the 747, by landing in Palermo, would deliver him into the hands of friends. Through the Vizzini fund, he had put Sicily high on his list of priorities. He had been phenomenally successful in dealing with the violence there. He was disliked by the Romans and by the Italian government. All that made him supremely popular on the island.

No sooner had Massoni made his announcement, to the fury of the average Sicilian, than they started to converge on the airport. No one knew why exactly, except that Thomas was still Pope to them and deserved a special welcome. By the time the green and red colours of the 747 became visible, descending out of the midday sky, thousands had already arrived at the airport and the roads serving it were clogged by many more.

The Italian government, trying to be clever, had banned RAI, the state television service, from covering Thomas's arrival in Sicily. But this was Italy: there were countless private TV stations which the government couldn't control and they delightedly sold their pictures, via satellite, to anyone who wanted them.

Gina sat next to David, keeping him fortified with cups of black, bitter coffee. He noticed that her make-up had run: she had been crying. Together they watched the television screen as, the scene being Sicily, the people who descended on Punta Raisi, Palermo's airport, were not content merely to wait on the observation deck, behind barriers, but spread all over the airport, even up to the runway. As the captain of Thomas's aircraft got the runway on visual, he must have been appalled to see, virtually *alongside* the strip, rows of cheering spectators.

It was dangerous to land in such circumstances. The captain decided not to land the first time but to come in low, survey the scene, give the crowd a taste of the ferocious noise the jumbo was capable of, and then go round again. Air traffic control did what it could to respond to his request for the people to be pulled back but the airport was simply not equipped to deal with this size of crowd. And there was no chance of the army helping: they could not get to the airport with the roads still choked.

Eventually some sort of order was established, with most people keeping back fifty yards or so from the runway. A new cheer went up as the Cardinal Archbishop of Palermo, Francesco Ligorio, arrived, just ahead of the second run by Thomas's aircraft. A member of the commission which administered the St Patrick's Fund, he was one of Thomas's strongest supporters. Now the welcome would be complete.

And so the aircraft came in, low and slow. There was a small puff of blue smoke as the tyres of the 747 punched the tarmac on the runway, a blood-curdling roar billowed into the ears of the crowd as the engines were thrust into reverse, and the huge aircraft lurched to a stop, then immediately turned off the runway to the taxiway. Before it could reach the apron, however, the people, so many of them, simply would wait no longer. They surrounded the aircraft so that the captain just had to give up, and switch off the engines.

The archbishop had commandeered an airport truck carrying a flight of steps. Standing on the top of the steps, he managed to steer the driver through the crowds towards the door in the shoulder of the jumbo. After some manoeuvring, the door was opened, the steps moved alongside and the archbishop disappeared inside. There was a short delay and then the crowd below glimpsed, first, the scarlet of the archbishop's cassock, and then the white of Thomas's.

Immediately, the cry of 'Papa! Papa! Papa!' went up, soon becoming a chant as the two men emerged from the plane together and waved.

The archbishop's black limousine had, by now, fought its slow way through the crowd and had reached the foot of the steps. Seeing it arrive, the cardinal led Thomas down the steps. Thomas had to allow his hand to be kissed many times by the crowds surrounding the car. He smiled and waved his blessing.

Then began a slow procession from Palermo airport into the city. The cardinal's car drove slowly across the airfield, Thomas and Ligorio waving and smiling. Everyone leaned forward to be blessed by Thomas. Mothers held out their babies. It made an extraordinary television spectacle, not least because the coverage was so makeshift. The fact that it was *not* staged, that the cameras did not always have the best vantage point, gave the event an urgency, a presence, an impact beyond anything anyone had seen before. The emotional effect was stunning. Outside the airport other cars, trucks and motor cycles joined the cavalcade, blaring their horns and flashing their lights. Two police cars joined the procession but they were not needed. By now one of the more enterprising Sicilian TV stations had got a camera aboard a helicopter so that the world was able to watch as the amazing cavalcade moved down the coast road between Punta Raisi and Palermo proper. With stony mountains in the background, it made an extraordinary sight: the cardinal's sober black car followed by forty or fifty others. Trucks, vans, buses even had joined in by now, all making an almighty din.

The procession entered the city by the Via della Liberta and the Piazza Castelnuovo. This was an area that hitherto had been strongly in the grip of the Mafia, and so had felt Thomas's help all the more keenly. Even in normal circumstances almost every house boasted a picture of Thomas. Now, as the procession arrived, everyone went wild. The limousine was held up and its speed reduced to walking pace as people filled the streets. Makeshift bands formed – guitars, woodwind, drums.

Palermo was choked. The crowds, hearing the news and the commotion, ran up the Via Emerico Amari from the docks. The theatre in the Piazza Verdi was surrounded. Cars were abandoned in the Principe di Scordia. It took Thomas and Ligorio another two hours to get to the cardinal's residence, next to the cathedral. Shops were closed, newspaper kiosks abandoned, buses immobilized.

The cathedral had a small piazza in front of it and a garden to one side. By the time the procession arrived, both were packed and overflowing. Some technician had had the foresight to install cameras overlooking both the cathedral and the archbishop's residence so what was rapidly becoming the world's longest-running unscripted TV show could continue uninterrupted. For half an hour the black limousine, swamped in people, struggled to cross the cathedral square. Thomas couldn't get out: he would have been crushed.

Eventually the car made it. Thomas and the cardinal stood up, opened the doors and were bundled inside.

But this was Palermo, not some northern city. No one went home. This was a chance for Sicilians to show their dislike of Rome: they weren't going to pass it up. The chanting began, slowly at first, and quietly. But soon rising in tone and tempo.

'*Papa vero! Papa vero! Papa vero!*' sang the crowd. 'We want the real Pope, the real Pope, the real Pope!' Soon the whole square was chanting. The whole city. Car horns blared the new rhythm: 'One-two, three-four; one-two, three-four'. '*Pa – pa ve – ro! Pa – pa ve – ro!*'

Twenty more minutes and then a great shout went up as first one window of the archbishop's residence was opened, and then another, to reveal two enormous loudspeakers. Then the great high doors to the balcony were opened and two men, one a priest, manoeuvred out two microphones. The chanting gave way now to singing, songs of the Sicilian mountains, songs from the mysterious south coast, sarcastic anti-Roman tunes. Everyone knew the words. Ten thousand Sicilians cleared their lungs, filling the air with a clear beauty. It was intensely moving.

A few more minutes then, beyond the balcony, the vivid scarlet of the cardinal's cassock was glimpsed and, maybe, the white too. The singing stopped and the chanting resumed – though this time with a difference.

'*Pa – pa ve – ro! Ma – ssoni ma – le! Pa – pa ve – ro! Ma – ssoni ma – le!*' 'The real pope!' 'Evil Massoni!' 'The real pope!' 'Evil Massoni!'

The great balcony doors opened further and the white figure of Thomas appeared, the cardinal at his elbow. The two men embraced – to renewed cheers – and then the cardinal held up his hands for silence. He waited as the excitable Sicilians calmed down.

'My friends!' It was a big voice for such a small man and it claimed everyone's attention. 'My friends, a prayer. A prayer for the miracle that is Thomas – *Papa vero* indeed. A prayer of thanks that he has been brought to us now . . . When we needed him, he did not fail us.' The cardinal knew when to pause. 'Now he needs us, we shall not fail him!' A cheer broke out but he stilled it. 'A prayer of thanks that we may be worthy of him, that we may help him as much as he has helped us. A moment's silence, my children, for all of us to be alone with *Il Papa Vero*.' And there was silence. For almost a minute there was silence. Not everyone kept their eyes down, or closed. Many looked up at Thomas as he looked down at them. But all were silent. Even the children.

But then, as Thomas moved to the microphone, another cheer swelled in the throats of the ten thousand crammed into the square. Thomas stood on the balcony, waving, acknowledging the cheers. The cameras swept back and forth, from him to the crowd. At length the noise subsided and Thomas could speak. He held his arms high.

'I give thanks to God for Sicily.' More cheers. 'For its people, its church, its independence.' Cheers again. He smiled down at them. 'For its airport.' Everyone laughed.

'I am told I cannot go to Rome.' He paused, took hold of the archbishop's hand, and raised it. He leaned forward, closer to the microphone. 'But who needs Rome, when one has all of Sicily?' Rapturous applause and wild cheering.

'I will not stay here, my friends, not long. Sicily has a great spiritual leader in Cardinal Francesco Ligorio. You are lucky' – again a smile – 'but then so is he.' Again everyone laughed.

'I ask you for one night, my children, my brothers and sisters. One night – and then, who knows? The world may be very different. In a moment I want you to go home, peacefully.' He raised his voice. 'But be here at this time tomorrow. Your cardinal and I, we may have some news. And pray for me tonight. I will bless you before you go.'

The crowd hushed as Thomas's soft voice swept in perfect Latin around the square. He turned and moved back to the huge doors. But, before he could disappear entirely, from somewhere in the crowd a woman's beautiful voice began singing the most beautiful Sicilian song of all. 'The Almonds of Marsalen' tells how the island's famous almond trees failed to bloom after Garibaldi invaded Sicily in the nineteenth century and annexed it to Italy. Its sad story was a metaphor for the way many Sicilians felt about the mainland. She was allowed one verse of the slow, shadowy song, then the other voices in the square joined in. Even Cardinal Ligorio was singing. Like many in the square, he was crying openly. It was an emotional climax to a shattering day. Ten thousand voices, as if as one, sharing the bitterness and pain of many years. Of now.

In the White House Roskill watched the proceedings in Palermo with a mixture of disgust and admiration. 'Shit!' he said, turning to Cranham Hope. 'You can tell Thomas is a goddam American: he refuses to know when he's beat. The guy oughtta been a politician, goddammit, not Pope.'

In the Vatican, Massoni had no mixed feelings. He didn't like television, he didn't much care for Sicily and he hated Thomas. The broadcast over, he paced up and down the study, telling himself he mustn't panic or exaggerate Thomas's power. He, Massoni, held the real power. The Italian government would do anything he asked, he held a firm grip on the Vatican finances, its channels of communication, its diplomatic corps, its physical territory. All Thomas had was emotion, emotion that would fade the minute the world realized he could not sustain himself.

In Rome proper, David went back to Bess's apartment and tried to get through to the archbishop's residence in Palermo. It was impossible. He'd known it would be impossible but he tried anyway. The whole world would be trying to get through. He was desperate to speak to Bess – lord, what she must have been through in the past few days.

After two hours of dialling Palermo every few minutes, he gave up. Should he go to Sicily? He thought not. As soon as she could, Bess would call the apartment, or Gina's. So long as he stayed by the phone in one or other place, she would reach him when she could. He therefore took his dinner at Gina's where he could also continue to watch the television.

In Italy the regular programmes had been scrapped that evening. What was happening to the Church was too important. The remarkable scenes of the day, beginning with the announcement of the election of a new Pope and the designation of Thomas as Anti-Pope, and proceeding to the events in Palermo, were re-run and re-run. Studio discussions followed in which pundits examined the options Thomas had before him. One Vatican observer voiced a rumour that Thomas was searching for a safe haven, away from Rome and away from America: Rio or Quebec were favoured. Another man, quoting unnamed sources inside the Vatican, said that Thomas was going to resign after all, and would then be allowed to remain in Sicily. David was frantic. If only Bess would call, he'd know the truth.

It was one of those nights when no one wanted to go to bed, in case they missed some sensational development. Television went on late, reduced to reporting what tomorrow morning's papers were going to say, the papers themselves based on what had been seen on television. David eventually decided to turn in around a quarter to two. There was still no word from Bess. He was just cleaning his teeth when the phone rang. He ran across the flat and snatched at the receiver. 'Yes?'

'David!'

314

'Darling. At last! How are you? You must be exhausted. Shall I come to Palermo? If I drive all night I could be there some time tomorrow.'

'Oh David, it's so good to hear your voice. How's the apartment? Did you hang the silks?'

'How's the *apartment?* How can you? A religious storm raging around you, and you want to know about the apartment?'

'I want normality, darling. I want to know there's firm ground somewhere. How are you?'

'I'm fine. I tried to get you on the phone for two hours but the archbishop's residence was always "*occupato*". I figured you'd call me as soon as you could.'

'Now is the first chance I've had to do anything even remotely personal. Thomas sends his blessing, by the way.'

David lowered his voice, as if to slow the pace of their conversation. 'Tell me, Bess, what's going on? All these rumours on television. And shall I come to Sicily? You didn't answer. Don't you want me – ?'

'Darling! One thing at a time. First, don't believe *any* of the rumours. They're all untrue. Second, I can't tell you what's happening, partly because it's not absolutely certain yet, but partly because there have been so many leaks that I'm under strict instructions to say as little as possible. But third, and this is the main reason I'm calling, apart from a wish to hear your voice, is that the Holy Father would like you to do something for him.'

'What on earth – ?'

'David! Hear me out. There is no one else in Rome who, in this particular matter, we can trust.'

David held his breath. Then: 'Go on.'

'We want you to see Massoni – '

' – what?'

'On our behalf. As Thomas's emissary.'

'He'll never see me!'

'Oh yes, he will. We shall prime him. We shall tell him to expect you and that you'll be acting on our behalf and with our authority. Only we shan't tell him in advance what it is we want. For this to stand any chance of working we need to knock him off balance.'

'And what is it you want?'

'The St Patrick's Fund.'

'You can't be serious! What if he says no? He's not just going to hand it over, is he?'

'I'm coming to that. Remember that exposé in the Naples newspaper, *Il Mattino?* The one about your report on the way the Fund was made to fail?'

'You mean the one which disclosed that Massoni's brother ran the bank which mishandled the funds?'

'Yes. Well, I guess that was only the tip of the iceberg. With so much

315

fund money being moved around, Aldo Massoni – the brother – started playing what bankers call "night games".'

'You mean – ?'

'In between investments, the brother would leave the money on deposit with another bank overnight. Or he would buy foreign currency at, say, six in the evening, and sell it again at eight the next morning. With the millions in his care, he could make several thousands in as many hours. When he did we – the fund – never saw them.'

'How do you know all this?'

'As I say, your report started it. And before he was killed, John Rich had set inquiries in motion. From his time in New York he had friends in the American Securities and Exchange Commission and they had contacts in Switzerland. Despite his kidnap and murder, or maybe because of it, they dug deep – and came up with what I just told you.'

'Powerful stuff. It's a pity it only touches the brother. We'd have a much stronger hand if the cardinal himself was directly involved.'

'But he is! I haven't got to the juiciest part yet. Thomas was saving it, in case Massoni refused to resign when we got back from the Far East. Remember, I told you we had something that would force him out. Now, in view of what's happened, you're free to make use of it. Massoni – the cardinal, I mean, not his brother Aldo – has his own bank account in Switzerland. At Aldo's bank, of course. There's over a million dollars in it but, more important, the dates on the account show that he also received money from his brother's "night games". The dates of the deposits all fit. Can you believe it, David? At the very time he was criticizing the fund, Massoni was milking it. I could weep.'

'You have proof of all this?'

'We don't have a signed confession from the brother, if that's what you mean. But we do have the number of Massoni's bank account, the dates of the deposits, and the balance at the close of business yesterday.' She read the figures over to him.

'I'll do as you ask, Bess. Of course I will. Anything to help Thomas. I just hope I don't let him down.'

'Darling, this is just up your street. You're the only person we can trust. You'll make it work, I know. You can think on your feet and that's what we need. Now I'm going to give you another number; it's the archbishop's private line here and you can call us tomorrow after you've seen Massoni. If you don't hear from me again, assume your appointment with Massoni is for noon. Then call us *immediately* after. It's important we know how you've done as soon as possible. Good luck!'

'I shall need it. I feel nervous already.'

'Don't be. You'll be fine. Remember, Massoni's the one with the troubled conscience. He's the one at your meeting tomorrow who'll

316

have had a rough night, not you. Goodnight, darling. Again, good luck.'

Despite what she said, and despite the fact that it was well after two when he climbed into bed, David was wide awake, and up, by six the next morning. He was immediately on edge, not sure what to expect at his meeting with Massoni, not sure what approach to adopt. Moreover, there wasn't any research he could do that would make his task easier. The best he could do was to take refuge in the papers.

Most of them showed the same instincts. It had been hundreds of years since two men had claimed to be Pope so the image of two men in white, Thomas on a balcony in Palermo, Massoni leaning out of a window in the Vatican, was simply too good to pass up. But David was more interested in what the morning papers had to say. For example, the Italian government's response to the crisis. The Prime Minister had thrown his weight firmly behind Massoni, saying disparagingly that Thomas's antics in Palermo merely showed how unfit he was to rule as Pope. To be on the safe side, Italian troops, with Massoni's permission, had been drawn up on the perimeter of the Vatican in Rome, to stop any anti-Massoni agitators from getting in. The Mayor of Rome had also weighed in on Massoni's side, allowing himself to be photographed kneeling in front of the new pontiff. There was no doubt where the political muscle was. Some of the papers also carried historical articles on the anti-Popes of the past. David knew about the great schism vaguely, when one set of Popes had reigned from Rome and another from Avignon but he hadn't realized there had been so many.

It was a sunny day but cold, November-cold. Even so, he sat outside Gina's in the square. He had asked her to warm some croissants for him and she had brought a large pot of coffee.

'Signorina Bess – you hear from her yet?' To David Gina's voice had always been more beautiful than her face.

David told her about their late night conversation. Enough of it to reassure her.

Gina looked down at him. 'You know why Signorina Bess and me get on?'

David pursed his lips thoughtfully. 'You both like *fettucine*?'

Gina shook her head, unamused. 'No. We have something else in common. We talked about it one night.' She paused. Then, going inside, she said over her shoulder, 'Each of us, we love two men. It's hard to decide between them.'

David buttered his croissant. It was the first he'd ever heard of Gina's love life. And what did she mean about Bess's two loves? The other man, he supposed, was the pontiff. Ah well, that was a different kind of love. He peered at Gina, now inside the bar. She *did* mean that, didn't she? It was a funny thing to say.

317

He finished his food. He had nearly two hours to kill before his meeting with Massoni – the cardinal would never be the Pope to him. Should he call the office in London? No – Sally would ask questions: he wanted to keep his mind clear for his meeting with the cardinal. On an impulse, he felt like walking. It was a good way to pass the time. He shouted goodbye to Gina and moved off. He walked down the Via Monserrato and past the Palazzo Farnese. He crossed the Via Arenuta and went by the synagogue. Over the Ponte Palatino and into Trastevere. The Via Luciano Manaro, he knew, led to the Janiculum, the wooded hill overlooking central Rome and the Vatican. A perfect place to clear his brain. He walked up the *passeggiata* to the Piazzale Garibaldi, which overlooked the slopes, and sat on a bench. What would the grand old soldier have made of these latest twists? Garibaldi would rather have had *no* Pope: now there were two.

David got up and wandered slowly down through the trees to the back of what was now the Palazzo Corsini but was once the Palazzo Riario. Here Queen Christina of Sweden had lived for many years after abdicating and converting to Catholicism. Would Thomas abdicate, perhaps? David didn't know. He looked down on the Riario. Christina had been a great collector – pictures, sculpture, bindings. Yet she had died unhappy, had never adjusted to her abdication, and had tried several times to gain other crowns. Once you have power, he reflected, it always hurts to give it up. What would Thomas do? He would never be the same again if he failed. And neither would he, David, if Averne beat him at the board meeting next week. Today was make-or-break day for them both. The meeting with Massoni was less than an hour away. And Michael Stone arrived from Milan tonight to authenticate the Leonardo.

David moved north along the Lungara towards St Peter's. As he had read, the army were out in force, their grey-green uniforms and squat, angular vans posted at every crossroad, every bridge, every traffic light. He followed the Lungotevere and turned left into the Corridori Borgo Sant Angelo. This brought him, at ten minutes to 'twelve, to the Porta Sant' Anna. As on other – if very different – occasions, he was expected. A Swiss guard, in blue breeches, took him up the slight slope to the papal apartments on the left and rode with him in the elevator. At the third floor, when the elevator stopped and the doors had opened, he was received by a figure he didn't recognize, presumably one of Massoni's new secretaries. The papal apartments were subtly different from the last time he had been here, to discuss the big sale all that while ago. Two Swiss guards now stood in the corridor. Either Massoni was making the most of the ceremonial his new position entitled him to, or he really was afraid of being invaded. There were other differences, too: pictures had gone from the walls and there were no flowers anywhere. The place was as austere as a monastery.

318

David was shown into the same office where Thomas had first produced the list of art works which he wanted to sell. The same large table,
the same view down on to St Peter's Square, though the weather now
was different: the early morning sunshine hadn't lasted, the sky had
clouded over and threatened rain.

David was kept waiting: the psychological game had begun. Eventually he heard movement beyond the double doors at the far end. They
opened and Massoni swept through. He seemed taller in white. Taller
but paler, a deathly pale. His high, cadaverous skull seemed about to
break through his skin at any moment, so thin, so transparent did it
appear.

There were no formalities. He stood by his desk and said, in Italian,
'Mr Colwyn, I forget how good your Italian is. Shall we need an
interpreter?'

'No.'

Massoni turned to the young man who had entered with him and
nodded. The young man left, closing the double doors behind him.

Massoni sat and David did the same, opposite him across the desk.
'Well,' said Massoni. 'I am told you are here on behalf of the – of
Thomas Murray.'

'Yes, sir.' David couldn't, wouldn't, call Massoni 'Holiness', but that
was no reason to be needlessly disrespectful.

Massoni was silent. He wasn't about to make things easy for David.

Outside the window a helicopter clattered by. Somewhere someone
was whistling. David said, 'Thomas feels that since the St Patrick's Fund
was his doing, his own idea, and that since it is so closely identified with
him, he feels he should be allowed to take it with him.'

What then happened David had never seen before. Massoni grinned.
It was alarming. His lips curled back to reveal teeth long, slightly
curved, slightly too big for his mouth. It was an ugly sight, reminiscent
of an ape's war grimace. 'He would, would he? Seven hundred million
dollars? He would like me to give him seven hundred million dollars?
Just like that? He *is* crazy. And what would he do with the money? –
no, don't tell me, I can guess. He would carry on spending the same
as before. So the world would be plagued with these ill-advised schemes
of his for years to come.'

Massoni slapped the desk between them. 'Not only is *he* mad, Mr
Colwyn, but you are, too, for accepting such a hopeless assignment.
Does he, do you, really think I will hand over cash like that, just for
the asking? I tell you: you are all still living in the past, Mr Colwyn.
It's over. Thomas is no longer Pope.' He drew himself up. 'I am.'

David reached into his jacket and took out a slip of paper. He placed
it on the desk between them.

Massoni glanced down. He looked more closely. Then he snatched
at it.

'Yes, sir,' said David. 'Your Swiss bank account. And your personal fortune, as of last evening.'

'How did you get this?'

'So it *is* yours.'

'How did you get it?'

'You are not the only man with friends in Switzerland, sir.'

Massoni stared at David. 'There's nothing wrong with cardinals having bank accounts. I shall close it now, of course. Now that I am Pope.'

'It's not the account itself, or the very large balance, that I have come to discuss, sir, but rather how certain payments – from the St Patrick's Fund – found their way *into* that account. You will recall it was I who noticed the pattern of investments in the first place – a pattern that was suspicious and drew attention to your brother's involvement. Now we have a pattern of transfers into your account. That is suspicious also. More than suspicious. While you were conducting your own crusade against the fund, and against its achievements, at the same time you and your brother were stealing from it. That is frankly criminal. I'm not surprised you feel so insecure you need the Italian army guarding your doors. If – when – this is all made public, even they won't keep you in that chair.'

Massoni still held the scrap of paper. For a long time he stared at it, as though the writing were hard to decipher. Eventually, he looked up. 'This is all you have, isn't it? A set of figures, and some dates perhaps. If you could prove the slanders you have just uttered, you would have the documentation with you. But you haven't. You haven't because there isn't any. Not since your own report. Your own interference warned us to destroy a lot of the evidence, Mr Colwyn.'

Calmly Massoni looked across at David. 'There's no documentation is there?' His stare burned into him. 'Is there?'

When David didn't reply, Massoni scrunched up the slip of paper and threw it contemptuously into a waste basket. He began to rise, terminating the meeting.

David improvised desperately. 'Thomas says he won't leave Sicily until he's got the fund.'

The cardinal lowered himself slowly back into his seat. The toothy grin reappeared. 'Let him stay,' he said at length. 'You know what will happen if he stays on, Mr Colwyn? He will outlive his welcome. Oh, there's high emotion down there at the moment, I grant you that. But it won't last. It can't. Nobody lives at that emotional intensity for long. Then, when the emotion has died down, one of two things will happen. Either the government will arrest him and deport him – they are firmly on my side, Mr Colwyn, and will do everything they can to support me. Or, the Mafia will get him. He may have wonderful friends in Sicily but that's where his most vicious enemies are too.' He got up and stood above David. 'If I gave Thomas the seven hundred million he's asking for, there'd have been no point in all that has happened in the past forty-eight hours. He'd be afloat in the world somewhere, and still able to do whatever damage he wanted.'

'Some people don't see charity work as damage,' said David.

'But damage it is. Can't you see that? Selling off all those wonderful treasures was damage. Interfering in Central America was damage. Meddling in Beirut was very damaging. Tampering in Northern Ireland was damage. Taking on President Roskill was both damaging and foolish. Plotting behind the Iron Curtain was in some senses the most damaging of all, potentially the most dangerous certainly.'

As he was speaking, Massoni sat down again and turned on the chair so that it was his profile David saw. David gasped. It was the same view he'd had that day in the restaurant off the Piazza del Risorgimento, when he'd eaten deep-fried anchovies and Massoni had been at another table with a jowly man David thought he'd seen before but couldn't place. Now he could: Massoni's action in sitting and turning had cleared his memory. That and the talk about damage behind the Iron Curtain. David made the connection and gasped. A quiet strength gripped him.

'You're not the one to talk about damage, *cardinal*.'

Massoni looked across, suddenly wary.

'I now understand the damage *you* have worked to cause.' The certainty in David's voice carried him over Massoni's objection. 'And I think you *will* give Thomas the money he wants.'

'Never – !'

'Oh yes! You see, I know who it was who tipped off the Hungarians and the Russians about the Vatican's secret cardinal. I know who divulged the identity of Cardinal Kharkov.'

Massoni's face had frozen.

*'And I know how you did it, Massoni. I was there, watching you.'*

Still Massoni didn't move. His reaction, as loud as any words, said that David was right.

'I should have worked it out before. It was Dorzhiev, the new director at the Hermitage, wasn't it? I saw him eating with you at that restaurant off the Piazza del Risorgimento. I should have smelled something when he so quickly replaced Shirikin. Or when I saw him in the same photograph as the spy Edgar Seton. I mean, it's a perfect cover. A Russian museum director can mix in the most capitalist company without raising the slightest suspicions. He can travel a lot, to conferences, exhibitions, auctions.' David closed in. '*You* told Dorzhiev about Kharkov. *You* destroyed Thomas's plans. You were willing to commit murder, simply to thwart him. You sent innocent Hungarian men and women to their certain deaths when you informed on Kharkov.'

'You . . . can't prove it.'

'I won't need to. I have all the times which will check out. You knew

321

Kharkov's identity, you talked with Dorzhiev. Coming after Seton's defection the world will know I'm right. Don't think Roskill will stand by you then, or the Italian government. Nobody will want a Pope who betrayed his own. You'll be a prisoner here. Maybe there'll be yet another Pope elected.'

'You're exaggerating. And bluffing.'

'Okay, risk it!' David pointed to the door. 'Let me walk out of this room and start calling my friends in the media. Thomas will be told in time for his speech tonight. A speech the whole world is waiting for. Then see what happens.' David got up, as if to leave. Massoni was right; he *was* bluffing. It was the greatest bluff of his life. But Massoni couldn't be sure and that uncertainty was all David had on his side. He picked up his coat and put it on. He did up the buttons. He picked up his briefcase where it had been leaning against his chair and turned.

Massoni said, 'Sit down, Mr Colwyn.'

David sat.

Massoni's eyes moved rapidly in their sockets. David couldn't tell whether it was through fear or anger. He knew the emotions were very similar, since he himself was experiencing both. 'You are a bad actor, Mr Colwyn. Stick to auctioneering. However, although you are obviously bluffing I choose to play safe. Therefore if Thomas leaves Sicily today – and he never mentions the Kharkov business – I will send the St Patrick's Fund, less one hundred million dollars – '

'Why the deduction?'

'The "Pietà", Mr Colwyn, it's on the market again. I want to buy it back.'

David thought fast. Should he hold out for the full amount? No. His position was not strong. Still, there was one matter he had to press. 'I accept. But you must transfer the money quickly. I will stay here to represent Thomas. If we receive nothing within forty-eight hours, Thomas will go public on Dorzhiev.'

Massoni stood up. 'Very well. Do you remember shaking hands with Thomas Murray, the first time you came to the Vatican? I remember the occasion very well. It started this whole sorry business. Will you shake hands with me, now? To finish it?'

David got to his feet. Massoni's arm was extended. David reached across the desk and clasped the dry, old man's skin.

# 16

Once outside the Vatican David grabbed the first free taxi he saw and told the driver to head for the Via dei Banchi Vecchi as quickly as he could. He took the steps up to Bess's flat three at a time. In the apartment he shook off his coat and dialled the number Bess had given him. It was answered on the second ring – by Bess herself.

'Yes or no?' she said quickly as soon as she realized it was David.

'Yes,' he said. 'But there are complications.'

He heard her shout across the room, 'It's a "Yes"!' A dim cheer and a murmur of approval could be heard. 'Okay,' she said, coming back to the phone. 'What are the details?'

He explained the deal he had struck with Massoni, the trade-off about Dorzhiev, the deduction for the 'Pietà', the fact that he would stay on in Rome over the weekend to handle the financial transaction.

Bess was aghast at what Massoni had done to Kharkov. But this was not the time for looking back. 'There you are darling. I told you you were the right person for the job. Great! You'll probably get an anti-Papal honour now, to go with the Papal one you already have.'

He smiled into the phone. 'At least you're joking again, Bess. Things must be looking up. What's happening?'

At the other end of the line Bess was shouting across the room again. 'OK! Coming! David, *I'm* sorry. I have to dash. Things are *really* crazy here, as you can imagine. Look, watch Thomas on television. When it's over give me half an hour to get back to this phone then call me. Or I'll call you. We'll have time to talk then, I promise. I really promise. OK?'

'I shall need a good long fix. And no excuses. I miss the old Mississippi drawl.'

'It's a deal. Thomas will probably want to talk to you too.'

David looked at his watch. It had already gone one. He went down the stairs and across to Gina's for lunch. The rain had started at last, and the place was crowded. In the bar the television was already switched on. Government ministers who wanted their say about the two Popes were being interviewed but no one was paying much attention.

The exact timing of Thomas's speech was not certain, but no one wanted to miss it so they just had to hang around. Amid all the uncertainty there was only one thing beyond doubt: no work was being done in Italy today except for bars, television companies and the police.

Gina appeared to have put on her best dress for the occasion. She came and sat with David, arriving with the whisky she knew he liked. Despite the dress, a cheerful green, Gina was feeling low. She hated Massoni, but she chose to believe the rumour that Thomas would resign that afternoon and remain in Sicily. David wished he could tell her about his meeting with Massoni and the deal that had been worked out.

It was clear from comments around the bar that customers were split between Massoni and Thomas. Although many Romans had been against Thomas for some time, even they did not like the way Massoni had seized power. On the other hand there were some who clearly relished the split and simply treated the two Popes like rival football teams.

Lunch arrived, *linguine* followed by *lombatina*. Gina stayed and ate with David.

The television was now covering international reactions to Massoni's coup. A film clip showed Roskill on the steps of the White House, saying he was saddened by the split but that Massoni promised a return to traditional Roman ways. 'That,' he said, 'is wiser, duller, safer, slower, sedate and sober. Better.' *Pravda* was quoted as saying that the decline and fall of Thomas's Roman empire merely showed western religion to be as corrupt as ever, and pointed out that even Popes, or would-be Popes, were not above a little unholy subterfuge. Some things, David thought, *Pravda* got right. Fidel Castro in Cuba made no direct comment but announced that the Cuban government and the American government had reopened negotiations on the Guantanamo Bay naval bases. A picture of David's dead former wife Sarah suddenly flashed on the screen and behind the Italian commentary David caught the voice of Michael Greener, from London, saying he hoped Northern Ireland would now enjoy an easier peace and that a foundation was being established, the Sarah Greener Foundation, which would give scholarships to enable foreigners to study in Northern Ireland and see the problems at first hand, so that worldwide understanding of the situation would grow. The Nicaraguans said the Vatican coup didn't make any difference: one Pope was as bad as the next. But the President said he admired Massoni: 'He's obviously been reading the right Trotskyist text  oks.'

Lunch was over. The bar was filling up now, the hubbub was deafening and the tobacco smoke so thick it gave a blue tinge to everything. On the screen attention had switched back to the cathedral square in Palermo. The square was a solid mass of bodies. There were people on the fountains, in the trees, leaning from every window. Overnight TV crews had arrived from everywhere: Rome, Africa, Madrid, Geneva, Marseilles. The *carabiniere* were out in force, but friendly, to judge from the TV pictures. Amazingly, the entrepreneurs had been busy during the early hours and already T-shirts and hats with '*Papa vero*' on them were on sale. Flags with pictures of Thomas and the archbishop were everywhere. Unlike in Rome, the weather was glorious, the sun poured down.

Just before four o'clock the chanting started. '*Pa-pa ve-ro! Pa-pa ve-ro! Pa-pa ve-ro!*' The chanting got louder, faded, got louder again. Then, as the cathedral bells started to clang the hour, the chanting changed into 'The Almonds of Marsalen'.

On cue, as the last words faded, a glimpse of scarlet and white could be seen through the windows behind the balcony. A cheer went up and the windows opened, the cardinal archbishop leading the way. Applause, whistles, trumpets, all sorts of welcome greeted Ligorio and he waited patiently. As the din continued he smiled, nodded and waved to people he knew.

The longer the noise went on the higher the tension rose. But eventually it dropped away. Ligorio waited until all voices had been stilled, until everyone would be able to hear clearly what he had to say. That too raised the tension. People were eager for words.

He gave them two.

'*Abbiamo Papa*'.

'We have a Pope.'

The crowd cheered madly. The whistles and trumpets blared again. No one knew what more was coming but they recognized the words as the traditional announcement after a conclave, spoken by the *camerlengo*, the Papal chamberlain, signifying that the election of the new Pope had been completed. What Ligorio meant was that Thomas was not going to resign.

The archbishop now stood back and the white-robed figure of Thomas came forward. A deeper, throatier cheer was now raised and people waved their flags or banners or hats and the square was, for a few moments, a huge field of lifted, swaying arms. As Ligorio before him, Thomas stood and simply smiled or waved, waiting patiently for the reception to die down.

Eventually, the noise and clatter started to subside. Thomas brought his hands together in an attitude of prayer and all in the square followed and became still.

'Friends, a prayer of thanks. For our blessings. For this beautiful day, for the lovely babies I can see before me, the trees in the park over there, the friendship that all of us, in this square, feel for one another. Especially at a time like now, when we are beset by terrible problems, we must remember the beauty that is about us, the beauty that God has provided.

'Of all the beauty God has created, however, I think that perhaps the beauty of friendship, the understanding of one person for another, is the most precious of all. I want you to think for a moment of the most unlikely friend you have, perhaps a very different person from yourself, and a long way across the world. A person who, despite the fact that he or she is very different from you, nonetheless shares with you understanding and affection. Just remember for a moment that feeling of friendship. It is important for the news Cardinal Ligorio and I are bringing to you.' There was quiet in the square. 'In the name of the Father, and of the Son, and of the Holy Spirit, Amen.'

'*Amen*'.

They waited for the news Thomas had promised. There was no more cheering, no more singing. They were there to listen.

'Friends, if my voice sounds weak, it is because Cardinal Ligorio and I have been up all night. And he is a fine man, your cardinal. A great support. Something wonderful happened yesterday. Your reception, your greeting, was so magnificent, so moving – and, I might say, so well televised – that as soon as the singing had finished in this very square I began to receive phone calls from all over the world. It seems that you Sicilians are not the only friends I have. It's true. Bishops, cardinals, mothers, monks, hotel receptionists, a doctor in Australia, a policeman in Holland, a headmistress of a school in Chile, a violinist in Singapore. All saying the same thing. "Don't resign. Fight! Fight back! Fight on!" All saying that what we have been doing, trying to change things – in Sicily, in South and Central America, in Hungary, in Ireland, in cities with racial troubles – is what they want to see happening. Is the lead they wish to follow.

'It was all very encouraging. So encouraging, in fact, that I telephoned some of the cardinals back. Then I discussed an idea with Cardinal Ligorio. He agreed with me – wholeheartedly, I might say. He's a giant of a man. The momentous news I am about to share with you is as much his doing as mine. Throughout the night he and I contacted every cardinal we could. We called Argentina, Taiwan, Switzerland, Nigeria, Brazil, Ireland, Chad and Luxembourg. We called Paris, Chicago, La Paz, London, Vienna, Venice, Beirut, Johannesburg, Sydney and Guatemala City. There are, at the present time, one hundred and twelve cardinals in the sacred college. In the past few hours Cardinal Ligorio or I have talked with eighty-four of them. The others were either impossible to reach or, in twenty cases, they refused to talk to us. But, as a result of our conversations, we now know where we stand.

'I have also talked to Cardinal Massoni, twice, and he knows where *he* stands.

'Now I come to the important point, friends. Some of you may recall the occasion when James Roskill, the American President, first called for my resignation. He said I should follow the example of my distinguished predecessor, Boniface. Well, President Roskill is a politician and used to bending the meaning of words. And perhaps we shouldn't expect a politician to be historically sound. But the fact is that Boniface, when he resigned as Pope in the fourteenth century, did so in order to avoid a schism in the Church. There is of course no schism in the Church today. Or, at least, there wasn't until Cardinal Massoni, by his divisive act, his *coup*, if you like, created a situation where we do, apparently, have two people who both claim to be Pope. During the night, therefore, Cardinal Ligorio here and I have been trying to establish just who in the Church supports which Pope. And we have found that there are many people who feel as you Sicilians do. They are morally outraged by what Massoni has done and they withhold their support from him, giving it instead to me. It has been a hectic night but I can report to you now that, henceforward, certain areas of the globe will no longer recognize Rome as head of the Church. Instead, they choose to recognize my Papacy wherever I place it. And that, I can tell you as a result of yet more calls during the night, will be in Rio de Janeiro, Brazil, where as you know certain functions of the Vatican have been devolved already and where, thanks to the generosity of the Brazilian government, the Church owns land. Already there, in Rio, is the Pontifical Commission on the Americas, Cor Unum, the Commission on Latin America, on the Family, the Laity, the Congregation for the Causes of Saints. So, friends, we already have a fine base on which to build.

'And now I give you the list of countries who will be joining you, my friends, in support for me.' Everyone in the square was spellbound. 'In Europe: Ireland, Portugal, Lebanon, Foligno, Sicily.' As Thomas called out each country a loud cheer went up.

'In Africa, friends, Nigeria, Chad and Zaire will follow us. In the Far East, Hong Kong, Korea, Portuguese Macao, the Marquesas Isles and the Philippines have offered their support. Most important, *every* country in South America, except Argentina and Paraguay, is with us.' Cheering broke out again, spiced with singing. Thomas held up his hand. 'Finally, Quebec is with us too.' Flags were waved, a horn picked up the '*Papa vero!*' rhythm.

'I say "finally", friends, but it might not be. Only one country in the world cannot decide which side it is on.' He paused. 'The bishops of the United States are divided. They are so numerous and so much at odds, they are to call a special congress to decide!

'Only time will tell but to those bishops listening or watching now, I say this: Roskill will not always be President. America is a rich nation, the richest. But that only emphasizes that, more than any other country, it should concern itself most with the poor.'

327

Thomas paused and looked around the square. 'I have more good news. In addition to his position as Archbishop of Palermo, Cardinal Ligorio has also agreed to accept a new title I am creating. He will administer the Church in Europe, and that will include the dangerous but important task of running the Invisible Vatican behind the Iron Curtain. I have therefore created the position of Patriarch of Europe and will crown Cardinal Ligorio in this position, in your cathedral here, before I leave this afternoon.'

Thomas turned and Ligorio stepped forward. Both acknowledged the delighted applause and cheers from the crowd. Their own church at last! The Sicilians loved it. The singing started again but this time Thomas waved for them to be quiet for a moment. 'You know, I've been here but a few hours and yet I feel more at home in Palermo than I ever did in Rome. But now, friends, in a few short hours I have to leave. I have to keep my side of the bargain. We shall be apart but not separated. This is a new alignment, a new way of looking at what is around us, a new force for good. Your cardinal and I, your *Patriarch* and I, have negotiated with Massoni, the anti-Pope, to take with us the St Patrick's Fund. We shall need a small part of that for administration but we shall still endeavour to provide money for relief work wherever it is needed. No doubt President Roskill will still find our activities irksome but he'll just have to get used to them. No one else offers help of the kind we can offer, or on the same scale, and we can be proud of it.

'And so I leave you for a new Rome, a poorer city perhaps, but richer in spirit. Less elegant but more deserving. Less historic – but only for now. Smaller but with your help its influence will soon be enormous. It will be a working church, friends, and we hope that some of you will come on pilgrimages.'

He straightened his body and lifted his arms. His cape spread like the wings of a bird. He was coming to the end of his speech. 'I do not know when I shall see you again. But while we are apart remember this: be proud of what we have achieved together in the last hours. Each one of you, every man, woman and child, every mother, father, daughter and son, just by being here, being seen by the rest of the world, has played a part in history. Rome tried to destroy us. Washington tried to destroy us. They could not. Perhaps we are not as strong as we were but we are as strong as they are!'

The sun caught Thomas's face and in that moment everyone in the square, everyone across the world, saw the glint of tears on his cheeks.

'Now – ' His voice broke. 'I give you my blessing.' They stood, the thousands in the square, many of them weeping too, as the ancient Latin words drifted down to them.

'And now, friends, thank you. Thank you and farewell.' He turned but the Sicilians had still to bid him goodbye. The singing started, not tentatively as on the day before but strong and muscular, the voice of an independent dignified people. Thomas stood for several moments listening to the song. Then he quietly turned again and went inside. The door was closed behind him, the balcony was empty but the singing continued. The Sicilians were singing for themselves now.

In Gina's, people were silent, overwhelmed by the weight, the striking beauty of what had happened. David asked Gina to bring him a whisky. Thomas's words had affected him very deeply. He was a Catholic, even if he wasn't a Sicilian. And as for Bess – these last two nights she had been at the centre of truly historic events. He envied her that. Hers was hardly a conventional life. It was lived at a daunting intensity, and he wondered how much of it he would ever be able to share.

He didn't go home. For once he couldn't face being alone. He finished his whisky, slowly, listening to the arguments that now began to rage about him. Some thought Thomas's plan brilliant, some thought it was foolish. Then he asked Gina if he could make a long-distance call, to Bess. Gina took him behind the bar, away from the crush, where the noise level was slightly lower.

Bess didn't answer the phone, but she was soon brought to it.

'David?'

'Talk to me. I'm here, in Gina's. Surrounded by people and horribly alone. Tell me what's been happening. Tell me what happens now, to us. Talk to me.'

'Thomas wants a word with you, darling.'

'Gina says you love two men – '

'Yes, she always says that, she thinks it's what we have in common. But when I told her that I didn't mean it the way she thought. There are so many different kinds of love, David. Yes, I love Thomas. I love him like a father. I love my job too . . . but none of this is the same as the way I love you. Oh, these last two days – if only you could have been here. They started out so bad, David. That night on the plane – flying back from the Far East – everything was coming apart, and it was all so *sudden*. We were isolated – just Thomas, the pilot of the jumbo and me. In one moment our purpose, our destination even, was taken away from us. Or that's the way it seemed. It wasn't until it was taken away that I realized how important it all was. Or rather, and this is the important thing, that nothing else came close.

'Sitting there – we were in the cockpit, using the pilot's radio – I watched Thomas shrink. I started to cry. I remember thinking we must have flown hundreds of miles while we just sat there. And how much I would miss not doing what I had been doing for months. But then something else happened. I witnessed the most incredible piece of courage on Thomas's part. An act of will, almost a resurrection. He wasn't just sitting in the co-pilot's seat, moping as I was, licking his

329

wounds. He was *thinking*. We talked a lot that night, after the idea had come to him to sound out his support around the world. And I have to tell you this, David, it wasn't any one thing, any one word or sentence that Thomas said that persuaded me. It was just the thrust of what he said, and the way that he said it, over a long time. Work, the improvement of the world, the channelling of human nature into ever better outlets was, is, to Thomas, far more important than any private life ever could be. And maybe it's that way for me too, David.

'There was a parallel too in what he said and something I once read about Verdi, the composer. I can't remember exactly and I certainly can't remember who said it, or wrote it. But it was to the effect that Verdi's music is too vital, in too much of a hurry to be beautiful. Verdi's music is obviously very beautiful but the point of the remark, so it has always seemed to me, is that Verdi realized there are more important things than beauty: in music he needed to explore new forms, invent new things, get on and try this or that. Beauty isn't the be-all and end-all of everything. The same applies to happiness. Happiness is overrated.

'I asked Thomas that night whether, if Sarah hadn't been killed, he would have allowed your dissolution. He said he wouldn't, that what Hale had come up with was a loophole, an absurd one at that, which it would not have been in the Church's interest to approve. But later he also said that he was, in a way, relieved that he never had to make the decision. He badly wanted me to stay as his aide and he would have hated seeing me go. So had Sarah lived he would have had a dilemma – he would never know how much his refusal of your dissolution was for genuine reasons and how much for his own personal, selfish motives.

'It was that frankness, the fact that even a Pope is puzzled by the simple moral questions and yet always had the courage to face them, that I found – I find – so comforting. At the same time I know now that I cannot leave him. He needs me.'

She paused. David was stunned. He didn't know what to say. Through crackles on the line he heard her clear her throat. When she spoke again her voice was strained. 'David . . . David . . . I can't give up now. *We* can't give up. I don't *want* to. It's just starting. It may end in chaos, in disaster. That's a risk I'm willing, eager to take.'

'Bess, I need you – '

'Don't say anything – not yet. I want you to talk to Thomas. He's just coming. Hold on!'

David heard the receiver being put down. There were voices far off. Then the receiver was picked up again.

'Mr Colwyn? David?'

'Holiness.'

'I heard Elizabeth's joke yesterday, about the anti-Papal honour. Good idea, when I can get round to it.' He laughed.

'I don't need any honours, sir.'

'Maybe not honours, David. But a reward. I think I have one, of sorts.'

'Oh?'

'I need someone to run the St Patrick's Fund.'

David said nothing. It was like his first meeting with Thomas, in the Vatican picture gallery. His mind refused to function.

'I'm taking Elizabeth away from you. You could come, too.'

'But that's crazy! I'm an auctioneer. Art is my life.'

'My life was Rome, David. Not any more. If it weren't for such upheavals the world would never change. Not everyone wants their life to be a crusade but sometimes you just have to follow where events lead. It's not comfortable but it's strange how addictive discomfort can be.'

'You mean come to Rio?'

'Yes. Elizabeth will be there. You'd spend a lot of time in Europe and America, looking after the fund investments. You'd have time for some art scholarship. Look at it this way: there'll never be another auction like the Vatican sale. You've had the best. It might be time to change.'

'I'll . . . I'll have to think about it.'

'Of course. We need you in Rome for a few days anyhow. To make sure Massoni doesn't try to wriggle off the hook. Keep in touch through Elizabeth.'

David continued to stand there, behind Gina's bar, holding the phone. A blank still occupied the centre of his mind. Then Bess came on the line again. 'I wish I was there to see your face now.'

'No you don't. You wouldn't recognize me. Was all this your idea – or Thomas's?'

'Thomas's, I swear. But I sort of helped him along.'

'I honestly have no idea what to do. What would happen to Ned?'

'Nothing. He'll have lovely holidays in Brazil and get on with becoming a goldsmith without his father always looking over his shoulder.'

'But it's all so uncertain.'

'Yes.' She paused. There was no hope of talking that fact away. 'Only one thing is certain.'

'And that is?'

'Come and we'll have us. Stay and we won't.'

'Yes, I know. I want you – '

' – then come.'

It was fantastic. Bess had already accepted, had accepted long ago that her place was on one side of a divide. She needed her work and she needed it to be important. Important to mankind. David knew that his work, art dealing, wasn't important in that way. In the past that had never worried him. As Thomas himself had said, not everybody wanted their life to be a crusade. So, what now? Could he, David, ever go back to his old uncomplicated ways?

'When are you leaving, Bess?'

'Straight after the ceremony to crown Ligorio. Around ten.'

'I need time to think. It's crowded in here. Can I call you before you go? I'll give you my answer then. And Thomas too.'

'It won't get any easier, you know, David. That's what I learned from Thomas. The really tough decisions take courage because even after you have taken them, you still can't be certain you've done the right thing. We're leaving here at ten. I'll call you at the apartment half an hour before. Okay?'

'Fine.'

David replaced the receiver and walked back round the bar. Gina looked across but he wouldn't catch her eye; he just picked up his coat and went out into the rain. This time he aimed for the Piazza Navona. It was getting dark and over there was a maze of narrow streets he could lose himself in. The rain had emptied the streets. Before long he found himself on the Via della Scrota. He turned right, where there was a bar opposite a church. He was a long way now from Gina's and the apartment: there would be no one he knew. He entered, sat down and ordered another whisky.

He turned over in his mind Thomas's offer. Was it silly to be rushed into a decision? Did he simply want to appear good in Bess's eyes? Could Thomas really make a go of things in Brazil? Would Roskill continue his vendetta? David's job was under pressure at Hamilton's but was it right to throw in the towel, give up something he knew he was good at? Tomorrow he would learn the truth about the Leonardo – perhaps that would reinforce his faith in himself. At the next meeting of the Renaissance Society he would reveal his discovery about the 'Virgin of the Rocks'. He *liked* the scholarly life. It was something he knew, enjoyed, and was valued in. Lord Afton, and Sally, would think him crazy if he threw it up.

A fresh thought struck him and he shivered. He should have thought of it sooner. He wondered whether Bess had thought about it, or Thomas. He went cold as its implications took hold of him. It suddenly mattered to him whether Bess had thought of it and had disregarded it or whether she hadn't. Once he mentioned it to her, she might change.

He looked at his watch – eight-fifty. It was time to be getting back. The rain was still as bad but it was, in its way, comforting. By the time he had reached the apartment, dried his hair, poured a drink and switched on the television, it was nearly nine-thirty. Almost immediately the phone rang. It was Michael Stone, just in from Milan. David was thrown. What if Bess couldn't get through? If she was short of time she would leave for Rio without speaking to him! He forced himself to be polite with Stone but cut short the conversation as quickly as he decently could, arranging to meet the American the next day at his hotel. They could proceed to the Palazzo Montaforno together.

He replaced the receiver. The TV set showed people leaving the cathedral at Palermo: the coronation was over. The phone rang again. This time it *was* Bess.

'Darling, before I give you my answer, I have a question. It won't take long.'

He reminded her of how disastrously he'd failed to identify Dorzhiev in time to stop Massoni's coup. Then he put the question he had to ask, 'Has that already occurred to you?'

There was silence at the other end of the line. Then, 'Yes.'

'And Thomas? Did it occur to him? Have you discussed it with him?'

'Yes. Twice.'

'Before or after he offered me a job?'

'Before.'

'And he still thinks I'm up to it? Isn't he angry with me? Aren't you?'

'It's *over*, David. Things could have been different, but they are the way they are. You performed brilliantly today, that's all that matters – I'm coming!' She shouted across the room. 'We're moving out, David. There's not much time.'

But all David could think of was that he had had it in his power to stop this tragedy from ever happening. He had even overheard Massoni and Giunta discussing the 'secret letter' in the archive, the very letter which had provided the pretext to topple Thomas. But his mind had been busy elsewhere and he simply hadn't noticed. That was the awful truth. The only consolation was that his decision had been made for him. His duty was clear. He couldn't live in London, and leave Thomas and Bess to struggle without him in Rio. He had been responsible for sending them there.

'Bess?'

'Yes, darling?'

'The offer still stands . . . ?'

'I'm *coming!* . . . I have to go David.' Then more softly, 'Of course the offer still stands.'

'Then I accept.'

'He accepts!' Bess relayed the news to Thomas. 'Then I won't say goodbye.'

'No. How about *ciao?*'

'How about getting off the line, so I can leave? How about booking your flight to Rio? There's a carnival in Rio, David. Like Fat Tuesday. Or are you going to come by tanker? How about kissing Gina for me? How about – '

' – if I agree to kiss Gina what'll you do for me in return?'

A pause.

'I'll wear Ned's brooch at our wedding.'

'You mean – '

'Yes! After all this, I at least need a stable home life. Don't forget what you unhooked in me, darling. All those memories, all those sensual flashbacks. I want them . . . you . . . again.' There was a silence along the line. A peace as powerful and as permanent as the Mississippi. 'Now I *must* go! If you watch us leave on television, you might just recognize what I'm wearing.'

'I'll watch it all on television. In between clinches with Gina. Tell Thomas I promise not to run off with the money.'

'I'll tell him.'

And she was gone.

David went across to Gina's. It was still raining. The lights of the bar sparkled in the wet dark, welcoming him. Gina was in her normal place, behind the cash register. David went up to her and kissed her. 'That's from Elizabeth.' He kissed her again. 'That's from me.'

'You're going, too, eh?'

'There's no reason to stay.'

Gina looked sad. 'I wonder how much a bar would cost in Rio?'

'But your two men – wouldn't they miss you?'

'They both support Massoni.'

David sat at the bar where he could chat with Gina, and from where he had a better view of the television. He bought a whisky, and a second. He would eat later, after the broadcast had finished. Thomas was still dominating all other news. The coronation of Ligorio as patriarch of Europe, Gina said, had been a glorious affair. The cathedral had been flooded with flowers, the organ had been supplemented by the Palermo Opera Orchestra, and the singing had been led by Renata Capalbio, the prima donna whose voice had led the singing in the square the day before. Because of the speed with which everything had to be arranged, Ligorio was crowned with Sicilian laurel. This was the way Frederick II, Holy Roman Emperor of the twelfth century, who had made his court in Palermo, was depicted on ancient coins, with a crown of laurel. And Frederick had campaigned ardently against the power of the Popes in Rome. The Sicilians loved that.

By now the television companies had cameras positioned at strategic points between the centre of Palermo and the airport at Punta Raisi. The whole way was illuminated, sometimes by TV arc lights, sometimes, as is the Sicilian fashion, by hundreds and hundreds of candles. Sicily, usually the dour heel of Italy, was for once coming into its own, producing a pageantry at the same time original and matched to the emotion of the occasion. All along the route the crowds were six or seven deep, everybody determined to say a personal farewell to Thomas. The car, which he shared with Ligorio, moved forward at times barely faster than walking pace and it was nearly midnight when the entourage reached the airport. David, growing hungry, was eating a simple plate of pasta. The bar was full but subdued. Not until Thomas had actually left the ground could the schism be truly said to have begun. Everyone waited, therefore, for this symbolic moment. The picture on the screen occasionally flashed from Sicily to Rome, to the Vatican which was marked by darkness and silence, with the sinister, half-hidden army guards on its perimeter.

The airport at Punta Raisi was a blaze of lights and crowded with people. A band was playing. As Thomas walked through the airport building, struggling to find a way past a throng of mothers and babies, nuns and police, farmers and engaged couples who hoped for his blessing, the chorus broke out again.

'Papa vero! Papa vero! Papa vero!'

Massoni had kept his word: a privately chartered Tristar, bearing no colours, was drawn up by the main terminal building. Thomas led the way towards it.

By the steps was a small platform with an array of microphones. The Sicilians would not let him go without a final message. Thomas mounted the platform. He stood alone: this time even Ligorio remained out of the light. Every camera was on Thomas.

'Goodbye Sicily. Thank you. Pray for me; pray for your patriarch; pray for Cardinal Massoni. This is not an ending, my friends, but a beginning. Ours is not an exodus, it is a genesis. Be proud of what we have achieved this day: always remember – Sicily did not fail its Pope.' He spread his arms wide. 'This is not night, it is morning.'

He got down from the platform and embraced Ligorio. At the foot of the steps to the Tristar, he turned, fell to his knees and prayed. The television commentators fell silent. The world watched as Thomas leaned forward and kissed the ground. The lump grew in David's throat.

Thomas stood. He waved and shouted, in most un-Pope-like gusto: 'Arrivederci!'

The crowd at the airport yelled back ten thousand times; 'Arrivederci Papa!'

By then Thomas was halfway up the steps, his limp more pronounced. Others followed him, among them Bess who was wearing the green silk shirt. David could see her speaking animatedly into an intercom of sorts. The latest gadget of its kind, no doubt. He turned and smiled contentedly across at Gina.

At the top of the steps Thomas turned, for a moment, and waved. Then he moved inside and was gone.

The steps were wheeled away, the engines to the Tristar began to turn. Their note rose, fell, rose again and, as it fell a second time, the aircraft moved off, wheeling to its right. Sleepily, it moved across the apron under the last of the television arc lights and out into the dark. The cameras followed the pencil-thin line of cabin lights as the Tristar taxied to the runway. The commentators were already discussing Thomas's arrival in Rio. Juliana Caratinga, the blind girl who could now see again, would be there. John Rich's mother would be there. Every president, every bishop, every cardinal from South America, save for the Argentinians and the Paraguayans, would be there. The mayor of Rio had said his city would rival Palermo in the welcome it extended to Thomas.

The aircraft reached the start of the runway, a quarter of a mile off. The television cameras could barely pick out the line of cabin lights. Still everyone watched for the symbolic moment of take off.

The aircraft remained stationary. The pilot made his checks, air traffic control double-checked its plans, and gave permission for take off. Then a throaty roar was heard as the pilot opened up his engines. The Tristar was seen to lumber forward. It gathered speed. Aboard the aircraft the pilot could feel the slap-slap-slap of the front wheel hitting the reflectors which marked the middle of the runway.

The Tristar approached 100 knots, 120, 130. It could fly at 161. It reached 140. 150. At 155 the co-pilot screamed: 'No!'

Ahead, just in vision as the Tristar's headlights picked them out, were two rows of black, metal spikes drawn tight across the runway.

'Let's go!' the pilot yelled, lunging at the throttle. The Tristar's engines had something left – the aircraft wasn't full – and they responded. The plane surged forward, lifting its blunt nose.

Even as it did so, the tires rode over the spikes and the rubber was shredded. The plane slewed – and settled, running on the metal hubs of its wheels. Showers of sparks shot back under the Tristar's wings. By now the aircraft had left the runway and was ploughing into the grass at its edge. As the starboard wing dipped towards the grass a spark ignited Number Two engine.

A yellow-red ball of flame erupted from under the starboard wing of the Tristar. The rest of the aircraft rolled into it. The fire fed on itself and surged into the black sky. The aircraft, still moving at 140 knots, cartwheeled back over the runway, a turning, blazing, upside-down cross of angry flame and deadly kerosene. Once, twice, it wheeled and then it fell, still burning, to the ground. There was a pause – in Gina's they could hear the rain outside – and then the Tristar exploded, the central fuselage first, the flightdeck next. For many long moments the TV screens were filled with crimson and scarlet and orange pillows of flame, folding in on each other. The rumble of the explosions went on.

At Gina's someone reached up to the television set and turned the volume down. Like many others he was weeping silently. The rain outside made the only sound, mocking the clear night air in Palermo, where the Mafia had, at last, claimed their revenge.

Instinctively, Gina looked across to David sitting at the bar. But he had gone.